CW00853964

Adoption

ADOPTION

Essays in social policy, law, and sociology

Edited by
Philip Bean

Tavistock Publications
London and New York

First published in 1984 by
Tavistock Publications Ltd
11 New Fetter Lane, London EC4P 4EE

Published in the USA by
Tavistock Publications
in association with Methuen, Inc.
733 Third Avenue, New York, NY 10017

Printed in Great Britain at
The University Press, Cambridge

British Library Cataloguing in Publication Data
Adoption.
1. Adoption — Great Britain
I. Bean, Philip
362.7'34'0941 HV875.7.G7

ISBN 0-422-78410-9

Library of Congress Cataloging in Publication Data
Main entry under title:

Adoption: essays in social policy, law, and sociology.
Bibliography: p.
Includes index.
1. Adoption — Addresses, essays, lectures. 2. Adoption — Great Britain — Address, essays, lectures. 3. Adoption — Law and legislation — Addresses, essays, lectures.
4. Intercountry adoption — Addresses, essays, lectures.
5. Social policy — Addresses, essays, lectures. I. Bean, Philip.
HV875.A33 1984 362.7'34 84-8553
ISBN 0-422-79410-9

Contents

Notes on contributors vii
Acknowledgements xiii
Foreword by Tony Hall xiv
Introduction 1

Part I Adoption and social policy

1 Adoption: perspectives in social policy 9
Gillian Pascall
2 The role of voluntary societies in adoption services 24
Mary Bromley
3 Obtaining birth certificates 38
John Triseliotis
4 Older child adoption and the knowledge base of adoption practice 54
Miles Hapgood
5 Causes and treatment of behaviour problems in adoptive children 83
Martin Herbert
6 An alternative family 100
Rob and Marian Clayton
7 Growing up adopted 113
Martin Shaw

Part II Adoption and the law

8 Adoption law: an overview 131
Brenda Hoggett

9 Step-parent adoptions 146
Judith Masson
10 Freeing a child for adoption - wardship 161
David Spicer
11 Aided conception: the alternative to adoption 174
Peter M. Bromley
12 The role of the court in the adoption process 194
Hugh K. Bevan
13 Subsidized adoption 203
Michael D.A. Freeman

Part III Transcultural adoption

14 Adoption of black children by white parents in the USA 229
Rita J. Simon
15 Reflections on bicultural adoption 243
Marilyn and Loyal Rue
16 Parentless refugee children: the question of adoption 254
Ron Baker
17 Latin American children in intercountry adoption 273
Rosa Perla Resnick
18 The influence of western adoption laws on customary adoption in the Third World 288
Maev O'Collins

Name index 305
Subject index 310

Notes on contributors

Editor

PHILIP BEAN

Philip Bean is Senior Lecturer, Department of Social Administration and Social Work, University of Nottingham. Prior to this he was a Research Officer for the Medical Research Council, and prior to that a probation officer in the Inner London Probation and After Care Service. His major interests are in the fields of criminology, mental health, and social philosophy where he has published widely; his publications include *The Social Control of Drugs* (Martin Robertson 1974), *Rehabilitation and Deviance* (Routledge and Kegan Paul 1976), *Compulsory Admissions to Mental Hospitals* (John Wiley and Sons 1980), and *Punishment: A Philosophical and Criminological Analysis* (Martin Robertson 1981). He has edited three books: *Mental Illness Changes and Trends* (John Wiley and Sons 1983), *Approaches to Welfare* with Stewart MacPherson (Routledge and Kegan Paul 1983), and *In Defence of Welfare* with John Ferris and David Whynnes (Tavistock 1984). He has held two visiting professorships, one in Canada (1979) and one in the USA (1983).

Contributors

RON BAKER

Ron Baker currently works as Research Officer (P/T) with the British Refugee Council, tutor at LSE and the National Institute of Social Work, and consultant/tutor to a range of statutory and voluntary welfare agencies. In 1983 he was National Children's Home Convocation lecturer and had the title of Senior Research Fellow conferred by Southampton University (Social Work). He was the first occupant of a new chair as Professor of Social Work at UNSW (1977-81) and previously Senior Lecturer and Lecturer at Monash (1974-77) and Bradford (1970-74) Universities. Prior to this he was a social worker in the mental health field for eight years and trained as a mental and general nurse for six years. He has personal refugee experience. His published work includes six book chapters, numerous articles, and two books: *The Interpersonal Process in Generic Social Work* (PIT Press 1978 2nd edn) and *The Psychosocial Problems of Refugees* (BRC 1983). In preparation is another book *Understanding and Dealing With Stress and 'Burnout' in Social Welfare Practice.*

HUGH BEVAN

Hugh K. Bevan is Professor of Law at the University of Hull. He is also a barrister and a Justice of the Peace. He was appointed a lecturer in Law at Hull in 1950 and a Professor in 1969. His interests are in family law and his publications include *A Source Book of Family Law* with P.R.H. Webb (Butterworths 1964), *The Law Relating to Children* (Butterworths 1973), *The Children Act 1975* with M.L. Parry (Butterworths 1978); he was joint Editor for *Butterworths Family Law Service* (1983).

MARY BROMLEY

Mary Bromley, MA, DPSA, Dip.Ed., has been a social worker with Doncaster Adoption and Family Welfare Society Ltd. since 1980. She trained and worked as a child care officer before lecturing on Post Graduate Work courses. While her own children were young she trained for and practised as a junior/infants teacher. This has given her a wide experience of work with children and of teaching a variety of age groups. Over the years she has worked in both statutory and voluntary agencies.

PETER BROMLEY

Peter M. Bromley was born in 1922 and educated at Ealing Grammar School and the Queen's College, Oxford. He was first appointed to an academic post in the University of Manchester in 1947 and has been Professor of Law there since 1965. He is also a barrister. He is the author of a textbook on *Family Law* (6th Edition 1981) and is the general editor of *Butterworths Family Law Service.*

ROB AND MARIAN CLAYTON

Rob and Marian Clayton are the parents of two children.

MICHAEL FREEMAN

Michael D.A. Freeman is Professor of English Law at University College London. He formerly taught at the University of Leeds. He is also a barrister. He is the author of a number of books including *The Legal Structure* (Longman 1974), *Violence in the Home - A Socio-Legal Study* (Saxon House 1979), *Cohabitation Without Marriage - An Essay in Law and Social Policy* with Tina Lyon (Gower 1983) and, most recently, *The Rights and Wrongs of Children* (Frances Pinter 1983). He has been on the Legal Committee of BAAF and is active in *Justice for Children*. He teaches on social work courses as well as to law students.

MILES HAPGOOD

Miles Hapgood received his Ph.D. and his MA in social work from the University of Nottingham. He has been engaged in local authority social work practice for ten years. He is currently employed as a social worker by Devon County Council and works in Exeter.

MARTIN HERBERT

Martin Herbert was educated at Durban High School and Natal University, South Africa. He did his professional clinical psychology training at the Institute of Psychiatry, Maudsley Hospital London in 1958 and was later awarded a Ph.D. in Clinical Psychology. In 1966 he went to the University of Leicester; first in the Psychology Department, later in the School of Social Work where he became Director and Professor, and now as Professor of Clinical Psychology in the Psychology Department. He has practised as an Honorary Consultant in the National Health Service for many years and directed his own child treatment research unit. He has published widely, including papers on childhood problems and therapeutics, and his books include *Conduct Disorders of Childhood and Adolescence* (John Wiley & Sons 1978), *Behavioural Treatment of Problem Children* (Academic Press 1981), and *Psychology for Social Workers* (Macmillan 1981).

BRENDA HOGGETT

Brenda Hoggett is Reader in Law at Manchester University where she has taught since 1966. Her main interests are in family law and the personal social services. She was the joint general editor of the *Journal of Social Welfare Law*, author of *Parents and Children* (Sweet and Maxwell 2nd Edition 1981) and *The Family Law and Society: Cases and Materials* with David Pearl (Butterworths 1983). She became a Law Commissioner in 1984.

JUDITH MASSON

Judith Masson studied for a Law degree at Clare College, Cambridge and was appointed as a lecturer in law at Leicester University in 1975. She now specializes in Family Law, Child Welfare Law, and empirical socio-legal research, and also teaches child care law at Leicester University School of Social Work. After joining the Legal Group of British Agencies for Adoption and Fostering she and Daphne Norbury were in 1978 commissioned by the DHSS to undertake part of the monitor for Parliament of the Children Act 1975. During this period Judith Masson also completed her Ph.D. thesis on 'Step-parent Adoption - a Social-Legal Study'. In 1981, as a Harkness Fellow, she studied 'Decision-making about Children' at the National Institute of Child Welfare, School of Social Work, University of Michigan, USA.

MAEV O'COLLINS

Maev O'Collins undertook undergraduate studies in Australia and then worked as a social worker and later Principal Adoption Officer at a family welfare agency in Melbourne. Following graduate studies at Columbia University New york where she obtained a DSW she initiated social work training at the University of Papua New Guinea and since 1979 has been the professor of an interdisciplinary department which includes anthropology, sociology, social work, and archaeology. Her research and teaching interests are in adoption, social welfare and the law, family planning, non-formal education, and youth in society, which are reflected in articles published in professional journals and seminar proceedings. The results of a major project on youth in Melanesia will be published in 1984.

GILLIAN PASCALL

Gillian Pascall is a lecturer in Social Administration at the University of Nottingham. She has a Diploma in Social Administration from the London School of Economics and a Ph.D. from Nottingham. Her main interests are in health and women's studies and her publications include *Women and Social Policy* (Tavistock

1985). In 1981 she went on an Inter-Universities Council visit to Papua New Guinea.

ROSA PERLA RESNICK

Rosa Perla Resnick holds a Ph.D. in Humanities and Education, University of Buenos Aires, Argentina; a Master of Science in Social Work, Columbia University; and a Doctorate in Social Work, Yeshiva University, USA. For many years Rosa Resnick was a professor of social work at Latin American universities. In the USA, alongside her teaching, she was Research Associate, International Association of Schools of Social Work, and Special Consultant to the UN Social Development Section. As an active participant in international conferences, she produced many significant papers on Latin American social welfare. Co-author of *The World Guide to Social Work Education* (New York: IASSW 1974); author of *The Indigenization of Social Work: Conscientization and Social Work in Chile*, unpublished doctoral dissertation, Yeshiva University 1976; Dr Resnick was Project Director of the study *Intercountry Adoptions between the United States and Colombia* (New York: ISS 1982), which was co-authored with Gloria Munóz de Rodríguez. Currently she is an Associate Professor at Hunter College School of Social Work, City University of New York.

MARILYN AND LOYAL RUE

Marilyn and Loyal Rue live in Decorah, Iowa with their three children, Carl Anders Boonsong, Anna Christine Sirikit, and Elena Marso Surin. While they are not engaged in family matters they work at Luther College where Loyal is Registrar and Associate Professor of Religion and Marilyn is a counsellor in the area of psychological services.

MARTIN SHAW

Martin Shaw practised as a social worker in the child care field before moving into social work education. He is currently a senior lecturer at the University of Leicester School of Social Work. Apart from a number of research reports on children in care, his main publications are a contribution to *Behaviour Modification in Social Work* (ed. D. Jehu, Wiley 1972), and the co-authorship with Tony Hipgrave of *Specialist Fostering* (Batsford 1983).

RITA J. SIMON

Rita Simon is Dean School of Justice at The American University,

Washington DC USA. She was formerly Professor of Sociology, Communications Research and Law, University of Illinois Champaign-Urbana. She has published widely, and is author of eight books and editor of six others. Her publications relating to adoption include *Transracial Adoption* with Howard Alstein (Wiley-Interscience 1977) and *Transracial Adoption: A Follow Up* also with Howard Alstein (Lexington Books 1981).

DAVID SPICER

David Spicer received his law degree at Manchester University in 1972 and was called to the Bar in 1973. After a brief period in practice he was appointed to a legal advisory post with Nottinghamshire County Council and since 1978 has occupied a senior post with particular responsibility for social services matters.

JOHN TRISELIOTIS

John Triseliotis is the Director of Social Work Education at the University of Edinburgh. He has written books and articles on adoption and fostering. His most recent book, co-authored with J. Russell, is *Hard to Place: The Outcome of Late Adoptions and Residential Care* (Heinemann 1984).

Acknowledgements

I would like to thank all the contributors to the volume as well as Mrs Ann Hodson who helped co-ordinate the project and did a great deal of typing. I am very grateful to the members of the Department of Social Administration and Social Work, University of Nottingham, and particularly to Stewart MacPherson who bore the brunt of so much discussion. Professor Arthur Willcocks gave useful advice and encouragement for which I am most grateful.

I also wish to acknowledge the special help given by my wife Valerie whose initial idea the book was and by our two sons Ian and Lee.

Philip Bean

Foreword

TONY HALL,
Director and Secretary, British Agencies for Adoption and Fostering

This book reflects some of the many changes which have occurred in the field of adoption during the past fifteen years. After reaching a peak of almost 25,000 in 1968, the number of adoption orders in England and Wales declined to 10,240 in 1982, echoing a trend experienced by many other countries. Changes in the availability of and attitudes towards contraception, and in abortion law, served to reduce the number of babies born unwanted by their parents. Changes in social attitudes and services made it possible for single mothers more frequently to keep and bring up their children themselves.

The greatest decline was in the number of illegitimate children adopted by 'strangers' - the group which has dominated the public image of adoption since the early years - from 14,500 in 1968 to 3,300 in 1982. Of the last group only 2,000 were children aged less than one year.

An equally significant social trend was the rapid rise and even more rapid reduction in the use of adoption to formalize arrangements in reconstituted families following divorce, and for illegitimate children when their single mothers married for the first time. These step-parent adoptions numbered 4,000 in 1962 and represented only 25 per cent of all adoptions; by 1974 there were 15,000 accounting for 60 per cent of the total. By 1982, following a change in the law, the numbers had fallen again to 5,800.

These demographic and social trends precipitated a revolution in adoption policy, law, and practice in Britain. In the late 1960s adoption was still widely regarded as a service for childless couples; a way of providing 'healthy white babies' for couples wanting a 'normal' family of their own. Ten years later it had become a service not for parents but for the children themselves.

While retaining sympathy and providing practical help for childless couples exploring the many ways in which they can cope with their childlessness, most British agencies today focus primarily on the needs of children needing families. In particular they are concerned with children in public care deprived of a family of their own. Ten, even five years ago many of these children would have been considered unsuitable for adoption and would have remained in care throughout their childhood and beyond. Agencies now routinely seek family placements for a range of children with 'special needs' - mentally and physically handicapped children of all ages, older children and adolescents, and sibling groups. Family finding, preparation, placement, and support of such children is, of course, not easy, requiring an immense range of skills and new methods of working. These have developed rapidly during the past decade, helped by the example of agencies facing similar trends on the other side of the Atlantic.

In identifying some of the main changes in practice, I do not wish to exaggerate or create the impression that such developments are universal throughout British adoption agencies: some traditional agencies still exist, seemingly untouched by the changes around them. But many more have made great efforts to adapt quickly to the new problems and opportunities, and the general picture is encouraging.

During the 'baby boom' of the 1960s, for adoption agencies it was a 'seller's market'. This was evident in the methods used for selecting suitable parents from the many queueing at the doors of the agencies. Selection criteria were rigorously applied. Couples had to be young and usually middle class, with a secure and healthy income, a house and garden. The change in focus to special needs children has forced agencies to adapt and develop rather different approaches to family finding, selection, and preparation.

There can no longer be a general, ideal-type model of a suitable couple. Care is now taken to identify the needs of individual children, and to find and prepare a couple, or a single parent, able to meet those needs. As a result the characteristics of adoptive parents are changing in terms of their social class, age, income, marital status, family type and size, and accommodation. Further change will occur now that local authorities are able to pay adoption allowances, making it possible for people on very low incomes to adopt children who might otherwise remain in care. Traditional methods of assessment (which used to be described by the dreadful term 'vetting') are also widely accepted as inappropriate. Many agencies have developed group methods of education and preparation in which a large measure of the responsibility for making the decision to continue lies with the would-be parents themselves.

The question of how to find adoptive parents for special needs children has created perhaps the biggest changes, stretching the ingenuity and imagination of many practitioners. Much has been learned from American example and from industry. There is now widespread use of family finding features and advertising in local and national newspapers, and on local radio. The use of television to present children needing families began in Britain in 1974 and is now firmly established; the advent of video offers new opportunities for the next ten years. In 1980 British Agencies for Adoption and Fostering (BAAF) launched *Be My Parent,* Britain's first national photolist of children needing families, and its success has given rise to other local and regional lists. High street adoption shops, pioneered in the voluntary sector, are now a growing feature of local authority as well as voluntary adoption services.

It is not by chance that one third of the essays in this book are concerned with transcultural adoption. In a field which is full of social, philosophical, and moral dilemmas none is more potent than those concerning adoption and race. Over the past fifteen years, as the number of babies available for adoption in Britain has declined, interest in adopting black babies from overseas has increased. The numbers involved are far smaller than in most other European countries where the practice is institutionalized, but the issues and emotions raised are no less great.

At the same time, most urban local authorities in Britain have in their care a large and disproportionate number of black children needing substitute families. From the late 1960s the response of most agencies was to place black children with white families, both for adoption and fostering. At first, this was out of perceived necessity; later it was out of habit. It is now clearly possible, if the right methods are used, to find black families for black children, although not yet in the numbers required to meet the needs of the thousands of black children in care.

Both inter-country and transracial adoptions continue despite warnings from America about the political backlash against such placements. In the past two years, for the first time in Britain, British black groups are voicing similar protests and agencies are rapidly rethinking their strategies for looking after the black children in their care.

Whatever the outcome of these debates about the rights and wrongs of transcultural adoption, I have no doubt that in the next few years we must see substantial new initiatives to find ways of recruiting more substitute parents from black communities. Some good work has already been started, but there is a great deal more to do.

Finally, I would like to congratulate Philip Bean on this collection of essays. All are interesting; some are outstanding. The book as a whole contains some fascinating perspectives and insights into the increasingly complex and changing phenomenon of adoption in Britain and I recommend it to anyone who has a professional or personal interest in the subject.

For those who wait . . .

Introduction: adoption - some reflections and considerations

PHILIP BEAN

Whilst the origins of adoption can be found at least as far back as Roman times it was not until 1926 that England and Wales had its first fully fledged adoption legislation aimed at regulating the transfer of a child of birth parents to others. In the last fifty years or so adoption has been viewed in different ways and assumed different functions: as a solution to infertility; as a recognition that step-parents might become legitimate parents; as a means of caring for unwanted children; and more recently with the adoption of older children or of children with special needs or from a different ethnic background, as a means of meeting children's needs. And with these changes there have been corresponding changes in adoption practice.

The adoption statistics

According to the Office of Population Censuses and Surveys (29 March, 1981) there were 9,284 adoption orders registered in England and Wales in 1981. That was a decrease of 12 per cent over the previous year. Specifically the number of adoptions of legitimate children fell by 623 (a 14 per cent decrease) and there were 702 fewer adoptions of illegitimate children (a fall of 12 per cent). However the proportion each group formed of the relevant annual total was virtually unchanged. After levelling off between 1979 and 1980 the general downward trend in the annual total number of adoptions resumed. About one quarter of the children adopted in 1981 were under eight months old, one quarter were children between nine months and five years, and half between five and fourteen years: virtually the same proportion as in 1980.

Two points can be made about these figures. The first concerns the information available from the figures themselves. Throughout this book a number of writers complain about the absence of basic socio-demographic material in the official statistics - even this is slightly inaccurate for there are no *official* statistics as such. Data have to be gleaned from a variety of sources, some of which may be unreliable. The information provided by the OPCS, for example, emphasizes factors such as the legitimacy of the children and the status of adoptive parents; that is as joint adopters or sole adopters, parental adopters or non-parental. There is information about the age and sex of the children but nothing about their social origins and nothing on their 'special needs' - if indeed there were any. It is as if legal definitions are seen as more important than social ones - a distinction maintained throughout these figures. The information on the types of courts making the order (High Court, County Court, or Magistrates Court) is quite extensive; but no information is provided about the agencies involved - whether they were statutory or voluntary. A great deal of social data is routinely gathered by the guardian *ad litem* for adoption hearings but it is not easily available to researchers. As long as it continues to be assumed that adoption is primarily a legal exercise we shall continue to know of little other than legal matters and be unable to provide a comprehensive evaluation of adoption practice - a matter I would regard as long overdue.

The second point concerns adoption practice itself. If we assume for the moment that adoption is prescriptive - and this point will be returned to later - it seems extraordinary that the numbers of children adopted have decreased over recent years. There was a slight rise in 1982 to 10,240 but according to Michael Freeman (Chapter 13) this was attributable mainly to an increase in step-parent adoptions. We have very large numbers of children in care, probably more than 50,000, and whilst it cannot be known how many are available for adoption, or indeed would benefit from it, the numbers must be high. We also have many prospective adopters, probably as many or more than the number of the children themselves. And we now have more social workers employed in adoption practice. The opportunities for increasing the number of adoptions are unprecedented. What then are social workers doing?

In asking this question it is recognized that adoption has to be seen within the context of the provision of services generally. Resources for adoption have to stand in competition with demands made in other fields and adoption itself is a time-consuming exercise. Adoption workers have to spend a great deal of time on applications, and this procedure must be dependent to a large extent on the priority given to adoption in financial or other terms. And adoption is about making judgements: it is not about some quasi-medical definition determined by experts examining a defined category of behaviour, whether of the child or the adoptive parents. Those judgements must in the nature of things be difficult and time-consuming.

But serious doubts remain about the activities of those involved in adoption, including senior welfare administrators who fail to give adoption an adequate priority. Doubts also include field social workers who, according to adoption workers, often fail to identify and refer the children or, if they do, refer them inappropriately. But the real root of the trouble is the tendency to view adoptions as being suitable only for babies, and particularly suitable when the physical characteristics of the adoptive parents are matched with those of the child's birth family (a way of implicitly denying the adoption anyway). There is a reluctance to see older children as adoption candidates.

The number of babies for adoption is unlikely to increase in the near future and adoption practice needs to adjust to this demographic change. There are, on the other hand, opportunities to develop adoptions amongst older age groups, where many children have been in care for some time and are likely to remain there. It is this group that adoption workers should be considering. Yet the number of older children adopted has hardly changed in the last few years; it has not increased as the number of babies being adopted has decreased (Miles Hapgood, Chapter 4). On humanitarian and economic grounds there is a prima-facie case for increasing adoptions of the older child. Of course social workers need to be careful about the children and about the adoptive parents they choose. It would be quite wrong to place children for adoption if they could return to satisfactory birth homes, but it is equally wrong to deny some children the opportunity for adoption, especially when the number of suitable adoptive parents remains so high.

Adopting the older child involves a risk and a great deal of work. The older child is a person in its own right to be considered with demands and expectations of its own. The initial placement period will never be easy and the potential legal wrangles often accompanying older child adoptions can be harrowing. Adopting older children is different from adopting babies, for the social worker, the child, the adoptive and the birth parents. But it is a worthwhile endeavour none the less, especially when the choice is as bleak as it often is. It is no accident that the voluntary societies have taken the lead (Mary Bromley, Chapter 2); now the statutory agencies must follow.

Adoption as a technical exercise

Too often the debate about adoption has taken place within a specified cultural milieu concentrating on detailed but somewhat mechanistic aspects of social work practice. (i.e. how to assess adoption applications), or on legal arguments producing similar practical results (i.e. what does the law allow).

Of course there are technical questions to be considered and it is right and proper to do so. There are technical questions about how to obtain birth certificates and technical questions about how to assess prospective adopters - although Chapter 6 by Rob and Marian Clayton suggests that improvements may be overdue in some areas. Brenda Hoggett's chapter (Chapter 8) provides a summary of the legal requirements.

It was said earlier that adoption depends upon and serves wider social demands, but to date analysis has not often recognized this. Yet if we wish to understand adoption and its place within the order of things, a wider model is required. In this volume adoption is linked to medical ethics (Peter Bromley, Chapter 11) and to child-rearing practices dominated by that elusive concept of 'bonding'. In Chapter 11 the ethical and legal problems are discussed which stem from attempts to supplement the shortage of babies by 'growing one's own'.

The area that has sharpened up the whole debate has been the adoption of black children by white parents, where accusations are made that adoption represents a subtle form of colonialism, (Rita Simon, Chapter 14), or that adoption of working-class children by middle-class parents represents class hegemony (Gillian Pascall, Chapter 1). Both arguments take adoption away from its comfortable technical shroud to place it where it must rightly belong - within the social world. For whilst everyone, or nearly everyone, can view adoption prescriptively when an unwanted baby is handed over to a potentially caring and loving couple (who may also happen to be childless as opposed to childfree), adoption becomes more of a social issue when the child is black and the adoptive parents white, or the child is working class and the adoptive parents middle class. And even more so when the adopted child is an older child who has already acquired a cultural background and a set of cultural responses which will have to be unlearned if he or she is to acquire a new cultural identity.

There is a darker side to adoption: it can be used to further selected interest groups irrespective of the needs of the child by trading on the honourable motives of the adopting parents. That darker side is a cause for concern when the child is a refugee and the birth parents hand the child over reluctantly, hoping and planning for a reunion one day, (Ron Baker, Chapter 16). It is worrying in some traditional societies where the application for adoption upsets traditional kinship patterns - where without the adoption application the child might have gone to appropriate relatives (Maev O'Collins, Chapter 18). And it becomes downright sinister when the child is illegally exported from the Third World, perhaps even against the wishes of a birth parent, in favour of those who see the trade in children as lucrative (Rosa Resnick, Chapter 17). But in all this (less so for those involved in illegal activities!) there still remains the laudable desire to provide a child with a better home than it might have otherwise had, especially where the alternatives are as stark as having a home and having no home at all. Chapter 15 by Marilyn and Loyal Rue raises these questions sharply and shows the dangers of making simple blanket statements about whether one form of practice should be banned and another not.

When all is said and done the track record of adoption remains good (Martin Shaw, Chapter 7). Adoption may be a comparatively recent legal phenomenon in Britain but the need for it exists and so it will remain in some form or other.

PART I
Adoption and social policy

1 Adoption: perspectives in social policy

GILLIAN PASCALL

'The traditional social policy has contributed greatly to our understanding of the operation and effects of individual social policies. The new social administration can provide the broader context in which it is possible to start making sense of social policy more generally' (Wilding 1983:13). Thus concludes a recent essay which assesses the contributions of different approaches within social policy. This essay is an attempt to review these approaches insofar as they apply to the adoption of children. It sets out first to review a number of perspectives which fall broadly within 'traditional' social administration; here, in fact, most of the relevant literature lies. It then goes on to ask whether the 'new social administration' has anything to offer within this area. Under the 'traditional social administration' I shall discuss approaches which view social policy issues from the inside, from the point of view of policy-making and prescription. Under the 'new social administration', I shall consider approaches derived from political economy and feminism, which are concerned with the relations of social policy with the broader contexts of economy and family.

Solving social problems

One of social administration's traditional tasks was to identify and solve social problems; allied to this was the need to assess the results of existing social policies as solutions to problems. A lot of adoption literature, including some from the psychologists, falls broadly within this framework. Sometimes the problem is posed as the problem of childlessness (e.g. Humphrey 1969); much more often it is posed as the problem of bringing up children born illegitimate, or children who for other reasons have come into the care of the local authorities or voluntary agencies. Success may be discussed in terms of parental satisfaction; of child development; and of the creation of integrated families. Or the problem may be seen as one of matching children in need to adults who wish to adopt. And success then may be discussed in terms of the numbers of children remaining in local authority care who would be better placed with permanent families.

If the problem is put this latter way, it looks well-nigh insoluble. Benet remarks that 'In most of the European countries, there is a desperate shortage of babies to adopt, combined with a crisis in the numbers of children being cared for by the state' (Benet 1976:82). Bureaucratic inertia is not the only reason for this, though it is one of them. Other barriers, particularly relationships with original families, exist between these children and new families. From the point of view of would-be adopters in Western countries the availability of children has never been sufficient. While a lot of the literature suggests that traditional adoption policies were directed to meeting the needs of the childless, it has to be said that adoption has never been a solution for the majority of childless people. Even when non-parental adoptions were at their height in the 1960s there were more would-be adopters than available children (Kellmer Pringle 1967:1). The subsequent decline in children placed for adoption has thus left childless couples at the mercy of long delays, multiple applications to the variety of agencies, and frequent disappointment. The growth of support and information groups for those interested in adopting older and handicapped children is a measure of the pressures on the childless.

If the problem posed this way produces rather gloomy answers, posed the other way, in terms of the 'success' of adoptive families, the answers are much happier. The primary focus of research has been the children, and in particular on how well adopted children fare compared with their contemporaries in other kinds of family. The question is not a simple one, since 'how children fare' is a question as ambiguous as one could find. However, in terms of the kinds of developmental assessments available to researchers, the answer has been clear enough. Adopted children do as well as or better than others on most such criteria. For example, the National Child Development Study concluded that 'in all the aspects of ability and attainment which were examined, they did either as well as, or even better than, all the other children in the cohort' (Seglow, Kellmer Pringle, and Wedge 1972:140–41).

With growing interest in placing older children and in transracial adoptions, the question has had to be posed again. Tizard, for example, has done an appealing study of children adopted from institutions after the age of two. In the light of well-known theories of infant attachment the success of these adoptions seemed uncertain; yet she found a high proportion of adoptions where close attachments had been formed, and where children were developing satisfactorily:

> 'at the age of eight the great majority of the adoptions were successful, judged by any of the criteria considered, except behaviour at school. Even children placed as late as seven and seven and a half were successfully integrated into their new families, although intellectually they had not shot ahead and behaviour problems were more frequent than in younger placements. Compared with the alternative placements available to these children, that is, continued institutionalisation, long-term fostering, or restoration to their natural families, adoption seems clearly the best solution to the children's needs.'
>
> (Tizard 1977:217)

Similarly, Gill and Jackson, investigating transracial adoptions, have found no evidence that in general the children they studied were developing less well than other children: 'Nor is there any evidence to suggest that life is so difficult for such children that they will be unable to operate effectively at school. If anything, the evidence on academic progress at least seems to be that these children are on average doing rather well' (Gill and Jackson 1983:55). Furthermore, both parents and children saw themselves as making successful families: 'For the majority of families there seems a consistent and happy picture of the parents and the children defining each other in a mutually warm, supportive, caring and positive way' (Gill and Jackson 1983:39). What is remarkable about these conclusions is that they emerge despite the authors' unease about transracial adoptions; none of the expected problems of identity and self-respect was in fact, prevalent in the study children.

Thus the overwhelming evidence is that as a way of providing substitute family life for children and of making families for the childless, adoption is a successful solution. While it is not a solution for the majority of childless people or for the majority of children in care, for reasons already discussed, those families that are built by adoption seem to work. Their family life and the development of their children have much more in common with families in general than they have differences from them.

It is no detraction from the significance of these studies to point out the limits of the approach. Indeed, the authors of the last two studies mentioned in particular show an acute awareness that when adoption is considered within a wider context it poses much more painful and political issues. Tizard, for example, has an important discussion of the family context within which adoption policies operate (Tizard 1977:1-6). And Gill and Jackson are so concerned about the implications of transracial adoption for the black community that they wish to see an end to it despite the 'success' of the families they interviewed. The point is that to define the 'problem' as providing substitute care is to set severe limits on the kinds of questions that can be dealt with. In particular it is to beg questions about why substitute care is needed, about the wider political impact of adoption policies, and about who cares for whose children.

Rights

A well established theme within traditional social administration is the analysis of the welfare state as consisting in the development of citizenship through social rights (Marshall 1949). Allied to this is the political movement for the defence and development of rights for groups whose tenure has been marginal. Among these, of course, are children.

On the whole the debate about rights has centred on older children and their families, particularly children who have been in care for extended periods and could be the subject of adoption proceedings. It should be remembered that insofar as these children do get to the stage of adoption proceedings they are a small minority of the total adoptees. However, concern about the issues surrounding them has produced a plentiful literature. Other groups have received some attention: children caught between parents and step-parents raise a somewhat different series of issues, and there has been some concern, including one impassioned feminist plea (Shawyer 1979), for the rights of single mothers involved in adoption decisions over their babies.

The first group, the children in care, were the subject of a key study by Rowe and Lambert, *Children who Wait* (1973). This was an extensive study concerned with 'the continued existence of a large number of children being brought up in care' (Rowe and Lambert 1973:35). Important conclusions were that 'if a pre-school or primary school age child has been in care for as long as six months, his chances of returning to his parents are slim' and that 'Over the country as a whole, there are probably at least 6,000 children of pre-school or primary school age who are in the care of social agencies and who need a substitute family' (Rowe and Lambert 1973:37–47). This meant that the children's social workers thought that they needed an adoptive or foster home. The fate of such children was often chronic insecurity of placement. Few were considered for adoption: 'most staff seem much more comfortable with foster care and therefore tend to foster a child unless adoption has been specifically requested by a parent' (Rowe and Lambert 1973:87). As pressure groups supporting children in care have pointed out, another feature of the children's lives was chronic powerlessness in relation to the bureaucracies which were responsible for them.

Also influential was *Beyond the Best Interests of the Child,* which started from psychoanalytic principles to argue in the Bowlby tradition about 'the need of every child for unbroken continuity of affectionate and stimulating relationships with an adult' (Goldstein, Freud, and Solnit 1973:6). Biological parenthood was less important than 'psychological parenthood'. If the relationship with biological parents did break down, the emphasis should be on early decision-making about rehabilitation or substitute parents.

The implication drawn from such studies was that children in care should have rights. 'Rights are important because without them we have a master–slave or authoritarian relationship. Rights then, are important moral coinage. Those who lack rights are poor, indeed. To have rights is to have dignity and respect. That is why we must insist that children are accorded rights and what goes for children applies with equal force to these children who lack, or lack adequate, parents' (Freeman 1981:6). Some of the rights most commonly discussed are the rights of children in care to a voice about their futures and - most to the point here - rights to permanent placement (Rawstron 1981). Organizations for adoptive parents, such as PPIAS (Parent to Parent Information on Adoption Services), have contributed to the movement to take at least some of these children out of care and into permanent new families. In this role they can be seen as defending the rights of children in care to normal family life.

However, the discussion about rights, as the participants in it admit, is a bit more complicated than it seems at first sight. As Freeman points out 'most rights are in fact freedoms so that in asserting "rights" we are more often demanding that others should lack rights' (Freeman 1981:7). Groups such as the Family Rights Group argue that distressed families lack rights; that their rights have been sacrificed in a local authority deluge of parental rights resolutions whose aim is to move children quickly to new families. According to Tunnard, 'Over half the queries that come to the Family Rights Group's office concern problems of access between children in care and their families. Most are from parents who want to be able to see their children more often, but have had their access arrangements changed, reduced, or ended' (Tunnard 1983:100). And the issue of rights for parents does not end there. Despite the protestations of politicians about the importance of the family, it is precisely families with children who have suffered most from recent trends in taxes, benefits, incomes, and employment (Coussins and Coote 1981). A high proportion of the parents of children in care are single parents, who are under special pressures. Groups supporting such families therefore press for basic rights to housing and income, and they argue, with justice, that while these are not fulfilled, parents may be deprived of their children through no fault of their own (Laurance 1982).

Thus a discussion of adoption in terms of rights poses a dilemma. Are the rights of original parents, children, and adoptive parents compatible with one another? One formula which partly resolves the issue is to assume that children are most likely to achieve permanency if they retain ties with their original families, rather than staying in care. (This fits with research findings about the extreme instability of placements in care.)

> 'We must put our resources into finding new families for children where rehabilitation with their natural parents is out of the question. But we must not put the cart before the horse. Every help, both financial and social work, must be given to parents to keep families together. The proposals in Finer or others like them must be implemented before we take further steps to dilute the natural family. This done, we must consider the rights of children.'
>
> (Freeman 1981:13)

A similar argument (though couched in more liberal terms of protection of families from state intervention) is put by Goldstein's second book *Before the Best Interests of the Child* (Goldstein, Freud, and Solnit 1979). While this goes some way towards accommodating the rights demanded for birth parents and the rights demanded on behalf of their children, the dilemma remains. It remains, first, because of the non-implementation of Finer and like proposals and the consequent continued deprivation of families, especially one-parent families. It remains, second, because resources are not all. As I shall argue in the next section, it is illuminating to consider issues of child care and adoption in relation to inequality and deprivation; but it does not tell us everything about relations between parents and children. It has to be concluded that there is nothing simple about the fate of the many children in care who might be better off in substitute homes. As Shaw and Lebens concluded in their study *What shall we do with the Children?* 'The realisation that at least half the children in one's residential establishments could be better placed elsewhere perhaps indicates a need for quite radical organisational change. But organisational change does not solve ethical dilemmas' (Shaw and Lebens 1978:22).

To pose the issue of the adoption of children from care in terms of rights thus exposes conflicts as much as it solves them. This is no criticism. Analysis in these terms, as well as practical action on behalf of all the groups concerned, is valuable. It does have limitations. First, it is easier to claim rights for children than it is to make a real difference to the lives of children in care, who are still, strictly, powerless. It is easier to take rights from parents than it is to give them to children. Mandell warns 'When parents lose legal rights over their children, it is not the children who gain more legal rights, it is the state' (Mandell 1973:64). Second, the fight for rights is a fight for recognition within a given framework. Relevant frameworks in this case are the structures of inequality and deprivation and the structures of 'normal family life' of which children in care may be seen as the victims. To step outside the rights approach may then be expected to yield other insights.

Inequality and distribution

An important tradition in social policy analysis is the concern with issues of inequality and distribution. Rather few writers on adoption have directly confronted these issues. One of the strengths of this type of approach lies in its ability to ask awkward questions about the distributional impact of social policies and to bring detailed empirical data to bear on them.

The writers on adoption who have used this approach have not been helped by official statistics (Fruin 1980). However, there is little room for dispute, within the limited available data, about the distributional results of adoption policy, both nationally and internationally. Thus, Robert Holman collates results from a number of empirical studies to show that adoptive parents are disproportionately middle class (Holman 1978:13); among these, the national survey *Growing up Adopted* shows that 'the proportion of children living in social class I homes was more than twice as large among the adopted as among the whole cohort or the population as a whole' (Seglow, Kellmer Pringle, and Wedge 1972:84–5).

Thus if adoption is seen as a resource for people who want children then it is one to which access appears very unequal. In the current climate of declining numbers of children available for adoption the prospects for working-class adopters must be particularly bleak.

Even more sensitive nerves are touched when the occupational background of adopters is compared with that of original parents. Again, official data are unhelpful, but the broad outlines are clear enough. Poor countries export children to rich ones, black parents to white, poor parents to better off. Where children are adopted from public care, they are more likely to have come from working-class families. Parents who cannot afford to keep their children surrender them to others who can. Alvin Schorr (writing about the USA) even suggests that 'adoption agencies are a system for redistributing children from the poor to the middle classes' (Schorr 1975:188). Similar patterns in the international sphere have made some of the most widely publicized political issues in adoption; but, within Britain too, the widening of legislation for transferring parental rights without the consent of the original parents, brings this analysis to particularly sharp focus, even if the numbers adopted through these procedures are comparatively small.

Allied to concern about the distribution of children is a concern about the distribution of resources within agencies. The allocation of agencies' resources between, on the one hand, preventive and support work with families and, on the other, adoption and family finding work, has distributional implications. Thus according to Macleod:

> 'the development of substitute care in foster homes and adoption homes has expanded recently following the 1975 Act. It takes place at the expense of expanded advice services and cash grants to natural families. The implicit statement in all this is either that it is not cost effective to support struggling families, or that substitute families quite frequently provide a better enviroment for children than natural families.'
>
> (MacLeod 1982:57)

Given the tendency for adoptive families to be better off than original families, agency commitment to adoption may mean fewer resources for their poorest clients.

This distributional analysis raises important issues. It takes us outside the immediate concerns of social work practice, and beyond issues of psychological development, to ask about the way advantage and disadvantage are reflected in adoption exchanges. To do this it uses class as a descriptive category (in the Registrar General's mode) rather than as an explanatory tool (as in Marxist political economy). It fits clearly, and sometimes explicitly, within the Titmuss paradigm of social policy. Schorr, for example, argues that public services for children should be seen within the context of private ones, analyses the distributional impact of public and private on different occupational groups, and argues for a universalized system of child support (Schorr 1975:204–09). All of this Titmuss himself would surely have approved. The relevance of such child support in the context of adoption policy is made explicit today by the groups aiming to support the rights of poor families where custody of children is at stake.

The strengths of this approach are clear. Mandell has a point when she argues that 'a class analysis of adoption and foster care will pinpoint the problems of the systems more precisely than does a purely psychological analysis of individual motivation and personality dynamics' (Mandell 1973:3). However, weaknesses are also apparent, weaknesses which have led social administration studies to other approaches. There is no space here to elaborate all the debates between different approaches to social policy; intead I shall select some key issues.

The limits of 'traditional' social administration

The approaches discussed so far belong within the framework of 'traditional' social administration. They study welfare 'from inside'; they are committed to 'description, evaluation, and prescription' (Wilding 1983:11). They ask questions of immediate practical interest to child welfare and adoption workers and they pose issues as decisions of policy. They also share, if rather broadly, certain ideological assumptions and commitments. Among these are an idealistic concern with justice and equality; a commitment to achieving these ideals through state welfare policy (and a tendency to optimism about the good nature of the state apparatus); and a commitment to the modern family (with occasional reservations).

Perhaps the most powerful force behind the 'new' social administration has been disillusionment about the success of state welfare policies over a broad front. Several decades of diligent policy analysis and prescription have not ended poverty, unemployment, poor housing, or the neglect and abuse of children. The 'traditional' approach has been seen to be lacking the power to explain these failures, in particular the continued inequalities which it documents so thoroughly. Political economists have stressed the need to examine the nature of the state in capitalist societies, rather than to assume that it can be used straightforwardly for welfare; they have argued that the nature and purpose of state welfare services can only be understood within an analysis of the class relations of capitalism. Feminists have questioned the rather comfortable view of family life in the traditional approach. They have attempted to reveal the extent of the abuse of women and children, arguing that these are not just matters of family pathology, or of poverty and deprivation; rather that they are intrinsic to the particular form of male-dominated family which is actually supported by the welfare state. The issue of who cares for children is also central to any feminist analysis.

Thus, both these strands within the 'new' social administration find the traditional lack of the broader context not just limiting but in some ways misleading. Both demand a direct concern with the nature of the state and a study of social policies which connects them directly to the fundamental relationships of the wider society - capitalist class relations in one case and patriarchal family relations in the other.

The 'new' social administration

It should be said in criticism of the new approaches that an analysis of social policy as a function of these contexts can lead to a kind of determinism in which it seems that nothing can be done. And it may also be remarked that developments in the new social administration have been somewhat one-sided. Thus the dominance of political economy has produced a transformation in the study of health and education; but this analysis has had a less dramatic effect on discussions of the family and personal social services. In the dialogue between political economy and feminism, the former's lack of an adequate perspective on the family has been made painfully obvious. While neither body of thinking has a 'social policy of the family' up its sleeve, which is in any way adequate to deal with the complex issues of child welfare and adoption, each does suggest that there are reasons in general for stepping outside the traditional approach and points to some of the directions one might go.

Both political economy and feminism share a concern with the nature of the state, and both have analysed its relation to children through the education system. In doing so they have attempted to show how children's experience of education is shaped by the state's service of a capitalist economy, as well as how schools reflect and reproduce the family patterns of the wider society. Numerous different positions can be taken on these issues, but what they share is a conviction that the state's relation to children's needs is at best ambiguous. While it is probably true that child welfare services are less determined than education services by the relations of capitalist production, this literature nevertheless provides a vast resource for an analysis of the state in child welfare. In particular the feminist version, in which the family is seen as part of a triangle of relations, is a relevant resource for raising questions about the state's relations to children.

A small study which poses some of these questions in the area of child welfare and adoption is *Whose Child?* (MacLeod 1982). In it the author traces the vicissitudes of state policy towards the family, with particular reference to parental rights. Her argument is that under the Poor Law 'Paupers had no inalienable rights to family life (MacLeod 1982:17). The state destroyed families as a condition of benefits. More positive attitudes to the family in the intervening period are now being eroded. 'This reduction in the rights of parents and the increased removal of children from their original families to other caring families has much in common and reflects some of the views of the 1834 Poor Law Act' (MacLeod 1982:59). Other interpretations of these events are, of course, possible. The point here is that the questions raised are central ones about the relations between state, parents, and children and the character of state intervention with children.

As has already been remarked, traditional social administration has pointed to the inequalities within the adoption process. However, it is to political economy that one has to look for a credible explanation. This is partly because the descriptive use of class in the studies referred to so far is a very different matter from its use in Marxism as an explanatory tool. Of itself, it tends to generate explanations in terms of the 'middle-class' characteristics of the adoptive parents, or the prejudices of social workers. However, the international scope of unequal exchanges in children seems to belie explanations at this micro-level. As Benet remarks: 'adopters need not fear that a look at adoption as a political phenomenon will cast them as the villains of the piece' (Benet 1976:13) and 'Adoptive parents do not have to shoulder the blame for family break-up and the relinquishment of children. Rather they can help to place the blame where it belongs: on the social system that impoverishes and punishes certain groups of people' (Benet 1976:21). She goes on, interestingly and revealingly, to locate the international traffic of children within underdevelopment theory, an offshoot of political economy. For 'underdeveloped' countries it is the relationship to the western capitalist world which produces the drain on resources and the inability to support children. The children themselves then become an export. While this explains the patterns of adoption on an international scale it also has relevance within countries.

> 'For it is only the developed countries that have this century been able to care for their own children - and then only for the children of the groups that form part of the capitalist world, not for the children of the satellite groups within the developed countries. Even in the most affluent parts of the world, there are patches of underdevelopment and consequent inability to care for children - one thinks of American blacks, southern Italians, the Gastarbeiter of Germany.'
>
> (Benet 1976:123)

The 'solution' of adoption works well for those children who find new homes, but the impoverishment and family dislocation produced in this way makes a different story for countless other children. Benet comments that the necessity to abandon children 'has been forced upon poor people by Western social welfare practices ever since the first Poor Laws; it is one of the first and longest-lasting Western exports to the countries that come within the orbit of world capitalism' (Benet 1976:125).

Thus relating adoption to the wider economy raises important issues, issues which, for countries within the orbit of Western capitalism, are best understood in the context of a political economy approach. Child care, however, is also about the family, and about the state's relation to the family. Here a feminist analysis has more to offer, raising as it does questions about the nature of the family and the particular kind of family system which is supported by state welfare services. Feminists have emphasized the welfare state's relation to the domestic world, in contrast to political economy's preoccupation with the world of paid work. Elizabeth Wilson goes so far as to describe the welfare state as the 'state organisation of domestic life' (Wilson 1977:9). Certainly the welfare state reflects norms of family life, but both through ideology and through the details of practical provision it also supports family life of a particular kind. Policies connected with adoption are some of the most direct expressions of this concern. Social policy is concerned in general terms with which kinds of family will be supported and to what extent (e.g. one-parent, two-parent). It is concerned more individually with which parents shall be considered capable and which incapable of bringing up their children. And it is concerned with remaking families, with which applicants shall become adopters and which shall be rejected. Thus a study of these issues should concern itself, not just with the issue of the distribution of resources between families, but with the character of the family that is being fostered by state policy.

In general, feminists have argued that social policies support a male-dominated, female-dependent family (Wilson 1977) and that far from being the comfortable haven depicted in much sociology and social administration, this family is the focus of a great deal of violence, of abuse of women and children. Furthermore, this family form is one in which a mother's responsibility for the care of her children is almost total and where women's main satisfaction in life is seen to come through bearing and raising children. Thus we have the sad picture of some mothers isolated and over-burdened by the demands of small children (and plenty of evidence that there is a high incidence of depression among these mothers); while other women, involuntarily childless, are denied their main function in life, as it is decreed by the ideology which supports this kind of family.

The relation of adoption to these issues is by no means straightforward. Adoption may be a way in which the rigidities of the classic nuclear family pattern are maintained (for example through pressures exerted on single mothers to relinquish their children which seem to have operated particularly severely in the 1960s). It may be a way in which the victims of such a family structure are 'rescued', though without disturbing the character of the family itself. On the other hand it may be, in some kinds of family system, a way in which community responsibility for children is expressed in contrast to the individual responsibility of isolated family groups. Benet concludes that 'in groups and nations that have practised widespread adoption, those who care for children do not do it on their own. Family, friends and society itself share the responsibility in tangible ways' (Benet 1976:219). The very considerable shifts in adoption policy and practice in Britain over recent decades could well be considered in relation to these questions of family structure and the care of children.

Conclusion

This paper has reviewed several approaches to adoption and adoption policy which fall broadly within the scope of 'traditional' social administration. In suggesting that there is some point in turning to newer approaches there is no intention of rejecting this kind of work. However, the 'new' social administration has had a radical impact on ways of thinking about social policy. Primarily, it offers ways which are not bound by the structures of the society whose problems social administration has traditionally sought to solve; it offers new ways of looking at the state; new ways of understanding such basic issues as inequalities and violence; and new ways of relating social policy issues to the structures of economy and family. However, its development has been somewhat one-sided, and its impact has been much greater in areas such as health and education than in family policy. This paper has therefore attempted to suggest some of the ways in which the understanding of adoption and child care policy can be extended within the newer paradigms.

References

Benet, M.K. (1976) *The Character of Adoption.* London: Jonathan Cape.

Coussins, J. and Coote, A. (1981) *The Family in the Firing Line: A Discussion Document on Family Policy,* London: NCCL/CPAG.

Freeman, M.D.A. (1981) Rights of Children in Care. In D. Rawstron *Rights of Children.* London: BAAF.

Fruin, D. (1980) Sources of Statistical Information on Adoption. *Adoption & Fostering* 100(2):25-36.

Gill, O. and Jackson, B. (1983) *Adoption and Race: Black, Asian and Mixed Race Children in White Families.* London: Batsford, BAAF.

Goldstein, J., Freud, A., and Solnit, A.J. (1973) *Beyond the Best Interests of the Child.* New York: The Free Press.

Goldstein, J., Freud A., and Solnit, A.J. (1979) *Before the Best Interests of the Child.* New York: The Free Press.

Holman, R. (1978) A Class Analysis of Adoption. *Community Care* 26 April: 13.

Humphrey, M. (1969) *The Hostage Seekers.* London: Longmans.

Kellmer Pringle, M.L. (1967) *Adoption - Facts and Fallacies.* London: Longmans.

Laurance, J. (1982) Captive Families: When Parents Lose their Children. *New Society* 27 May: 332-33.

MacLeod, V. (1982) *Whose Child? The Family in Child Care Legislation and Social Work Practice.* London: Study Commission on the Family.

Mandell, B.R. (1973) *Where are the Children? A Class Analysis of Foster Care and Adoption.* Massachusetts: Lexington Books.

Marshall, T.H. (1949) Citizenship and Social Class. In T.H. Marshall *Sociology at the Crossroads.* London: Heinemann 1963.

Rawstron, D. (ed.) (1981) *Rights of Children.* London: BAAF.

Rowe, J. and Lambert, L. (1973) *Children who Wait.* London: ABAA.

Schorr, A. (1975) *Children and Decent People.* London: Allen & Unwin.

Seglow, J., Kellmer Pringle, M., and Wedge, P. (1972) *Growing up Adopted.* London: NFER.

Shaw, M. and Lebens, K. (1978) *What Shall We Do With The Children?* London: ABAFA.

Shawyer, J. (1979) *Death by Adoption.* New Zealand: Cicada Press.

Tizard, B. (1977) *Adoption: A Second Chance.* London: Open Books.

Tunnard, J. (1983) No Access for Parents. *New Society* 20 January: 100-01.

Wilding, P. (1983) The Evolution of Social Administration. In P. Bean and

S. MacPherson (eds) *Approaches to Welfare*. London: Routledge & Kegan Paul.
Wilson, E. (1977) *Women and the Welfare State*. London: Tavistock Publications.

2 The role of voluntary societies in adoption services

MARY BROMLEY

The central experience of all people participating in adoption from 1926, when the first Adoption Act was passed in this country, to the present day, is one of change. The voluntary pioneers of the 1920s could not have foreseen the present work of an organization such as 'Parents for Children'. During that time the expansion of knowledge, exchange of ideas, and the growth of awareness about changing needs has been enormous. Those working in voluntary societies in particular have been challenged to justify their existence by adapting to newly perceived needs.

In 1966 there were seventy-three voluntary societies who were members of SCSRA (the Standing Conference of Societies Registered for Adoption) (Rowe 1966:9). By 1970, sixty-six voluntary societies acted as adoption agencies in England and Wales (HMSO 1970:9), and by 1980 the total had declined to forty-three (DHSS 1980:3). The fall in numbers is not an accurate reflection of decline in quality of contribution. The record of failure to adapt, as the number of white, healthy babies placed for adoption decreased and costs of other adoption provision escalated, is counterbalanced by a vibrant response to new opportunities and changing demands, which is the ideal characteristic of the voluntary contribution to the welfare of society. New agencies came into being, challenging traditional expectations.

In the 1960s the Agnostics Adoption Society offered the chance of adoption to a wider field of adopters; the International Social Service promoted the new British Adoption Project to find families for infants of mixed racial inheritance; and Standing Conference tried to raise standards in the voluntary agencies by appointing an adviser and tutor.

In the 1970s the beginning of the Association of British Adoption Agencies (later to include fostering in its scope) brought a closer relationship between voluntary and statutory bodies. It replaced the former Standing Conference which had a membership of voluntary societies only. The Adoption Resource Exchange (ARE), developing out of the British Adoption Project, gradually established, not only that any child can be adopted but that, to achieve this, agencies must co-operate on an agreed basis of standards and procedures. Parent to Parent Information on Adoption services (PPIAS) and Parents for Children, alongside ARE, found new ways of bringing together adopters and children.

This catalogue of change in the 1960s and 1970s indicates considerable strengths in new and existing voluntary agencies. I hope to make clear the nature of their contribution in the past and assess their present and future role in the comprehensive service which will become mandatory when Section 1 of the Children Act 1975 comes into force.

Changes 1950-83

STRUCTURES

Over the last thirty years, provision has been very patchy indeed, developing on an *ad hoc* basis. In 1950, the creation of SCSRA, helped into existence by the National Council of Social Service, marked a notable commitment to disseminate knowledge about adoption policy and practice, not only among its own members, but also among those children's departments doing adoption work. The voluntary societies ranged from small Diocesan or independent groups serving local communities, to regional and national agencies providing adoption as part of their general child care service. Some adoption work was begun in a few local authority children's departments. After the Adoption Act 1958 (Sec. 28) gave the local authority power to make and participate in arrangements for the adoption of children, whether or not the child is in the care of the local authority, the work increased. The Adoption Agencies Regulations replaced the Adoption Societies Regulations (Goodman 1972:1100-109) so that, for the first time, both statutory and voluntary agencies came under the same regulations. It was a public recognition of adoption developing as a statutory as well as a voluntary service. It took ten years before both types of agency joined in a common specialist association, when the Association of British Adoption Agencies (ABAA) began in May 1979. It is important to remember that, alongside this dual structure, many adoptions, apart from those where parents adopted their own children, were arranged on a private basis through what became known as a 'third party'.

In the late 1950s, the proportions of adoptions arranged by voluntary societies and through children's departments were still quite small (McWhinnie 1964:9-25). The figure has been quoted at between 10 and 25 per cent. By 1966, considering only those adoptions not involving a parent as adopter (62 per cent of all adoptions), 65 per cent were arranged by adoption societies, 27 per cent by local authorities, and 8 per cent by a third party. It was envisaged that at least another 10 per cent would be done by local authorities, as the adoption societies were stretched to capacity (*Child Adoption* 1969:2). Opinion began to be against third-party placement and in favour of placement by approved agencies. However it was not until 1983 that Section 28 of the Children Act 1975 was implemented, making third-party placement illegal.

During the 1960s the will to provide an accessible service, with less rigid idiosyncratic criteria and standards, provided another motivation for change (Association of Child Care Officers 1969). Lancashire County Council Children's Committee's decision to act as an adoption agency (*Child Adoption* 1959-60:22-3) reflects local authority thinking. They accepted that there were too few voluntary societies to meet the national need, thought they could accept adopters whom societies rejected, and wanted to prevent private placements. They did not want to usurp but to complement the work of the voluntary societies. Development of a nationwide adoption service came very slowly. In 1966 fewer than half of the 172 local authorities (67) in England and Wales acted as adoption agencies (*Child Adoption* 1966:50) despite the fact that they had been empowered to do so since 1958.

As late as 1969 two-thirds of agency placements were made by voluntary societies (Rowe 1972) although the total of local authorities now acting as agencies had risen to 94 (HMSO 1970:10).

In 1983 out of the 116 reorganized local authorities listed in *Adopting a Child*, 106 (91 per cent) acted as adoption agencies (British Agencies for Adoption and Fostering 1983). The thinking of the 1960s reflects not simply a negative struggle for control of adoption practice between the newer statutory bodies and the voluntary societies, but a basic and general concern about standards of practice and universally available provision. As a result there emerged not merely pressure for new legislation to enact advances in practice, and a reorganization of the structural basis of provision, but the pioneering of new approaches to adoption. Whilst some traditional voluntary societies began to close their doors as fewer healthy white babies were needing adoptive families, others began to find homes for infants, first of mixed racial inheritance, then with physical or mental handicap and latterly for any child needing a new permanent family. The changes involved a new approach away from 'parochial' provision to an inter-agency basis. In addition, adoption began to be recognized as an integral part of an overall child care provision.

The British Adoption Project reflected growing awareness of the possibility of transracial adoption. It was initially sponsored by International Social Service and reflects the pioneering drive of voluntary agencies combined with the research experience of a university. Out of this emerged the Resource Exchange to help agencies co-operate in seeking families for non-European children. Much work had to be done to overcome mistrust and to establish mutually acceptable standards (ARE 1980). By spring 1968 the Exchange had 20 members; by 1983 the total was 93 with 67 members being local authorities and 26 voluntary agencies. Despite the voluntary societies being in a minority, they provide as many adoptive parents for the Exchange as the local authorities. The whole emphasis of the Resource Exchange has been one of inter-agency co-operation to find homes for 'hard to place' children.

The structure of the service has changed over thirty years from a piecemeal, largely parochial, voluntary basis to the enactment of a comprehensive structure in which statutory and voluntary agencies can make mutually respected contributions, although as we shall see there still exist conflicts and ignorance of each other's strengths.

PERSONNEL

As early as 1953 the editor writing in *Child Adoption* No. 9 foresaw problems facing the voluntary societies in trying to employ properly trained workers and pay them salaries commensurate with those paid by the local authorities. The problem still exists, as paying the same salaries as local authorities puts additional financial pressure on voluntary societies. The societies were concerned about standards of work and in the mid-1960s Jane Rowe wrote up her findings following visits to 69 of the 72 voluntary agencies in Great Britain (Rowe 1967). She reported enormous variation in size, structure, and practice. The largest group of 28 had developed from Church of England Moral Welfare work. In another 24 adoption was only one part of general child care provision, while 7 societies were national in scope and only concerned with adoption placement. Most of the remaining 13 had grown out of local councils of social service.

The length of training which staff had undertaken varied from a few months to years of professional training and only nine societies were without any trained worker. At the same time the Association of Child Care Officers (ACCO) described a 'deep concern' that some adoption agencies showed no understanding of the need for training or qualifications (ACCO 1966).

The Seebohm Report (HMSO 1968:175) also expressed concern about lack of trained local authority social workers. The truth seems to be not that voluntary societies had lower standards of training than local authorities, but that both groups were very variable in their standards of training. The new adoptions officer working in a small city children's department in the 1960s, surrounded by fully qualified staff was seconded for three months to one of the leading voluntary societies to observe and plan how to establish the city's adoption service. Both groups had enough confidence in their own standards to respect each other.

The real problem in hindsight seems to have been, not simply lack of training in the voluntary societies, but a rapid rise in demand for a service which could not be met by the existing network. In the early 1970s the local authorities also had to face the upheavals of the new social service departments and the local government reorganization. At the same time the Houghton Committee was collating evidence on adoption and formulating recommendations (HMSO 1970). Resources for change were severely tested. There seemed to be some repercussions in staffing in the voluntary societies as some of the child-care oriented staff of the previous children's departments transferred into the larger voluntary societies. In the 1970s all agencies gained from a general increase in training for social work but concern has been expressed about the lack of specialist training on social work courses.

The affects of post-Seebohm organization highlight the fact that the voluntary agencies are specialists and have less conflict over priorities than the general social service departments. The conflicts between generic or specialist do not affect them to the same extent. This is typified by an organization such as 'Parents for Children' which not only demonstrates the drive to bring new parents and children together but the amassing of very specialized knowledge about the kind of work involved in placing children with individual special needs. Whilst accepting the need for trained workers, a voluntary group can also free those workers to break new ground to meet a need, without being seen to have obligations to a wide range of other social work tasks. The local authority counterpart is the creation of specialized units within the social work service.

The changes in personnel in the voluntary agencies and the pressure towards training have meant a rethinking of the contribution of their true volunteers who are motivated by a belief in the value of adoption and the importance of good parenting in a child's development. Volunteers still provide many hours of skilled and experienced service. Management committees and adoption panels are fortunate to be able to rely on the services of doctors, lawyers, adoptive parents, ex-social workers, and accountants to provide the relevant framework for a specialist organization. Their contribution often goes uncosted but many voluntary organizations could neither carry the caseload nor maintain the same standard without them. Their participation reflects a more 'personal' organization. An extension of this is the increasing involvement of adoptive families in helping other adoptive families. This ranges from individual families talking of their own experiences in training groups, to an organization like Parent to Parent Information Advisory Service (PPIAS), founded in 1971 by two adoptive mothers. PPIAS acts as an information exchange, supports adopters, acts as a pressure group, and promotes the needs of children seeking new families. The self-help aspect is a vital contribution to the adoption service.

The changes in personnel in both statutory and voluntary agencies have been characterized by increased training but the voluntary societies in particular have maintained the close involvement of adopters and volunteers with relevant expertise.

CONCEPTS OF NEED

The peak year for the adoption placement of infants for adoption was 1968 (*Child Adoption* 1970:48) when 24,831 children were legally adopted. This figure includes children adopted by birth parents. By 1981 the total adoption figure was down to 9,284. The pattern for adoption was placement of very young, healthy, white babies. In the 1960s 80 per cent of the children from the voluntary societies and 50 per cent from the local authorities were under six months when placed with their new family (Goodacre 1966:56). In 1981 only 20.5 per cent of adoptions were of babies under nine months on the day of their adoption. The decline began in the 1970s. Voluntary societies who had been placing between 150 and 200 babies a year in the 1960s were placing about a third of that number by the mid-1970s (*Child Adoption:* Reports from Societies 1960–75). In the 1960s societies referred to some babies as being not acceptable for placement, which now seems strange, but many societies did not have facilities to care for babies where there was a history of handicap. Some of the large societies and the local authorities would receive into care babies thought not 'suitable' for adoption. By 1969 however the editor of *Child Adoption* anticipated an increase in the placement of infants with a variety of handicaps and predicted that in future the main focus would be on searching out homes for all children who needed parents (1969:9–10). The development of this service is referred to elsewhere, but the 1970s saw an increase in the identification of older or handicapped children who needed families (Rowe and Lambert 1973). By 1972 the Adoption Resource Exchange extended its service to *all* children needing adoptive families. And it was not just the newer voluntary agencies like the Resource Exchange and Parents for Children who made this striking transition. Some smaller societies gradually placed older children or handicapped children and some larger societies were beginning to specialize in finding homes for children with special needs. The Yorkshire Branch of Dr Barnardo's was described (*Child Adoption* 1974:49–51) as referring 'ordinary babies' to other societies, all the children they placed having special needs. They worked closely with local authorities in the area and still do. Indeed this is true of all voluntary agencies now placing children for adoption. Some of them do not have facilities to care for children. Instead local authorities refer children to them. They specifically act as placement agencies. Even those agencies who had facilities to care for children in foster homes or children's homes found it a much more expensive process than the virtually direct placement of babies.

The other aspect of the decline in numbers of infants placed for adoption and the increase in 'special needs' has been the necessity to go out and seek adopters rather than find them queueing on the doorstep. The PPIAS newsletter, which goes to individuals and groups nationwide, and the *Be My Parent* book launched in 1976 actively seek out adopters. The biggest single impact was made in the Granada TV programme 'World in Action' shown in April 1974. Publicity on this scale calls for more than the average social worker's skills. One of the important contributions of the new voluntary societies has been in public relations with the media. The focus of their work is on reaching out to find people and show them the need.

Alongside this, the individual voluntary societies no longer select and vet their adopters in the same way as they did in the 1960s, when they were criticized for their rigid rules and class bias.

Despite the advent of the Agnostics Society in 1965 and the

existence of some independent societies without a religious foundation, it was thought that the local authorities would give more choice to would-be adopters. In reality the decline in the number of infants to be placed has meant a continuation of criteria as a way of limiting applications. Many workers see a need for a counselling service for childless couples rather than simply viewing them as prospective adopters. The idea of criteria for adopters of hard-to-place children is inappropriate and has been replaced by a training, experiential process to help people understand all that is involved before committing themselves to a child. The trend has been towards self-help and the involvement of experienced adopters. Far from voluntary effort being superceded (*Child Adoption* 1975:2-3) there is a real movement towards its development. Prospective adopters are not seen as clients but as resources, in the voluntary agencies at least. The social worker's role is more of a catalyst, bringing two sets of people together and enabling them to realize each other's needs and potential. This kind of adoption may be compared to marriage - for the older child it is often a second or third marriage. Twenty years ago the voluntary agencies saw themselves as providing a service either for the unmarried mother, or for the baby, or for the adopters. Now they often provide a service for hard-pressed, busy local authorities.

Adoption has its roots in a triangular relationship of child, birth parent, and adoptive parent. Even where a child has had no contact with the birth parents for years, the past is still within him. For the new relationship to succeed, several social workers need to work together and need to work alongside all the people involved. This approach may be more easily made in a small informal setting. One adopter said recently of the agency, 'It's become part of the family'. A large local authority carries a stronger image of authority. It does not follow that individual social workers in either setting can or cannot work alongside people, but the pressures within an organization and people's perception of it can make it more or less difficult.

Whilst the children being placed have changed and the adopters have changed - from an emphasis on childless couples to any couple or single person who meet a particular child's needs - the relationship of social worker with birth parent has also changed. Many of the societies, whose basis was rooted in moral welfare, closed when casework with unmarried mothers was transferred to the new local authority personal social services (Wainwright 1976). Social acceptance, financial help, contraception, and abortion have all contributed to the decline in numbers of unmarried mothers placing babies for adoption. From the 1960s more voluntary societies refer in their annual reports to mothers keeping their babies. Those societies still placing infants often also offer ongoing support to mothers keeping their babies. Usually they have less contact with the birth parents of children in care. This dichotomy can cause conflicts between the birth family's social worker and the adoption worker, either in the voluntary agency or in the local authority adoption section, particularly if a hearing is contested. It can be difficult for one social worker to reconcile the sometimes conflicting interests of the child, the birth parent, and the adopters.

Roles and relationships

A new comprehensive service is at last within sight with the proposed implementation of Section 1 of the Children Act 1975 which makes it the duty of each local authority to provide such a service either directly or in conjunction with other agencies.

Some of the fears of voluntary societies that they would be unnecessary have proved false, especially for those who have adapted to changing needs, standards of service, and who have, most importantly, found ways of financing their work.

FINANCIAL BASIS

While local authorities have their own financial pressures, the voluntary societies seem to live closer to the financial brink. They have to balance constantly what they would like to do with what they can afford. On the one hand the grant from the local authority may seem 'erratic and wholly inadequate' (Richards 1971:49) when half of the work is devoted to hard-to-place babies who would otherwise stay in care. On the other hand, there is a danger that if a voluntary agency is almost wholly funded by a grant from a local authority, control of the agency's future existence could become externally based. In the 1960s token grants were given by several authorities to local voluntary societies and bore little relationship to the cost of maintaining the service (*Child Adoption* 1967, 1968:48; Rowe 1978). This practice has to some extent been replaced by the inter-agency fee paid for each child placed. The work of the Association of British Agencies for Fostering and Adoption (ABAFA) and ARE, now the British Agencies for Adoption and Fostering (BAAF), in negotiating fees relevant to expenditure of time and energy of staff, has had an incalculable effect on the position of the voluntary societies who provide the Exchange with roughly half the families used. The balance of money from local authority grants, fees, traditional fund-raising, and covenants from adopters seems to vary from agency to agency. Infant adoption does not attract fees and has still to be financed in other ways. One effect of the 'professionalization' of workers in the voluntary societies may be less commitment to fund-raising. If this is so one can foresee a gradual loss of independence in direct ratio to the reliance on local authority grants. To remain independent the voluntary societies need their financial eggs in a variety of baskets and independent fund-raising is important. One other possible source of grant aid is central government. The DHSS played an important part in initially funding Parents for Children. Over the years the voluntary societies have achieved remarkable successes with limited and precarious incomes, partly because of the number of hours worked by unpaid volunteers. The pressure to maintain a sound financial basis still plays an important part in any voluntary society.

PIONEERS IN PRACTICE

It is certainly true that initiative and exploration of new areas of work can be seen in both voluntary and statutory agencies. The original provision of infant adoption, the movement to place infants of mixed racial inheritance, infants and, later, older children with handicaps, adolescents, and sibling groups owes much to voluntary agencies. The more 'open' attitude to adoption, the use of the media, and the involvement of adoptive parents were pioneered by national groups such as ARE, PPIAS, and Parents for Children, as well as by the older established voluntary societies like Dr Barnardo's and smaller independent societies. Although the number of voluntary agencies has declined by half, possibly two-thirds, the amount and quality of work being done by voluntary societies deserves recognition. Development of service depends not only on a pioneering spirit but on sound research and it is important to remember the contributions of charities like the Buttle Trust, Rowntree, Gulbenkian, or societies like the Guild of Service, to the discovery, dissemination, and sharing of knowledge throughout all agencies. In some areas voluntary societies are actively contributing to training in local authorities by leading seminars and workshops on adoption.

WORKING TOGETHER

Pioneers may fill gaps of their own choosing, given that they can convince their financial backers. The other side of the coin is that the local authorities have to be the anchor men of any nationwide, comprehensive service. They will carry the mandatory burden. In this sense they cannot choose to withhold service. The small society covering one area of service is safe in the knowledge that the local authority has to provide the rest of the comprehensive service. This can cause friction with the voluntary agency being seen as an easy or protected place to work, less weighed down by accountability and less torn between a variety of priorities. On the whole, hierarchies are small in voluntary societies. The team is small; committees are less remote from field workers and committed to the specialism rather than responsible for a vast spectrum of services. Approval by the Secretary of State will, rightly, make the voluntary societies maintain standards. The relationship between the local authority and the DHSS is slightly different: the DHSS can advise the local authorities, but it cannot inspect them. Sadly, the relationship between voluntary and statutory bodies is in many areas non-existent, with each knowing little of the other's work. One may well agree with Bacon and Rowe (1978) that the idea of regional planning for family care is premature. In the region they studied they found little policy of co-ordination between statutory and voluntary services. In the Yorkshire and Humberside region, planning towards a consortium does not include the voluntary agencies of the area despite good individual relationships between some of the local authorities and the voluntary agencies. Distrust and sheer lack of knowledge are inevitably reflected in stereotyped thinking about 'amateurs' and 'bureaucrats'.

A more positive picture and hope for a truly comprehensive service, in which both participate, are seen in those areas where consortia of both types of agency work together to share expenditure and resources. Each time co-operation succeeds, each time a local authority social worker successfully places a child in a voluntary society's family, the stereotypes begin to crumble. Out of the Soul Kids Campaign (1977) came a Black Families unit, sponsored jointly by the Independent Adoption Society and the London Borough of Lambeth. In Doncaster the local authority gives a grant to the Doncaster Adoption and Family Welfare Society Ltd., which undertakes all infant adoption and the placement of children in care referred for adoption by the local authority. Other local authorities have worked out special relationships with a nearby independent agency. Change to closer working relationships calls for a closer look at one's own practice and requires patterns of referral and placement to be worked out. The best working relationship is founded on the primacy of the child's needs, rather than that of the worker involved. The adoption workers have to value the local authority's first responsibility to keep families together where possible, and the way decisions about a child's future are made: the social workers in the local authority have to recognize the adoption workers' expertise in preparing and supporting families. The gradual introduction of specialized adoption and fostering units in some local authorities has created some of the same tensions about 'handing over' children or families.

While one still comes across mistrust of other social workers and misconceptions about present-day adoption, there has been interchange of ideas through regional BAAF groups, through the setting of standards in the Resource Exchange, through PPIAS, and through the successful co-operation of individual social workers. Voluntary agencies grow out of private commitment to solving a problem. Statutory agencies grow out of public recognition of a problem. The solution to the problem is hopefully embodied in legislation, either mandatory or permissive. The work of the local authority emphasizes people's rights to a service. Voluntary societies represent people's awareness of obligations towards others. This can result in either paternal or participatory services available only to a few. At their best they represent a cohesive force in society, free to go beyond rights to obligations. This does not mean that individual workers in one agency are more concerned than those in others. The state can legislate larger and larger burdens which have to be allocated places in priority lists. The voluntary societies, on the other hand, have a more specific commitment. Their unique combination of paid and unpaid workers may well be important in the future in a society where the boundaries of paid work, leisure, and voluntary work will need to be increasingly flexible to allow people to move between all three.

Conclusion

Adoption is a mixture of a very private experience and a public process. Workers in both types of agency need to balance their position of authority with a catalyst role. The comprehensive service should provide equality of provision but it cannot of itself ensure a personal, flexible approach which actively involves all participants. National and regional networks including both statutory and voluntary agencies, are needed to bring together the families and the children; having done this the focus of work becomes very personal and will best be sustained by small agency or adoption units. Adoption has to be part of a wide variety of child care and family provision but it does not necessarily follow that it must be solely based within local authority departments. Links with outside agencies are vital to share resources. To be truly comprehensive the service needs to be on an inter-agency basis, not simply to bring children and parents together, but to stimulate the exchange of ideas. To keep it vital and responsive, it needs to maintain the participation of non-professional adopters and foster parents.

Voluntary groups and voluntary agencies, together with the local authorities, can sustain not merely the letter but the spirit and thinking behind the legislation for comprehensive service. The roles and relations will differ throughout the region depending on the existing strengths and interests of the existing agencies. To work successfully together to improve the service the agencies need to respect each other's experience and expertise.

The last thirty years have seen considerable changes in practice, despite the slow implementation of legislation. The changes reflect a willingness, in both statutory and voluntary agencies, to discover and adapt to changing patterns of need. The present-day voluntary agencies seem to have a future as independent specialists with considerable expertise.

References

Adoption Resource Exchange (1980) *A Dramatic Record by Anyone's Standards.* London.

Association of Child Care Officers (1966) Future of the Personal Social Services. Quoted in *Child Adoption* 50:53.

______ (1969) *Adoption - The Way Ahead.* Monograph 3, London.

Bacon, R. and Rowe, J. (1978) *The Use and Misuse of Resources.* London: ABAFA.

British Agencies for Adoption and Fostering (1983) *Adopting a Child.* London: BAAF.

DHSS (Children's Division) (1980) *Approval of Adoption Societies by the Secretary of State.* Report of DHSS Working Party, London.

Goodacre, I. (1966) *Adoption Policy and Practice.* London: Allen & Unwin.

Goodman, L. (1972) *Clarke Hall and Morrison on Children.* (8th edn) London: Butterworths.

HMSO (1968) *Report of the Committee on Local Authority and Allied Personal Social Services.* (The Seebohm Report) London: HMSO.

______ (1970) *Working Paper Containing the Provisional Proposals of the Departmental Committee on the Adoption of Children.* (The Houghton Report) London: HMSO.

McWhinnie, A. (1964) Adoption Work of a Scottish Society. *Child Adoption* 45:11.

Richards, K. (1971) The Independent Adoption Society. *Child Adoption* 65:49–50.

Rowe, J. (1966) Training: The Preliminary Work. *Child Adoption* 50:9.
______ (1967) Present Standards and Future Needs. *Child Adoption* 51: 17-22.
______ (1972) Adoption in the New Social Service Departments. *Child Adoption* 68:26-8.
______ (1978) The Voluntaries: Adapting to Partnership. *Adoption and Fostering* 93:10-13.
Rowe, J. and Lambert, L. (1973) *Children Who Wait.* London: ABAA.
Soul Kids Campaign 1975-6 (1977) London: ABAFA.
Wainwright, D. (1976) The Future of the Diocesan Adoption Societies. *Adoption and Fostering* 84:51-6.

3 Obtaining birth certificates

JOHN TRISELIOTIS

Introduction

Section 26, of the Children Act of 1975 gave effect to the recommendation of the Houghton Committee that adopted people in England and Wales who have reached the age of eighteen years should be entitled to a copy of their original birth certificate (HMSO 1972). At the same time the Act placed a duty on the Registrar General, local authorities, and approved agencies to provide a counselling service for adopted people who apply for information, enabling them to obtain their birth certificate. In effect, information from the birth records is subject to the acceptance of counselling by adoptees. In this chapter I shall be discussing the background to this piece of social legislation and what happened after Section 26 came into operation in November 1976.

Based on the findings of my first study which was carried out in Scotland where access to birth records has been possible since 1930, my written and oral evidence to the Houghton Committee concluded that 'no person should be cut off from his origins'. My subsequent studies in adoption, foster care, and residential care have on the whole confirmed and extended the key concepts identified in the original study. It can now be claimed with some confidence from the available evidence that there is a psychosocial need in all people, manifest principally among those who grow up away from their original families, to know about their background, their genealogy, and their personal history if they are to grow up feeling complete and whole. In this respect, Section 26 of the Children Act 1975 is a legislative response to a psychological need, something almost unique in social legislation. In effect, the Act has recognized the importance of genealogical information to the formation of a positive concept of self. Adoptees trying to bring about legislative change in other countries are appropriately arguing that their psychological needs should constitute a fundamental right. The argument is based on the research findings, which suggest that the development of a positive sense of identity and mental health are at risk when vital background and personal information are missing.

Some ideas relating to the need for background information and for personal history material to be made available to the growing child have now been translated into everyday social work practice with children. For example, social workers, in their efforts to enable children to maintain their identity through care, try and help them construct family trees or history books which include background information, photographs, letters, and so on. When a seven-year-old boy recently joined his new family and arrived with his personal history book clutched under his arm, the family's own daughter asked why she didn't have one.

While some of these books have been excellent, there have also been instances when children have been overwhelmed with information inappropriate for their age and stage of development. Though it is important for the child to know the truth about his circumstances, the pace of revelation and sharing of information have to take account of his age and readiness to cope particularly with complex or unpalatable material. Information about murder, abandonment, incest, or cruelty should be withheld, in my view, for a later stage, sometimes after childhood.

The Rationale of Access

The passing of Section 26 was welcomed not only by adopted people in England and Wales but by many groups of adoptees, particularly in English-speaking countries such as the USA, Canada, Australia, and New Zealand. There was hope that the evidence from research and the example given by the British Parliament would influence legislators in these countries. Sadly these hopes have not yet been realized, though a Government Commission in Ontario, Canada has recommended such legal reform (1976). A Departmental Committee set up by the Northern Ireland Office in 1976 to review, among other things, legislation and schemes relating to the adoption of children, found itself divided on the question of retrospective access to birth records and made no recommendation. In a press release in June 1982, the Parliamentary Under Secretary of Health and Social

Services in Northern Ireland did declare his intention to ask Parliament to approve the 'retrospective option'. His statement was accompanied by the important comment that there was 'lack of evidence of seriously adverse consequences' arising out of the open access arrangement pertaining in the rest of the UK. In most states of the USA, adoptees wishing to gain access to their original birth records must convince the court that it should authorize access to such information.

The arguments in favour of access to birth records may now sound academic in Britain, where adoptees have won this basic right. It is nevertheless helpful to remind ourselves about the supporting evidence. McWhinnie (1967) and Triseliotis (1973, 1974, 1980, 1983) link genealogical and personal information to the development of a positive sense of identity and of a whole self. In effect a full concept of self is not possible when important links in the person's background and development are missing. The psychological need to know is present in all, but the evidence suggests that it is intensified where secrecy and evasiveness predominate and where relationships are not satisfactory. Yet my own studies also show that when a number of factors are considered together, such as quality of relationships, availability of background and personal information, and community perceptions, the paramount factor is the quality of relationships. Background and personal history information are important, but hierarchically the quality of caring and relationships come first. Put simply, 'love' by itself can go a very long way to make up for other deficiencies. Not surprisingly, it is usually where relationships in general are satisfying, honest, open, and sharing that the child is also most likely to be fully aware of his status and circumstances. Erikson (1968) writing from a theoretical rather than a research perspective, also viewed the development of a person's identity in a psychological context relating to the individual's sense of genealogy in his or her life cycle. He implies that ignorance about important stages of one's past brings about a break in the continuity of the life cycle. He also adds that, especially in adolescence, it is difficult to plan for the future if parts of the past are blacked out.

Clinical observations by Paton (1954, 1960), Sants (1965), and Stone (1969) raised concerns about the impact on the adoptee's identity of ignorance about important aspects of the past. As early as 1953, the Hurst Report on the adoption of children stressed the need to tell a child of his or her adoption. (HMSO 1953). Not surprisingly, detailed arguments to support this declaration were missing because of the lack at that time of relevant research. A number of witnesses told the Committee that adopted people in

England, as in Scotland, should have the right to genealogical information from the birth records, adding that 'it is not in the interests of adopted children to be permanently precluded from satisfying their natural curiosity'. The Hurst Committee, however, made no recommendations in this direction. It referred to the possible risks involved for the birth mother, who might be sought out, and urged that this possibility should be explained to her when she consented to the adoption. The opponents of access in the 1970s were to use the absence of such explanation to the mother as the basis for their objection. There is also no evidence to suggest that adoption workers in Scotland were explaining to parents surrendering children for adoption that the children would have a right of access to information when they reached the age of seventeen.

My study (Triseliotis 1973) was followed by a few others, some relying for their samples on members of adoptees' groups or seeking volunteers through newspaper and radio appeals. In spite of these sampling deficiencies and with minor exceptions, most of the published material supports the key concepts and ideas identified earlier on. Notable among these papers are those by a California-based group, Sorosky, Baran, and Pannor (1974, 1975), and an Australian study by Picton (1980). Autobiographical writings, such as the forceful account given by Fisher (1973) of her own efforts to locate her birth parents, added to the weight of opinion supporting access. The quest for origins displayed by groups of adoptees in the 1970s seems to have generated a whole industry of fiction books, plays, and semi-autobiographical films. Their central theme has been the quest for roots, origins, and reunions. It can also be claimed that the adoption studies of the last 10–15 years have yielded insights into the subject of identity which are relevant to the development of self - not only among adoptees but in all children, particularly those growing up in situations where one or both carers are not the child's birth parents. The early 1970s was a period when adoptees in England and in other English-speaking countries organized 'Right of Access' groups, for political and legal action to bring about the opening of records through legislative changes. Movements such as ALMA (Adoptees' Liberty Movement Association) in the USA. Parent Finders and the Open Door Society Inc. in Canada, and Jigsaw and Adoption Triangle in Australia are a few examples of the many organizations that sprang up in the early 1970s. Those years were a period when other minority groups, besides adoptees, were asserting their rights.

It is not surprising that as a result of the movements for access many adoptive parents were feeling (and some still are) threatened and confused. The possible bewilderment of the adopted child who lacks genealogical information is often equal to the confusion felt by some adoptive parents. Some are unable to comprehend the issues and others see the movement for access as a threat to their parenting qualities. My contacts with some adoptive parents' groups illustrated to me their understandable fears, confusion, and ignorance. Paramount was their lack of information about the rationale for access, together with the feeling that access was in conflict with their interests as parents. Whilst adoptive parents were usually urged by adoption workers to tell the child about his adoptive status, the reasons for this and for providing background information were usually missing, as was the fact that the people who matter most to adoptees are those who bring them up and not those who give birth to them. Understandably, before the advent of the research findings adoption workers were themselves unaware of the reasoning behind such exhortations. Telling and so on was simply thought to be a 'good' thing. As late as 1968, the Child Welfare League of America, in its Standards for Adoption Services manual (1968), recommended that only limited information be given about the biological parents and discouraged detailed descriptive data.

The various studies agree that about half of those seeking access are only after additional information to 'complete' themselves and are not seeking meetings or reunions with original parents. As many put it to us 'we already have parents'. Basing one's personality on the concept of two sets of 'families' or 'parents', far from proving confusing, offers the adopted person the necessary reality on which to construct him or herself. It is only when the adults around the child are not clear or display shame or hesitation that the child is likely to get confused. Adoptive parents also need to know that openness and sensitivity to their children's feelings about their first families is less likely to lead to a quest, although they should try not to see a quest as bad in itself. The wish for access to birth records should not be seen as reflecting on the parenting qualities of the adoptive family. The figures, after all, suggest that the wish for access remains a minority response among adoptees and those hoping for reunions with the original parent(s) are still fewer. Available evidence also suggests that the results of reunions are mixed: many contacts are broken off soon after they are established, though a minority seem to lead to constructive relationships. It does not follow that the finding and establishing of a positive relationship with a birth parent or half-sibling will necessarily lead to the abandonment of an existing relationship. Shaffer, writing from a study of young infants, commented that being attached to several people 'does not necessarily imply a shallower feeling towards each one, for an infant's capacity for attachments is not like a cake that has to be shared out. Love, even in babies, has no limits' (Shaffer 1977:108). Sorosky commented from a small study which concentrated on the reunion of adoptees with birth parents that the reunion 'less frequently ... results in a meaningful relationship and rarely in a typical parent-child association.... Furthermore, the reunion does not appear to have had any serious effect on the existing relationship between the adoptee and adoptive parents in most of the cases studied' (Sorosky, Baran, and Pannor 1974:13-17). After all, non-adopted adults may pursue relationships with older men or women, who may or may not be related to them, and this is not seen as a reflection on the parenting qualities of their parents.

Background to the Children Act of 1975

Successive Adoption Acts provided for anonymity in a number of areas, particularly in concealing the identity of the parties involved in the adoption procedure. The element of secrecy was partly aimed at protecting single parents and their offspring from the stigma of unmarried parenthood and illegitimacy. It was also aimed at ensuring that birth parents would not interfere in the relationship between the child and his adoptive family in a way that might upset the stability of the arrangement. The 1920s and 1930s were also years when adoption was not all that popular and it was thought that the guarantee of secrecy would encourage more adopters to come forward. The law may have been well-meaning but unintentionally it conveyed secrecy and evasiveness, and possibly shame and stigma, among adoption agencies, adoption workers, and adopting couples. Some adoptees, for example, noticed a degree of embarrassment or shame in their parents when they were talking about adoption. Others felt 'second class' or not 'a proper person'. Until 1976 the only way that an adopted person in England and Wales could obtain a copy of his original birth certificate was under an order of the High Court, the Westminster County Court, or the court by which the adoption order was made.

The so-called 'sexual revolution' of the 1960s, changes in the social situation of women in relation to sex and parenthood, the changing attitudes towards illegitimacy, the availability of contraceptive and abortion facilities, and the increasing emphasis on the rights of minority groups, all created a climate of greater tolerance and of social change. Some of these changes had an impact on the institution of adoption as perceived at the time, including a reduction in the number of infants being released for adoption. There was also dissatisfaction with aspects of the 1958 Adoption Act, so the then Home Secretary was prompted to set up a Committee of Inquiry. The Committee was appointed in 1968 under the Chairmanship of Sir William Houghton and a working paper was first published in 1970. Within its wide remit 'to consider the law, policy and procedures on the adoption of children and what changes are desirable' the Committee also decided to consider the issue of access to birth records. I was then commissioned to carry out a study 'to investigate the circumstances under which adoptees made use of the access provision in Scotland'. Almost all the organizations which gave evidence to the Committee, with the exception of the Children Officers' Association and of the National Council for the Unmarried Mother and her Child, were against access. Most of their concern was with the potential distress that might be caused by children seeking out their birth parents. It is of interest to note that in other countries such as the USA, Australia, and New Zealand it is again the professional social work (Adoption) organizations which mostly oppose change. In another study we carried out in Scotland, also for the Houghton Committee, about two-thirds of mothers surrendering children in 1970 said they would not mind being contacted by their children later on, if this would be of help to them (Triseliotis and Hall 1971). The Houghton Committee in its White Paper in 1970 recommended no change in the provision of access in England and Wales. Depending also on the results of our study on the subject, the Committee seemed prepared to consider recommending the withdrawal of this facility in the Scottish law. The Hurst Committee had also toyed with the same idea twenty years earlier but in the end left this part of the Scottish law alone. The Houghton Committee's change of attitude is reflected in the main report published in 1972, by which time the results of our study had been made available. The findings demonstrated the overall beneficial effect of the access provision. More important, no evidence was found of any abuse of the provision *or* of harassment of natural parents (Triseliotis 1973). In addition the Deputy Registrar General for Scotland was able to tell the Committee that he could not recall any complaint made by natural relatives who had been traced through the Registrar General's records. The evidence pointed to the fact that no Pandora's box existed, except in the assumptions and imaginations of those individuals and organizations who were reluctant to accept the research findings. Courageously, in my view, the Houghton Committee concluded that the weight of the evidence 'as a whole was in favour of more access to background information' and went on to recommend that 'an adopted person aged 18 years or over should be entitled to a copy of his original birth certificate'. There was no suggestion for compulsory counselling in the report.

The Children Act of 1975

In 1974, a Children's Bill proposed by Dr David Owen had to be abandoned because of the unexpected dissolution of Parliament. The next round was in 1975 when Dr Owen, then Under Secretary of State for the Social Services in the DHSS, presented the Bill on behalf of the new Government. The Bill was first debated in the House of Lords. Under Clause 24, it provided for access to birth records with no pre-conditions. The Lord Chancellor introducing Clause 24 (eventually 26 in the Act) on 21 January, 1975 tried to reassure the House of Lords that there was no evidence 'to suggest that the exercise of this right has encountered any difficulties there' (i.e. in Scotland). While some peers argued in favour of the provision, the main opposition came from Baroness Young. She suggested that an adoptee who wanted a meeting with a birth parent should have to ask the local authority to act as an intermediary between him/her and the birth parent, if needed. This system, it was argued, would offer protection to the birth parent(s). (In the State of Minnesota the legislation provides that when an adoptee presents himself to the Department of Public Welfare seeking access to his birth records and perhaps a meeting with his original parent(s), the agency views the records, abstracts relevant information, and assigns responsibility for the search to the most appropriate local child-placing agency. The latter then begins a series of attempts to locate the birth parent and ask for his/her written consent before the adoptee can be granted access to his birth records. A typical form of approach is to telephone people in the state or county who happen to have the same surname as that of the original parent(s). The phone may be answered by a husband, a wife, or child. If it turns out to be the sought parent, formal correspondence then follows. This approach seems to carry more risks for the birth parent(s) than the very circumspect process followed by most adoptees found in our studies (Weidell 1980).

A mixed reception awaited the Children's Bill in the House of Commons. Strong support was voiced by a number of MPs, notably Tom Houson, Leo Abse, and Phillip Whitehead. Mr Houson commented that 'it is psychologically important that an adopted child should have the right to know as much as possible about his or her biological origins - I have been convinced to that point of view in the course of discussions and considerations'. Mr Abse said that 'children want an answer to the queries "Who am I?" . . . that is a basic human right that every child should know his origins'. And Mr Whitehead, an adoptee himself, said more information was important for the adoptee to feel 'psychologically whole'. However, both Abse and Whitehead were also concerned about the possible misuse of the information and supported the insertion of a clause providing for compulsory counselling where retrospective access was sought. Whitehead, who had met his birth mother at the age of thirty, said 'I know that it is a traumatic experience for both parties', but he still supported access as long as counselling was made available. Strong opposition came from Jill Knight, who spoke about the probability of adoptees 'wrecking another person's life', because, she went on, 'this would happen under Clause 25' (26 in the Act itself). She later spoke of the possibility of 'blackmail'. Similar opposition was expressed by Linda Chalker. Norman Fowler supported 'a counselling in different ways, in its final form it was meant to be a check or restraint against possible hasty actions by adoptees'. Mrs Knight, however, was not satisfied with the inclusion of the counselling provision. The portrayal of adoptees and of other children growing up in substitute care as potentially vindictive or as blackmailers seems to be a remnant of popular mythology which featured particularly in the English literature of the nineteenth century. I am not saying that an individual adoptee may not turn out to be vindictive or a blackmailer, or try to harass, but non-adopted people can turn out like this without having their rights curtailed as a group. The attitudes portrayed by some of the media and even by some professional organizations, during the discussion of the Bill in the House of Commons, tended to convey a view of adoptees as potentially vindictive 'second-class' citizens. When the Clause providing for access was passed, all kinds of hazards, dangers, and harassments were anticipated by the Press. As examples we can look at headlines in the *News of the World* (10.10.76) 'Mums in fear of knock at the door', the *Daily Mirror* (27.10.76) 'Haunted by the past', and the *Daily Telegraph* (11.10.76) 'Fears of emotional upsets over "reveal all" Adoption Law'. Six years later, there is no evidence to substantiate these fears and the predicted calamities have not materialized.

The impact of Section 26 of the Children Act 1975

It was to be expected that the wide publicity afforded to the issue of access would lead to an initial influx of applications to Register

House. During the early and the middle 1970s there was hardly a week when the issue of access was not debated either on television, on radio, in the press, or in women's journals. With the possible exception of non-accidental injury to children, no other child care issue received so much attention during this period. As a result, a fair amount of interest and curiosity may have been generated among adoptees who had not previously thought about the matter. The publicity may also have helped to make it easier for adoptees to seek access without guilt or anxiety.

In the thirteen months following the implementation of Section. 26 (November 1976 to December 1977) a total of 5,449 applications were received and another 2,220 in 1978. The highest number of enquiries was received in January 1977 but by April of that year numbers were falling off. Since 1979 the number of applications has evened out at around 1,700 a year (see Table 1). Whilst it was acknowledged that most counselling would fall on the shoulders of local authority social service departments, in anticipation of the influx of applications two social workers were also appointed as counsellors at Register House in London. (For details about the role of the counsellor in such cases see Triseliotis 1980.) In fact local authorities have been dealing with almost 90 per cent of all enquiries. Since the opening of the records there have been three known survey studies. These are Leeding (1977), Day (1979), and Walby (1982). The DHSS has also commissioned Professor Timms of Newcastle University to undertake further research into the matter and the results are expected soon.

Table 1 *Number of applications by adopted persons for access to birth records under Section 26 of the Children Act 1975*

country	*1976*	*1977*	*1978*	*1979*	*1980*	*1981*	*1982*	*total*
England and Wales	1,991 (Nov/Dec)	3,458	2,220	1,375	1,547	1,754	1,684	14,029
Scotland	167	254	253	269	325	331	337	1936

Note: Of the 14,029 applying to the Registrar General in England and Wales only 12,474 went on to have counselling and obtain access to birth records.

(All the statistical information appearing in this and the next table was supplied by the Registrar General of England and Wales and the Registrar General of Scotland, to both of whom I am most grateful.)

With approximately 600,000 adopted people in England and Wales over the age of eighteen, those applying for access to their birth records in each of the last three years represent approximately 0.3 per cent of adopted adults in England and Wales and 0.7 per cent in Scotland. Taking this annual rate over the whole period of the average lifecycle (i.e. from age 18 when access is possible to age 70) would still yield only about 15 per cent of adoptees in England and Wales making enquiries. Obviously this figure is approximate because there is no prospective study. Another way is to take all 18-year-olds applying for access and multiply the number by 52, that is, the difference between 18 and 70 years. In 1982, 70 adoptees or 0.4 per cent of the estimated number of adoptees reaching their 18th birthday applied for access. Multiplied by 52, this yields 21 per cent of adoptees enquiring over the whole of the lifecycle. In Scotland, where access has been available for exactly 52 years, approximately 7 per cent of 'adult' adoptees have so far sought access. Even allowing for the fact that something like one-third of adoptions were by parent(s) or relatives, and that very few such adoptees seek access, the annual rate would still be only 0.6 per cent for England and Wales and 0.9 per cent for Scotland. The higher rate of access applications in Scotland compared to England and Wales is difficult to explain. In fact, the percentage of those obtaining access in Scotland went up from 0.2 per cent in the late 1960s to approximately 0.6 per cent in the early 1980s. The fact is that, in spite of all the publicity of recent years, access to birth records is still a minority response among adoptees. *Table 2* summarizes the characteristics of those counselled between November 1976 and December 1982.

Table 2 *An analysis by age and sex of adoptees counselled for access to birth records under Section 26 of the Children Act 1975 between November 1976 and December 1982.*

sex	*age-groups* *under 20*	*20-24*	*25-29*	*30-34*	*35-39*	*40-44*	*45 and over*	*total*
	no. (%)	no. (%)	no. (%)	no. (%)	no. (%)	no. (%)	no. (%)	no. (%)
male	207(25)	635(33)	819(36)	1,130(35)	777(36)	327(36)	349(33)	4,244(34)
female	637(75)	1,311(67)	1,456(64)	2,131(65)	1,402(64)	588(64)	705(67)	8,230(66)
total	844	1,946	2,275	3,261	2,179	915	1,054	12,474(100)
% of total	(7)	(16)	(18)	(26)	(18)	(7)	(8)	(100)

There are a number of points to be made about these figures. First, significantly more females than males seek access to their birth records (66 per cent as against 34 per cent). The imbalance of female to male is particularly noticeable among those under twenty. Yet of all adoptions completed over the last fifty-six years, the ratio of males to females is about the same, if anything with males somewhat exceeding the number of females. Another conclusion to be drawn from these figures and from the Scottish experience is that adoptees are not bursting to gain access to their original birth records on reaching the age of eighteen. The figures support my earlier contention that access to birth records spreads over the whole of the life-span and is related to continued events, happenings, or crises in the adoptee's life. When the age of those obtaining access is related to the possible numbers of adoptees in each of the seven age-groups (these are very approximate figures) the percentage differences between age groups are insignificant.

Four months after Section 26 was implemented, Leeding (1977) analysed information collected on 279 adoptees who applied for counselling and information in 13 local authorities in the West Midlands. Something like three-quarters were judged to have had a 'good' adoption and at least 20 per cent a 'poor' one. Half of them had learned about their adoption after the age of 5 and over, a third when over 10. Over half of those enquiring wanted only information. The rest intended to trace their birth parents but only about 20 per cent wanted also to meet them. This compared with 60 per cent who wanted to trace and if possible meet their parents in my first study (Triseliotis 1973). According to Leeding only 2 per cent of the total sample gave some cause for concern to social workers about the way they intended to trace and meet the birth parent(s). About one in every ten of the applicants told social workers that they had traced a parent or relative. Of 28 contacts with the birth family, 11 were described as 'good' or 'happy' and the rest 'uncertain'. Leeding concluded that this finding largely agreed with my study: 'we feel that there is every justification for a system through which adopted people can obtain detailed knowledge of their parentage' (Leeding 1977). Social workers found the interviews and subsequent reporting on behalf of adoptees time-consuming but interesting and rewarding. A second study was carried out by Day, who was one of the two social workers attached to Register House in London, with the aim of providing counselling to enquiring adoptees (Day 1979). Day prepared his report on the basis of the first 500 interviews acknowledging that the recording of adoptive history was secondary to the counselling purposes of the interview. Over half of those enquiring said that they were told about their adoption by their adopters in infancy or childhood. The rest either found out for themselves in childhood or later in life. Almost one-fifth were told or found out as teenagers or as adults. Telling in adolescence was experienced by adoptees as most distressing. More than 20 per cent of adoptees reported adverse factors in their adoption and half of these were intent on tracing their first families. Like Triseliotis (1973) and Leeding (1977), Day found that very few applicants were content with the birth details supplied at the interview. Almost two-fifths, compared to about half found by Leeding and two-fifths by Triseliotis, had no intention of tracing the original family. What they needed was simply information. Another third were still 'undecided' and the rest, three out of every ten, were intent on tracing with a view to arranging a meeting with a birth parent or relative. The great majority wanted to do this through an intermediary. Day adds that 'in view of this, it would seem that ill-considered, unwise, or precipitate confrontations, if the figures are reliable, are not likely to occur on any great scale' (Day 1979). Only 3.6 per cent of applicants gave possible cause for concern because of the way they might set about tracing.

Day concluded by saying that the number of adoptees seeking access was fewer than expected. In fact because the anticipated numbers did not materialize, one of the two counsellors attached to Register House was removed. He also concluded that the great majority of applicants 'appeared to be stable and well-adjusted' and confirmed Triseliotis's earlier findings that applicants with an unhappy adoptive experience were 'much more likely to trace' (Triseliotis 1973:158). Applicants felt strongly that adopted persons had the right to know and that more openness was needed in adoption. Overall neither Leeding nor Day found evidence of misuse of the information and all the dire predictions of the media were found to be baseless. The Secretary of State reported to Parliament in 1979 that the surveys by Leeding and Day 'found that the majority of applicants had a mature and responsible attitude towards the implications and possible consequences of their action in obtaining their birth records' (HMSO 1979).

Walby's study was different from the previous two in that she carried out interviews in considerable depth with a small number of adoptees who had had both counselling and access to their birth records (Walby 1982). Three-fifths of the thirty-two adoptees found the service very helpful or quite helpful but the rest thought it was a 'waste of time'. Adoptees did not like what they called 'red tape' and generally expected much more practical advice and help than was generally forthcoming. A non-directive, reflective approach seemed to reinforce the adoptees' expectation of disapproval. Overall, however, counselling served a useful purpose in increasing awareness of relevant issues and in giving support and approval to the 'good intentions and responsible attitudes of the majority' (Walby

1982). It also served a useful purpose in reducing the possibilities of precipitate action on the part of a small minority. Walby found that the counselling service for many was the first opportunity to talk with an 'informed, interested, and objective person' about their adoption experience. She also stressed the importance of the counsellor being familiar with adoption work and particularly with issues of access, identity, and so on. Walby concludes her detailed and sensitive study with the comment that the findings lent support to Leeding, Day, and Triseliotis, and that any differences apparently concerned only minor points. She also adds that 'the fears expressed in 1976, often in extreme and hysterical parlance, were largely groundless' (Walby 1982).

As one of the responsibilities of counsellors is to provide background information to the adoptee and direct her/him to other possible sources of information, a major issue for adoption agencies is how to keep up to date the information they have on the birth family and on the adoptee. As well as adoptees having access to such material, the birth parents too should be able to call at the agency and ask for news about the child they surrendered years ago.

Summary and Conclusions

Only a minority of adopted people seek access to their birth records under Section 26 of the Children Act 1975. The calamities anticipated by sections of the media, politicians, and some organizations have not materialized. The various studies carried out so far suggest that the vast majority of adoptees act thoughtfully and with great consideration for the feelings of both their birth and adoptive parents. The value of access facility is not now in dispute. The studies so far have mostly concentrated on adoptees who sought and obtained access to their original birth records. A reasonable criticism to be levied at all of them is that they do not constitute a representative sample of adopted people. One could argue that a proper sample of adopted adults might explain why some adoptees have a deep psychological need to obtain more information, or establish contact with a birth parent, while others are not interested in taking action of this sort. A study we carried out recently of 44 adoptees who were in their twenties at interview, and who were adopted when over the age of 2, identified 4 (or 9 per cent) who had tried to obtain access to their original birth certificates (Triseliotis and Russell 1984). Two of these would have liked to meet one or both of their birth parents. A third of the total sample said they would have liked more information about their background and a few might have welcomed a meeting. The vast majority of adoptees had no intention of setting out on a quest. Their main explanation was that they had parents, their adoptive ones, they were leading a 'happy' life and they were not interested in quests or in meetings with an original parent. Raynor (1980) also found from her study of adoptees who were in their early twenties that at the time of the interview 75 per cent were unconcerned about their birth parents. Only 4 per cent showed any interest in establishing a relationship with birth parents, but almost a fifth said they would like to 'communicate with one or both just once, or see them once'. It is difficult to escape my earlier conclusions that though there is a curiosity and deep psychological need in every adoptee to know about his background and personal history, the need for access to records, for meetings or reunions with birth parents is frequently a characteristic of those who were not given reasonable explanations and information about their origins, of those who have recently gone through some major event or crisis in their lives, or of those who may have experienced unsatisfactory growing-up experiences. Contrary to some assumptions identity confusion does not necessarily go with adoption. Studies have shown that the vast majority of adopted people have a firm and secure sense of self.

References

Child Welfare League of America (1968) *Standards for Adoption Services* (5th edn). New York.

Day, C. (1979) Access to Birth Records: General Register Office Study. *Adoption and Fostering* 98(4):17–28.

Erikson, E. (1968) *Identity*. London: Faber & Faber.

Fisher, F. (1973) *The Search for Anna Fisher*. New York: Arthur Field Books.

HMSO (1954) *Report of the Departmental Committee on the Adoption of Children*. The Hurst Committee, Cmd 9248. London.

______ (1972) *Report of the Departmental Committee on the Adoption of Children*. The Houghton Committee, Cmnd 5107. London.

______ (1975) *Children Act 1975*. London.

______ (1979) *Children Act 1975*. First report to Parliament. London.

______ (1982) *Adoption of Children in Northern Ireland*. Belfast.

Leeding, A. (1977) Access to Birth Records. *Adoption and Fostering* 89(3):19–25.

McWhinnie, A. (1967) *Adopted Children: How They Grow Up*. London: Routledge & Kegan Paul.

Ontario Ministry of Community and Social Services (1976) *Report of the Committee on Record Disclosure to Adoptees*.

Paton, J.M. (1954) *The Adopted Break Silence*. Acton, California: Life History Study Centre.

_____ (1960) *Three Trips Home.* Acton, California: Life History Study Centre.

Picton, C. (1980) *Persons in Question: Adoptees in Search of Origins.* Social Work Dept, Monash University, Australia.

Raynor, L. (1980) *The Adopted Child Comes of Age.* London: Allen & Unwin.

Sants, H.J. (1965) Genealogical Bewilderment in Children with Substitute Parents. *Child Adoption* 47:32-42.

Shaffer, H.R. (1977) *Mothering.* London: Fontana/Open Books.

Sorosky, A.D., Baran, A., and Pannor, R. (1974) The Reunion of Adoptees and Birth Relatives. *Journal of Youth and Adolescence* 3(3):195-206.

Sorosky, A.D., Baran, A., and Pannor, R. (1975) *The Effects of the Sealed Record in Adoption.* Paper presented at the Annual Meeting of the American Psychiatric Association, Anaheim, California.

Stone, F.H. (1969) Adoption and Identity. *Child Adoption* 58(3):17-28.

Triseliotis, J. (1973) *In Search of Origins.* London: Routledge & Kegan Paul.

_____ (1974) Identity and Adoption. *Child Adoption* 78(4):27-34.

_____ (1980) Counselling Adoptees. In J. Triseliotis (ed.) *New Developments in Foster Care and Adoption.* London: Routledge & Kegan Paul.

_____ (1983) Identity and Security in Adoption and Long-term Fostering. *Adoption and Fostering* 7(1):22-31.

Triseliotis, J. and Hall, E. (1971) Giving Consent to Adoption. *Social Work Today* 2 (17):21-4.

Triseliotis, J. and Russell, J. (1984) *Hard to Place: the Outcome of Late Adoption and Residential Care.* London: Heinemann.

Walby, C.M. (1982) *Adoption: A Question of Identity.* Thesis submitted to the University of Wales for the degree of M.Sc Econ.

Weidell, R.C. (1980) Unsealing Sealed Birth Certificates in Minnesota. *Child Welfare* 59(2):113-19.

4 Older child adoption and the knowledge base of adoption practice

MILES HAPGOOD

This contribution is made up of two separate but interrelated sections, the first examining the development of adoption services for older children, and the second reviewing the knowledge base available to those engaged in adoption practice. It is written from the perspective of a practitioner employed in local authority social work.[1]

Older child adoption

The issues to be examined in this section include the pattern of older child adoption in recent years, the current need for placements of this type, and the ethical, casework, or organizational factors which may be constraining practice in this area. Older children will be defined as those aged five or over, and only those children adopted in England and Wales where neither adoptive parent is a birth parent are under consideration.[2]

OLDER CHILD ADOPTION AS A PLACEMENT CHOICE

As a result of the very inadequate organization of the statistical returns from adoption agencies we do not have comparative figures for the numbers of older children adopted through voluntary or local authority agencies. We know the numbers of adoption orders made within different age groups but have no accurate information on important issues like the age of the child at the time of placement, care status, or parental consent. The extent of this problem is well documented by Fruin (1980). The Department of Health and Social Security is currently piloting an adoption unit return which should improve our understanding of different agency practices. However, given the structure of child care services in England and Wales it seems safe to assume that the vast majority of non-parental older child adoptions concern children who are in the care of local authorities and placed with adoptive families by them.

It seems generally accepted by both the supporters and critics of older child adoption that in recent years it has occupied an increasingly important place in the range of options available in planning for children in care. This range of options would have previously been more limited to rehabilitation, residential care, or non-adoptive family placements. The apparent focus on adoption as a placement option for older and other 'special needs' children, particularly physically or mentally handicapped children who may also be aged five or over, has been linked to any of four recent developments:

(a) A gradual realization from surveys of children in care that there were many children in foster homes or residential care who were available for adoption should social workers choose to pursue such plans, (i.e. there would be grounds for the making of an adoption order if a suitable placement were established).
(b) Legal changes recommended and enacted during the 1970s and partially implemented since then, establishing a more favourable legal framework for such placements. These include the widening of the grounds for the dispensation of parental consent, the rights of foster parents to make independent applications after five years and, more recently, the possibility of subsidized adoption.
(c) An increased demand from prospective adopters for older and other special needs children caused by the steady decline since 1968 in the numbers of infants and young children available for adoption.
(d) Research findings, predominantly American, suggesting that older child adoptions could have high success rates.

As a result of these developments there appears to have been greater professional and public interest in older child adoption and a growing controversy about the practices involved. Before examining these it is necessary to consider the extent to which the above developments have influenced the actual numbers of adoption orders made in respect of older children.

THE NUMBERS OF OLDER CHILD ADOPTIONS

The numbers and proportions of older child adoptions for 1951, 1968, and 1976-81 are shown in *Table 1* below.

Table 1 *The numbers and proportions of adoption orders for legitimate and illegitimate children adopted in England and Wales where neither adopter is a parent, or where there is a sole adopter, by age, 1951, 1968, 1976-81*

year	*adoptions, children 0-4*		*adoptions, children 5+*	
	number	%	number	%
1951	7,674	79.6	1,965	20.4
1968	15,243	93.4	1,071	6.6
1976	4,781	82.5	1,013	17.5
1977	3,983	80.2	982	19.8
1978	3,725	79.6	952	20.4
1979	3,452	79.6	884	20.4
1980	3,447	77.3	1,012	22.7
1981	3,258	77.1	969	22.9

Source: Derived from Table 1 in 'Adoption Trends and Illegitimate Births 1951-77' *Population Trends 14*; and from Table 3 in *OPCS Monitors* Series FM3 with the permission of the Controller of HMSO. Crown © reserved.

The highest number of older child adoptions was during the years immediately after the Second World War. The proportion fell dramatically during the peak years of infant adoptions, such that in 1968 it constituted only 7 per cent of all non-parental adoptions. Between 1976 and 1981 the proportion of older child adoptions gradually increased from 17.5 per cent to 22.9 per cent.
However, the table clearly shows that this proportional increase is due to a greater rate of decrease in the numbers of younger children adopted. Their numbers have declined annually such that there were 1,323 fewer adoption orders made for this group in 1981 than in 1976, a number substantially higher than the total number of older child adoptions in either year. The proportional increase in the numbers of older child adoptions has tended to disguise the fact that their *number* has remained relatively static over this period. Indeed, the highest annual figure during the period 1976-81 was in 1976, and the 1981 figure of 969 represents almost exactly the mean figure for the previous five years (968.6).

The figures provided by the annual DHSS report on children in care, and by the reports by the Secretaries of State for Social Services and for Wales, show that there has been a small increase in the number of children leaving care through adoption. The DHSS figures, which do not include Wales, indicate that the number of children leaving care each year as a result of being adopted alternated between 1,400 and 1,500 during the period 1976-80. The figure for 1981 (1,598) is slightly higher than previous years, but not markedly so. The recent report on Social Services for children in

England and Wales (HMSO 1983) suggests a clearer trend towards the adoption of children in local authority care, increasing from approximately 1,500 in 1979 to provisional figures of 1,700 for 1981. However, the official figures do not include details of the ages of the children adopted. Any apparent increase in the numbers of children adopted from local authority care may well be explained by the decrease in the number of voluntary adoption agencies in recent years and the greater involvement of local authorities in the adoption of pre-school children.

The fact that increased professional and public interest in older child adoption has not resulted in more adoption orders may be due to one of three possible explanations:

(a) that the need for older child adoptive placements is relatively constant and is being met,
(b) that an unmet need for these placements has led to changes in adoption practice which are adequate but have yet to be reflected in the numbers of orders made,
(c) that an unmet need for older child placements has led to changes in practice which are proving inadequate.

These alternative explanations will be considered below.

THE NUMBERS OF OLDER CHILDREN REQUIRING ADOPTIVE FAMILIES

In recent years there have been a number of important studies undertaken into the family placement needs of children in care. The first and most important of these was that by Rowe and Lambert (1973). They examined 2,812 children aged under 11 who were in the care of 33 voluntary or statutory agencies, asking these children's social workers about their placement needs. Of the sample 22 per cent were assessed as requiring some form of family placement. Converted into national terms, these figures suggested that there were about 7,000 children in that age group who required family placement. The study also explored the types of family placement preferred by the children's social workers. A direct adoptive placement was the first choice in only 6 per cent of these cases with the more open-ended 'fostering with a view to adoption' preferred for 26 per cent of the cases. The remainder were assessed as requiring permanent foster homes (40 per cent) or foster homes for an indeterminate period (28 per cent). Rowe and Lambert noted that the low preference for adoptive placements did not necessarily reflect a low availability for adoption. In any event, combining the early and delayed categories, their findings suggested that, by social worker rating, there were approximately 2,240 children aged under 11 requiring adoptive families on a national basis.

A comparable study by Bacon and Rowe (1978) revealed a similar pattern. They examined half of all the children aged under 14 who were in the care of 5 Midlands authorities and who had been placed in residential care for at least 3 months. Of the 514 children in the sample, only 228 were assessed by their social workers as appropriately placed in the long term. Of the remaining 286 children, only 2 were viewed as requiring a direct adoptive placement with a further 35 (13 per cent) assessed as requiring long-term fostering with a view to adoption. The main placement choices were long-term fostering (52 per cent) followed by alternative residential care (27 per cent). On these figures, only 70 of the children in the whole region who were aged under 14 and in residential care were viewed as requiring some form of adoptive home. Bacon and Rowe commented: 'Social work reluctance to consider direct adoption placement for older children even when adoption is the desired outcome and long-term foster homes are in such short supply, is a striking factor' (Bacon and Rowe 1978:5). Other research studies have reported similar findings.[3]

All of these studies have relied on social worker assessments of the placement needs of children in care. The British Agencies for Adoption and Fostering (BAAF) have attempted to provide an independent estimate of the overall need for permanent or long-term substitute family placement for children in care. They estimate that there are approximately 20,000 children in this position. This includes children of all ages and those in hospitals and indicates that social workers may tend to underestimate the real need for family placement. There is no estimate for the number of adoptive placements required, but using the 32 per cent figure requiring early or delayed adoption suggested by Rowe and Lambert (1973), such an estimate would be in the region of 6,400, the majority of whom would be older children.

If we look again at the three explanations suggested above for the relatively constant annual number of older child adoptions in recent years, it is possible to draw the following tentative conclusions:

(a) that the need for older child placements is not being met. This appears to be the case if one uses the social worker's own assessments or that of an independent agency.
(b) that it is possible that there have been changes in social work practice which are not yet reflected in the official statistics. Given the time taken by local authorities in developing new policies and practices and the longer-term nature of the work itself, it is possible that a trend towards more older child adoption may yet emerge.
(c) that the absence of any clear evidence of such a trend emerging,

some ten years after the publication of *Children Who Wait* (Rowe and Lambert 1973), suggests that any developments which have taken place are unlikely to meet the level of need indicated above. Furthermore, the research evidence has highlighted several factors inhibiting practice developments in this area, particularly the suggestion that social worker preference for adoption as a placement choice appears consistently low.

THE CONSTRAINTS ON OLDER CHILD ADOPTION PRACTICE

The apparent gap between the need for older child adoptive placements and the willingness of social workers to pursue adoption as a placement choice may be due to certain constraints facing local authority social workers in this field of work. The remainder of this section will consider the nature of these possible constraints.

There are three types of constraint which may be operating:

(a) Philosophical or ethical constraints: the result of social workers retaining professional doubts about the validity of adoption as a placement choice for older children in care.
(b) Casework constraints: the result of particular problems in the management of child care cases preventing any increase in older child adoptions.
(c) Organizational constraints: the result of structural factors within Social Services Departments inhibiting the development of social work practice in this field.

Philosophical and Ethical Constraints

Older children adoption is a controversial area and the intensity of the controversy within social work and the allied professions reflects the general lack of consensus which exists about certain fundamental child care principles. This lack of consensus is essentially about values, but also exists at a legal level.

The main value issue concerns the primacy of the birth parent-birth child relationship. This controversy seems to have developed through three distinct phases. The first can be called post-war child care practice, influenced by the views of Bowlby and other developmental psychologists. This stressed the importance of the initial birth mother-child bond. Every effort was made to support the bond and to maintain birth parent-child contacts in the event of separation. Such a climate of opinion was unfavourable for older child adoption which required the severance of such links. The ideal long-term placement for a child in care was either within a children's home or a foster home affording as much access as possible to the birth parent. The justification for this practice was not so much an ethical belief in the rights of birth families to retain contacts as a pragmatic belief in the primacy of early bonding such that no other type of child care practice was viewed as likely to succeed.

It was this pragmatic belief which was challenged during the second phase of the debate. Predominantly American findings on older child adoption suggested that any emphasis on early bonding as a bar to later attachment might be misplaced (Clarke 1981). These studies seemed to indicate that it was possible to place older children in adoptive families successfully. The emerging interest in older child adoption gradually developed into what is now termed the permanence movement. The principles of permanence are that a comprehensive child care service requires three components, preventive services, rehabilitative services, and long-term family care. The primary goal of permanence is to allow the child to remain within its own family through the provision of preventive and rehabilitative services. However, if genuine and skilled attempts at the first two fail, a stable long-term alternative is required: 'For the overwhelming majority of children who are unable to return to their own family within a reasonable time, an adoptive family who can assume all the rights and responsibilities of parents will be the best alternative' (BAAF 1983:10). Some children in long-term care will require fostering or residential care, but these should be the minority.

Both the first and second phases of the debate centred on the theoretical nature of the birth parent-birth child relationship and how this should be translated into practice. The third and current stage of the controversy is less about the relative effectiveness of different social work methods, but about their ethical basis, and in particular the moral right of an authority to sever a birth parent-birth child relationship against the wishes of the parent. Jordan views the permanence movement as potentially increasing the degree of polarization between family and state. He sees social workers confusing the concepts of prevention and substitute care by viewing them as opposites rather than complementary. The notion of prevention, he argues, should apply to children already in care such that substitute care should include all the significant people in the child's life.

> 'I am suggesting that in future the art of preventative work will be not so much in preventing receptions into care as in preserving links and creating long-term security for children, even when they cannot return home quickly. We will have to become more aware of how we often contribute to the breaking of links and of what skill and determination and goodwill are needed to maintain

links. None of this can become clear and be acted upon while prevention and substitute care are seen as opposing principles or even as alternatives.'

(Jordan 1981:21)

These arguments have been taken up and developed by various organizations and pressure groups, particularly the Family Rights Group, who have published a set of papers by social workers, psychiatrists, and lawyers, which challenge the principles of permanence (Family Rights Group 1982).

The above controversy at the level of basic child care values also occurs at a legal level. The legal context of child care practice seems unreasonably weighted in favour of the local authority in three important areas, all of which have been the subject of external criticism and internal debate. First, the system by which local authorities assume the parental rights of children in their care has been heavily criticized. Research by Adcock, White, and Rowlands (1982) and by Lambert and Rowe (1974) has indicated that existing legal safeguards may be inadequate and that there are wide differences in local authority practice. Second, the discretionary powers exercised by local authorities over children subject to different types of care orders are viewed as excessive by many observers. These powers enable the authority to act as they see fit for the interests of the child, and include the power of refusing access and refusing to disclose a child's whereabouts to his or her birth parent. Third, birth parents seem to have restricted legal rights in some other important respects, including no right to independent representation in Juvenile Court care proceedings and no right to wardship proceedings to challenge local authority planning for a child in care. (Legislation designed to improve the rights of birth parents with regard to both access and appeals is currently before Parliament in a Health and Social Services Bill.)

The implications of these debates at both the value and legal levels for older child adoption are profound. The social work profession seems ethically and philosophically divided over the management of cases where children are likely to remain in long-term care. The emphasis on adoption advocated by those who support the principles of permanence is vigorously challenged by those committed to retaining the physical and emotional links between children in care and their birth parents. Such widely differing perspectives must have a constraining influence on social work practice. At one level, within such a climate of opinion, it is hard for individual authorities to commit themselves to clear and explicit placement policies. At another level, it is harder still for individual practitioners to involve themselves in the complex issues of older child adoption with any degree of professional confidence.

Casework Constraints

Further constraints limiting the numbers of older child adoptions may be due to more practical difficulties experienced in the management of long-term child care cases. Such difficulties may arise with regard to legal obstacles precluding a successful adoption application, the lack of motivation of existing caretakers, or financial pressures on present or potential caretakers.

The first issue, that of legal availability, may cause the fewest constraints. The various studies on children in care all indicate that the majority of children who have been in care for over six months have very limited contact with their birth family, and as many as half have no contact at all. In these circumstances, adoption applications involving well planned and stable placements have every chance of success. Should parental consent not be forthcoming, the grounds for dispensation are sufficiently wide to ensure that an order is likely to be made if adoption is clearly in the interests of the child. The legal climate remains favourable, but adoption applications will only succeed if the social work planning and case management have been of a high professional standard.

The second casework constraint, the motivation of existing caretakers, is a more difficult problem to gauge given the lack of research in this area. It is certainly the case that many long-term foster parents who have successfully fostered a child for a number of years are unwilling to commit themselves to the total assumption of responsibility for the child required by adoption. In their survey of children boarded out, Shaw and Lebens found that of the cases where social workers said they would be willing to support adoption applications, foster parents expressed willingness in only half. They noticed a lack of communication between foster parents and social workers on this issue and, although made several years ago, their comments are probably still relevant today:

> 'Turning to the question of adoption, there is among foster parents quite a high level of interest, while among social workers there is a high level of willingness to contemplate the idea - we might call it "interest" except that social workers rarely seem to discuss the possibility with foster parents. Such non-communication leads to a situation where when approving the idea of adoption, social workers and foster parents are found to be enthusing about different children. We thus find a considerable area of (tacit) disagreement between the two parties

about intentions and reactions to possible intentions. One sad corner is occupied by children whom foster parents would like to adopt and whom social workers would like to see adopted, but where there is no discussion and social workers assume foster parents to be uninterested.'

(Shaw and Lebens 1976:25)

Triseliotis (1980), in a follow-up study of foster care, interviewed 40 young adults and their foster parents. He noted that many of the children would have liked to have been adopted. At least 12 of the foster parents would have seriously considered adopting the child in their care if encouraged by the local authority.

The changes brought about by the Children Act 1975, which increased the opportunities for successful adoption applications by long-term foster parents, led several observers to predict a sudden rush in applications. Rowe *et al.*'s study (1980) of the Act's impact indicated an initial increase in applications, but concluded that the number of applications by long-term foster parents remained very low. The reluctance of many foster parents to apply to adopt their foster children has also been noted in America. It would seem that many long-term foster parents see responsibility for the child as a shared task between themselves and the agency. They have neither the commitment nor the confidence to make the bonds permanent and may feel a need to retain an escape route in the event of future difficulties.

These motivational constraints are probably linked to the terms under which the placement was originally established. It appears that adoption applications are most likely to result when the adoptive intent is explicit and well defined from the start such that all parties, including the child, are clear in their expectations. The temptation to avoid the issue at the initial stage, referring to the possibility of future adoption in vague terms, seems more likely to result in differing aspirations and expectations at a later stage.

The third possible casework constraint concerns the financial implications of adoption for foster parents receiving boarding-out allowances for the children in their care. This constraint will probably be removed in the near future with the recent Government approval of various pilot schemes for subsidized adoption. In any event, this may not be a particularly serious obstacle to older child adoption. The experiences of American agencies, where subsidized adoption schemes exist in the vast majority of states, is that there has been little change in the number of applications in respect of older children.

Organizational Constraints

The research into the placement needs of children in care identifies various organizational constraints which inhibit family placement practice. Shaw and Lebens concluded that the shortfall on family placement could not simply be attributed to thoughtlessness or drift on the part of social workers, but that 'the evidence is of systems inadequacy rather than of individual incompetence' (Shaw and Lebens 1978:21). They compared social work practice in residential care, which was commonly viewed as a full agency responsibility, with practice in family placement where the responsibility fell very much on the individual worker. The differences are illustrated by the reviewing practices for children in different types of care. Those in residential care tend to have regular reviews requiring the attendance of everyone who is professionally involved, and the reviews are usually chaired by a senior officer. Foster children tend to be reviewed less regularly, often outside the statutory time limits, and their reviews may be restricted to the child's social worker and their senior social worker. Foster parents are present only in a minority of statutory reviews. These discrepancies in social work practice for children in different types of care were highlighted in the recent DHSS report on boarding out of children:

> 'It is clear from these inspections that children in care of these authorities who were boarded out received less attention than other children in care, less attention than the minimum requirements of the statutory regulations and less attention than the objective reality that their situation warranted. These omissions in the care of children arise from deficiencies in policy, management, supervision, and social work practice.'
>
> (DHSS 1982:26)

To understand the organizational constraints facing local authority workers it is necessary first to identify the main organizational requirements for successful practice and compare these to existing working conditions. The prerequisites for successful practice seem to be threefold: accurate identification of children who would benefit from adoptive placements; selection and training of suitable adoptive families; skilled case management of adoptive placements. These three issues are now examined in detail.

The main skills required for accurate identification of children who would benefit from adoptive placements are the ability to assess the individual needs of children in care and to gauge their capacity to respond to an adoptive placement, combined with an ability to consider each case within its legal context and make realistic plans accordingly. Skilled social work practice in both these respects depends partly on the quality of initial training and partly on the acquisition of relevant experience.

With very few exceptions, the limitations of social work qualifying courses in these areas are well known within the profession. These limitations were identified in two recent surveys of social work practice in this area, one conducted by the DHSS (1982) and one conducted for the National Children's Bureau (Parker 1980). The former report reviewed the skills required for family placements and concluded: 'The sum of this is probably beyond what can normally be acquired in basic professional training courses and in-service training is clearly essential for the development of good practice' (DHSS 1982:3). However, the level of in-service training within most departments has been considerably reduced in recent years due to financial constraints.

The second requirement for skilled practice in this area, the acquisition of relevant experience, is even more problematic. If we assume that local authority social workers are responsible for all the non-parental older child adoptions each year, averaging at just under 1,000, and that the number of fieldworkers employed during the past six years has been in the region of 14,000 per year, the number of older child placements made per local authority worker each year is less than 0.1. If we then assume that the average amount of post-qualification fieldwork done by local authority social workers is five years, the number of older child adoptions each fieldworker might undertake averages out at approximately 0.3.[4] Therefore, without considerable specialization, the opportunities to acquire experience in this field are very limited. The National Children's Bureau report drew attention to the loss of specialist skills and identified several deficiencies in the level of child care skill and knowledge, including insufficient acquaintance with the relevant law and detailed procedures, lack of close knowledge of children's past and present circumstances, an inadequate understanding of the developmental aspects of childhood, and too little first-hand experience with children together with insufficient skill in communicating with them (Parker 1980:27–30).

The second prerequisite for successful adoption practice concerns the selection and training of suitable adoptive families. The two requirements for good practice here are the acquisition of experience and allocation of adequate time by the agency. The selection of adoptive families is a complex task requiring skills of communication, personal detachment, and assessment. These skills can only develop with considerable experience, which, for the same reasons as those outlined above, it is hard for the typical local authority social worker to obtain.

Those workers experienced in the placement of older or 'special needs' children all comment on the considerable time commitment required to produce a relatively small number of approved adoptive families. Sawbridge commented on this problem in describing her agency's work in placing special needs children:

> 'It is obvious to us why children on the caseloads of generic social workers do not get placed. This kind of work does not fit easily alongside the pressures and crises of generic work. It is expensive of time, we meet and talk with many people who do not pursue an adoption; we spend a great deal of time getting to know and preparing individually and in groups the families who do pursue it; we spend as much time again with some of the children, helping them sort out their past and preparing them for the future; we undertake to support the families after placement for as long as may be necessary and we are already finding out how much some of them welcome close support in the early days. We are privileged to have only this to do, and to be able to specialize, but we are very aware that the task would be virtually impossible any other way.'
>
> (Sawbridge 1977:10–11)

An illustration of these issues, based on actual local authority experience, is given in the notes at the end of the chapter.[5]

The last requirement for successful adoption practice is the skilled case management of adoptive placements. The tasks here include those of matching child to family, and the subsequent management of the different stages of a placement. The twin requirements for good practice are the same as above: experience and time. The matching decision in particular requires considerable feel and sensitivity, with both the child and the family feeling anxious and dependent on the social worker's judgement. The importance of experience at this level is obvious.

With regard to time, the management of an adoptive placement should be almost as time-consuming as the selection of adoptive families. The social worker has initially to gain the child's confidence, get to know the selected family, arrange and monitor introductions, participate in planning decisions, and support the placement, particularly in the early stages and at the time of an adoption application. Over and above this the worker will need time to discuss all these areas with appropriate colleagues. Done thoroughly, a placement will require at least one session with the child each week and probably more during certain important phases of the placement process.

To enable social workers adequately to perform these three key tasks of identification of children, selection of families, and case management an organizational structure must enable the following:

(a) The acquisition of first-hand experience to permit the development of skills. It is clear that this requires specialization, which in turn poses further structural problems. Social workers will only be drawn away into specialist fields if the level of remuneration is directly comparable to what they might obtain in other, probably managerial, posts, and also if there are avenues back into the mainstream.
(b) The guarantee of training opportunities to develop skills and keep up to date on legal and practice developments.
(c) The provision of the amount of time necessary to carry out the work thoroughly. This is probably impossible within the context of standard generic social work for the reasons given above by Sawbridge.
(d) The provision of expertise and supervisory skills within the agency to help social workers in this field. The low level of older child adoptions and the limited fieldwork experience acquired by many existing managers during the organizational changes of the past decade have both resulted in agencies having limited expertise at advisory or supervisory levels.

> 'Experience and specialized knowledge are needed for successful family placement of older children. If the work is to be done by generic staff, a lot of supervision and support will have to be given by seniors who believe in substitute family care and who have themselves had the necessary experience.'
>
> (Rowe and Lambert 1973:102)

Many of these organizational constraints apply to other areas of local authority social work, but they are particularly relevant to older child adoption. The solution to many of the problems encountered in managing specialist areas within generic departments will probably be found in an analysis of the absurd career structure of local authority social work, but this is beyond the scope of this contribution. It should be clear, however, that the organizational constraints on local authority social workers are considerable, and that in these circumstances it is not surprising that the level of all types of family placements for older children remains very low. The social worker's dilemma is neatly described by Shaw and Lebens:

> 'Certainly, for the ordinary, generic social worker, understandably paralysed by the enormity of the task, the temptation – perhaps at times the only professionally responsible course of action – is to play safe and do nothing, i.e. to leave the child in residential care.'
>
> (Shaw and Lebens 1978:22)

CONCLUSIONS

Despite the considerable attention given to the field of older child adoption in the past fifteen years, the number of adoption orders has remained steady, and shown a decline from earlier levels. From the available evidence provided by the surveys of the placement needs of children in care and the estimates by BAAF, the number of children in care currently requiring adoptive families *may* exceed 6,000, and most of these will be older children.

The apparent failure of local authority social workers to meet these needs and, indeed, their apparent low rating of direct adoption as a placement choice for older children occurs despite the likely availability of such children for adoption, and the research findings to date suggesting that adoption may be at least as successful as other placement options. Instead, the problem seems best defined in terms of the various constraints affecting social work practice in this field. These have been identified as ethical constraints (the failure of the profession as a whole to agree on certain basic child care principles), casework constraints (particularly the motivation of existing caretakers), and organizational constraints. There appears to be an enormous gulf between the conditions under which local authority social workers currently undertake this work, and the minimum standards which are required to do the job properly. It is difficult to be optimistic about the placement chances of those older children needing adoptive homes until these constraints are better understood and at least partially resolved.

The knowledge base of adoption practice

INTRODUCTION

Social workers in adoption practice are engaged in a unique form of social engineering, involving the artificial transfer of a child from one parenting situation to another. The decisions taken by those responsible will profoundly influence the lives of all concerned: the child, the birth family, and the adoptive family. Given the complexity of these decisions, particularly with older child adoptions, it is necessary to examine the foundations on which they rest - that is, the knowledge base available to social work practitioners to help them ensure that their decision-taking is something more than a statement of personal values.[6]

In considering the term knowledge base with regard to any form of professional practice it is important to distinguish between the knowledge gained from evaluative research and the knowledge held by skilled practitioners and sometimes described in published guides to practice. This brief review focuses on the former - the body of knowledge developed from methodologically valid research. This is not to deny that there is a wealth of expertise within many adoption agencies, some of which has been written up in books or articles. However, such expertise should not be viewed as constituting part of a profession's knowledge base until it has been evaluated. Regrettably, one of the main features of adoption practice, and also of other branches of social work, is the lack of controlled evaluative research about what may well be excellent practice methods.

The principal types of decisions required for each adoptive placement can be grouped as follows:

(a) The selection of children to be placed for adoption.
(b) The selection of adoptive families.
(c) The matching of child and family.
(d) The management of the adoptive placement.

The knowledge base available to practitioners with regard to each group of decisions will be considered in terms of:

(a) Necessary knowledge: that which is needed to give decision-taking an adequate base.
(b) Useful knowledge: supplementary information which would enhance adoption practice.
(c) Available knowledge: that which is currently available to practitioners.

THE SELECTION OF CHILDREN TO BE PLACED FOR ADOPTION

In examining children who are selected for adoption, distinction must be drawn between those children who are a placed by an agency at the request of the birth parents, and those children who are already in the care of an authority which initiates the adoptive plan with or without the consent of the birth parents. The scope of the agency's influence in the selection of children placed for adoption will be more restricted for the first group than the second.

Children placed at the request of the birth parents

The majority of agency placements are those of infants or young children who are voluntarily placed for adoption by their birth family. The central issues facing practitioners in this area are twofold: first, the extent to which agency structure and policy may affect the decisions of birth parents and, second, the relative merits of different practice methods used in placements of this type.

	Necessary knowledge	Available knowledge
A	The practice methods most likely to result in a resolved decision for the birth parent, including: (a) the management of the initial referral; (b) the involvement of wider family; (c) the counselling techniques used; (d) participation in groups.	None. This is an area which has received little attention and there appear to be no significant studies allowing a controlled evaluation of practice methods.
B	The placement techniques most likely to satisfy the birth parents, including: (a) involvement in the selection of the type of adoptive family; (b) meeting with the adoptive family; (c) exchange of information with the adoptive family; (d) the timing of the placement.	As above.
C	The placement techniques most likely to satisfy the adoptive parents, including: (a) involvement in the selection of the child; (b) meeting with the birth family; (c) exchange of information with the birth family; (d) the timing of the placement.	Again, there has been no controlled evaluation in this area. Raynor (1980), in her follow-up study of different adoption placements, did find that families who undertook a period of fostering prior to the adoption application would have preferred earlier adoptions. There are no studies comparing direct-from-hospital placements of infants with those involving an initial period of fostering with people other than the applicants.
D	The influence of placement techniques as variables in the successful outcome of adoptive placements.	Almost none. The small number of outcome studies, usually with a specific focus, have been inadequate in this respect. For example, agency practice is likely to determine the methods used by adoptive families in helping adopted children to understand their origins, but there are no controlled studies in this crucial area. Raynor (1980) found the overall

Necessary knowledge (cont.)	Available knowledge (cont.)
	satisfaction ratings of families who experienced early and delayed adoptions did not significantly differ.

Useful knowledge	Available knowledge
A The extent of agency variations with regard to: (a) the ratio of referrals to head of population; (b) the ratio of placements to referrals; (c) the types of placements arranged - e.g. direct from hospital or pre-adoption fostering.	None. The difficulties in obtaining comparable data from different agencies concerning even the most basic referral and placement figures have been described by Fruin (1980).
B The comparative outcome for those children where adoption is seriously considered but not pursued.	Almost none. The research by Tizard (1977) provides some information about children initially placed in a residential nursery and then restored to their birth family. She found that in certain respects these children compared less well with children from the nursery who were adopted and with children in a control group. However, the sample sizes are very small and no firm conclusions can be drawn.

Children placed on the initiative of the local authority

Over the past six years an average of 1,500 children each year have left care because they have been adopted. Most of them were older children. Various research studies described in the previous section suggested that there remain a large number of older children in care who require adoptive placements and whose needs are not being met. For these children the decision as to whether they are selected as suitable for adoption rests with their social workers, who will consider adoption as one of a range of placement options.

The state of the knowledge base for practitioners concerned with the selection of children for adoption is as follows.

	Necessary knowledge	Available knowledge
A	The success of adoption as a placement option when compared to other types of placement in terms of stability and other outcome criteria.	There appears to have been no research comparing adoption to other placement options with the exception of the small scale study by Tizard (1977) on younger children. A significant proportion of children in care placed for adoption are older or black. These pleacements have been evaluated in different research studies, although not in a comparative manner. Clarke, in a useful review of both British and American adoption studies, concludes: 'Studies of late adopted children, including some who were received by their permanent families very late, also give us cause for cautious optimism. Scientifically these studies, like others from different domains, are of importance in casting very grave doubts on the notion that there exists in early life a critical period for later satisfactory development' (Clarke 1981:28). With regard to colour, Gill and Jackson (1982) concluded that transracial adoptions appeared successful using conventional measures of adoption outcome but suggested possible concerns with regard to the child's sense of racial identity. The success rates found by these follow-up studies in terms of placement stability and quality seem generally high. If representative they would certainly compare favourably with other placement options.
B	Specific selection criteria which may affect outcome, e.g. sex, age at time of placement, intelligence, parental consent.	None. There appears to have been no systematic attempt to identify key variables in this respect.

Useful knowledge	Available knowledge
A The extent of agency variations with regard to: (a) the ratio of adoptive placements to the number of children in care; (b) the types of placement undertaken, e.g. according to age of child, parental consent.	Almost none. Turner (1980) studied the differences in the boarding out practices of authorities within the same region but there are no similar studies on adoption practices. The DHSS is piloting a new adoption unit return for agencies which should provide more information in this respect.
B The extent to which above variations reflect identifiable differences in agency policy or practice methods.	There has been some research in this area which has been discussed in the first part of this chapter. These findings suggest that social workers have failed to agree on some of the complex issues raised by older child adoption. Few agencies have comprehensive child care policies and most practitioners operate within something of a policy vacuum.[7]

THE SELECTION OF ADOPTIVE FAMILIES

The majority of adoption agency placements are made with families whose initial approach to the agency was made without any specific child in mind. In these circumstances the agency will initially consider each application in terms of sex, age, colour, or handicap of the child preferred and decide whether to proceed with the applicants. If so, the application will be assessed in general terms with no linking to specific children before approval.[8]

The state of the knowledge base for practitioners involved in the selection of adoptive parents is as follows.

Necessary knowledge	Available knowledge
A The existence of any demographic variables which may be linked to successful outcome - e.g. social class, ages of applicants, current family circumstances, marital status, marital history, geographical mobility.	Almost none. There have been no studies offering controlled evaluation of variables of this type. Raynor's follow-up study (1980) provided some relevant findings: that adoptees tended to be less satisfied with older parents, and that neither the

Necessary knowledge (cont.)	Available knowledge (cont.)
	employment of the adoptive mother nor the adopted child's place in the family seemed to be associated with successful outcome.
B The existence of any other variables, including attitude variables, which may be linked to successful outcome, e.g. academic expectations, acceptance of birth family, religious beliefs.	Very limited. Again, there have been no studies offering controlled evaluation of variables of this type. Some research findings offer guidelines in this area but do not constitute a knowledge basis. Raynor (1980) found that poor academic showing was the most frequent frustration for adoptive parents in her sample. A more serious frustration was any perceived failure of the child to acquire the family's value system. A significant success variable seemed to be the assessed emotional climate of the adoptive home. There are some indications that the process of telling adoptees about their origins may influence the need for later information and be an important success variable (Day 1980; Leeding 1980; Triseliotis 1973). Tizard (1977) found that this process may be problematic for many adoptive parents. The importance of attitude variables in this area seems to be highlighted by those adoption studies carried out by developmental psychologists. These have suggested that: (a) the IQ of adoptees is more likely to show correlation with birth parents than adoptive parents (Scarr and Weinberg 1978); (b) adoptees with birth parents who experience schizophrenia or alcoholism may themselves be at a greater risk of experiencing

Necessary knowledge (cont.)	Available knowledge (cont.)
	similar problems than other children (Plomin, Defries, and McClearn 1980); (c) adoptees seem more likely than other children to experience problems of educational and social adjustment during childhood, but these may be resolved by adulthood (Bohman 1973; Bohman and Sigvardsson 1980; Tizard 1977; Raynor 1980; Lambert and Streather 1980).

Useful knowledge	Available knowledge
A The extent of agency variations with regard to: (a) the types of selection methods used; (b) the ratios of approvals to applications.	There has been virtually no research into agency selection practices. My impressionistic conclusion from discussions with colleagues in different agencies and with BAAF is that agencies vary enormously in terms of approval standards and practice methods. Wide differences in practice can be found in terms of the overall length of the selection process, the number of interviews undertaken, the involvement of different family members in the selection process, the interviewing of referees, the standards of medical approval, the use of training groups, the presentation of the completed assessment, and the management of the approval decision.[9]

THE MATCHING OF CHILD AND FAMILY

An adoption agency will generally retain a number of approved families who will be considered for the children selected for adoptive placements. The degree of choice available to those making the matching decision will vary according to the difficulties of the child. For most pre-school children the agencies will match from within their own resources. For harder-to-place children an inter-agency placement may be necessary.

The notion of matching has changed considerably in recent years. An initial concern with the physical matching of child and adoptive parents has been largely replaced with a greater emphasis on matching in terms of the child's individual needs and what a family has to offer. The significance of matching decisions for all those involved is profound, but the knowledge base available to practitioners again seems limited.

	Necessary knowledge	Available knowledge
A	The existence of any matching variables which may be linked to successful outcome, e.g. physical similarities, social backgrounds, assessed intelligence, position in the family, degree of choice of adoptive families.	Almost none. Matching by physical characteristics has been a subject of debate in the past, but few agencies currently follow this method. However, Raynor (1980) found that successful outcomes were significantly associated with feelings of family likeness between child and parents. She concluded that this issue should be re-examined. With regard to social backgrounds and assessed intelligence, the findings concerning IQ, mental illness, and alcoholism mentioned in the previous section may be of relevance to matching decisions, but any such relevance is unexplored. The involvement of adoptive families in the matching process has received some attention, and techniques like adoption parties have been described, but not yet evaluated (Davis *et al.* 1982).

	Useful knowledge	Available knowledge
A	Agency variation in the matching principles and methods used.	None.

THE MANAGEMENT OF THE ADOPTIVE PLACEMENT

Having matched child and family the social worker must then decide on the most appropriate methods to use, first in effecting the child's move into the adoptive family, and second in supporting the placement. The knowledge base for practitioners in this area is as follows:

	Necessary knowledge	Available knowledge
A	The extent to which successful placement practice may be linked to the types of introductions undertaken or the timing of the adoption application.	None. There appear to be no controlled studies into different introductory methods nor into the relative merits of early or delayed adoption applications, particularly for older children. In both instances there would seem to be considerable agency variations in placement practice (Fratter, Newton, and Shinegold 1983).
B	The extent to which successful placement practice may be linked to different working methods with the child - e.g. the use of preparatory techniques for children awaiting placement, the use of specialist placement centres or of pre-placement group work.	In recent years there have been many new developments in social work with children undergoing family placement. Most of these have been described in various BAAF publications. Regrettably there has been no controlled evaluation of the new methods comparing the outcome of placements where they are used to those where they are not (Fahlberg 1981).
C	The extent to which successful placement practice may be linked to different working methods with the adoptive family - e.g. the use of groups, preparatory work with children of the family, adoptive family participation in the decision-making procedures.	None.
D	The extent to which successful placement practice may be due to organizational variables within the agency.	In the previous section it was argued that local authority social workers experience various organizational constraints which impinge on their adoption practice. There

Useful knowledge (cont.)	Available knowledge (cont.)
	has been no research directly comparing the work of different agencies or organizational types in adoption practice.

Conclusions

This brief review suggests that social workers engaged in adoption practice operate within a very restricted knowledge base. It is clear from various publications in recent years that there is considerable expertise within the profession. Furthermore, many practice developments are very recent, so much so that follow-up study has not yet been possible. Nevertheless much of this expertise and these recent developments have not been subject to any form of systematic evaluation, and until this situation improves our knowledge base will remain restricted.

Our understanding of the four principal areas of adoption practice discussed above can be developed through two avenues of research. In the first place, outcome studies could be used to monitor the progress of adoptive placements according to certain key variables. Such variables might include demographic variables of the child, demographic variables of the adopters, the selection methods of the agencies for both children and adopters, the matching methods of agencies, the preparatory methods of agencies for both children and adopters, birth parent consent, the timing of the placement, the explaining of adoptive status to the child, attitude variables of the adopters. With some of these variables follow-up research could begin relatively soon after placement, while other issues - e.g. racial identity in transracial adoptions - would require a much longer-term study. The scope of the research would also depend on the nature of the variable being studied. Some would ideally require larger-scale studies involving several agencies. Current funding restrictions may make this an unlikely goal in the immediate future.

The other avenue of research might cover smaller-scale evaluative or comparative research not necessarily linked to placement outcome. Topics lending themselves to this type of study, conducted either from within the agency or from an academic setting, would include the perceptions of birth parents and adoptive parents on direct-from-hospital placements, an evaluation of different counselling techniques used with birth parents, the ratio of children placed for adoption to the number of children in care for different agencies, the ratio of adoptive parent applications to approvals within different agencies, the perceptions of adoptive parent applicants concerning different selection procedures, comparative agency practice with regard to selection procedures, matching procedures, or the management of adoptive placements.

The importance of developing a stronger knowledge base through well designed longitudinal research and better evaluative studies extends beyong the needs of practitioners in this field. For children in care, adoption should be viewed as one of a range of placement options, but even now its use as an explicit placement plan is comparatively rare. Furthermore, objections from various legal and social work pressure groups to aspects of social work practice in this area are gaining increased recognition.

Given this level of controversy the onus must fall on the proponents of adoption to justify its place as a primary placement option for children in care. Such justification will properly require the types of carefully researched arguments which are not available at present. The above review indicates that our understanding of adoption as a placement choice is very limited. At best, adoption practice is based on possibly skilled but largely unevaluated methods, whilst at worst it is based on an unsatisfactory blend of guesswork and goodwill.

Notes

1 I would like to acknowledge the influence of many of the children, families, and colleagues with whom I have worked in recent years. My experiences with them are reflected in the contents of this chapter and I hope it meets with their approval. I must also acknowledge the assistance received from the British Agencies for Adoption and Fostering and in particular from their director, Tony Hall.

2 Non-parental adoptions constitute the minority of older child adoptions. In 1981 the number of older children adopted where at least one adopter was a parent totalled 4,040, compared to 969 adoptions where neither adopter was a birth parent (OPCS 1983).

3 See, in particular Turner (1980) and Shaw and Lebens (1976). Turner examined the children boarded out in 6 different authorities, and considered the planning for the 203 children in the sample who had been boarded out with the same family for at least 3 years. He found that adoptive plans were in process for 9 per cent of the cases, that a further 17 per cent would require subsidized adoption, and that 'further investigation' was required

in 16 per cent of the cases. There were no adoptive plans for 50 per cent of the sample. Turner found that the level of birth parent involvement was very low with almost half of the children never seeing a birth parent and only 16 per cent having contact more frequently than once a quarter.

Shaw and Lebens also examined children who were boarded out and who had been in care for at least six months. They found, like Turner, that the majority were expected to remain in care with little or no parental contact. Adoption was rarely considered as a placement option and communication between social workers and foster parents on the subject seemed poor.

4 The estimated number of fieldworkers is based on DHSS statistics (1982) which put the number of field social workers in England alone in September 1981 at 13,933. It should be noted that these do not include social workers employed in Wales, although the adoption figures cover both England and Wales. The estimate on post-qualification practice is taken from the NCB study (Parker 1980) which suggested an annual turnover rate of field social workers of about 20 per cent.

5 This example sets out the predicted amount of social work time involved in obtaining six families approved for older child adoptions. The following assumptions, all based on actual experience, shall apply:

(a) that the ratio of initial enquiries to final approvals is 5:1;
(b) that approximately one-third of the enquiries will be withdrawn before an initial visit;
(c) that a further 25 per cent will withdraw after initial discussions;
(d) that a further 10 per cent will be advised to withdraw after initial discussions;
(e) that of the remaining 32 per cent undergoing full assessment, two-thirds will be approved.

On the basis of these assumptions, in order to obtain 6 approved families one would need 30 initial enquiries with 10 withdrawing at once, 11 withdrawing or being advised to withdraw after initial contact, and 9 undergoing a full assessment. The social work time involved can now be estimated as follows:

(a) the management of initial enquiries: receiving referral, sending information, offering interview - 20 minutes per referral;
(b) undertaking initial assessments of 20 applications: 2 × 1½ hour interviews, 1 hour travel; 2 hours administration and case discussion per application;
(c) full assessment of 9 applications: 8 × 1½ hour visits, 4 hours travel, 8 hours administration and case discussion per application;

(d) training for 9 applications assuming 3 social workers involved in one group: 7 sessions of 2 hours each and 2 hours preparation and evaluation per session;
(e) presentation before panel for decision: 1 hour per application;
(f) time allowed for delays and mistakes: 2 hours per application.

The total time involved is 462 hours, an average of 77 hours per approval, almost exactly two full weeks of a social worker's time.

6 As in the previous section, I shall be referring only to the adoption practice of local authority or voluntary adoption agencies involving the placing of children with families where neither parent is a birth parent of the child.

7 The few exceptions to this include Lothian, Rochdale, Essex, and Lambeth. See, for example, Hussell and Monaghan (1982) and two short articles on child care services in Essex (*Adoption and Fostering* (1981) 1:6-7 and *Adoption and Fostering* (1982) 2:6).

8 Some more specialist agencies, including Dr Barnardo's and Parents for Children, are moving away from this practice, preferring instead to recruit families with specific children in mind (Sawbridge (ed.) 1983).

9 The presentation of applications is becoming more standardized as a result of the increasing number of agencies which are affiliated to BAAF and which use their comprehensive set of family placement forms. The use of such forms helps to ensure that similar areas are covered. This is a significant advance but will not in itself lead to greater standardization of approval standards and methods.

References

Adcock, M., White, R., and Rowlands, O. (1982) The Role of the Local Authority as Parent. *Adoption and Fostering* 6(4):14-18.

Bacon, B. and Rowe, J. (1978) *The Use and Misuse of Resources.* London: ABAFA.

Bohman, M. (1973) 'Unwanted' Children - A Prognostic Study. *Child Adoption* 72:13-25.

Bohman, M. and Sigvardsson, S. (1980) Negative Social Heritage. *Adoption and Fostering* 4(3):25-31.

British Agencies for Adoption and Fostering (1983) *Children in Care: Evidence to the House of Commons Social Services Committee.* London: BAAF.

Clarke, A.M. (1981) Adoption Studies and Human Development. *Adoption and Fostering* 5(2):17-29.

Davis, L., Lord, J., James, S., James, R., and Yielder, J. (1982) *Adoption Parties.* London: A Voice for the Child in Care.

Day, C. (1980) General Register Office Study. In T. Hall (ed.) *Access to Birth Records.* London: BAAF.

DHSS (1981) *Staff of Local Authority Social Services Departments at 30.9.81, England.* London: HMSO.

______ (1982) *A Study of the Boarding Out of Children.* London: HMSO.

Fahlberg, B. (1981) *Helping Children When They Must Move.* London: BAAF.

Family Rights Group (1982) *Fostering Parental Contact.* London: FRG.

______ (1982) *Accountability in Child Care - Which Way Forward?* London: FRG.

Fratter, J., Newton, D., and Shinegold, D. (1983) *Cambridge Cottage Pre-Fostering and Adoption Unit.* Hertford: Barnardo's.

Fruin, D. (1980) Sources of Statistical Information on Adoption. *Adoption and Fostering* 4(2):25-36.

Gill, O. and Jackson, B. (1982) *Adoption and Race: Black, Asian and Mixed Race Children in White Families.* London: Batsford, BAAF.

HMSO (1983) Social Services for Children in England and Wales 1979-1981. London.

Hussell, C. and Monaghan, B. (1982) Child Care Planning in Lambeth. *Adoption and Fostering.* 6(2):21-6.

Jordan, B. (1981) Prevention. *Adoption and Fostering* 5(3):20-2.

Lambert, L. and Rowe, J. (1974) Children in Care and the Assumption of Parental Rights by Local Authorities. *Child Adoption* 78:13-23.

Lambert, L. and Streather, J. (1980) *Children in Changing Families.* London: National Children's Bureau.

Leeding, A. (1980) The Local Authority Experience. In T. Hall (ed.) *Access to Birth Records.* London: BAAF.

Office of Population Censuses and Surveys. *OPCS Monitors Series FM3 1976-1983.* London: OPCS.

Parker, R. (1980) *Caring For Separated Children.* London: Macmillan.

Plomin, R., Defries, J., and McClearn, G. (1980) *Behavioural Genetics: A Primer.* San Francisco: W. H. Freeman.

Raynor, L. (1980) *The Adopted Child Come of Age.* London: Allen & Unwin.

Rowe, J. and Lambert, L. (1973) *Children Who Wait.* London: ABAFA.

Rowe, J., Hundleby, M., Paul, H., and Keane, A. (1980) Long Term Fostering and the Children Act 1975. *Adoption and Fostering* 4(4):11-18.

Sawbridge, P. (1977) Report on Parents for Children. *Adoption and Fostering* 1(3):10-11.

______ (ed.) (1983) *Parents for Children.* London: BAAF.

Scarr, S. and Weinberg, R. (1978) The Influence of 'Family Background' on Intellectual Attainment. *Amer. Social Rev.* 43:674-92.

Shaw, M. and Lebens, K. (1976) Children Between Families. *Adoption and Fostering* 84:17-27.

Shaw, M. and Lebens, K. (1978) *What Shall We Do With the Children?* London: ABAFA.

Tizard, B. (1977) *Adoption; A Second Chance.* London: Open Books.

Triseliotis, J. (1973) *In Search of Origins.* London: Routledge & Kegan Paul.

______ (1980) Growing Up in Foster Care and After. In J. Triseliotis (ed.) *New Developments in Foster Care and Adoption.* London: Routledge & Kegan Paul.

Turner, M. (1980) Waiting in Foster Care. *Adoption and Fostering* 4(4):17-21.

5 Causes and treatment of behaviour problems in adoptive children

MARTIN HERBERT

Most parents, with little or no training - and parenting is in large part a skill - rear their children (with the help of other socializing agents) into socially acceptable and broadly norm-abiding adults; and normality is defined in terms of the social criteria, i.e. social standards that children learn. There seems to be a fair amount of latitude in learning conditions for those children with intact central nervous systems, healthy bodies, and relatively unvolcanic temperaments. They acquire an understanding of, and willingness to abide by, society's conventions, despite parental inconsistency, double-binds, and ambiguous rules. For them, parental inexperience or poor judgement seem no more than a minor hindrance in the business of growing up. For others, predisposed to problem formation by *handicaps* - temperamental lability, physical and/or mental impairments - a more predictable and persistent learning environment becomes essential. The demand characteristics of such children - the high rate, high-intensity behaviours of a coercive kind so often associated with handicap - interact with parental sensitivities and other attributes to produce an environment which often is fraught, unpredictable, and unpersevering!

But does the fact of being adopted constitute such a handicap, predisposing the child or, indeed, the family to the development of problems? The evidence concerning the nature and risk of psychological disorders in adopted children is, as Shaw points out in Chapter 7, somewhat ambiguous. It is difficult to disentangle the complex relationships between such problems and a variety of influences: the fact of adoption *per se*, the special perceptions people have toward adopted children (which may affect the problem-labelling process and the threshold at which a referral is made), and attributions about the causes of behaviour in these youngsters which can turn into self-fulfilling prophecies.

We are left with doubts as to whether there is a *raised incidence* of psychological disorder in adopted children or whether there are *special problems* associated with the status of adoptee. If there is a bias in the nature of the problems displayed by these youngsters when they do manifest difficulties, it is in the very broad direction of conduct disorders. They are more likely to be referred for help with conduct problems than emotional (i.e. neurotic) disorders (Humphrey 1963; Reece and Levin 1968; Offord 1969). But what does this mean? What has emerged from past and present studies of childhood disorders is a consensus about the classification of these many and diverse problems into two main 'symptom clusters' (Achenbach and Edelbrock 1978). The various researchers find, despite great diversity in subjects, instruments, raters, and statistical analyses, that empirical investigations consistently elicit syndromes of the *undercontrolled type* (conduct disorder, aggressive, externalizing, acting out) and the *overcontrolled type* (emotional disturbance, personality disorder, inhibited, internalizing, anxious).

I shall focus in this chapter on the causes and treatment of conduct problems of adopted children. Parents find these the most difficult to cope with as, indeed, do therapists. The fact that emotional disturbances of childhood tend to be relatively benign (i.e. transient) whereas the conduct disorders - at least in their extreme manifestations - have more serious prognostic implications, provides the basis for this choice. The fact - if such it is - that adopted children display more conduct problems than emotional disturbances does not differentiate them from non-adopted youngsters (Herbert 1978). Nor does it necessarily stigmatize them as a 'high-risk' group. Biased sampling, the generalization of findings from clinic-attending adopted children, has led to many erroneous conclusions. It is not surprising that when groups of 'special-risk' (i.e. referred) children are examined, relationships between specific parental patterns (for example) and subsequent behaviour disturbances in the offspring are found which then disappear when they are looked for in the more general childhood population.

What we do not know from aetiological studies of restricted clinical samples is how many run-of-the mill children have suffered the allegedly 'pathogenic' influence (and this would seem to include being brought up adopted by non-biological parents if one is to believe writers like Humphrey 1963) *without* any particular ill-effect. What we can affirm on the basis of more broadly based surveys is that, in all the risk categories invoked in the literature on psychopathology (be they prenatal or perinatal pathology, parental characteristics, family problems, adoptive status, or whatever), it is possible to identify significant numbers of children who, although subjected to these influences, nevertheless developed normally. The National Child Development Study (see Shaw, Chapter 7), which is a broad-based longitudinal survey, certainly confirms such an assertion in the case of adopted children.

The common theme running though the rather heterogeneous collection of problems making up the category 'conduct disorders' is antisocial disruptiveness, and the social disapproval offenders earn because they flout society's sensibilities and rules and because the consequences of their actions are so disturbing or explicitly harmful to others. Thus the problems range from legally defined delinquent acts to a variety of non-delinquent behaviours, including the more or less involuntary forms of what are referred to as coercive or oppositional problems: commanding, screaming, crying, pestering, tantrums, negativism, and so on.

Children labelled as problematic have often been regarded in the clinical and social work literature - often at the cost of effective practice - as passive victims of external forces. One still hears occasionally what used to be a popular and simplistic catch-phrase: 'There are no problem children only problem parents.' But not only is the *presence* of parents apparently pathogenic but so is their *absence*! Sadly it is mothers who are most frequently inculpated among the noxious and simplistic influences.

Maternal deprivation and problem development

In searching for causes of problem behaviour, researchers and theorists have focused on the earliest influences in children's lives - the period within the family, when they learn their first lessons and enjoy (or suffer) so many new experiences. Milton expresses this notion of predisposition: 'Childhood shows the man as morning shows the day.' It is thought that early childhood experiences are not ephemeral but determine later behaviour and attitudes.

A commonly held belief which can be very worrying to adoptive parents is the notion that infants who are deprived of maternal care and love (evident in the history of some of the older children who are adopted) are affected adversely in their ability to form affectional bonds and also in their development of a pro-social repertoire of attitudes and behaviour. Much has also been made (because of the respectable-looking conceptual links between psychoanalysis, embryology, and ethology) of the 'critical period' hypothesis - an idea which provided a theoretical underpinning for much maternal deprivation theorizing. An attitude of therapeutic nihilism was created in the minds of many social workers when considering problems in older children who were adopted, or the breakdown of fostering arrangements. This resulted from their concept of fixed and irreversible attributes. One wonders how many difficult youngsters have been written off as psychopathic because of the postulated link between their experience of early maternal separation/deprivation and the acquisition of a so-called *affectionless* personality (Morgan 1975). An intolerable burden of anxiety about the child's future is placed on parents who adopt older youngsters. But what is the evidence for such misgivings?

Infant-to-parent attachment

Behaviour which is characteristic of infantile attachment may readily be observed in its many forms in human children as well as in the young of birds and non-human mammals. Examples of chicks or ducklings following a person have been seen by many people in nature films. Although normally attached to their birth mother, such infants can become attached with ease to an 'adoptive' parent or (in the laboratory) to a moving inanimate object. Lorenz (1935) found that during a restricted period - just after hatching - goslings instinctively follow the first large moving thing they see. These young creatures not only tend to follow this moving object but they come to prefer it to all others, and after a time will follow no others.

This type of early learning is referred to as imprinting. The newborn of mammalian species capable of locomotion soon after birth - as are most herbivores, such as cows, horses, or deer - also appear to form attachments by exposure to figures in their immediate environment, which usually, of course, happen to be their mothers. Other young mammals, including infra-human primates, such as monkeys and apes, show strong ties to their mothers and sometimes also to other individuals. It is by no means certain whether these attachments can be explained in terms of imprinting-like learning (Sluckin 1970). Regardless of how acquired, the specific attachment of a young animal to a particular adult or adult substitute is known as *infantile* attachment.

A great deal has been written on the subject of the affectional ties of human infants to their parents, particularly in the context of maternal deprivation. The fascinating question that arises from studies of imprinting is whether human attachments, preferences, or other behaviours are acquired (and perhaps even 'fixed') during restricted periods of development on an imprinting-like basis. The most influential writings have been those of John Bowlby (1953, 1969). His early opinion was that the child's strong attachment to its mother was necessary for normal, healthy development. Bowlby argued that the period in the infant's life when a major new relationship (e.g. to the mother) was being formed was a vital one for determining the nature of that relationship. At that time he thought that deprivation of maternal affection, or protracted maternal separation, was liable to result in maladjustment which could show itself in a variety of ways, including delinquency. He was suggesting then that not only the presence of adverse influences (e.g. a harsh rejecting mother), but the absence of crucial stimulation (e.g. the lack of a mother or mother-surrogate), disturb - possibly irreversibly - the child's ability to make relationships with people. Bowlby's later view, following an examination of detailed empirical research findings, was that the child's separation from its care-giver did not inevitably result in the maladjustment of the child. This is not to deny the vital importance of the presence of a mother-figure - especially before the age of about five years - in facilitating the child's healthy psychological development. The debate about the relationship between infantile attachment and maternal deprivation continues; fortunately the 1970s have produced some very useful critical reviews on the effects of maternal deprivation and other types of early experience, also on current theories of infantile attachment (e.g. Rutter 1972; Schaffer 1979; Clarke and Clarke 1976). An influential review of the evidence indicated the more optimistic conclusion that early experience is no more than a link in the chain of development, shaping behaviour less and less powerfully as age increases (Clarke and Clarke 1976). What is probably crucial is that for some children early learning and experience (of an adverse kind) are continually reinforced and it is in this way that long-term effects appear. And there is also the possibility that later problems and deviance are the result of *later* experience or reinforcement and not only early learning experiences.

The idea of a critical period implies that parents are all-powerful, all-responsible. Such an ideology places a great burden on parents to 'get things right'! In fact, our knowledge of cause and effeect in behaviour development is elementary, and therefore our conjectures about what parental practices are appropriate or beneficial need to be tentative, and our inferences about the outcome of conditions - combinations of parental attitudes, home and school circumstances, reinforcement contingencies, genetic influences, and so on - must be extremely cautious.

There is (for example) no hard evidence of a relationship between *specific* early childrearing practices and the child's adjustment and personality development (Caldwell 1964; Lee and Herbert 1970). Available evidence suggests that what is important in childrearing is the general social climate in the home - the attitudes and feelings of the parents which form a background to the application of specific methods and interactions of childrearing.

Rearing adopted children

The Egyptians, Romans, and Greeks all sanctioned adoption. In earlier periods adoption was utilized primarily to serve adult ends. Specifically, adoptions were arranged to acquire heirs in order to provide continuity for a family line. Views on adoption have shifted markedly over the years. Today's philosophy is unmistakably child-centred and aspires to provide permanent homes for children. In essence the value of adoption in modern society is that it safeguards the child by providing a permanent family arrangement; some commentators might add that such advantages are counterbalanced by certain adverse features inherent in the nuclear family as a context for rearing children. This is not the place for a debate on the virtues and vices of the nuclear family. The fact is that adoptive parents - like biological parents setting out to rear an infant - are faced with the rather daunting task of transforming helpless, unsocial, and self-centred infants into more or less self-supporting, sophisticated, and responsible members of the community.

Not all infants are as co-operative as they might be in this process of socialization. Parents are sometimes taken by surprise by the 'difficult' temperament of their newborn baby, and by resistance to changes of routine and even the simplest training requirements (Thomas, Chess, and Birch 1968). In many ways a child's behaviour can have as much effect on his parents' actions as their behaviour has on his (Bell and Harper 1977). So when parents meet these temperamental or inborn factors - this powerful individuality -from a very tender age, they can be overwhelmed for a time, and change the way they bring up their child. These individual characteristics may show themselves in moodiness, over-activity, defiance, over-sensitivity, physical problems, general irregularity, and unadaptability - that is, a noisy unwillingness to adapt to changes in routine. The impact may be greater on adoptive parents because they may ascribe the difficult behaviour to deprivation experiences, rejection of themselves by the adopted child, or even 'bad blood'.

In defining to themselves what is normal in their offspring, parents have a set of expectations with which the child's progress and behaviour are compared. The criteria to which the child is asked to adjust in the name of social life are guidelines of intellectual, social, and moral behaviour. It may be that adoptive parents have particular sensitivities or special expectations because their child has the status of being someone 'special'. However, there is no evidence that their attitudes and expectations are unique, or differ markedly from parents who are biologically related to the children in their care.

Antecedents of conduct problems

Many of the children with conduct problems seen by the author at the Child Treatment Research Unit in the Psychology Department of the University of Leicester seemed to be arrested at a demanding (egocentric) stage of development - whatever their age (Herbert 1978). The period between approximately one and three years of age is often, according to research conducted at the Unit, a 'sensitive period' with regard to the development (and therefore prevention) of many conduct disorders. Disorders take root because of the inability of parents (there were several adaptive and foster parents in our sample (Herbert and Iwaniec 1981) for a variety of reasons - emotional or social - to confront their child's coercive behaviour (in some youngsters of an extreme nature) in a manner that will launch him into the vital later stages of moral development and those processes of socialization which have to do with empathy and impulse control.

Patterson (1975) lists the following possibilities for the child's failure to substitute more adoptive, more mature behaviours for his primitive coercive repertoire: (a) the parents might neglect to condition social skills (e.g. they seldom reinforce the use of language or other self-help skills); (b) they might provide rich schedules of positive reinforcement for coercive behaviours; (c) they might allow siblings to increase the frequency of aversive stimuli which is terminated when the target child uses coercive behaviours; (d) they may use punishment inconsistently for coercive behaviours; and/or (e) they may use weak conditioned punishers as consequences for coercion.

The literature tells us that well-adjusted children tend to have parents who are warm, nurturant, supportive, and controlling with high expectations. Baumrind (1971) has produced evidence for the assertion that firm control is associated with independence in the child, provided that the control is not restrictive of his or her opportunities to experiment and be spontaneous. Studies of parent-child relationships have been made possible by using special psychological measures and statistical techniques of analysis; they may make it possible to reduce the rich variety of maternal behaviour to a few main dimensions.

There are two main underlying, independent dimensions of parental attitudes and behaviours:

(a) attitudes which are warm (or loving) at one extreme, and rejecting (or hostile) at the other;
(b) attitudes which are restrictive (controlling) at one extreme, and permissive (encouraging autonomy) at the other.

The combination of *loving and controlling* attitudes is indexed by behaviours which are restrictive, overprotective, possessive, or overindulgent in content; *loving and permissive* attitudes are shown by actions which are accepting, co-operative, and democratic. The combination of *rejecting and controlling* attitudes is indexed by behaviours which are authoritarian, dictatorial, demanding, or antagonistic; *rejecting and permissive* attitudes are indicated by actions which are detached, indifferent, neglectful, or hostile. Children's reports of their parents' behaviour suggest three rather than the conventional two orthogonal factors: the additional one being a dimension of firm versus lax control. It is possible for children to perceive their parents as firm but allowing autonomy at one and the same time; or indeed, lax but still controlling. The outcomes of the various combinations listed above - trends of course - are many but most worrying in the case of the last-mentioned category as they predispose towards aggressive, anti-social patterns in children and adolescents.

Love alone is not enough in moral training; precise teaching has to be provided in seemingly endless moral learning situations - with much attention paid to the detailed consequences of transgressions on the part of the child. The factors that facilitate the development or moral and social awareness and behaviour (Hoffman 1970; Wright 1971), and which have to be given due attention when planning therapeutic interventions, are as follows:

(a) strong ties of affection between parents and children;
(b) firm moral demands made by parents on their offspring;
(c) the consistent use of sanctions;
(d) techniques of punishment that are psychological rather than physical (i.e. methods that signify or threaten withdrawal of love and approval), thus provoking anxiety or guilt rather than anger;
(e) intensive use of reasoning and explanations (inductive methods).

A variety of family conditions preclude the operation of these factors in the lives of some children. Typically, children with persistent conduct disorders come from families where there is discord and quarrelling, where affection is lacking, discipline is inconsistent, ineffective, and either extremely severe or lax, and where supervision is inadequate. Often the family has broken up through divorce or separation. In addition, the children may have had periods of being placed 'in care' at times of family crisis (Koller and Castanos 1970).

Of course, these overinclusive concepts can be misleading. In the case of broken homes, for example, many factors must be taken into account (e.g. the sex of the lost parent, the cause of the loss, the age of the child at the time of the loss) if the circumstances of parental loss are to have any explanatory value. Rutter (1977) throws some light on this issue of moderating variables in his detailed study of the families of psychiatric patients with children of school age or younger. He found that a separation from both parents that had lasted four weeks or more was associated with antisocial problems in boys; however, this correlation held up only in homes where there was a very disturbed marital relationship between the parents.

Mention of the effects of parental rejection and hostility in contributing to the development of conduct disorder brings us to a commonly held belief about the evolution of maternal affection, i.e. the issue of mother-to-child attachment (bonding). Sadly, this belief about the ties of affection - given much publicity in the media - is quite likely to engender apprehension and pessimism in would-be adoptees. Just as an infant becomes attached to its mother, so also a mother can be attached to her infant or infant-surrogate. This kind of attachment is known as maternal attachment. The social work and paediatric literature is full of dire warnings about the consequences of failures or distortions of mother-to-child bonding. It is widely believed that, as with some mammalian species, human mothers become bonded to their infants through close contact during a short critical period soon after birth. In this concept we have 'echoes' of the nihilistic applications - at least in their early manifestation - of maternal deprivation theory!

What evidence is there for the close-contact, critical-period view of mother-to-infant-bonding? One strand of evidence is ethological, since it is rooted in studies of animal behaviour. The other has to do with observations of human mothers, both those who have had extended contact and those who have had little or no contact with their newborn infants. Klaus and Kennell in their book *Maternal-Infant Bonding* reviewed the evidence from those sources and concluded that 'an essential principle of attachment is that there is a *sensitive period* in the first minutes and hours after an infant's birth which is optimal for the parent–infant attachment' (Klaus and Kennell 1976:65–6). Furthermore, 'early events have long-lasting effects. Anxieties a mother has about her baby in the first few days after birth, even about a problem that is easily resolved, may affect her relationship with the child long afterward' (Klaus and Kennell 1976:52). These views and the notion of the importance of post-partum skin-to-skin contact between mother and child (also put forward by Klaus and Kennell) have been very influential. The consequences of the 'doctrine' of maternal bonding - as it has become - are positive *and* negative, and will be discussed later. What is important to note is the growing scepticism about the validity of the concept (Chess and Thomas 1982).

In a book *Maternal Bonding* by Sluckin, Herbert, and Sluckin (1983) the authors review the concept of mother-to-infant bonding, and the evidence for the theory of a sensitive or critical period. The ethological support for the bonding doctrine was based upon some early experiments with ewes and female goats. The findings appeared to show that those animals learned the smell of their offspring in a rapid fashion immediately following birth. After this they would repudiate any lamb or kid other than their own. This reported mechanism of bond formation was initially referred to as olfactory imprinting of mother on infant.

The postulating of maternal olfactory imprinting seemed to explain the original experimental results; but this interpretation of the data could not be sustained - in the long run - in the face of further experimental findings. The most recent studies at Duke University in the USA. have shown more clearly how the mother of a recently born lamb or kid responds to the situation (Herbert, Sluckin, and Sluckin 1982). To put it briefly, what happens is that female sheep and goats reject any incorrectly 'labelled' young. They butt away all those infants tainted with alien smells. Any young, on the other hand, that are free from the wrong smells, or that by some means have been freed from them, are accepted and allowed to nurse. It follows therefore that in these particular ungulates maternal attachment cannot be said to be due to close olfactory or tactile contact shortly after parturition.

Sluckin, Herbert, and Sluckin (1983) make the point that in no mammalian species has rapid maternal bonding been demonstrated. In some species, including humans, lactating females are not strictly discriminatory in suckling young infants. Foster mothering does sometimes succeed in animals and can be very successful (as is adoption) in the human species. It is noteworthy that acceptance and adoption of the young do not necessarily occur immediately after parturition. Despite recent evidence and, more important, the dangers of drawing parallels between animal and human behaviour, practitioners concerned with mother-to-infant bonding in human beings still frequently quote sheep and goat studies to support the maternal bonding doctrine (Klaus and Kennell 1976). If we must extrapolate from animal to human behaviour then it would make most sense to observe what occurs in our nearest mammalian relatives, the various infra-human primates. Here there is *no* reported evidence of the rapid post-parturition bonding that is said to occur in human mothers.

The more critical confirmation of the notion that rapid bonding occurs in the *human* species would come from studies of mothers who, shortly after giving birth to a baby, have either been separated from it or have been allowed much skin-to-skin contact with it. There have been quite a number of such follow-up studies during the last decade (Sluckin, Herbert, and Sluckin 1983). The earliest studies seemed to indicate that extended-contact mothers were in some ways initially more attached to their babies, as measured by certain criteria of attachment (not all of obvious significance), than mothers who have little or no skin-to-skin contact after birth. However, these more marked signs of attachment were of very short duration. Differences in attachment behaviour between extended-contact and no-contact mothers were found to vanish as time went by. The most recent, carefully controlled investigations - American and Swedish - have shown that close contact soon after birth makes no difference to mothering effectiveness or to mother-love, as reported by mothers or as inferred from their behaviour (Herbert, Sluckin, and Sluckin 1982). There is no support for the belief that skin-to-skin contact is necessary for the development of mother-love; and, what is more crucial (especially from adoptive parents' point of view) is that mother-to-infant attachment does not depend on such contact occurring during a sensitive, or critical period of short duration after the birth of the baby. If it did it would be difficult to explain those studies which report a high proportion of successful parenting by adopters (Tizard 1977).

The practical implications of what is now known about bonding are very significant. On the positive side there has been a salutary highlighting of the psychological needs of the mother and her baby, and a welcome emphasis on the importance of a humane flexible environment in which they can get to know one another. The cost of the dogmatic application of 'bonding theory' is that would-be adoptive parents could be deterred from adopting an older child, especially if they accept uncritically the received wisdom about the genesis and implications of maternal bonding. Strong mother-to-infant bonds are thought to be a prerequisite of true mother-love, of good maternal care, and of the absence of rejection and child abuse. Bowlby (1951) used the metaphor for mother love of something as essential for mental health as vitamins and proteins for physical health. Given such powerful ideologies, it is perhaps not surprising, if regrettable, that some present-day obstetric and nursing procedures provide for skin-to-skin contact between a mother and her newborn at almost any cost - even if the mother is ill or in pain, even if the infant is premature. All this because it is considered to be essential for bonding. Although early close mother–infant contact is usually highly desirable (mothers tend to like it, mother and baby have the opportunity to get to know one another, lactation is facilitated, and so on, it is by no means a necessary or sufficient condition for the development of mother-love or mother-to-infant bonds. Therefore no adoptive mother should worry because she has not been bonded to her infant at the 'proper' time.

It is quite bad enough that many adoptive mothers may call into question the depth and sincerity of their maternal feelings. It is perhaps worse when distortions or lack of maternal bonding are blamed for a variety of problems such as unsuccessful adoptions, fostering breakdowns, infantile autism, and, especially, child abuse. We have seen that adoptive parents tend to do vey well as parents (Seglow 1972; Tizard 1977), and there is simply no hard evidence that children are battered by their mothers when the latter have not been successfully 'bonded' to the former. There is plenty of evidence, however, that child abuse occurs in certain types of home and social environment. Sluckin, Herbert, and Sluckin (1983) explore this theme further, and we indicate how exposure learning, different forms of conditioning, imitation, and cultural factors, all influence the development of mother-to-infant and father-to-infant attachments. Maternal bonding should not conjure up an image of a kind of rapidly working 'superglue' fixing or bonding the mother to her infant. A more appropriate image is that of a growing mother-to-infant attachment - a process which consists of learning gradually to love one's infant more truly and more strongly, a process which is characterized by ups and downs, and which is often associated with a variety of mixed feelings about one's child or children (Harlow 1971).

Identity and self-perception

The issue of identity and self-image is said to be a significant one in adopted children (see Shaw, Chapter 7). Psychological problems are very much bound up with the child's favourable or unfavourable perception of himself - his self-image - and his perception of, and relationship with, other people. This perception is related, in turn, to acceptance and approval by parents and others. But many other factors contribute to this vital component of personality (Herbert 1966). So many of the difficulties which a youngster has to cope with are social ones - the problems of getting on with other children of the same age, with teachers, with his own parents, and, by no means least, getting on with himself. He needs to like himself, to rely on himself, and to know himself. Positive self-attitudes are the basic ingredients of positive mental health, and negative self-concepts among the critical predispositions to maladjustment (Coopersmith 1967).

There is clear evidence that all human beings old enough to have acquired even a rudimentary self-image need to perceive themselves in at least a moderately favourable light (Herbert 1974). A reasonable agreement between the self-concept ('myself as I am') and the concept of the ideal self ('myself as I would like to be') is one of the most important conditions for personal happiness and for satisfaction in life. Marked discrepancies arouse anxiety, and are associated with psychological problems. Whether such discrepancies are a *particular* feature of adopted children as a group is not established. Where such problems happen to be a feature of certain individual adopted youngsters, there are a variety of counselling and/or therapeutic interventions available (Herbert 1975).

Helping adoptive parents

When it comes to the conduct disorders (which adoptive parents, like other parents, find most troublesome), the sort of help provided at the Child Treatment Research Unit is based on the rationale that maladaptive social and moral learning lies at the root of many of the problems (Herbert 1981). Such a notion points to the logic of treating such disorders in the child's home with the care-givers as the main mediators of change. The approach of the Unit (based on the so-called *triadic* model) has provided encouraging evidence of the ability of parents to help themselves and their problematic children (Herbert 1978). The theoretical basis for the work is that childhood learning takes place within a social nexus where rewards and punishments as well as other events are mediated by human agents and within attachment and social systems; they are not simply the impersonal consequences of behaviour. Behavioural interventions do not rest solely on an assumption of a critical role for the social environment in shaping and maintaining human behaviour but, as Ross insists, they also 'make room for such concepts as self-control, self-observation, observational learning and cognitive mediations such as anxiety and anger' (Ross 1974:3).

The social learning-based behavioural approach has crucial implications not only for the way in which the therapist works, but also - as we have seen - for the location of the work. If it is accepted that problematic behaviours of childhood occur in part as a function of faulty learning processes, then there is a case for the proposition that problems can most effectively be modified where they occur - by making good the deficits, or by changing the social training of the child and the contingencies supplied by social agents. The triadic model recognizes the profound influence that parents have on their children's development and mental health, an influence far greater than that which any professional could exert even with intensive intervention. It presupposes a co-operative working alliance between the parent and the helping professional, both of whom are interested in the welfare of the child. Training or retraining children is a potentially long-term endeavour, given that slowly evolving, complex psychological attributes must be fostered (e.g., learning rules, developing a conscious resistance to temptation, empathy, and self-control). Some of these are internalized quickly (depending on self rather than external reinforcement); with others, parents have to go on prompting and cajoling month in and month out, and sometimes year in and year out. Some remain forever situationally determined. Time scales vary, depending on the age and maturity of the child and the nature of the behavioural task, but parents - going about the business of rearing their offspring -should not (and usually do not) expect the child to acquire and maintain certain lessons without setbacks and repetitions.

Therapeutic methods

The methods elaborated at the Unit involve a multi-faceted package depending for its final shape on the behavioural assessment (Herbert 1981). It might involve developmental and/or personal counselling. Behavioural programmes might include: differential reinforcement (positive reinforcement - social and sometimes material - of prosocial actions and removal of reinforcement or application of punishment contingent on antisocial behaviours), time-out from positive reinforcement (periods of six minutes for children below ten years of age), response-cost, and over-correction procedures. Incentive systems (token economies) are negotiated and contracted between parents and children, and some are linked to behaviour at school. With the older children, we tend to use more cognitively orientated methods including self-control training (assertion and relaxation training, desensitization of anger, role play, behaviour rehearsal), problem-solving skill training, and social skill training. A technique that has proved invaluable with hyperactive, impulsive children is self-instruction training - the development of children's skills in guiding their own performance by the use of self-suggestion, comments, praise, and other directives. Frequent use is made of alternative response training, a method that provides children with alternative modes of response to cope with provocative and disturbing situations, or activities that are incompatible with the desired behaviours.

Contingency contracts between parents and their children (particularly adolescents) have also proved of great value, not least because of their function in modelling skills in finding solutions to conflicts and learning to communicate and compromise. Such contracts are also useful in fostering situations and in residential settings; conduct problems often lead to a breakdown in substitute care (Child Treatment Research Unit Reports 1971-77). Parents and significant others (and also child clients) are trained to use reinforcement effectively, and are shown how to negotiate compromises and to bring about positive changes in ways other than by sheer coercion. This type of work can also involve communication training.

Family discussions

We also encourage family discussions in our work. It is helpful, as children get older, to hold family meetings in order to decide important family concerns such as holidays, but also to review matters of importance to the child; for example discipline, rules, pocket money, bedtime, or when to return home from a party. Children are privy to all aspects of *their* therapeutic programmes.

Traditionally, parents have tried to keep a lot of information about life and about their own affairs from children. This may be ill-advised. Keeping a child in ignorance may produce more anxiety than if parents openly explain the true facts. Children develop all kinds of disturbing fantasies about matters kept hidden from them, and yet they dare not discuss these fantasies with others. Moreover, to be told the truth - given that they are old enough to understand - offers them a chance to talk it out with someone instead of finding out later for themselves, and having to face it alone. Such matters are part of the day-to-day discussion we might have with parents. The notion that behavioural work somehow excludes 'talking therapy' because of a main emphasis on 'action' is (these days) quite erroneous.

References

Achenbach, T.M. and Edelbrock, C.S. (1978) The Classification of Child Psychopathology: a Review and Analysis of Empirical Efforts. *Psychological Bulletin* 85:1275–301.

Baumrind, D. (1971) Current Patterns of Parental Authority. Development Psychology Monograph 4 (1), Pt 2, 1–103.

Bell, R.O. and Harper, L.V. (1977) *Child Effects on Adults.* Lincoln: University of Nebraska Press.

Bowlby, J. (1951) *Maternal Care and Mental Health.* Geneva: World Health Organisation.

_____ (1953) *Child Care and the Growth of Love.* Harmondsworth: Penguin.

_____ (1969) *Attachment and Loss, Vol. 1.* London: Hogarth Press.

Caldwell, B.M. (1964) The Effects of Infant Care. In M.L. Hoffman and L.W. Hoffman (eds) *Review of Child Development Research.* New York: Russell Sage Found.

Chess, S. and Thomas, A. (1982) Infant Bonding: Mystique and Reality. *American Journal of Orthopsychiatry* 52:(s2), April.

Clarke, A.M. and Clarke, A.D.B. (1976) *Early Experience: Myth and Evidence.* London: Open Books.

Coopersmith, S. (1967) *The Antecedents of Self-Esteem.* London: W.H. Freeman.

CTRU Reports (1971–77) Child Treatment Research Unit: Empirical and Case Reports. School of Social Work, University of Leicester.

Harlow, H.F. (1971) *Learning to Love.* San Francisco: Albion.

Herbert, M. (1966) The Development of the Self-image and Ego-identity. *Common Factor Monographs* 4:61–8.

_____ (1974) *Emotional Problems of Development in Children.* London: Academic Press.

_____ (1975) *Problems of Childhood: A Complete Guide for All Concerned.* London: Pan Books.

_____ (1978) *Conduct Disorders of Childhood and Adolescence: A Behavioural Approach to Assessment and Treatment.* Chichester: John Wiley.

_____ (1981) *Behavioral Treatment of Problem Children; A Practice Manual.* New York: Grune & Stratton, London: Academic Press.

Herbert, M. and Iwaniec, D. (1981) Behavioral Psychotherapy in Natural Home Settings: An Empirical Study Applied to Conduct Disordered and Incontinent Children. *Behavioral Psychotherapy* 9(55):55–76.

Herbert, M., Sluckin, W., and Sluckin, A. (1982) Mother-to-Infant bonding. *Journal of Child Psychology and Psychiatry* 23:205–21.

Hoffman, M.L. (1970) Moral Development. In P.H. Mussen (ed.) *Carmichael's Manual of Child Psychology* 261–359. London: John Wiley.

Humphrey, M. (1963) Factors Associated with Maladjustment in Adoptive

Families. *Child Adoption* 43:25-31. Reprinted in *Child Adoption - a Selection of Articles on Adoption Theory and Practice* (1977). London: BAAF.

Klaus, M.H. and Kennell, J.H. (1976) *Maternal-Infant Bonding*. St Louis. Mosby.

Koller, K.M. and Castanos, J.N. (1970) Family Background in Prison Groups: A Comparative Study of Parental Deprivation. *British Journal of Psychiatry* 117:371-80.

Lee, S.G.M. and Herbert, M. (eds) (1970) *Freud and Psychology*. Harmondsworth: Penguin.

Lorenz, K.Z. (1935) Imprinting. In R.C. Birney and R.C. Teevan (eds) *Instinct* (1961). London: Van Nostrand.

Morgan, P. (1975) *Delinquent Fantasies*, London: Temple Smith.

Offord, D.R. (1969) Presenting Symptomatology of Adopted Children. *Archives of General Psychiatry* 20(1):110-16.

Patterson, G.R. (1975) Architect or Victim of a Coercive System? In L. Hamerlynck, L.C. Handy, J. Mash (eds) *Behavior Modification and Families: I Theory and Research: II Applications and Developments*. New York: Bruner/Mazel.

Reece, S.A. and Levin, B. (1968) Psychiatric Disturbances in Adopted Children: A Descriptive Study. *Social Work* 13(1):101-11.

Ross, A.O. (1974) *Psychological Disorders of Children: A Behavioral Approach to Theory, Research and Therapy*. New York: McGraw Hill.

Rutter, M. (1972) *Maternal Deprivation Reassessed*. Harmondsworth: Penguin.

______ (1977) Individual Differences. In M. Rutter and L. Hersov (eds) *Child Psychiatry: Modern Approaches*. 3-21. Oxford: Blackwell.

Schaffer, R. (1979) *Mothering*. London: Fontana.

Schechter, M.D., Carlson, P.V., Simmons III, J.Q., and Work, H.H. (1964) Emotional Problems in the Adoptee. *Archives of General Psychiatry* 10(2):109-18.

Seglow, J. (1972) *Growing Up Adopted*. London: NFER.

Sluckin, W. (1970) *Early Learning in Man and Animals*. London: Allen & Unwin.

Sluckin, W., Herbert, M., and Sluckin, A. (1983) *Maternal Bonding*. Oxford: Blackwell.

Thomas, A., Chess, S., and Birch, H.G. (1968) *Temperament and Behaviour Disorders in Children. London: University of London Press.*

Tizard, B. (1977) *Adoption: A Second Chance*. London: Open Books.

Wright, D.S. (1971) *The Psychology of Moral Behaviour*. Harmondsworth: Penguin.

6 An alternative family

ROB AND MARIAN CLAYTON

No case history is typical. We have been married fifteen years and have adopted a family during those years, but *our* sense of the experience involved is that it is too personal to shed much useful light, either for students of society or for potential adopters. Also, we began our enquiries in the mid-1970s when there were still some babies available for adoption, whereas in less than a decade the pattern seems to have changed and the chance to create an adopted family from babyhood is much rarer. Even so, our account may perhaps illuminate the *process* of adopting as one encounters it in England, for it was in this area that we met our problems. In Chapter 15 of this book, there is a moving account of problems experienced in America by a couple in the years after they had adopted their son. Our load has felt heavy at times, but clearly other loads can weigh much more.

We have always had an abundance of interests. In the early years of marriage there was the challenge of a big city: contributing to an improvement in its living conditions, enjoying its many diversions, being part of two cultures (for we are of two separate racial and cultural groups), bringing up Marian's daughter.... We took apparently effective precautions against any more children because 'a family' was not a priority. In secret the very thought was unreal for Rob; and the inevitable marital arguments often froze thoughts of a family before they had taken shape. Nor were we surrounded by parturient friends or living on a housing estate where nappies would flap - visible from every window - on whirlabout drying posts.

But a half-hearted decision to have a child got taken and, in due course, nothing happened. It made no sense. We were both in the prime of life and notoriously energetic, not to mention that Marian had a daughter; and in Rob's vain daydreams 'a family' meant effortlessly producing a tribe of what a contemporary song was calling 'coffee-coloured people by the score' - superpeople.

It was our friendly, avuncular GP who brought shadows into the picture. He sketched the womb's geometrical relationship to the vagina and suggested that Marian's backside should be propped by cushions to ensure efficient sperm drainage. He suggested that Marian's innards might have been damaged by aggressive male penetration earlier in her life - at which Rob bit his tongue. He suggested that Rob 'treat her like a prostitute sometimes' - at which Marian looked at the floor in bewilderment. It is curious how these chance remarks lodge in the memory, for in reviewing our story in order to put it onto paper, one of us has often forgotten what the other has remembered with searing clarity.

In due course, Marian went to be tested. Neither of us took the business too seriously or really knew what was to be involved. In the event a foreign doctor with no explanation investigated her genital parts hamfistedly, injected her, and caused great pain. Afterwards he revealed what she now remembers as 'You OK, you have baby now'. Rob stormed off and demanded to know what had happened and what its purpose had been. There was no encouragement to husbands to be involved so he cooled his heels a long while until the day's patients had been dealt with. Finally, an anonymous registrar made a brief, opaque, and now forgotten explanation.

It may well be common experience that, in the medical and social work fields, a 'lay' person has few rights in matters affecting his or her own life. One feels acutely uneasy about taking issue with the 'experts' because not only have they important knowledge, but also the power: to operate or not to operate, to say 'no' to services or decisions that are desired.

It emerged that Marian's fallopian tubes were blocked, one seriously, and that abdominal surgery would be the next step.

Seemingly as an afterthought Rob's sperm were to be counted in case the operation was not necessary. Thus to the Women's Hospital in seedy trepidation, one bit of the brain brooding on the absurdity of it, one breezily devising words to ask the nurse's help in the matter, a third bit fearing inadequacy. It is a sharp realization that this visit was to be Rob's only physical humiliation beside Marian's protracted ordeal. He was required to masturbate into a vaseline bottle behind a shower curtain, and observed that his vaseline bottle was rather less full than others on the window-sill where they were stored. Apparently it was not the stuff of super-tribes, but it was adequate. Just as siring children is simple compared with gestating them, so the husband's part in the trauma of female infertility is very cursory.

This article is not designed to be a wringing confessional or a whimsical narrative. The events are part of the process of 'adopting a family' in that later, when we applied to adopt, one of the initial criteria for getting on the waiting lists was that each couple had done all possible to produce a child and to verify that they were not likely to produce one. At the stage of surgery and sperm tests, however, we were not thinking of adoption.

So Marian was cut open for 'major surgery', an investigation into what was blocking the tubes. It was painful and debilitating, and was to be followed later by our GP telling us that the specialist saw almost no possibility of fertilization. He was gentle and friendly in suggesting that we stop thinking in those terms and consider adopting, but we did not truly believe him because it was just not acceptable that a lengthy operation could fail. More, it was an affront to our respective adulthoods: he seemed to be talking down to us. Marian cried visibly on occasions and much more in private. It has taken years for her to come to terms with what she saw as her failure as a woman, to bear children within marriage, and it has been too delicate a subject for us to exorcize by talking it through.

This medical saga was to span nearly five years. We did what many another has done and tried privately with a prestigious gynaecologist. He was as genial and direct as the other had been distant. He encouraged Rob to come to consultations, which was itself a boost to our confidence. It compensated us for our unease in insisting to a disapproving GP that we had another opinion. But the events were as uncomfortable - dyes, probes, inflations, X-rays - and as unpromising. Ironically we remember not only this man's humour and sense of authority, but also his fierce disapproval of the tentative 'test-tube baby' experiments that were occasionally making news. Marian also remembers him holding the X-rays up to the window and saying to himself, 'it's a bit like flogging a dead horse'. She has recalled this every time her period has come with a mixture of distress and defiant hope that somehow she will prove him wrong.

We now agreed in principle to attempt to adopt, but instead suddenly found ourselves fostering four young children at twenty-four hours' notice. They were aged between three and seven and had been separated and sent to three locations after their parents were badly injured. This seemed so incredible and so misguided that we - who had space and knew the family somewhat - gathered them back into a unit and kept them for six months. So we met the Social Services for the first time. Three days after the children were ensconced they produced some bedding and a month later they sent papers to the character referees whom we had named, asking whether we would be suitable *adoptive* parents. Despite these administrative shortcomings, the children were a pleasure to have and astonishingly amenable in spite of the traumatic events. What happened then has no bearing on our adoptive history apart from the delay it caused, but it transpired that, when their mother limped out of intensive care six months later, the family's house had been demolished unknown to us in a clearance programme. Again we saw how others' loads could be much heavier than our own.

Before we proceeded towards adoption, we heard of another distinguished gynaecologist arriving with a reputation for up-to-the-minute knowledge. The thought that the new fertility technologies might help led us to sign up with him, but we drew yet another blank. It was amazing during this period how many people we met who turned out to be sharing our problem. Busy successful couples who we would never have guessed were yearning for children, or more children. Equally we noticed teenagers becoming pregnant without visible means or competence to bring up the unexpected children. A ribald, succinct West Indian proverb expresses it: 'Wantee, wantee can't get, Gettee, gettee don't want.'

We are not a pair to discuss everything at length and thus to know each other's every thought; actions often precede talk and Marian especially lives in the present not the future. She was busily involved but in limbo, the shame of infertility in the background. Rob was maturing to a more realistic sense of the meaning of parenthood and, with our daughter in her mid-teens, a vision was appearing of a void without family. Yet still adoption seemed such a final acceptance of the doctors' cold verdict, and such a second-rate kind of 'family'.

But we stumbled hesitantly towards the practical decision, each privately thinking it was more for the other's sake than our own. A phone call to the County Social Services . . . but they simply had no babies and they advised us of the maximum ages at which couples were permitted to adopt: 40 for men, 35 for women. To our horror we were almost there, almost out of court before we had got on court.

They did suggest we try a private agency and as it happened a religious adoption society was just about to initiate a batch of intending adopters. The meeting was mid-week at 11 am, a time that seemed as incovenient as possible, though we concluded that it would be a test of everyone's serious intent to get there - there were five couples, a social worker dispensing tea, and a senior to conduct the session. The meeting made a deep impression on us both and could not have presented the implications of what we were groping half-blindly towards more sympathetically. The points from it that now register were that one should not decide to adopt for the sake of the child, or to do society 'a favour', but for one's own sake because one wanted one's own family; that discovering infertility would have meant distress and a period of 'mourning' for the uncreated children and this period must have been passed through; that no-one can guarantee that adoptions will work and, if a child is returned to care after the collapse of the adoption, the 'false start' for the child will be a handicap it may never recover from; and that one's police and medical records would be checked as a preliminary. We were invited to feel no shame if we decided to drop out, but simply not come to the following meeting - which three couples in the event attended. The meeting was lengthy and grave in tone as each of us internalized these searching points and asked questions. One was wondering about 'matching' children to adoptive parents, another about coping with handicap. Someone was perturbed about the ways in which parents did not adapt to awkward children and how one could tell that a breaking-point had been reached. Marian said nothing but dreaded that she would never be able to love another woman's child. Questions presumably were answered, but what we remember are not the answers but the questions forming in our minds.

We also discovered that there would be a lengthy process of assessment with no guarantee as to our eventual suitability. Apparently, 'harder-to-place' babies were easier to come by, and this daunting phrase meant handicapped or part-black (not Anglo-Indian babies who were apparently 'easier to place').

The central experience in the period between this meeting and the final adoption of our second child was the uncomfortable and unnatural one of being assessed by other people for 'suitability'. It goes against the norm of parenthood, by which couples find themselves pregnant and have to come to terms with the imminence of a dependent life. Many had not intended, many are not couples, and many are not emotionally or financially 'ready', but their babies come steadily and inevitably. No-one sits in judgement. Yet our motives for wanting a child were probed in interviews and chats, and our domestic management was evaluated with at least one visit being unannounced. Referees and relatives were consulted about our attitudes to life and our teenage daughter had her special interview though she did not find it easy to put her feelings into words that would, so to speak, be used in evidence.

One sees that there is a legitimate reason for all this, for the agencies have many hopeful couples for any baby and adoptions can go wrong. But they use standards of 'perfection' rather than the random standards of natural parenthood. They want *guarantees* that a couple won't separate and will handle the stresses that children generate. They want a guarantee that couples will handle the subject of adoption openly with the children rather than suppress it. Perhaps they are also trying to guard against the pressure exerted by the abnormal time-scale of adoption. One of its great 'losses' as a means of gaining a family is the absence of 'nest-building'. A pregnant girl may find it hard to decide definitely to hand over her baby after birth. She has the legal right to change her mind up until the court hearing. So she probably says she will allow adoption before birth, but must confirm this immediately after birth when the child goes to a foster-mother, again before the adoptive parents take it, and again before the hearing.

At the receiving end this means huge, unknowing waits while the agency mulls over potential futures for unborn babies, matching them against couples on the list; but the adoptive parents know nothing and cannot be told until the child is born, its health assessed, and its mother's reactions are clear.

So one waits. For our first we waited six months, for our second nineteen months. There is no point building up hope, so one must act as normally as possible to minimize the fretting. Suddenly the call comes and there are perhaps two weeks to adjust mentally and domestically. The 'loss' is the absence of gradual build-up, the intimacy of knowing a child is present as a growing foetus, of feeling it, the togetherness of parents in their anticipation. Rob missed this particularly, being one who had never handled a child and had retreated to far corners in the presence of all babies.

Our first social worker was admirable - punctual to the second, neat, well-prepared, and managing not to 'crowd' us or seem too critical. If anything she hinted that she was obliged to go through the interview procedures but that we were unlikely to be rejected. So we came to rely on her as a pleasant professional, however unsettling it was just to wait. Rob fretted - as he thought to himself - about the 'matching' and particularly hoped for a child of academic potential.

Then one day there was word of a baby boy in good health and of mixed race, which was what we wanted, 'But I'm afraid he may be a CSE baby not a GCE baby,' whispered the social worker apologetically. Rob realized what Robbie Burns says we so seldom see unaided, 'How others see us'.

At last the fretting became focused and turned to excitement . . . a pram . . . a cot . . . a funny plastic feeding bottle. The social worker was warning us that intending parents can actually be turned off a baby on sight, so not to be frightened of admitting it should this occur. We were contemplating the brief biographies of the parents whom we would never see, as the mother must have pondered whatever the agency said about us. Rob anxiously read huge significance into brief phrases, or facts such as the mother's height . . . Marian trusted her instinct that it was no use crystal-gazing but that she would warm to the baby and her motherhood would flood back.

Curiously, the maternity allowance goes to the natural mother, who probably has her child for a day, rather than to the adoptive parents who suddenly have to find everything within a fortnight.

So we drove a great distance on a trip to a mystery. Conversation was unreal and under the thin ice of excitement yawned fears of failure. The social worker was already there and the foster-mother who had had the child for ten weeks was welcoming. Marian simply looked at him in his cot and picked him up with a cry of excitement, and he was ours, without hesitation - she knew it and he knew it. Both the outsiders, and Rob, watched proudly, at this 'birth encounter'. The foster-mother understood perfectly the requirements of the moment and had arranged that the baby needed feeding about then so mothering began, he was fed and burped and rocked. Rob watched from a safe distance as this primary connection was established between mother and child. It was in lieu of nine months' pregnancy. But later it was his turn to hold it, to put his fathering capacity to the test of this specific baby, and the 'outsiders' understood to slip outside. He gingerly took delivery of the sleeping bundle, held it briefly, and returned it with the half-grin that millions of clumsy unlearned men must have found on their faces; and his corner too was turned.

We should simply have left then, but there was paperwork to complete and courtesies to be part of. We were told of our son's eating and sleeping habits, that he frowned a lot but liked looking at the black and white tiles in the kitchen. He had a bizarre clutch of names quite unlike the simple one we had in mind, but luckily the names were only on paper at that age and now are quite meaningless when we come across them in the strong-box. We had borrowed a Polaroid camera to leave the loving but unattached foster-mother a record of us and the child, but even at this time we wondered about the birth mother. The agency suggested we write her a brief anonymous letter after he had settled, so presumably she received, via many hands, this simple note:

Dear Susan,
You know a little about us. We have now brought René to our home and he is settled happily. He is healthy and strong and good-looking, and we know we shall love him very much. Thank you for letting us have him.

Yours sincerely,
His new mum and dad.

This boy is now seven and is not particularly academic, but those early anxieties have no bearing on his growth or our perception of him. He is handsome and energetic, though a bit quarrelsome with his younger brother. He has a problematic kidney, an inseparable friend, a slightly nervous temperament as apparently many eldest children have, he runs and rides his bike maniacally, loves stories, speaks well . . . how can we convey our view of our child. We are conscious of an 'x' factor, the input that pre-dated ours, but there is no shadow of a sense that our adopted child is other than our own absolute child. The day he came home friends and neighbours came to congratulate us and we found ourselves with twenty-six baby blankets among other items. Though we now know how baby blankets soon become obsolete, at the time it seemed that a great many had sensed our loss and now shared our delight.

Our religious agency has now closed in favour of local authority officials, in the shrinking baby market. But it imposed another hazard on prospective parents - that of demonstrating an appropriate degree of faith.

Marian was more or less a regular member of the Church, Rob a hostile non-attender; though sufficiently friendly with the vicar to have been invited to heckle the sermon one evening with counter-arguments. Unfortunately, this show-stopper never materialized, but we were grateful that it had been spoken of when we realized that the vicar had to write a reference for us. Also implicit in the arrangements was that there should be a religious framework to the children's lives, initiated by a formal service of baptism for each. We thought we knew that the vicar would not damn our chances, but it was another unnerving period. Not only was there the sense of another outside intrusion into our private business but the dread that an ill-chosen phrase might cast doubts at HQ. where the decision would get taken by a committee, a committee that we were warned could override our local social worker's recommendations.

However, this Church angle provided us with the last chuckle for, when our second application was being processed, we were told that the criterion had been modified by a new director. No longer had one to be a 'member of' the Church in the rigorous sense that had led to Rob's earlier evasions but to be 'in a state of pilgrimage through life' so that ultimate arrival in the Church was 'a real possibility'. We could accept this with a fuller heart. As it has worked out, the children attend a tiny Sunday School in the village that would not offend the most zealous marxist, and the religious agency has withdrawn below our horizon.

In retrospect the harrowing anxieties of applying and waiting are mellowed by years of normal family activity, but whilst in progress they dominated our lives. We made our second application on the first day permitted by the agency, i.e. when our first boy was eighteen months old, but it was to be another nineteen months before we received a baby. The entire rigmarole of interviews, assessments, local authority double-checks, vicarial references, and so on had to be undergone again. Only the preliminary group sessions were not required. But another social worker officiated, who took less on trust, turned up hours late for interviews she had arranged, never put on paper any record of, for example, receiving our doctor's medical report, and generally gave us the impression that in her capacity as God and the Stork (i.e. assessing us and bringing us a child if we passed the assessment) she had a difficult decision on her hands. The questions hovered endlessly round our motivation for wanting a second child, round Rob's willingness to sacrifice interests of his to be at home, round whether we fully understood the reactions the first boy might have to a rival, even round whether our sex life was normal. And always the statistic that more second adoptions break down than first, however improbable this sounded to us and may appear to a reader. They were valid questions, along with many others, and our reply was always, yes we realized there might be difficulties and yes we thought we would be able to cope but that we could only cross the bridges when we came to them. But back came the questions in other guises until this friendly, well-intentioned social worker had us edgy, defensive and, according to long-suffering friends, apoplectic. No progress was visible. No specific dates got fixed for further contacts with her . . . long gaps . . . then it transpired that our vicar's reference had been lost for months in the files.

To us it appeared thus: we were getting older, the gap between first child and hoped-for child was enlarging. We thought we were making a fair job with number one. We had a large safe garden and a large old house. We had many interests and pursued them to a reasonable level. We were a mixed couple and we sought a mixed-race child. So were there not grounds for confidence and urgency? To the social worker it seemed that we were unreasonably demanding in the face of her duty to enquire fully. After a three-month hiatus we decided we would be justified in complaining - but how could one complain to a higher echelon without offending the agency or the individual.

We felt very vulnerable. The social worker's loss of an important document focused our sense of grievance sharply but the agency had complete control, in that they alone knew where babies were and they alone could prosecute our interests, vigorously, slowly, or not at all. A friend crystallized it thus, that we were 'supplicants rather than applicants'.

On tenterhooks we did write to the senior social worker an enquiry about the delays, the text of which was drafted a dozen times and hawked round friends for assessments of how every phrase might be construed, and whether it would alienate the entire agency. At the other end there was a flurry of activity . . . and some ruffled feathers. But fortunately the process re-started. In the fullness of time the committee in London passed us and we were back onto the waiting lists.

Later, word came of a baby. The details were sketchy but it had stopped breathing at birth for a few minutes and there might be brain damage. There might be deficient hearing but it would not be clear for months whether or how much. Did we want to go ahead?

Immediately we identified with the child. If we passed it by not only might we wait another year but what would happen to him - a lifetime in an institution? When we finally said no, the word 'rejection' echoed round the house like a guilty secret, though it was the correct decision. As the social work ads in the daily press remind us there are thousands of children seeking homes and one cannot meet all their needs. Our forte would be to give an active home to an active child.

Luckily one was born shortly after this - black rather than mixed. This foolish fact caused another stutter because the concept of 'the child we might have had' had taken root. Like so many other fantastical anxieties it was rendered absurd by events. The second boy has irrepressible energy and humour and conquers all who meet him. Perhaps in recompense for not watching our own birth children take our place gradually, our adoptive family contains two utterly unalike bodies and personalities each with his 'x' factor that we cannot alter or predict the growth of, each with part of us in.

There are two more practical stages to adoption that have been plain sailing for us but are hurdles that could have been traumatic.

Even with a private adoption agency the local authority comes in as 'welfare supervisor' and as 'guardian ad litem', i.e. it monitors the child's arrival and progress once it enters the locality of its new home; and it has power to recommend that the adoption is not confirmed in the courts. Our local authority social worker minimized this potential stress and on each occasion supported us towards the earliest permissible court appearance. Court too can obviously be daunting. The circuit judges are apparently very 'individual' in their attitudes, though in general predisposed in favour of birth parents should there be argument over custody. So those who knew scanned the lists to see which judge's circuit brought him to our town. Blessedly ours was benign and took the written reports as knowing more than he could hope to unearth in a court interrogation; so each adoption went through on the nod and finally we had our family.

The children know they are adopted, as it is enjoined on us that they should. We mention it when we go past the courthouse. Occasionally, they come out with heart-stopping references to 'my real mummy and daddy' but these are only uttered on the run. We do fear their teenage years when their adoptive status may boil up to something obsessive, or surface in arguments about other matters. We are anxious about what will happen when they are eighteen and have automatic right of access to their birth certificates and may take off to investigate their own 'x' factors. We shall be in our mid-fifties when these things happen - if they do - and we may find it hard to cope; equally one can only foresee difficult times for teenagers in the 1990s anyway without the additional hazard of identity crises. But these things are written into the small print of the adoption deal and we can only have faith that relationships will be sturdy enough when the time comes to cope with whatever arises.

'A family' is an unfinished story but our adoptive one is as instinctive and beloved as children could be. The commitment is not limited or reversible. Colour and race cease to mean anything in a way that it would be difficult for those not involved to grasp, though we are lucky to be able naturally to impart two cultures. The people who say 'Oh I do so admire you for adopting them, especially at your age!' are so far off target that one cannot begin to explain.

There is an instructive postscript to this account. Shortly after number two came an offer of number three - aged between the other two and with a tangled history: another boy, mixed-race, with a promising family history and at that stage living with his grandmother. Blithely we leapt at the chance. But this time we met the relatives not foster-parents and it transpired that grandmother wished to retain that role. We accepted without thinking too deeply and in due course took the child on holiday with us during which time we crossed a dozen little bridges with the children and seemed to be making magical progress. At the end of the week the grandmother changed her mind and required more time to decide whether she could relinquish the child. We were both disturbed, Marian especially. She sobbed uncontrollably as we handed him back. The agency stepped in and made it a condition that grandmother should agree to a full 'no-further-contact' adoption. She declined and took him to a Greek island to beachcomb for an indefinite period, while we licked our wounds.

Our family established its own four-person balance, until nearly two years later we had an urgent request from Greece that we now adopt him. Grandmother would still wish to keep contact but would not impede adoption, and she considered us the ideal family.

We agonized. Marian had doubts about whether she would be able to love the child and tolerate the grandmother but she suppressed them in the face of Rob's enthusiasm. She remained shy after being bitten previously, but Rob felt her pragmatism would cope with any problems.

It is unnecessary to narrate the details and problems of taking delivery, or of the grandmother's stalling, or of the stresses between us as Marian found the uncertainties crushing her, or of the unsettling effects on our eldest of a thrusting competitor. We had him nine months and felt we were gradually resolving these stresses when the grandmother took him back through a subterfuge. He departed, as we thought for three days, in pyjamas late at night with no toys and one change of clothes, but we have never seen him since.

The experience is 'instructive' in the sense that we got it all wrong, suffered considerably ourselves, and were yet another false start for a child who had had four such 'starts' before he came to us. We think it would have worked out marvellously if we could have taken this child as the other two, anonymously; even if we had inherited a grandmother who was stable. Our error was not in our handling of the children but in going it alone without outside official guidance on the problems, *psychological* and *legal*. The delays and frustrations of being dependent on an agency are perhaps the price of finally acquiring one's family this alternative way.

Now that this account is written we again wonder who will gain any practical use from reading it. Perhaps the doctors and social workers will see how their chancest remarks can lodge in their clients' awareness and how people under stress may misunderstand them? As a very general comment, and in the context of this book which reveals how adoption can take many forms, we can only say that our new family has brought us great joy. We cannot guess how the children would have grown up in what would have seemed on the surface less advantageous circumstances with their birth mothers, but we have found fulfilment with them. That there are so many childless couples in the country and so many children in care, frequently as a result of mothers or couples not actually managing to cope, seems a tragic and ironic feature of our society. If only somehow the needing children and the yearning parents could be brought into alignment.

7 Growing up adopted

MARTIN SHAW

In the course of preparing the material for this chapter, it became clear that an important theme running parallel to that of adoption reseach was that of the *politics* of adoption research. Study of the research findings in terms of this wider focus seems to indicate that some key questions about 'growing up adopted' are as yet not only unanswered but unformulated.

The background to early research studies

Legal adoption, involving the complete transfer of parental rights from one person (or married couple) to another, came late to English law, the first Adoption Act coming into effect in 1926. Initially, lawyers and the general public responded cautiously to the legislation: lawyers suspicious of the threat to well-established family law, with implications for legitimacy and inheritance in particular; and many of the general public seeing adoption as an unsavoury if not dangerous development, with overtones of babyfarming, cruel step-parents, and foster parents on the one hand, and bastardy, 'bad blood', and a threat to decent family life on the other.

Adoption agencies in the 1920s and 1930s faced a difficult task in attempting to promote adoption as a responsible and rewarding way of building one's family. They were not helped in this task by the dominant scientific and popular view of the time that 'nature' far outweighed 'nurture' in determining an individual's personality and abilities. Adoption workers responded to this challenge by engaging in extravagant claims to be providing 'the perfect baby for the perfect couple' and by exhorting their consultant paediatricians and psychologists to devise predictive tests which might demonstrate whether the newborn prospective adoptee would have the intelligence or the athletic, artistic, or business talents desired by the prospective adopters. The validity of these tests came to be questioned, though the tendency to confuse genetic and social factors in development lingered on for some time (Schapiro 1956) and is doubtless still with us today.

Ultimately, the proof of adoption is in the outcome, and interest shifted to investigating how adopted children 'turned out' later on. A major problem in such research lies in finding a truly representative sample, for adopted children, unlike their contemporaries growing up in institutional or foster home care, have gone through a legal process deliberately designed to ensure that they are to all intents and purposes indistinguishable from other children in the community at large. Consequently, adopted children cannot easily be studied until they come into public view for some reason other than being adopted. The most visible and - for a researcher - accessible adopted children are those referred to psychiatrists, psychologists, social workers, and the courts, and the 1960s saw a considerable volume of research emanating from clinical experience in psychiatric and child guidance settings (Schechter 1960; Schechter *et al.* 1964; Toussieng 1962; Humphrey 1963; Sweeny, Gasbarro, and Gluck 1963; Menlove 1965; Borgatta and Fanshel 1965: Simon and Senturia 1966; Jackson 1968; Reece and Levin 1968; Offord, Aponte, and Cross 1969).

For psychodynamically-oriented workers, adoption offers a rich field of study, ranging from early separation through the complexities of the oedipal phase to the question of adolescent identity. The emphasis on critically sensitive periods in early life and the generally pessimistic view of the human condition inherent in much psychodynamic thinking predisposed its adherents to regard adoption as a highly problematic enterprise for parents and children alike. According to this framework, many of the problems of growing up adopted derive from genealogical bewilderment, the confusion and doubts which stem from not knowing (or not knowing enough about) one's heritage (Sants 1964). To the extent that establishing an identity involves locating oneself in relation to the past as well as to the present, there are likely to be gaps in the adopted person's self-understanding, gaps which may be filled by fantasies of an unhelpful kind.

Some early clinic-based research was inspired by impressionistic evidence that adopted children were over-represented in referrals for psychiatric assessment and treatment. An influential paper by Schechter (1960) purported to show, on the basis of the fact that adopted children made up 13.3 per cent of his caseload as a psychoanalyst in California, that adopted children were one hundred times more likely than non-adopted children to be referred for treatment. Schechter's view that adopted children are very much at risk received apparent support from subsequent studies throughout the 1960s (Toussieng 1962; Sweeny, Gasbarro, and Gluck 1963; Simon and Senturia 1966; Reece and Levin 1968), although the degree of over-representation in most such studies was found to be at more modest levels. In an English study, Humphrey (1963) estimated adopted children to be at twice as much risk of psychiatric referral as non-adopted children.

A major hazard in research of this kind lies in the attempt to estimate how many adopted children there are within the catchment area of a particular psychiatric facility. A serious flaw in Schechter's work was that, lacking basic demographic data on which to draw, he took as his baseline for comparison the number of adoption applications filed during the period in question, which would give a fair picture of the incidence of applications but no indication of the prevalence, or cumulative total, of adopted children living in the area at the time. Partly in response to Schechter (1960) and Toussieng (1962), Johassohn (1965) offered a review of problems in adoption research arising from the lack of adequate measures and the misuse of existing data. On the same theme, Kirk and colleagues argued that the misinterpretation and misuse of data raised ethical questions for researchers (Kirk, Johassohn, and Fish 1966).

A further problem in some studies has been the idiosyncratic way in which adoption is defined. Toussieng included any children 'not related by blood to either parent' (Toussieng 1962:59), and the review of studies by Kirk and colleagues noted a range of definitions in which 'foster child, step-child, legal guardianship, informal day care, and even extended kinship visits were frequently, confused with legal adoption' (Kirk, Johassohn and Fish 1966:293). In one of these studies the senior practitioner regarded as adopted 'anyone not born into the family'.

A factor sometimes overlooked in studies of clinic populations is the nature of the psychiatric referral process itself. Opinion is divided as to whether adoptive status in itself increases or decreases the likelihood of referral for child guidance or other specialist attention. Arguments that adoptive status increases the risk of referral revolve around the notion of the self-fulfilling prophecy – that, because adoption is seen as inherently problematic, parents, teachers, doctors, and magistrates are more likely to refer adopted children for specialist attention. Support for this view is to be found in a survey of psychiatric outpatient clinics, which showed the adopted children referred to be significantly less disturbed than the non-adopted children, only 4 per cent of the former described as psychotic as against 14 per cent of the latter group (Borgatta and Fanshel 1965). A study of juvenile court cases in Connecticut indicated that, although the offences committed by the children in each group were similar, the court appeared to deal more harshly with the adopted children and was more likely to commit them to residential care (Lewis *et al.* 1975). More generally, it is sometimes suggested that adopters' anxiety to succeed as parents or their good experience of counselling at the adoption application stage makes them more likely than other parents to seek professional help if problems arise later with their children.

The obvious counter-argument to the last point is that, because of their previous experience at the hands of professional helpers, adoptive parents may be *less* likely than others to seek help with their children's problems. This view receives support from the evidence of Humphrey (1963) that adopted children tend to be older than non-adopted children at the point of referral, though this finding may equally well indicate that problems emerge later in adopted children, or indeed that problems of adolescence are the most difficult for adoptive parents to handle. Similar uncertainty surrounds the common finding in clinical studies that, by comparison with their non-adopted peers, adopted children are more likely to be referred for conduct disorders than for neurotic disturbances (Humphrey 1963; Menlove 1965; Simon and Senturia 1966; Jackson 1968; Reece and Levin 1968; Offord, Aponte, and Cross 1969). Do these findings reflect 'real' differences in symptomatology or a higher level of anxiety and greater readiness to seek help on the part of adoptive parents for their 'aggressive' than for their 'withdrawn' children?

Comparative studies of adopted and non-adopted children should also take into account a number of social factors which are associated with adoption but which in themselves may put the child 'at risk'. The child adopted from outside the family by a childless couple seeking to build their own family is more likely than his non-adopted counterpart to be a first child, an only child, acquiring parents who are more likely to be middle class and to be ten years older than the norm. Each of these factors places any child at greater risk of psychiatric referral and must be disentangled from adoptive status as an explanation for disturbing behaviour (Kadushin 1966). Several writers have sought to identify factors specific to adoptive status which may lead to difficulties. Humphrey (1963) suggests as contributory factors parental mishandling of the process of telling the child he is adopted, and 'genetic anxiety', a term describing the tendency to attribute misbehaviour to an inherited 'vicious streak' rather than to understand it in terms of own-family relationships. (For further discussion of this point, see Herbert, Chapter 5.) Offord, Aponte, and Cross (1969) suggest underlying hostility on the parents' part to the child's adoptive status; the child's acting-out of the unconscious hostile and sexual impulses of one parent; the once-popular strategy of telling the child he is 'special' or 'chosen', which makes it difficult for negative feelings to be expressed openly and freely discussed or faced; the nature of agency investigations, which may produce anxieties for the parents in setting limits for their children; the child's identity problem; and (surely somewhat speculatively?) the greater likelihood of out-of-wedlock children's having psychopathic natural parents. Psychopathic or not, mothers of children placed for adoption are likely to have had inferior antenatal care (Seglow, Pringle, and Wedge 1972), which may adversely affect the child's later development.

Follow-up studies

The quality of the adopted child's original parentage is a crucial question in another popular line of investigation, the follow-up study, of which there are numerous examples conducted with varying (and generally increasing) degrees of sophistication since the 1920s (Theis 1924; Brenner 1951; Witmer *et al.* 1963; Skodak and Skeels 1949; McWhinnie 1967: Kornitzer 1968: Ripple 1968; Lawder *et al.* 1969: Elonen and Schwartz 1969; Jaffee and Fanshel 1970; Bohman 1970; Raynor 1980; Bohman and Sigvardsson 1980). Reviewing a large number of studies carried out from 1924 to 1970 with widely differing populations, criteria, and methods, Mech (1973) arrived at an overall success rate of 75.4 per cent. The meaning of 'success' in absolute terms or relative to other modes of childrearing is a question to lead the investigator into a minefield of value issues. The understandable desire of the interested bystander to know whether adopted children grow up to be bank robbers or bank presidents contains the somewhat dubious assumption that these occupations are mutually exclusive (Jaffee and Fanshel 1970). However, to find that three out of four adoptions work out satisfactorily goes some way towards counterbalancing the more pessimistic expectations of some psychiatric investigators, even if it is not a success rate with which adoption workers will feel satisfied.

A common problem in follow-up studies, however, is the difficulty of establishing the baseline from which future progress may be measured. In the last few years there has been criticism (Goldhaber and Colman 1978; Clarke 1981) of the way in which some researchers, perhaps out of a concern to establish adoption's credentials, have exaggerated the benefits of adoptive family life by devaluing the quality of the endowment bestowed on the child by the birth parents. One series of studies of mentally handicapped children placed from institutions seemed to indicate an improvement on the part of the adopted children well beyond anything which might have been predicted, given their disadvantaged backgrounds (Skodak and Skeels 1949). It is possible, however, that the children's initial low intelligence was too readily deduced from information either that the mother's IQ was 75 or less, or that the putative father was of low occupational status. The statistical principle of regression to the mean would also ensure that, where parental intelligence was abnormally low, the children's IQ would be nearer the normal range, whether the children were adopted or not. Among more recent work, commentators on Kadushin's influential study of older children placed for adoption (Kadushin 1970) tend to overstate the degree of deprivation in the children's lives prior to adoption and to overlook the fact that a significant minority (31 per cent) had had a warm emotional relationship with their birth parents - a fact which ought to raise questions as to why such children were placed for adoption at all.

If clinic-based studies offer a more gloomy view of adoption outcome than common experience would support, follow-up studies risk falling into the opposite error. There is no cause to impute improper behaviour or motives to their authors, but the studies themselves - often carried out by researchers strongly sympathetic to adoption and needing the support and co-operation of adoption agencies themselves - collectively produce a split image of pre-and post-adoptive life, with everything bad attributed to the pre-adoptive state and everything good to post-adoptive family life.

The National Child Development Study

In the search for a more 'balanced' mode of investigation, the National Child Development Study seems to offer a more promising approach. The NCDS, following the fortunes of all the children born in England, Scotland, and Wales during the first week of March 1958, has been able to draw comparisons between adopted children, those living in one-parent families, and those in 'standard' two-parent families. An early report on the adopted children at the age of seven (Seglow, Pringle, and Wedge 1972) not only showed them to be making excellent progress on a broad range of developmental, social, and educational measures, but suggested that in some respects they were ahead of the legitimate children living with their birth parents, a finding likely to raise the rather disturbing thought that all children might be better reshuffled and adopted into a different family. Subsequent study of the children at the age of eleven (Lambert and Streather 1980), taking account of social class and economic circumstances, suggested that it is not adoption *per se* but the social benefits (greater economic security, better housing conditions, and so on) associated with adoption as traditionally practised which give this group of children advantages over some others, especially over those in one-parent families.

Analysis of the NCDS material (Lambert and Streather 1980; Bagley 1980) indicates that the adopted children had lost some ground by eleven years, and it has been suggested that the slight regression may be linked to the fact that many adopted children are by this age aware of their special status and are grappling with the additional 'developmental task' which this knowledge imposes. It is as well to remember that, in the general population, children's development is not invariably smooth or uninterrupted and that a fair proportion of children experience or present problems which are resolved without recourse to specialist help.

The overall picture of the adopted child presented in recent research, unlike the rather fragile creature shown in early clinical studies, shows a sturdy, thriving youngster holding his own in comparison with his non-adopted peers. More significant in terms of social policy is the progress made by children adopted after a period in public care (Lambert 1981). Furthermore, a study by Tizard (1977) suggests that the progress of children going on to adoption from residential care compares very favourably with that shown by children who are fostered or restored to their original families. So predictable are such findings now that research interest has moved away from 'traditional' adoptions to those involving children who by reason of age, health, or handicap would once have been considered hard (if not impossible) to place. Confidence in adoption and the remedial qualities of good nurturing care is such that it has become possible to re-open an area of study which has been taboo in adoption circles for several decades, the importance of hereditary factors for later development. A review of studies on the issue of intelligence (Munsinger 1975) came to the conclusion that the IQ of adopted children corresponds more closely to that of their biological than of their adoptive parents. Other studies have shown, in the words of one reviewer, 'perhaps a heightened risk but limited certainty' (Kadushin 1978:83) that adopted children whose biological parents were schizophrenic (Rosenthal and Kety 1968) or alcoholic (Goodwin 1976; Bohman and Sigvardsson 1980) might develop similar pathology.

The experiential dimension

An essay on the theme of growing up adopted calls for something more than the assurance that adopted children measure up well against a battery of tests of adjustment and attainment. Missing from much of the research already quoted is the experiential dimension - what is it like to grow up adopted? Simply to frame the question in this way highlights the fact that in the great majority of studies adopted children are research objects rather than subjects, tested to produce findings which are statistically significant but often, in terms of human experience, relatively unimportant. Adoption research remains largely in the world of product-testing, with the primary aim of boosting consumer confidence. The consumers in this context are adoptive parents - children not so much consumers as consumed.

A notable feature of most follow-up studies is that questions concerning the children's 'adjustment' or the overall satisfactoriness of the adoption are almost exclusively directed towards the adoptive parents or other adults such as teachers. McWhinnie (1967) and Raynor (1980) are exceptions to this rule, and the former study in particular - with a sample of placements most of which appeared less than satisfactory - identified some worrying features of adoptive family life, especially in the area of parent-child communication. In his study of older children placed for adoption, Kadushin (1970) acknowledges the gap in information which arises from not consulting the children themselves, but presents as a working assumption the view that, if the child performs his role functions to the parent's satisfaction, this suggests not only reasonably decent adjustment on the part of the child but also that the child is satisfied in the relationship. This assumption seems to take no account of the power imbalance in family relationships, rather as if one were to derive a measure of the happiness of Victorian marriage from interviews with husbands only. Jaffee and Fanshel (1970), in their follow-up study of children adopted in the decade 1931-40, note the political and practical problems of gaining access to the children themselves. In 55 per cent of their sample families, the adoptive parents refused to let their children be approached, the 'children' being by then anything up to thirty years old.

Access to adopted people other than through a protective screen of agency approval and parental consent has been made easier in England and Wales by a provision in the Children Act 1975 which gives adoptees themselves the right on attaining their majority to obtain their original birth certificate. This document opens the door to fuller information about the person's origins and, for some, is the first stage in the laborious process of tracking down the birth parents. In an earlier study in Scotland - where adopted people have had such a right for much longer - it was suggested that, where the adoption has gone well, the adopted person is generally interested only in fuller information; whereas the urge to seek out the birth parents is more often to be found in adoptions which have gone less well, and in particular where the adoptive parent-child relationship is unsatisfactory (Triseliotis 1973). In the latter applications, 'there was hope that the natural parents (if found) would make up to them what they had missed from other relationships' (Triseliotis 1973:159). Subsequent work in England (Leeding 1977; Day 1979) and Australia (Picton 1982) does not seem to support this distinction but shows adopted people as having varied and mixed motives for seeking information - personal identity, medical history, curiosity, concern for birth parents' welfare - and suggests that such interest is natural rather than, as has often been supposed, pathological.

From the small number of studies so far in which adopted people have been able to make themselves heard (e.g. Raynor 1980), there emerges a high level of acceptance by adopted people of their situation, even where things have by any objective standard gone badly. Even where relationships with adoptive parents are unsatisfactory, adoptees see them unequivocally as their 'real' parents, possibly reflecting everyday experience that relationships do not need to be free of stress to be worthwhile.

Telling children of their adoptive status

Probably no issue in adoption has generated more anxiety or more literature than that of telling the children about their origins. Adoptive parents receive much exhortation but little guidance in the matter, apart from the standard double message, 'make him your child but tell him he isn't really'. Discussion of origins raises in many cases the adopters' own feelings about their infertility, about illegitimacy and unmarried parenthood, and the primitive fear that the child will cease to love them once he learns they are not his 'real' parents. Kirk (1964) suggests that the obligation to reveal to a child his adoptive status conflicts with the still prevalent 'happy ever after' ideology of courtship, marriage, and parenthood, and also sets the parents the dual task of promoting the child's integration into and differentiation from the adoptive family, possibly at one and the same time.

Many studies (e.g. Goodacre 1966; Jaffee 1974; Raynor 1980; Triseliotis 1973) show 'telling' to be a problematic exercise producing a variety of approaches. Some adopted children never hear the truth of their status from their parents; some are told in anger under stress; some are left to hear from strangers, kindly or maliciously; others are 'told' once by their parents, usually at an early age, after which the matter is considered closed; and still others are told well and in good faith but the information, from the child's point of view, may be inadequate.

Notwithstanding the difficulties involved, there is now little dispute that adopted children should be told of their status. The minority case is offered by Ansfield (1971), a psychiatrist who argues (extrapolating boldly from the referred to the non-referred population) that most adopted children would do better not to know, and that, if they do have to be told, the later they are told the better - the formal reading of their parents' will being quite soon enough. The most imaginative section of Ansfield's book outlines strategies to help adopters live with this lie at the heart of their family relationships. More orthodox writers of the psychodynamic school (Schechter 1960; Schechter *et al.* 1964; Peller 1961) oppose the common view that children should be told as early as possible and argue that telling should be delayed until the child has negotiated the oedipal phase, by which time his social world has widened and he is less totally dependent on the relationship with his parents.

Studies such as those by Raynor (1980) and Triseliotis (1973) noted earlier show a wide measure of agreement amongst adopted people themselves that they do wish to be told, told early, and by their parents, with information updated in line with their intellectual, emotional, and social development. While some adoptees complain of a sense of rejection in being over-reminded of their status, the more common experience is of parents unable or unwilling to offer appropriate information and disinclined to take sufficient initiative in raising the matter for discussion. Several writers, such as Jaffee (1974) and Raynor (1980), note wide discrepancies in perception between, on the one hand, parents who believe they have been informative and open to discussion with their children and, on the other hand, the children themselves who feel they have been told too little and hold back from raising what they have learned to regard as a delicate subject with their parents. Typically, there develops a kind of stalemate, with each party waiting for the other to make the next move. While the majority of adopted people wish to be told early, there is little support in these studies for the notion of critical periods for telling or not telling. As with many aspects of child-rearing, adopted children seem able to tolerate a wide range of approaches, timings, and general mishandling of the whole matter, so long as telling takes place within an overall context of love and belonging.

Some unformulated questions

There is more to growing up adopted than being told about it but, with easier access directly to adopted people, there remains the difficult question of what it is we wish to know, or, more to the point, what adopted people may be in a position to tell about themselves. While preparing this chapter, the writer sought the help of a bright, insightful thirteen-year-old, with the question, 'what would you say it feels like to be growing up adopted?' After a long pause, there came the reply, 'I'm not sure I can say much about what it is like to grow up adopted because I've never grown up any other way'.

It would be difficult to devise a more succinct formulation of the problem facing the researcher seeking a new direction in the study of the adoptive experience. Having established that adopted people are not flocking into prisons and mental hospitals, it nonetheless remains all too easy to settle for a problem-centred stance - 'what do you find difficult about being adopted?' - perpetuating a situation where adopted people are seen only as having (or being) problems. Sociological research to date has offered a less individualized but still somewhat pathological perspective on adopted people as a minority group. Kirk (1964), borrowing from Lewin, offers helpful insights into adoptive *parents* as a deviant minority and a corresponding study of adopted adults might prove equally illuminating. It is as well to remember, however, in a period when a wider diversity of lifestyles is achieving greater acceptance, that the 'normal' family - a married couple with their 'own' dependent children - is also approaching the status of a minority group.

To the extent that society is made up of minority groups, research may more fruitfully investigate minority group experience and perceptions from a standpoint which sees such groups as different rather than deviant or substandard. Are there differences, for example, in the ways in which adopted children (or black children, handicapped children, or girl children, for that matter) perceive and tackle Erikson's developmental tasks (Erikson 1959)?

A surprisingly neglected area of psychological research is that of micro-level parent–child interaction in adoptive families. Advocates of adoption maintain that the high success rates in adoption are not simply a function of social and economic advantage in adoptive families but derive also from the commitment which adopters bring to the parenting task. Critics would suggest that the drive and determination necessary to become an adopter are not necessarily conducive to healthy, relaxed parenting thereafter, and would argue that the educational difficulties experienced by boys in particular may well stem from undue pressures by their over-zealous adoptive parents (Lambert and Streather 1980). The absence of research into adoptive parent–child relationships means that this debate has to remain at the level of speculation.

The question of identity is much discussed but relatively little researched in adoption, either from a sociological or psychological standpoint. One study which addresses this issue directly is by Triseliotis (1983), who defines identity in terms of a childhood experience of feeling wanted and loved within a secure environment, knowledge about one's background and personal history, and the experience of being perceived by others as a worthwhile person. The study suggests that, in comparison with people who have grown up in foster care, the identity of adopted people is less ambiguous and uncertain. With the increasing tendency to allow adopted people access to birth records, the question arises as to how far the establishment of one's identity is an historical or an existential quest. Foster (1979) argues that we create our identity, defining and redefining it in daily living, and that preoccupation with the past is self-defeating, a misdirection of energy. Conversely, some adopted people who feel they have benefited from their search for origins would maintain that the value of knowing one's roots is too easily underestimated by non-adopted people.

The next stage in adoption research may be helped by psychology's recently renewed interest in the 'self' – the person's central core which is more than a set of responses to external stimuli, more even than the sum of one's personal relationships. Self-understanding and self-presentation are still relatively unexplored areas of adoptive life, though of obvious interest to the non-adopted as well as of practical concern to the adopted person. As an adopted person, what do you tell other people about your status? what do you tell yourself? It is sometimes said that the major concern of the adopted child is not that he was born to other parents but that he was given away by those parents, in some sense rejected, possibly as being not good enough. One is reminded of Kelly's recurrent theme that you are not the victim of your autobiography but you may become the victim of the way you interpret your autobiography (Maher 1969).

The adopted person may also become the victim of the way in which researchers formulate their questions. A greater appreciation of the history and politics of adoption research - and in particular of the extent to which the questions asked shape the answers given - might help us formulate better questions for the future.

References

Ansfield, J.G. (1971) *The Adopted Child.* Springfield, Illinois: Charles C. Thomas.

Bagley, C. (1980) Adjustment, Achievement and Social Circumstances of Adopted Children in a National Survey. *Adoption and Fostering* 102:47-9.

Bohman, M. (1970) *Adopted Children and their Families.* Stockholm: Proprius.

Bohman, M. and Sigvardsson, S. (1980) Negative Social Heritage. *Adoption and Fostering* 101:25-31.

Borgatta, E.F. and Fanshel, D. (1965) *Behavioral Characteristics of Children Known to Psychiatric Outpatient Clinics.* New York: Child Welfare League of America.

Brenner, R.F. (1951) *A Follow-Up Study of Adoptive Families.* New York: Child Adoption Research Committee.

Clarke, A.M. (1981) Adoption Studies and Human Development. *Adoption and Fostering* 104:17-29.

Day, C. (1979) Access to Birth Records. *Adoption and Fostering* 98:17-28.

Elonen, A.S. and Schwartz, E.M. (1969) A Longitudinal Study of Emotional, Social and Academic Functioning of Adopted Children. *Child Welfare* 48(2):72-8.

Erikson, E. (1959) *Identity and the Life Cycle.* New York: International Universities Press.

Foster, A. (1979) Who Has the 'Right' to Know? *Public Welfare* Summer: 34-7.

Goldhaber, D. and Colman, M. (1978) Untitled review of research on the adoption of older children. *Adoption and Fostering* 94:41-8.

Goodacre, I. (1966) *Adoption Policy and Practice.* London: Allen & Unwin.

Goodwin, D.W. (1976) *Is Alcoholism Hereditary?* New York: Oxford University Press.

Humphrey, M. (1963) Factors Associated With Maladjustment in Adoptive Families. *Child Adoption* 43:25-31. Reprinted in *Child Adoption - A Selection of Articles on Adoption Theory and Practice* (1977). London: BAAF.

Jackson, L. (1968) Unsuccessful Adoptions: a Study of 40 Cases Who Attended a Child Guidance Clinic. *British Journal of Medical Psychology* 41(4):389-98.

Jaffee, B. (1974) Adoption Outcome: A Two-Generation View. *Child Welfare* 53(4):211-24.

Jaffee, B. and Fanshel, D. (1970) *How They Fared in Adoption: a Follow-Up*

Study. New York: Columbia University Press.

Johassohn, K. (1965) On the Use and Construction of Adoption Rates. *Journal of Marriage and the Family* 27:514-21.

Kadushin, A. (1966) Adoptive Parenthood: a Hazardous Adventure? *Social Work* 11(3):30-9.

_____ (1970) *Adopting Older Children*. New York: Columbia University Press.

_____ (1978) Children in Adoptive Homes. In H.S. Maas (ed.) *Social Services Research: Reviews of Studies*. New York: National Association of Social Workers.

Kirk, D., Johassohn, K., and Fish, A.D. (1966) Are Adopted Children Especially Vulnerable to Stress? *Archives of General Psychiatry* 14(3):291-98.

Kirk, H.D. (1964) *Shared Fate*. New York: Free Press of Glencoe.

Kornitzer, M. (1968) *Adoption and Family Life*. London: Putnam.

Lambert, L. (1981) Adopted From Care By the Age of Seven. *Adoption and Fostering* 105:28-38.

Lambert, L. and Streather, J. (1980) *Children in Changing Families*. London: National Children's Bureau.

Lawder, E.A., Lower, K.D., Andrews, R.G., Sherman, E.A., and Hill, J.G. (1969) *A Follow-Up Study of Adoptions: Post-Placement Functioning of Adoptive Families*. New York: Child Welfare League of America.

Leeding, A.E. (1977) Access To Birth Records. *Adoption and Fostering* 89:19-25.

Lewis, D.O., Balla, D., Lewis, M., and Gore, R. (1975) The Treatment of Adopted Versus Neglected Delinquent Children in the Court: a Problem of Reciprocal Attachment? *American Journal of Psychiatry* 132:142-45.

Maher, B.A. (ed.) (1969) *Clinical Psychology and Personality: the Selected Papers of George Kelly*. New York: Wiley.

McWhinnie, A. (1967) *Adopted Children - How They Grow Up*. London: Routledge & Kegan Paul.

Mech, E. (1973) Adoption: a Policy Perspective. In B.M. Caldwell and H. Ricciuti *Child Development and Social Policy: Reviews of Child Development Research*, 3. Chicago: University of Chicago Press.

Menlove, F. (1965) Aggressive Symptoms in Emotionally Disturbed Children. *Child Development* 36(2):519-32.

Munsinger, H. (1975) The Adopted Child's IQ: a Critical Review. *Psychological Bulletin* 82:623-59.

Offord, D.R., Aponte, J.F., and Cross, L.A. (1969) Presenting Symptomatology of Adopted Children. *Archives of General Psychiatry* 20(1):110-16.

Peller, L.E. (1961) About Telling the Child About His Adoption. *Bulletin of the Philadelphia Association for Psychoanalysis* 1:145-54.

Picton, C. (1982) Adoptees in Search of Origins. *Adoption and Fostering* 6(2):49-52.

Raynor, L. (1980) *The Adopted Child Comes of Age*. London: Allen & Unwin.

Reece, S.A. and Levin, B. (1968) Psychiatric Disturbances in Adopted Children: a Descriptive Study. *Social Work* 13(1):101-11.

Ripple, L. (1968) A Follow-Up Study of Adopted Children. *Social Service Review* 42(4):479-99.

Rosenthal, D. and Kety, S. (eds) (1968) *The Transmission of Schizophrenia*. London: Pergamon Press.

Sants, H.J. (1964) Genealogical Bewilderment in Children with Substitute

Parents. *British Journal of Medical Psychology* 37(2):133-41. Reprinted in *Child Adoption - a Selection of Articles on Adoption Theory and Practice.* (1977). London: BAAF.

Schapiro, M. (ed.) (1956) *A Study of Adoption Practice.* New York: Child Welfare League of America.

Schechter, M.D. (1960) Observations on Adopted Children. *Archives of General Psychiatry* 3(7):21-32.

Schechter, M.D., Carlson, P.V., Simmons III, J.Q., and Work, H.H. (1964) Emotional Problems in the Adoptee. *Archives of General Psychiatry* 10(2):109-18.

Seglow, J., Pringle, M.L.K., and Wedge, P. (1972) *Growing Up Adopted.* London: NFER.

Simon, N. and Senturia, A. (1966) Adoption and Psychiatric Illness. *American Journal of Psychiatry* 122(8):858-68.

Skodak, M. and Skeels, H.M. (1949) A Final Follow-Up Study of 100 Adopted Children. *Journal of Genetic Psychology* 75:85-125.

Sweeny, D.M., Gasbarro, D.T., and Gluck, M.R. (1963) A Descriptive Study of Adopted Children Seen In a Child Guidance Center. *Child Welfare* 42(7):345-49,352.

Theis, S. Van S. (1924) *How Foster Children Turn Out.* New York: State Charities Aid Association.

Tizard, B. (1977) *Adoption: a Second Chance.* London: Open Books.

Toussieng, P.H. (1962) Thoughts Regarding the Etiology of Psychological Difficulties in Adopted Children. *Child Welfare* 41(2):59-66.

Triseliotis, J. (1973) *In Search of Origins.* London: Routledge & Kegan Paul.

—— (1983) Identity and Security in Adoption and Long-Term Fostering. *Adoption and Fostering* 7(1):22-31.

Witmer, H.L., Herzog, E., Weinstein, E.A., and Sullivan, M.E. (1963) *Independent Adoptions: a Follow-Up Study.* New York: Russell Sage.

PART II
Adoption and the law

8 Adoption law: an overview

BRENDA HOGGETT

The primary object of adoption law is to effect the transfer of the adopted person from one family to another. Whatever the cultural context and underlying purpose, only the law can create and recognize the artificial relationships involved. Subsidiary objects are to lay down the procedures, both for making the initial placement and for reaching the final decision. How the law approaches all three tasks will depend upon whether adoption is seen as essentially a private transaction between the two families, in which the agencies of the state will have minimal involvement, or whether it is seen as a matter of concern to the whole community, in which it may be necessary to involve expert placing agencies and the sanction of the state. There is a whole spectrum of variations between these two extremes.

Comparison of the institution of adoption in different cultures suggests that the importance attached to the parties' consent in adoption law may well be associated with the point which the institution has reached in that spectrum. Where adoption is a private transaction, consent will be essential, save perhaps when the birth family is not there to give it, or where the adopted person is his own master and can give it for himself. Where adoption is a matter for the whole community, the community may be increasingly prepared to place its own requirements above those of the individuals involved. Similarly, the point which the institution has reached on that same spectrum will reflect its cultural context and underlying purpose, but the connection will not be an entirely simple one.

Thus, if the point of the institution is to enable the rich and powerful to recruit new heirs from the surplus members of their own caste, as it was in ancient Rome and several similar societies (Crook 1967; Goody 1969), the element of private transaction will predominate. The adopting family will want to pick the adopted person from among those known to it. The adopted person will be male and usually adult. If he is still under the power of his own paterfamilias, a private transaction modelled on the conveyance of other forms of valuable property will take place. If he is his own master, the community will have to sanction the transfer, not in order to protect the individuals concerned but in order to ensure that it is proper to permit the extinction of one family in the interests of preserving another.

However, even when the main purpose becomes the transfer of responsibility for bringing up a child, as it is in modern Western society, the element of private transaction may still predominate for a while. This is certainly how adoption was seen by the Tomlin Committee (HMSO 1925), who gave a very cautious and reluctant blessing to its introduction into English law by what became the Adoption of Children Act 1926. There was no regulation of adoption placement and the adoption order did little more than give legal sanction to the de facto transfer which had already been agreed. The court's role was limited to checking that the birth parents had indeed agreed and that the child's welfare did not suffer. It was assumed that there were only too many unmarried mothers or poor couples wanting to dispose of their children and far fewer altruistic families wishing to take them on. The committee were by no means sure that either ought to be encouraged and were certain that the child should not become a full member of the adoptive family for purposes such as succession.

There can be no better illustration of the entirely different clientele and purpose of the modern institution than the exclusion of the very object for which in earlier times it had been principally designed. The development of English law since 1926 demonstrates quite clearly how these differences have led to the virtual abandonment of the private transaction model in favour of providing another weapon in the child care armoury of the state. There has been a corresponding decrease in the importance attached to parental agreement and a reappraisal of the aftermath of an order. This has proceeded to such a point that the traditional distinction between fostering and adoption, recognized by historians and anthropologists as well as by modern child care agencies, seems in danger of disappearing. Perhaps this should not surprise us. Goody (1969) suggests that the presence of adoption in pre-industrial times is associated with stratified societies having a limited supply of heritable property, lineal inheritance, and monogamous marriage. Those without monogamy could supply their heirs in other ways. Those without property, for example in Africa, made use of fostering for the upbringing of children. The features which produced the ancient form of adoption do not predominate today.

The decay of the private transaction

In English Law, events seemed to combine to produce an institution which increasingly strove to distinguish between adoption and other forms of care. The initial caution must have contributed to the stereotype which developed - an illegitimate but otherwise perfect white baby placed with usually infertile strangers in order to replace the child they had been unable to have. But such caution enabled legal development to concentrate upon strengthening and deepening the concept of a total transplant from one family to the other. The effects of adoption came to reproduce more and more closely those of a family of birth, just as they had in the ancient world. However, the element of private transaction began to fade, as the task of selecting and making placements was increasingly seen as one for the new breed of expert social workers. But at first those experts were trying to arrange something as close as possible to what would have happened if the child had been born to the adoptive parents.

The most recent comprehensive review of adoption law, by the Houghton Committee which reported in 1972, carried both these trends to their natural conclusion. The current law is still contained in the Adoption Act 1958, with changes made in the Children Act 1975 following the Houghton Report (HMSO 1972). (References will therefore be given to those Acts, but they have been consolidated in the Adoption Act 1976 which is not yet in force.) The effects of an adoption order reproduce the birth relationship almost in its entirety. The order vests all parental rights and duties in the adoptive parents. From that point on, it extinguishes those of anyone else, whether birth parent or child care agency (Children Act 1975: s.8(1)-(4)). The court cannot order the birth parent to go on maintaining the child, nor can the parent later come back to the court and ask for access or for the order to be revoked. However, parental rights and duties relate only to the upbringing of a child during his childhood (Children Act 1975: ss.85(1) and 107(1)). These provisions simply make adoption a more drastic form of custody order. But it is now much more than that. For almost every legal purpose, the child is transferred from one family to another

(Children Act 1975: s.8(8) and Sched. 1, esp. para. 3). Not only do the adoptive mother and father become his mother and father, but in theory at least all their relations become his relations. The latter does not apply for the purposes of inter-marriage (para. 7(1)), but it does apply for the purpose of property and succession. Any reference to a child, or to issue, or to any other relationship, in any statute or legal document now automatically includes a relationship traced through adoption unless this is expressly excluded. People disposing of their property are presumed to intend to benefit their adopted relations, including those to be adopted in the future, unless they say otherwise. This new network of relationships stays with the adopted person throughout his life. It does not come to an end when he grows up or his adoptive parents die. Even today, however, it cannot be used to supply heirs to peerages and other titles of honour, or to the property limited to devolve along with them (paras.10 and 16). Nor does the general principle apply for the purposes of nationality and immigration (para. 7(2)). This is to prevent evasion by means of adoption abroad, although the case of *Re H* (*A Minor*) (*Adoption, Non-patrial*) [1982] Fam.121 showed that it might still be possible by means of an adoption here.

The other purpose of the changes advocated by Houghton (HMSO 1972) was to complete the professionalization of adoption. All trace of the private transaction has now been lost. It is a crime for anyone other than an adoption agency to make arrangements or place a child for adoption, unless the proposed adopter is a relative of the child, or the person is acting under a High Court order (Adoption Act 1958: s.29(1) and (3)). Money must not change hands between the birth and adoptive families, or between either of them and an intermediary (Adoption Act 1958: s.50). The only exceptions are payments by prospective adopters of the agency's expenses, inter-agency fees, and payments under one of the approved schemes for adoption allowances. Under provisions which came into force in May 1984, agencies must supervise their own placements and report on them to the court (Children Act 1975: s.9(3)). The child must have had his home with the applicants, or one of them, at all times during the thirteen weeks before the order is made (Children Act 1975: s.9(1)). All applications which do not result from an agency placement must be notified to the local social services authority at least three months before the order. The authority must then supervise, investigate, and report (Children Act 1975: s.18; Adoption Act 1958: s.37 *et seq.*). Unless the applicant, or one of them, is a parent, step-parent, or relative, or the child was placed under an order of the High Court, the child must have had his home with them for the past twelve months (Children Act 1975: s.9(2)). The Adoption Agencies

Regulations 1983 try to put into words what a good adoption agency should be doing when it decides to plan for the adoption of a particular child, when it chooses potential adopters to go on its list, and when it matches the individual child to the individual home.

This reflects the main duty of both the adoption agencies and the courts. In reaching any decision relating to the adoption of a child, they must 'have regard to all the circumstances, first consideration being given to the need to safeguard and promote the welfare of the child throughout his childhood' (Children Act 1975: s.3). So far as practicable, they must also ascertain the wishes and feelings of the child regarding the decision and give due consideration to them, having regard to his age and understanding. Hence the court may appoint a guardian *ad litem* to safeguard the child's interests in the case (Children Act 1975: s.20; the Adoption Rules 1984 N.18). This was thought to be an essential protection when the court was giving sanction to a private arrangement, so that there could be a proper adjudication rather than a judicial rubber stamp (HMSO 1925). Now that adoption has become a professional process, it is thought that the professionals should be directly responsible to the court. Under the new rules the court must appoint an independent guardian in contested cases and may do so if there are 'special circumstances' and the child's welfare requires it. This is perhaps most likely in cases raising complex legal problems. These, for reasons which will appear, are increasing. But if so, it is strange that the guardian will still be a social worker or probation officer (from specialist panels set up under the Children Act 1975: s.103) rather than a lawyer. A social work guardian may be particularly useful where the child is old enough to have 'wishes and feelings' of his own, so that these can be properly explored. Cases of both sorts again are increasing in number. Nevertheless, the young child may be in just as much need of someone whose only duty is to serve his interests, rather than those of the adults and agencies involved. It is still the best, even the only, way yet devised by our adversarial legal process for ensuring that even uncontested cases receive some adjudication. In a genuinely child-centred process, the tyranny of two experts may be preferable to that of one.

Retreat from the stereotype

However, just as the law has been completing the process which had clearly been devised with the traditional stereotype in mind, the facts have been pushing that stereotype further and further into the background. The number of babies available for adoption has fallen rapidly from its peak in 1968 and is now less than a third of that figure. But the increase in babies available during the years leading up to 1968 was matched by an increase in the number of couples wanting to adopt. Indeed, it seems to have been more than matched, for couples were then being told that there were no babies available. More and more people began to see adoption as an acceptable way of creating or adding to the family and the Tomlin Committee's expectations in 1925 had been completely confounded.

The very existence of these couples may have prompted the reappraisal of the traditional view, but there were other pressures. Almost without anyone noticing it, people who did not conform to the traditional picture had begun to use adoption, not because they wanted a child, but because they wanted its legal effects. Mainly, these were mothers who had kept their children following an illegitimate birth, or a divorce, or the father's death, and who now wanted to replace the father whom the child had lost or never had. Fatherhood, it seems, usually requires some legal sanction, whereas motherhood, even by substitute mothers, does not (see *Re D.* (*Minors*) (*Adoption by Step-parent*) [1980] 2 F.L.R. 102).

However, some substitute mothers were beginning to feel the need for legal recognition. Traditionally, adoption and fostering had been kept quite separate. The Curtis Report on the Care of Children (HMSO 1946) had put adoption at the top of its list of preferred child care alternatives. Despite this, in practice, the activities of adoption and fostering were thought to be quite different, the people involved were different, and usually the agencies concerned were different. Fostering was a temporary expedient for children whose parents were unable to look after them for the time being. It was arranged on a footing of total insecurity for both foster parents and child. That insecurity was to some extent promoted by the responsibilities of the child care agency which were designed to protect the child. The foster parents were paid for their services, however inadequately, and were often chosen by reference to criteria which were the reverse of those by which prospective adopters were chosen. The preferred approach to fostering was that of a partnership between agency, foster parents, and birth parents (George 1970). Responsibility for bringing up the child would be shared between them. Parents should be encouraged to visit regularly. Foster parents should be selected for and encouraged in their capacity to see their role as one of preparing the child for his eventual return home. The image of that home and family should be kept alive and presented in a positive light (curiously, an excellent example of such fostering is supplied by Tizard 1977:206–8). Nothing could be further from the traditional view of adoption.

Unfortunately, not only did many long-term foster parents find this role impossible to sustain, but the very premise on which it was based was often unfounded. The way in which parenting tasks were shared between the three parties involved changes as time passed, even in those cases where it corresponded to expectations in the first place (Rowe 1977). Wherever the fault may lie (and there is good reason to suppose that it may often lie with the child care agencies rather than with the parents), the longer the child remains in care, the less likely he is to return home (Rowe and Lambert 1973; Shaw and Lebens 1978). There was ample evidence upon which unfavourable comparisons could be drawn between fostering (or other child care placements) and adoption. The outcome for the adopted children in the National Child Development Study could be seen as generally positive compared with that for the children who had spent long periods in care. But people were understandably slow to draw the conclusion that the fault lay in the structure of fostering itself, rather than in the practice of the individual social workers and foster parents involved.

Three distinct views emerged. Social workers such as Holman saw the solution in terms of more positive efforts to combat poverty and to reunite parent and child, combined with his 'inclusive' model of fostering, which was thought to be linked with more positive outcomes for the child (Holman 1975). Researchers such as Tizard pointed to the more satisfactory outcomes experienced by children in care who were adopted than by those who were returned to their families of birth and argued that adoption should now be seen 'as a form of child care, one among several possible ways of rearing children whose parents can't, or won't, look after them' (Tizard 1977:7). The suggestion was explicitly made that the wishes of such birth parents should be overborne in the interests of providing properly for their children.

A middle course was put forward both in the higher courts and by the Houghton Committee (HMSO 1972). The House of Lords decided that in wardship proceedings where the custody or upbringing of a minor was in question, the welfare of the minor should be the first and paramount consideration, even in disputes between birth parents and foster parents. The parental wishes and claims might be a secondary consideration in their own right, or they might be viewed as contributing to the welfare of the child in a very special way, but the child's welfare must come first, and most of their lordships thought that this decided the issue (*J.* v. *C.* [1970] A.C. 668). It is fair to say that the judges found it easier to understand the problems and dangers of uprooting a pre-adolescent child from the home where he had been happily settled since the age of three than the crisis of cultural identity and self-esteem which he might suffer a few years later. They may have been right. The evidence tends to suggest that the crisis occurs where the child is less than fully secure in his present and wanted environment or where he has been given a less than positive picture of his parents and why they had to let him go (Triseliotis 1973, 1980).

Wardship can grant both foster parents and child some security in their living arrangements, while allowing the child to retain his roots and identity. The High Court is particularly anxious to achieve this in cross-cultural placements where there is parental opposition to adoption (*Re A.* (1978) 8 Family Law 247). Wardship is, however, the only way in which foster parents can achieve this. Furthermore, without the local authority's co-operation, it is not available to those looking after children who are to remain in public care. It seems that the court will only intervene in the statutory responsibilities of local authorities at the instance of foster parents if the child is in voluntary care and the parent has asked for his return, so that the authority's responsibilities are almost at an end (*Re M. (An Infant*) [1961] Ch. 328; *Re S.* (*An Infant*) [1965] 1 W.L.R. 483). Even then, foster parents have to be unusually resourceful (in every sense) to pursue this avenue.

Hence the Houghton Committee suggested a middle course which would curtail the need for those adoption applications which they thought inappropriate. Legal custody (later dubbed 'custodianship') would give security in caring for the child, but would not deny the parents the possibility of access, the responsibility to maintain, and the chance of revocation. The child would remain a member of his original family for all other purposes. It would be particularly suitable for step-parent and other family adoptions which distort rather than replace the natural family relationships. But it would also be available for long-term foster parents who wanted to maintain their established relationship with the child. The length of time for which they would have to have cared for him would be one or three years, depending upon whether at least one of the people with legal custody over him was prepared to agree to the application. These proposals were enacted in part II of the Children Act 1975 and are to be brought into force by the end of 1984. The important question now is whether adoption is developing in such a way as to make the implementation of custodianship almost unnecessary, and if so, whether this is desirable. In effect, should adoption become another weapon in the child care armoury of the state? Has it, in fact, already done so?

Adoption as a child care resource

The transition from private transaction to professionalized institution, already described, has undoubtedly contributed to the integration of adoption into the child care system. Before the Houghton Report (HMSO 1972), there were many local authorities which did not act as adoption agencies, and most of the traditional placements were handled through the voluntary societies. But the Houghton Committee recommended the introduction of a comprehensive adoption service aimed at the needs of children, birth and adoptive parents, as part of the general child care functions of local authorities. The relevant provisions have not yet been implemented, and may still be delayed, but they have undoubtedly contributed to the changed climate of opinion.

Other changes recommended by Houghton have also contributed, despite the generally traditional view which the Committee took of the nature and purposes of adoption. One is the provision for adoption allowances already mentioned. These were intended to encourage the adoption of certain 'hard to place' groups but obviously blur the distinction between looking after someone else's child and bringing up one of your own. Another is the so-called 'five-year rule' (Adoption Act 1958: s.34A). This allows people who have looked after a child for five years or more to apply for adoption secure in the knowledge that no-one can take the child away from them pending the hearing of the case. By itself, the rule does not make it any easier for the applicants to persuade the court to dispense with the birth parents' agreement to the adoption. Nor, in practice, does it add much to the preceding position where the child is in care by virtue of a care order or resolution transferring parental rights to the authority. In those cases, there is no risk that the parent will summarily remove the child, and the local authority can only do so with leave of the court once an adoption application has actually been made (Adoption Act 1958: ss.35 and 36). The five-year rule simply gives the foster parents complete protection from the moment they give notice of their intention to apply to adopt, provided that they follow this up with an application within three months. In practice, local authorities have increasingly been prepared to encourage these applications, and can now give foster parents financial support for the costs of a contested hearing. More and more authorities began to make placements with an eventual adoption in mind, even though the birth parents had given no sign of agreeing to this.

The question of parental agreement is obviously one crucial aspect of the development of adoption in this way, but another is the view taken by the courts of the effects of an adoption order. Because an adoption order now results in the almost total legal transplant of the child from one family to another, it has sometimes been thought that an adoption where a total transplant cannot in fact take place is automatically undesirable. The reasoning is, of course, circular. Ormrod L.J. has been particularly insistent that the point is not so much whether some contact with the natural family is desirable, but whether the decision should be taken by the court, the child care agency, or by the prospective adopters (*Re F. (A Minor) (Adoption: Parental Consent*) [1982] 1 W.L.R. 102). Others have agreed that contact between the two families may well be perfectly acceptable in some cases, particularly if the prospective adopters believe that it will do the child good (*Re G (D.M.) (An Infant)* [1962] 1 W.L.R. 730; *Re B. (M.F.) (An Infant), Re D. (S.L.) (An Infant)* [1972] 1 W.L.R. 102). In exceptional cases (admittedly when agreed by the parties to the adoption of an illegitimate child by natural mother and step-father), the courts have been prepared to make access by the natural father a condition of the adoption order (*Re S. (A Minor) (Adoption Order: Access)* [1976] Fam. 1). In suitable cases, therefore, the courts have taken the non-doctrinaire attitude that the institution can depart from the traditional stereotype in order to suit the needs of the particular case.

This can obviously affect how they view the question of dispensing with parental agreement. Even if all other parental rights are vested in the local authority as a result of a care order or resolution, an adoption order cannot usually be made unless each parent or guardian has given free and unconditional agreement, with full understanding of what is involved, to the particular adoption proposed. (Parent means both mother and father of a legitimate child and mother of an illegitimate child. Guardian means a guardian legally appointed to act in the place of a parent who has died or the father of an illegitimate child who has custody under a court order.) Agreement can be dispensed with on a number of grounds (Children Act 1975: ss.12 and 107(1)). Mainly, these involve reprehensible behaviour towards the child, such as abandonment, neglect, persistent or serious ill-treatment (in the second case only if for this or any other reason the child's rehabilitation in the parent's household is unlikely), or persistently failing without reasonable cause to discharge the parental duties in relation to the child. Although no statistics are available, it appears that these grounds are not often used. They are not appropriate to the conventional baby placement, unless the mother has had time to neglect or ill-treat her child before she parts with him. There is no neglect, abandonment, or persistent failure to discharge her duties if she places the child with an adoption agency in order to find him a permanent home. Where a child has been in care for a long time, it may be difficult now to prove that the particular parent has neglected or ill-treated the child. The events which led to the separation are long past and the grounds for care proceedings do not require it to be shown who was in fact responsible for the child's condition. Once the child is in care there is often reasonable cause for the parent's failure to visit or give other evidence of parental concern and commitment.

Hence the ground most frequently chosen is that the parent is withholding consent unreasonably. The law on this has been clearly laid down in the House of Lords (*Re W. (An Infant)* [1971] A.C. 682; also *O'Connor* v. *A. and B.* [1971] 1 W.L.R. 1227). The court is not entitled to substitute its own view for that of the parent, for two reasonable parents can come to opposite conclusions on the same set of facts. But the test is what an objectively reasonable parent might do in all the circumstances of the case. It is not culpability in relation to the child. It is not callous or self-indulgent indifference to his interests. It is whether a reasonable parent, judged at the date of the hearing, could have come to the same conclusion as the parent in the case. The reasonable parent does not necessarily regard the child's welfare as the sole consideration, for she is entitled to take other things, including her own wishes and feelings, into account. But she will certainly give great weight to what is better for the child and in cases where she would regard it as decisive, the parent in the case must do so too. The fact that courts and adoption agencies must put the child's welfare first has not affected the courts' view of what the parent should do (*Re P. (An Infant) (Adoption: Parental Consent)* [1977] Fam. 25).

But this clear statement of the law still leaves a great deal of discretion to the individual judge in the county court. The Court of Appeal will only interfere with him if he has applied the wrong principles or is plainly wrong. In a baby placement to which the mother has initially agreed and then changed her mind, the issues are relatively simple. She cannot recover the child without leave of the court once she has signed her formal agreement (Adoption Act 1958: s.34(1)). From that moment onwards 'time begins to run' (*Re H. Infants) (Adoption: Parental Consent)* [1977] 1 W.L.R. 471). The court has to choose between the homes offered by mother and prospective adopters. If the mother has little to offer and the child is already well established in the adoptive home, the court is likely to dispense with the need for agreement. At least the mother did once give her consent and has now changed her mind.

Where the mother has never given her consent, the court has no such consolation. Nor is it usually faced with the choice between her home and that of the adoptive parents. A foster child in compulsory care will remain where he is and the only question is the basis on which he does so. Some judges have concentrated upon the child's need for security in his new home and on the foster parents' need to be free from the nagging fear that the local authority or the birth parent will try to take him away. These judges may be prepared to hold the mother unreasonable, even though there may be something to be said for continued contact between her and the child. The question is simply whether the foster parents should be allowed to decide upon this for themselves (Bridge L.J. in *Re S.M.H. and R.A.H.*, 14 February 1979, Court of Appeal; Ormrod L.J. in *Re F. (A Minor) (Adoption: Parental Consent)* [1982] 1 W.L.R. 102; also [1982] Journal of Social Welfare Law 165–70). Other judges have thought that the question turned upon whether contact between parent and child was in the child's own interests. If any reasonable parent would have realized that it was not, then agreement could be dispensed with (Dunn L.J. in *Re F.* above). Yet a third strand of opinion has stressed that although there has been a move towards a greater emphasis on the child's welfare, short of amending legislation or reconsideration in the House of Lords, there must be a limit to this move. A reasonable parent can have regard to the interests of all three parties involved and does not have to put the child's interests before those of the others. A critical factor may be the chance of a successful reintroduction to the birth parent, even though the child was removed from the home at an early age and is now thoroughly integrated into the family with whom he wishes to stay (*Re H. (A Child), Re W. (A Child)* (1982) 13 Family Law 144). Each case is to be decided by applying the correct test to its individual facts, but there is a fairly clear difference of opinion as to how the test should operate in these cases. The safest course is always to do nothing, but some judges are undoubtedly prepared to be more courageous. Like many others, however, they are influenced by the general climate of opinion, in which public sympathy veers from birth parents to foster parents and back again in a remarkably short time.

The new procedure for 'freeing a child for adoption', brought into force in May 1984, is intended to help in both the conventional and the foster-parent types of adoption (Children Act 1975: ss.14 to 16). The application will be made by the adoption agency, either with the consent of one parent or guardian, or where the child is already in its care and the agency is also applying for the agreement of each parent or guardian to be dispensed with. The procedure aims to end the agony of the mother who first gave up her child for adoption, signed the formal agreement some weeks later (for she cannot do this until the child is at least six weeks old), was later still approached by the child's guardian *ad litem* to check that this has been freely given, and even then could change her mind until the order was made. Instead, she will consent to the application and then give her formal agreement for the child to be adopted. She can remove the child while the application is pending. But once the child has been freed, there is nothing more she can do. A year later, however, she must be told whether the child has been adopted or placed for adoption, unless she has asked not to be kept informed. If he has not, the order may be revoked. In practice, agencies may not trouble to free these children at all. The chances of the mother changing her mind should in any event be reduced under the provision for her formal consent to be witnessed by a 'reporting officer' who will at the same time fulfil the role of the child's guardian *ad litem* in checking that it has been freely given (Children Act 1975: s.20; the Adoption Rules 1984 N.17).

Agencies are more likely to use the procedure to enable them to plan a secure future for a child already in their care. It will be much easier to do it in this way than by assuming parental rights by resolution under the Child Care Act 1980. A parent who did *not* consent to the application cannot remove the child while it is pending (Adoption Act 1958: s.34(2)). The agency will know that parental agreement has been dispensed with before the placement, whereas a resolution is no guarantee that the court will later dispense with parental agreement. The grounds for keeping a child in care under a resolution are also quite different from the grounds for dispensing with agreement to adoption. The difficulty lies in knowing how the courts will interpret these grounds in the context of a 'freeing' application. The most popular ground, unreasonable withholding of agreement, has hitherto depended upon measuring the parent's attitude against the particular adoption proposed, usually after the child has had ample opportunity to form a lasting relationship with his proposed adopters. It will be much more difficult to apply this to adoption in general than to adoption in particular. On the other hand, agencies may find it rather easier to use the fault-based grounds. The facts which led up to the initial separation between parent and child will be much fresher in everyone's mind and will not be coloured by the parent's later triumph over adversity. There will certainly be a temptation to 'free' the child as soon as possible, rather than to prejudice the case by attempts at reconciliation which may later prove to have been in vain. This problem has, of course, already been experienced in relation to parental rights resolutions on the 'consistent failure to discharge the obligations of a parent' ground (*W.* v. *Sunderland Metropolitan Borough Council* [1980] 1 W.L.R. 1101; *W.* v. *Nottinghamshire County Council* [1982] Fam. 1).

Conclusion

All of this suggests that adoption is indeed becoming a resource for the child care agencies, but not a particularly reliable one. We are very short of data on the past and present use made of the power to dispense with agreement, nor are we able to predict how things will develop in future. It could be that there will shortly be no call or cause for any halfway house between insecurity and adoption. Adoption is becoming increasingly possible for those children in long-term care for whom custodianship might otherwise have been appropriate. It is also learning to depart from the stereotype, not only in order to encourage the child's own knowledge of his origins, but also on occasion to allow him to make or keep in contact with them (which is a very different thing). Many will say that only adoption brings the complete and irrevocable commitment which inspires a family to welcome and care for a new and often difficult or demanding member. On almost all measures, adoption has hitherto proved a remarkably successful form of social engineering, so why not continue to develop it as such?

That view has great attractions. But no study has been able to compare the outcomes for each individual child, for obvious reasons. Few have been prepared through an all-out effort to make inclusive fostering work. Above all, there has been little attempt to provide security for the child and his foster family while retaining his original kinship links. It is a great mistake for adoption law to place so much emphasis on the 'needs of the child throughout his childhood'. To concentrate on the adopted person's needs is obviously right, but those needs continue throughout life and far beyond childhood. The security of a happy childhood will stand the adult in great stead, but we all need to feel part of a wider family than the simple household unit where we live. For some children, adoption may be the best way of supplying that wider family. But others may need security in their present home while retaining the relationship with their family of birth. There is still a need for a halfway house whether supplied by adoption or some other institution.

References

Crook, J.A. (1967) *Law and Life of Rome*. London: Thames & Hudson.

George, V. (1970) *Foster Care: Theory and Practice*. London: Routledge & Kegan Paul.

Goody, J. (1969) Adoption in Cross-cultural Perspective. *Comparative Studies in Society and History* 11:55-78.

Holman, R. (1975) The Place of Fostering in Social Work. *British Journal of Social Work* 5:3-29.

HMSO (1925) *First Report of the Child Adoption Committee*. (The Tomlin Report) Cmd 2401. London: HMSO.

_____ (1946) *Report of the Care of Children Committee*. (The Curtis Report) Cmd 6922. London: HMSO.

_____ (1972) *Report of the Departmental Committee on the Adoption of Children*. (The Houghton Report) Cmd 5107. London: HMSO.

Rowe, J. (1977) Fostering in the Seventies. *Adoption and Fostering* 90:15-20.

Rowe, J. and Lambert, L. (1973) *Children Who Wait*. London: ABAFA.

Shaw, M. and Lebens, K. (1978) *Substitute Family Care - A Regional Study. 2: What shall we do with the children?* London: ABAFA.

Tizard, B. (1977) *Adoption: A Second Chance*. London: Open Books.

Triseliotis, J. (1973) *In Search of Origins: The Experiences of Adopted People*. London: Routledge & Kegan Paul.

_____ (1980) Growing Up in Foster Care and After. In J. Triseliotis (ed.) *New Developments in Fostering and Adoption*. London: Routledge & Kegan Paul.

9 Step-parent adoptions

JUDITH MASSON

Step-families are different from other families because one of the adults, usually the man, has no legal relationship to some or all of the children. He is only a stepfather. This may have an effect on the way the family functions as a unit and on the way the adults and children view themselves and each other (Maddox 1975:152). It will definitely affect dealings with outside bodies - school and hospital authorities - who must always defer to the mother or the non-custodial parent as they are the children's guardians.[1] The stepfather may believe that he becomes the child's 'father by marriage'; he will find out (if he does not already know) that he is considered financially responsible for his stepchildren - supplementary benefit paid before the marriage will be withdrawn. However, only on the mother's death (by being named as guardian in her will) can the stepfather acquire a legal relationship to his stepchild unless there are proceedings for adoption or joint custody. The custom of children taking their father's family name while women take that of their husbands marks any family with a stepfather as different from others. To counter this the mother may wish to change the children's surname but, if the first marriage ended in divorce, she may not do this without their father's or the court's consent.[2]

Adoption recasts the step-parent in the part of a parent and gives him the same legal relationship with the child as legitimate birth. Thus the child gains a new parent, rights of inheritance, and adopted status. He also loses the corresponding rights against his birth, non-adopting parent. This transfer is marked by an adoption certificate which replaces the birth certificate and, usually, also by change of name. Adoption legally changes the whole family: the custodial parent becomes an adoptive parent, half brothers become full brothers, and the legal relationship with the non-custodial parent and his family is extinguished. Socially the effects of adoption are less clear cut. The court order may merely ratify what, in practice, has been the arrangement for some years; alternatively it may put down foundations for a new family. Fear has been expressed that adoption destroys relationships but there is little evidence of this (HMSO 1970:30, 1972:29). In a recent study only a tiny minority of birth fathers had contact with the children at the time of adoption and for most of these it was intended that visits should continue (Masson and Norbury 1982:10).

As a newcomer to an established family or as a person without parental rights the step-parent may feel insecure or unsure about his role (Maddox 1975:82; Thomson 1967:126). Although he is usually contributing to family finances the stepfather may wish to show that he has taken responsibility for the family, perhaps by adoption. A stepmother can consolidate her position through acts of caring and may therefore not feel the need to obtain a legal status. She will usually have changed her name so the fact that the family is a step-family will not be obvious. Whether for these or other reasons it is clear that over 95 per cent of families applying for adoption consist of a birth mother and stepfather (Masson, Norbury, and Chatterton 1981:89).

The motives of those step-families who seek to adopt and the very many more who do not are unclear. Helen Thomson suggests that the mother is usually the moving force because she wants to provide her children with greater security and remove complications from their lives (Thomson 1967:206). The Association of Child Care Officers attributes to her less commendable reasons: the desire to conceal her past, especially if it includes illegitimate birth, or to tie the new husband to her family (ACCO 1969:22). Other writers have also listed base motives such as the desire to exclude the birth father and sever his relationship with the children (Bissett-Johnson 1978:336, 1980:388; Williams 1982:214). Sometimes the stepfather is thought to press for adoption, perhaps because of feelings of insecurity (ACCO 1969:22) or to give himself status in the family (HMSO 1970:29; Bissett-Johnson 1978:337). It has been noted that there is a peak in applications for children aged four and ten years, suggesting that starting and changing school are events that encourage adoption (Leete 1978:13; Masson, Norbury, and Chatterton 1981:95). Similarly it has been found that applications are often associated with the birth of a child in the new family (Masson, Norbury, and Chatterton 1981:93). The application may be seen in the family as a solution to the practical problems of name difference, inheritance, or the position on the death of the birth parent.

These, of course, may be handled more simply, some would say more suitably, by name change and by will.

The wishes of the children or the needs of the family as a whole have rarely been seen as the focus for an application. However, in the cases included in a recent survey (Masson and Norbury 1982:7) some applicants made statements to the guardian *ad litem* or to the researchers which emphasized these. Most were unaware of the practical differences (except for name change) which adoption would make. They suggested that adoption was something the whole family wanted, sometimes encouraged especially by the children, the non-custodial parent, or members of the extended family. They wanted family unity or, as many put it, 'to be like a proper family'. Adoption aided this by permitting name change and making the parties members of the family, legally. Without adoption they could have pretended to be a family of first marriage but the step-parent would have been unable to prove a relationship with his stepchild.

Although the Adoption of Children Act 1926 was intended to provide a framework for existing *de facto* adoptions it was not enacted with step-parents in mind. Indeed, a late amendment treated step-families less favourably than relatives: the former, like strangers, could only adopt if they were twenty-one years older than the child. This prevented some step-parents adopting and the birth parent thus had to adopt alone (*Re C* (1937)). An adopted child was not completely severed from his birth family as these early adoption orders had no effect on inheritance rights. Some amendments were passed during the following years but it was not until the Adoption of Children Act 1949 that this was changed. That Act also recognized the use step-parents were making of adoption and abolished the age restrictions which had applied to them. In other respects applications from step-parents were not distinguished from the rest; new provisions requiring local authorities to supervise adoption placements and oversee the welfare of children applied to them. From then on step-parent adoption could no longer be seen as a simple way of obtaining legitimacy, security, and name change. It now clearly involved a transfer of a child to a new family and was subject to supervision by social workers.

In 1954 adoption law and practice were reviewed by the Hurst Committee. Whilst acknowledging without criticism that nearly one-third of all orders were granted in favour of parents (and step-parents) the Committee rejected the suggestion that different laws should apply to them (HMSO 1954:1,18). However, they accepted that 'welfare supervision' might not be necessary and could cause difficulties in such cases. Therefore they recommended that the courts should be able to give exemptions. The Adoption Act 1958, which enacted most of the Committee's recommendations, abolished welfare supervision for all applications involving parents. Once again it was more simple for parents and step-parents to obtain adoption orders but all orders had the same effect. It was not until the passing of the Children Act 1975 that there were provisions which restricted step-parent adoption.

Details of the numbers of orders granted were first published in 1950 (Registrar General 1950–73; OPCS: FM3 1973–). The number of step-parent adoption orders in respect of legitimate children rose from 762 in 1950 to a peak of 9,262 in 1975. For illegitimate children the increase was less steady and less dramatic: in 1950 there were 3,049 orders; 5,691 in the peak year, 1974. Orders in favour of step-parents formed less than one-third of all adoptions in 1950 but the proportion had risen to over two-thirds by 1975. This does not simply reflect a growth in the popularity of step-parent adoption – far more step-families were created during this period. No records are kept of the size of the step-family population but some estimates can be made from the numbers of illegitimate births, divorces, deaths, and remarriages. As far as changes in the population of illegitimate children living in step-families are concerned trends are uncertain (Leete 1978:10, 15; Leete 1979:4; Lambert and Streather 1980:54). The number may have been increasing with the illegitimacy rate but is perhaps more likely to be declining on account of planned illegitimate births to stable cohabiting couples (Leete 1978:15). Legitimate children may lose a parent by either death or divorce. Mortality rates are both low and stable amongst people under the age of forty-five where remarriage of the survivor is more likely to create a step-family. The number of divorces has risen considerably since 1950 with a dramatic increase following implementation of the Divorce Reform Act 1969. The number of children involved in divorce has risen proportionately and there has been a rise in the number of remarriages (Leete 1979:4; OPCS, FM2). It seems likely, therefore, that the increase in step-parent adoptions of legitimate children reflects the rise in the number of children living in step-families rather than increased use of adoption amongst the step-family population; indeed this may have been declining even before the law was amended.[3]

It has been calculated that nearly half of all divorced women with children remarry within five years (Leete and Anthony 1979:8). This implies that each year during the 1970s over 35,000 children under the age of sixteen lost a parent by divorce but gained a step-parent. During that same period the highest figure for step-parent adoptions involving children of divorce was less than 8,000. It is suggested that fewer than one-fifth of step-parents of legitimate children seek adoption (Masson 1981:93).

Little was written about step-parent adoption either to encourage or discourage the practice until the 1960s. In 1959 in her guide to adoption Margaret Kornitzer briefly explained the process of step-parent adoption (Kornitzer 1959:109). Helen Thomson countenanced caution in *The Successful Step-parent,* repeating Dr Spock's view that it was best to wait until the child was old enough to take part in the decision-making (Thomson 1967:206, 207). Illegitimacy still carried both considerable social stigma and legal disadvantage.[4] Judges gave more emphasis to biological relationships in cases concerning child welfare than is common today. Thus in *Re G (TJ)* (1963) an adoption application from a widowed step-mother was refused because this would cut the child off from his divorced mother even though she had shown no interest in him. However, illegitimacy put the matter in a different perspective. In *Re E* (*P*) (1969) the advantage of legitimacy brought by adoption far outweighed the possible benefits of a social relationship with the putative father. However, statements in reported cases do not necessarily reflect the views or practices of the majority of judges.

In the late 1960s, while their colleagues continued to recommend step-parent adoptions in their thousands, a few social workers voiced their unease. These views were encapsulated in *Adoption: The Way Ahead,* a report of the Association of Child Care Officers.

> 'This type of adoption appears to be an artificial and unnecessary legal arrangement which can produce little gain for all parties, and it is an irrevocable transfer of legal parentage which could have harmful repercussions in the long term, e.g. if the relationship between the child and his step-father never matures positively. There are obviously cases where it is in the child's interest to preserve his own identity rather than to confuse his status. . . . Adoption will not eliminate the reality that the child is illegitimate and is the child of another man. If the child is legitimate there is even less gain for the child and in some circumstances actual loss.'
>
> (ACCO 1969:22)

There was, however, no empirical research to support this opinion. Some child care officers had written to the association and Iris Goodacre, a child care officer herself, after reviewing her own cases had expressed concern about the possible outcome of some of them (Goodacre 1966:149). Judge Grant had set out his reasons for refusing an order in a fairly typical case (ACCO 1969:84). Adoption by parent and step-parent was outside the concept of adoption (professionally found families for children whose parents could not provide) which the ACCO wished to promote. Its use where only the legal status of adult and child was in question was inappropriate, was only a fiction, and could lead to the debasement of adoption, confused relationships, and loss of identity (ACCO 1969:16). It is interesting to note, however, that the definition of adoption in common law countries was already far narrower than under the civil law. The term is used there for the process whereby one adult may create a legal relationship (primarily for inheritance purposes) with another adult.[5] The ACCO recommended that the law of guardianship should be amended to allow step-parents to obtain rights which would be complementary to those of the birth parent.

Pressure for reform from the ACCO and the Standing Conference of Societies Registered for Adoption (SCSRA 1968) led to the setting up of the Departmental Committee on Adoption under the chairmanship of Sir William Houghton. The Committee's working paper adopted the views of the ACCO about step-parent adoption and expanded on them:

> 'These adoptions may hold particular problems of family relations. Often the adoption application follows closely on the marriage, before the family has settled down as a family unit, and when stability of the marriage is untested, the mother may have conflicts over sharing responsibilities for her child; the child will be a constant reminder to them both of a former liaison; the truth of his parentage may be hidden from him.'
>
> (HMSO 1970:29)

Although the Committee recognized that family circumstances varied they emphasized negative aspects - the cutting off of a child from a birth father and even siblings; a change of name against a child's wishes; the loss of inheritance rights; the possibility of breakdown of the second marriage. They concluded, 'The legal extinguishment of a legitimate child's links with one half of his own family . . . is inappropriate and might well be damaging' (HMSO 1970:30). Nowhere was it reasoned that alternatives were necessary to overcome the fact that the majority of step-parents did not use adoption and, consequently, had no legal relationship with their stepchildren. The Committee recommended that step-parent adoption should be abolished for legitimate children. While recognizing that a new distinction between legitimate and illegitimate children might be invidious they justified it because adoption brought the benefits of legitimacy to illegitimate children. In addition they suggested that adoption procedure should be changed so that the custodial parent could retain her natural status if her spouse adopted her child. The Committee proposed that guardianship, obtainable by court order as in other custody proceedings, should replace adoption for step-parents. This would enable a step-parent to obtain parental rights but would not affect the position of the non-custodial parent, inheritance rights, or name.

The report of the Committee repeated these views about the inappropriateness of adoption and the proposals for amendment of guardianship law but abolition of step-parent adoption for legitimate children was dropped because of 'overwhelming opposition from correspondents' (HMSO 1972:29). Instead it was suggested that courts should decide between the alternatives of guardianship and of adoption, giving first consideration to the child's long-term welfare. The proposal to amend adoption law so that the birth parent did not need to adopt was omitted because the Registrar General had given evidence that it was not practical to require two documents for proof of status and parentage. Thus adoption was to be available for families finally selected by the courts but not reformed in a way which could minimize its use for concealing the circumstances of birth.

Following the publication of the Houghton Report law reports suggested that a few judges had now begun to reconsider step-parent adoption. In two cases Sir George Baker, President of the Family Division of the High Court, who had himself given evidence to the Houghton Committee, criticized the making of such orders, particularly where the non-custodial parent opposed this (*Re D* (1973); *Re B* (1975)). Cumming-Bruce J. stated, 'it is likely to be difficult to discover any benefit to the child commensurate with the probably long-term disadvantages'. The lower courts continued to make orders and to dispense with parental agreement but cases were rarely actively opposed. Even the appellate courts did not go as far as the Committee; the judges had not apparently changed their attitude to unopposed applications, possibly because there were no alternatives to adoption. In the only reported case of a county court judge refusing an application made by a parent and step-parent and supported by the guardian *ad litem* the Court of Appeal reversed the decision (*Re S* (1975)). Megaw L.J. commented that Sir George Baker had not intended to lay down 'some infallible principle that applications should not be granted'. The pattern established in reported cases that unopposed applications should be granted but others treated with extreme caution was not reflected in the practice of magistrates' and county courts. Between 93 and 97 per cent of all applications were granted in the areas studied for the monitor of the Children Act 1975 and agreement was dispensed with in three-quarters of cases which were opposed (Masson and Norbury 1982:9).

The Houghton Committee's recommendations were introduced to Parliament, first in an unsuccessful private member's bill and then, in the 1974-75 session, by the Government. The bill included a clause which became subsection 10(3) of the Children Act 1975.

> 'Where the application is made to a court in England and Wales and the married couple consist of a parent and step-parent of the child the court shall dismiss the application if the matter would be better dealt with under section 42 (orders for custody etc.) of the Matrimonial Causes Act 1973.'

Part II of the Act made comparable but slightly different provision through the new process of custodianship for Scottish cases and cases where there had been no divorce.

Neither in Parliament nor in the media did step-parent adoption receive more than the slightest attention. Other provisions which were perceived as major changes or which were more controversial preoccupied all involved. There was no public debate about the value of the changes in step-parent adoption or the principles on which they were based. Moreover, when they were enacted there was no publicity to bring them to the attention of those whom they might affect (Masson, Norbury, and Chatterton 1981:124).

Subsection 10(3) of the Children Act 1975 came into force on 26 November, 1976 along with some other provisions including section 3, which required the court to give 'first consideration to the need to safeguard and protect the child's welfare throughout his childhood'. The Matrimonial Causes Rules were amended from 17 January, 1977 to allow a step-parent to apply with a divorced custodial parent for a variation of an existing custody order to their joint favour.[6] The custodianship provisions are still not in force largely because of the cost of implementation (DHSS 1980). Consequently, Scots law has not been changed. The Government has indicated that custodianship will be available by the end of 1984. More important, perhaps, the policy of discouraging step-parent adoption and of providing an alternative, by guardianship, applies only to step-families created after a divorce.

It is unfortunate that such distinctions, which have their origin in problems of procedure rather than differences in children's needs or families' structures, have come to exist. Implementation of custodianship would not remove them all. Although the orders probably have the same effect there are fundamental distinctions between the procedure and thus the practices in joint custody and custodianship. A parent and step-parent seeking joint custody apply to the divorce court for a variation of the original order. The judge must consider whether this is in the child's best interests; he has the power to call for a welfare officer's report but is unlikely to do so in an unopposed case (Eekelaar and Clive 1977:65; Davis, Macleod, and Murch 1983:129). In fact, he may merely rubber stamp the application, perhaps on the basis that the step-parent will be living in the household in any event. Applicants for custodianship, however, will be required to notify the local authority of their intentions and will be subject to a social work investigation similar to that undertaken by the local authority and adoption agency (Children Act 1975: s.40). And there is a minor difference in the wording of sections 10(3) and 37(1) which serves further to confuse. The former requires the court to dismiss the adoption application if it considers the matter would be '*better dealt with by custody*' while the latter requires the court to make a custodianship order if the child's welfare '*would not be better safeguarded by adoption*'. It therefore appears that if adoption and joint custody are equally good an adoption order should be made but if adoption and custodianship are equal the court should grant custodianship!

Since the implementation of subsection 10(3) a number of cases have reached the Court of Appeal. Initially appeals against refusals of orders were upheld but more recently a number have been granted (Rawlings 1982:637). In *Re S* (1977) the Court to Appeal upheld the refusal of an agreed adoption supported by the guardian *ad litem* and the children. The county court judge had refused the order because the advantages of adoption were 'vague and uncertain' even though the interest the birth father showed towards the children was 'admittedly minimal'. In a later case, also called *Re S* (1978), the court approved adoption *against* the wishes of the non-custodial father largely because adoption had already taken place de facto. More recently, in *Re D* (1980) and *Re S* (1981), step-parent adoptions have been permitted even though they might have the effect of legally severing links between a remembered birth father and his child. Ormrod L.J., who gave judgments in all these cases, has now enunciated his beliefs. The benefit of adoption lies in the integration of the new family and its disadvantage - the severance of links with the old family - will or will not occur irrespective of court orders.

The Children Act 1975 certainly had a dramatic effect. The number of step-parent adoption orders granted for legitimate children fell to 2,872 in 1983, the lowest number since 1965. There was a similar reduction for illegitimate children - in 1983 only 2,067 orders were made, the lowest number since records began in 1950. No statistics are collected for joint custody but it seems that only comparatively few orders have been made (Masson and Norbury 1982:9). Subsection 10(3) had three major effects. It discouraged would-be applicants - this may partly explain the decline in illegitimate cases. It led to an increase in the rate of refusal of orders, particularly in the first year following implementation. And it produced markedly different success rates in different courts. Masson and Norbury found that success rates ranged from 91 per cent to 9 per cent in 1978 in courts which had had roughly similar rates in 1975 and which were dealing with equivalent cases (Masson and Norbury 1982:9). This suggests that judges have difficulty applying the test in subsection 10(3) and have taken very different approaches to the assessment of the welfare of children living in step-families.

The Court of Appeal has attempted to get to grips with the notion of child welfare in step-families (Rawlings 1982:650) and thus to provide guidance for the lower courts. However, its method, the description of how the different statuses (adoption and joint custody) may feel to those concerned, must be regarded as speculation because of the lack of scientific research into child development in adopting and non-adopting step-families. The problem of interpretation, of setting the balance between adoption and custody, is not one of semantics as may have been suggested (Rawlings 1982:639, 641; Priest 1982:293) but of developing criteria, making prognoses and applying these to a given family. In what circumstances is refusal of adoption likely to be in the child's best interests? Extreme circumstances with, for example, neglectful step-parents, children who do not wish to be adopted, or non-custodial parents or their families who are actively and positively involved with the children but opposed to the adoption may not cause difficulty. What of more usual cases? The vast majority of birth fathers agree to the adoption and only a handful still visit their children. It seems unlikely that these absent fathers will play a part in their children's lives in the future (Masson and Norbury 1982:10). Some 95 per cent of applications are supported by the guardian *ad litem* (opposition is rare and will usually precipitate withdrawal of the case). The guardian spends far more time with all parties than the judge and usually includes information about the child's views in her report. An adverse factor such as concealment of the adoption from the child is likely to lead to the guardian recommending against adoption. Thus the judge is most likely to be faced with a united family where everybody wants adoption, information which shows that the non-custodial parent does not demur, and a social worker's assessment favouring it. Moreover, the applicants may well state that adoption will help them bring up the child better. The child too may say that he wants the stepfather to adopt them. In the face of such positive statements and no negative ones many judges will feel constrained to make the order (Masson 1983:17). A judge who refuses can justify his decision by using his own definition of welfare or from impressions gained in the brief court hearing which cast doubt on the validity of the guardian's recommendation. However, there has been no research on the outcome of these orders so he has only that recommendation against which to test his view of welfare.

Where judges are unwilling to hold that adoption is for the child's welfare this may be because they have been influenced by the authoritative statements of the Houghton Committee. It may also be related to an approach which underlies the court jurisdiction in custody cases and prefers continuing review to final, irrevocable orders like adoption. This philosophy runs contrary to the emphasis placed on permanency in current social work practice.

Although academic lawyers and others have expressed concern about the status of step-parents proposals like those of the Houghton Committee have not generally been made abroad. Step-parent adoption is widely practised in North America (Wadlington 1967:209; Maddox 1980:189; Bissett-Johnson 1980:382) but there are considerable variations even within the USA and Canada because adoption is a matter of state not federal law. Any comparisons with other jurisdictions must also take account of the general legal position. English law relating to step-parents differs from that of the USA; an American stepfather cannot be required to support his stepchild financially without an adoption order (Berkovitz 1970:212). In Canada, the position was uncertain but the Law Reform Commission of Canada recommended in 1976 that divorce courts should have power to order maintenance for any child 'who has been accepted and treated by the spouses as a child of their family' (LRCC 1976:40).

In neither Canada nor the USA is it generally possible for a step-parent to obtain rights in relation to his stepchild by alternative orders like joint custody or custodianship; the lack of such means has been criticized (Bodenheimer 1975:45; Wadlington 1967:208). In some states and provinces, for example Ontario, it is not even clear whether a step-parent may become the child's legal guardian on his spouse's death (Ontario Law Reform Commission 1973:106). Thus in North America adoption provides more concrete advantages to the stepchild and the step-parent than it does under English law. Moreover, the lack of alternatives clearly promotes adoption.

Despite the fact that the Ontario Law Reform Commission was aware of Houghton's recommendations when it made its own proposals on adoption and custody law in 1973 it did not follow them (OLRC 1973:36, 40). The Commission was concerned about the artificiality of a parent and step-parent adopting the parent's child. It sought to remedy this by providing that adoption by the step-parent alone should create a relationship without destroying that with the custodial parent. This has now been provided for in the Child Welfare Act 1981 s.86(1)(a). In addition it was proposed that testamentary guardianship should be permitted so that a mother could name her husband as guardian on her death. The difference in thinking between the Commission and the Houghton Committee is evident in this proposal; the stepfather as testamentary guardian would be the child's sole guardian and would not, as under English law, have to act jointly with the surviving (non-custodial) parent. This perhaps reflects views of the importance of autonomy and control for custodians which have been emphasized in *Beyond the Best Interests of the Child* (Goldstein, Freud, and Solnit 1973:38). The importance of the stepfather was underlined rather than the dangers and disadvantaves of the exclusion of the birth parent. In a later report on *Change of Name* the Commission again considered step-parent adoption. It was concerned that judges were refusing to allow the surname to be changed to that of the stepfather on the basis that he should apply for adoption (OLRC 1976:21). Although there is no indication how common this was the comment that 'The decision to adopt is a weighty and difficult one and should not legally be imposed on a couple' suggests a very different judicial practice from that in England following the Children Act 1975. More recently, in a consultative paper, the Ontario Ministry of Community and Social Services has suggested the provision of guardianship to replace adoption for step-parents (Ontario Ministry 1982:148).

The difference in approach between England and North America does not only relate to adoptions where the non-custodial parent agrees. Most jurisdictions require the agreement of a birth parent and, in the USA but not in England, this includes the father of an illegitimate child (*Re M* (1955); *Stanley* v. *Illinois* (1971). Step-parent adoption is encouraged in the USA; in some states non support of a child is grounds for dispensing with the defaulter's agreement and in others the agreement of the non-custodial parent is not required to step-parent adoption (Wadlington 1967:197). In Canada, Ontario, Manitoba, and Saskatchewan allow courts to dispense with agreement if adoption is in the child's best interests. This formula has led to step-parent adoption orders being made despite the objections of non-custodial parents (Williams 1982:220). However there are instances of courts emphasizing the rights of birth parents, the possible damage caused by severing links and refusing to grant orders.

It remains unclear to what extent such reported cases reflect the general practice of step-parent adoption. While there are no alternatives available to step-parents, even with broader and more flexible attitudes to family in the community step-parent adoption is likely to remain popular in North America.

Despite the concern in some quarters about the use of adoption by step-families there is general agreement that the law which fails to recognize the part many step-parents play in their new families is unsatisfactory. Like other families step-families should be able to arrange their affairs so that the step-parent may take an active part in family decision-making. This could occur if step-parents were granted some form of parental rights automatically on marriage to a custodial parent. However, there seems little purpose in providing rights when the custodial parent or the step-parent does not wish this. A better solution would be to allow them to decide to share parental rights and to provide a means for proving this where necessary. There would be no need for court proceedings - the non-custodial parent's rights would not be affected nor does it seem either desirable or possible to assess the suitability of step-parents for such shared rights. Exactly how the couple exercised their roles would be a personal matter as in other families, but the fact that this arrangement had been made would, for example, permit the stepfather to consent to the child receiving medical treatment and make him the child's guardian in the event of the mother's death unless she appointed someone else. A simple procedure leading to a comprehensible position should be more attractive to step-families than adoption, joint custody, or custodianship and thus lead to the majority of step-parents being full legal members of their families. Whether this would produce benefits in terms of family welfare-security, self-esteem, and good relationships is impossible to say. It would, however, end the legal fiction which recognizes step-parents as parent substitutes with duties but not with rights.

Notes

1 Even if the mother has been awarded legal custody on divorce the father still retains rights *Dipper* v. *Dipper* [1980] 2 All E.R. 722).
2 Matrimonial Causes Rules 1977 r.92(8); the court will give consent if the name change is in the child's best interests (*W* v. *A* [1981] 1 All E.R. 100, 105).
3 The ratio of step-parent adoptions to the number of children

whose parents divorced in the previous year declined from .07 in 1967 to .05 in 1973.

4 The Family Law Reform Act 1969 removed some of the legal disadvantages; further reform is planned (see Law Commission Report No. 118 *Illegitimacy* (1982)).

5 In France this is 'adoption simple': the ties with the birth family are retained but new relationships are created (French Civil Code Acts 363, 364). The effect is very similar to the result of the changes in guardianship law proposed by the ACCO.

6 This was done for step-parents married to a divorced parent by permitting them to apply for joint custody with the parent (Matrimonial Causes Amendment (No. 2) Rules 1976 r.9).

References

Association of Child Care Officers (ACCO) (1969) *Adoption: The Way Ahead.* London: ACCO.

Berkovitz, B.J. (1970) Legal Incidents of Today's Step-relationship: Cinderella revisited. *Family Law Quarterly* 4:209–29.

Bissett-Johnson, A. (1978) Step-Parent Adoptions in English and Canadian Law. In I. Baxter and M. Eberts (eds) *The Child and The Courts.* Toronto: Carswell.

______ (1980) Children in Subsequent Marriages. In J. Eekelaar and S. Katz (eds) *Marriage and Cohabitation.* Toronto: Butterworths.

Bodenheimer, B. (1975) New Trends and Requirements in Adoption Law and Proposals for Legislative Change. *Southern California Law Review* 49(10):44–51.

Davis, G., Macleod, A., and Murch, M. (1983) Undefended Divorce. *Modern Law Review* 46(2):121–46.

DHSS (1980) *The Cost of Implementing the Unimplemented Parts of the Children Act 1975.* London: HMSO.

Eekelaar J. and Clive, E. (1977) *Custody After Divorce.* Oxford: Centre for Socio-Legal Studies.

Goldstein, J., Freud, A., and Solnit A.J. (1973) *Beyond the Best Interests of the Child.* New York: Free Press.

Goodacre, I. (1966) *Adoption Policy and Practice.* London: Allen & Unwin.

HMSO (1954) *Report of the Departmental Committee on the Adoption of Children.* (The Hurst Committee) Cmd. 9248. London: HMSO.

______ (1970) *Adoption of Children.* (The Houghton Committee) London: HMSO.

______ (1972) *Report of the Departmental Committee on Adoption of Children.* (The Houghton Report) Cmd: 5107. London: HMSO.

Kornitzer, M. (1959) *Adoption.* London: Putnam.

Lambert, L. and Streather J. (1980) *Children Changing Families.* London: Macmillan.

Law Commission (1982) *Illegitimacy.* London: HMSO HCP.

Law Reform Commission of Canada (1976) *Studies on Divorce.* Ottawa: Information Canada.

Leete, R. (1978) Adoption Trends and Illegitimate Births 1951–77. *Population*

Trends 14:9–16.
______ (1979) New Directions in Family life. *Population Trends* 15:4–9.
Leete, R. and Anthony, S. (1979) Divorce and Remarriage: A Record Linkage Study. *Population Trends* 16:5–11.
Maddox, B. (1975) *The Half Parent*. London: Andre Deutsch.
______ (1980) *Step-parenting*. London: Allen & Unwin (a revised version of *The Half Parent*).
Masson, J.M. (1981) *Step-parent Adoption: A Socio-legal Study*. Unpublished Ph.D thesis Leicester University.
______ (1983) Decision-making: The Roles of the Judge and the Guardian *ad litem* in England. In S. Katz (ed.) *Resolution of family conflict*. Toronto: Butterworths.
Masson, J. and Norbury D. (1982) Step-parent adoption. *Adoption and Fostering* 6(1):7–10.
Masson, J., Norbury, D, and Chatterton, S.G. (1981) *Report to DHSS: Step-parent Adoption*. Published research report (1983) *Mine, Yours or Ours? A Study of Step-parent Adoption*. London: HMSO.
OPCS: *Marriage & Divorce Statistics, FM2*. London: HMSO.
OPCS: *Adoption Monitor, FM3* (1973-) London: HMSO.
Ontario Law Reform Commission (OLRC) (1973) *Report on Family Law, Part III Children*. Toronto: Ministry of Att. Gen.
______ (1976) *Change of Name*. Toronto: Ministry of Att. Gen.
Ontario, Ministry of Community and Social Services (1982) *The Children's Act. A Consultation Paper*. Toronto: Ministry of Community and Social Services.
Priest, J. (1982) Step-parent Adoptions: What is the Law? *Journal of Social Welfare Law* 293–94.
Rawlings, R. (1982) Law Reform with Tears. *Modern Law Review* 45(6):637–51.
Registrar General, *Registrar General's Statistical Review (1950–73)*. London: HMSO.
Standing Conference of Societies Registered for Adoption (SCSRA) (1968) *Report to the Home Office on the Working of the Adoption Act 1958*. London: HMSO.
Thomson, H. (1967) *The Successful Step-parent*. London: W.H. Allen.
Wadlington, W. (1967) The Divorced Parent and Consent to Adoption. *University of Cincinnati Law Review* 36:196–209.
Williams, C. (1982) Step-parent Adoptions and the Best Interests of the Child in Ontario. *University of Toronto Law Journal* 32:214–30.

10 Freeing a child for adoption – wardship

DAVID SPICER

The development of specialized placing arrangements for children identified as having 'special needs' by reason of handicap, age, or origin has removed an element of the frustration and difficulty experienced by professionals operating in the field of adoption placements. It is often more difficult to come to terms with those cases of children whose need is not for adopters with the special qualities necessary to cope with particular problems but for a family committed to providing a home for the life of the child. Such a family may still need to cope with the uncertainty and insecurity which can arise from ambivalence or direct opposition by a birth parent to the course proposed. Those working in the adoption field have looked towards Parliament and the courts for help in reassuring prospective adopters about the security of the placement of children in their care.

In considering how best to establish a secure adoption placement for children considered suitable for such placements, the Departmental Committee on the Adoption of Children (Houghton Report) readily acknowledged that it was of the utmost importance for a child to be placed in an adoptive home as early as possible in his or her life, since the early establishment of the parent/child relationship is vital for the good emotional development of the child (HMSO 1972: para. 155). The Houghton Committee considered the existing arrangements, under which it was not possible for a child to be secure from parental objection to adoption until a specific adoption application had been made while parental agreement, however frequently expressed, could have effect only when an adoption order was to be made. The Committee concluded that such procedures encouraged indecisiveness on the part of the birth parent and imposed unnecessary strain and confusion on her. The welfare of the child was seen to be at risk, either on account of the prospective adopters' anxiety and fear of totally committing themselves to the child, or as a direct result of the mother's uncertainty about the child being removed or his future remaining uncertain (HMSO 1972:147).

Research before and after the Report of the Houghton Committee indicated that a large majority of mothers faced with the question of adoption for their child made up their minds at an early stage and considered that the procedure for finalizing consent was too slow and too open to alteration (Raynor 1971). The need to consider adoption for large groups of children presently thought to be unsuitable for it has been highlighted. Thus Rowe and Lambert, in their study for British Adoption Agencies *Children Who Wait* (1973), estimated that 7,000 children in the care of the local authorities, mostly accommodated in residential homes, were unsuitably placed; on a professional assessment 2,000 required adoption while the remainder were in need of some form of permanent substitute family care.

The Houghton Committee noted that in some states of the United States of America the child is not placed for adoption until the parent has taken an irrevocable decision to have the child adopted and that, in some other countries such as New Zealand, parental rights and the ability to consent to an adoption are vested in a statutory agency prior to the consideration of an adoption application (HMSO 1972:148).

The Houghton Committee concentrated its attention on the inability of a parent to make a final early decision agreeing to the adoption of his or her child. It briefly criticized the state of the law regarding the provisions for dispensing with the agreement of a parent to adoption when that parent will not or cannot agree to the course proposed and yet leaves the child in the care of others or is incapable of providing a satisfactory home for the child herself. This situation is stated by Houghton to be 'inadequate' (paragraph 147). In practical terms the effect on the child of the inability to make a secure early adoption placement is identical, whether caused by an inability on the part of the parent to come to terms with the decision or whether there is at the outset a direct parental refusal to agree to an adoption.

A child may be adopted only if his birth parents agree to the making of the adoption order, or if their agreement is dispensed with by order of a court on any of a number of statutory grounds contained in Section 12 of the Children Act 1975. Until 1984, in all cases it has been the prospective adoptors who have made the application to dispense with the parent's agreement. It is they who have provided the court with a statement of facts in support of their application establishing the ground on which the court must rely to dispense with the agreement of the parent (Rule 8 Adoption (High Court) Rules 1976; Rule 7 Adoption (County Court) Rules 1976; Rule 6 Magistrates' Courts (Adoption) Rules 1976). It is clearly unsatisfactory to have a procedure under which the applicants in all probability know little or nothing of substance concerning those issues which go to establish the grounds for dispensing with agreement, and the principal provisions of which relate to critical comment on the conduct of the parent. The prospective adopters were thus faced with the possibility of lengthy and costly legal proceedings, which largely concerned matters of which they have little knowledge and no control. The outcome of such proceedings cannot be guaranteed and many adopters have felt that the direct confrontation, albeit anonymous, between themselves and the parents of the child was not conducive to establishing their relationship with the child or to dealing with future questions concerning the child's origins. It is not surprising that prospective adopters wish to avoid the possibility of involvement in such proceedings or that adoption agencies should seek to protect their adopters from the anguish, anxiety, distress, and possible disappointment arising from such applications. The increasing tendency of adoption agencies to offer assistance in the form of contributions towards legal costs, drafting of documents, and provision of information did little to assist the emotional strain. Unfortunately the inability to place a child with prospective adopters in confidence of a secure placement may lead to the postponement of the adoption placement, inadequate arrangements for a child's care involving constant moves, or inappropriate attempts at rehabilitation of the child with his birth parent. It may also lead to a decision not to intervene statutorily in a situation regarded as offering a child unsatisfactory home circumstances because of uncertainty over the ability to provide a satisfactory alternative.

As a result of dealing with cases of damaged and disturbed children for whom it was clear at an early age that adoption was appropriate, but not pursued because of the difficulties outlined, social workers and their professional colleagues looked increasingly towards Parliament to remedy the situation. The Houghton Committee limited its recommendations to the establishment of a procedure of 'relinquishment' by which consent to the making of an adoption order subject to certain safeguards would be irrevocable, so enabling the child to be placed with prospective adopters with security. Houghton concentrated on the problem of the parent who is susceptible to change of mind, while making no recommendation concerning cases in which it is necessary to dispense with the agreement of a parent (HMSO: 149–54). However, Parliament, influenced by continuing research and no doubt by public awareness of such tragedies as that of Maria Colwell (the subject of a report of a Committee of Inquiry published in 1974), went further than Houghton envisaged. It established in the Children Act 1975 Section 14 a procedure enabling the freeing of a child for adoption by order of the court on the application by an adoption agency, provided either that the parent agreed to the making of an adoption order or that the agreement of the parent could be dispensed with on one of the specified grounds contained in Section 12 of that Act. Where the application involves dispensing with parental agreement the child must be in the care of the adoption agency making the application and either have already been placed for adoption or be likely to be so placed.

There is no doubt that the operation of the provisions of Section 14 of the 1975 Act would have been of great assistance to those involved in the placement of children for adoption since 1975. The value of procedure under which the legal and professional arguments concerning the agreement or otherwise of a parent to adoption are brought significantly forward to a time at which the prospective adopters may not be involved, and at which decisions about the permanent placement of the child may be made at the earliest opportunity cannot be over-emphasized. Unfortunately, Parliament did not provide for the early implementation of these important provisions. The Act received the Royal Assent on 12 November, 1975. The provisions relating to freeing a child for adoption were to come into force on such date as the Secretary of State may by order appoint (S108 Children Act 1975). The Secretary of State has recently provided for their implementation with effect from spring 1984, some twelve years after the report of the Houghton Committee and some eight years after the Act received the Royal Assent. (S.I. 1983. No. 1946). The delay in the implementation of these provisions has been deplored by adoption agencies and those involved in adoption fieldwork.

The period during which the delay has occurred has coincided with a number of other important developments affecting in particular the operation of the statutory powers of local authorities, both as local social services authorities and as adoption agencies. At the forefront of these developments has been the tremendous increase in the quantity and quality of research and knowledge in the sphere of child welfare and in particular those factors leading to child abuse. That many cases of non-accidental injury to children, sometimes with fatal consequences, were being incorrectly diagnosed as accidents, was exposed as early as 1962 by Kempe in the American publication of his papers *The Battered Child Syndrome* (Kempe 1962). In Britain active interest was confined to very few within the medical profession and, despite the statutory responsibilities of social workers for the protection of children, there were very few papers published in the British Social Work Journals before 1973 (Jones 1982:43). Thereafter however interest and concern grew, fired by statutory enquiries such as that into the death of Maria Colwell and into the deaths of other children which highlighted the potentially lethal consequences of neglect and showed the overlap between neglect and physical injury to children (HMSO 1980; Berkshire County Council 1979; Essex County Council 1981). As expertise in the identification of cases of abused children grew so did the recognition that agencies and professionals should not operate in a vacuum. The Colwell Inquiry Report stressed that Maria fell through the welfare net primarily because of communications failure. It emphasized that social workers should reasonably expect matters of concern about individual families or children to be passed on to them by other agencies. The Department of Health and Social Security responded to the growing concern, involving in particular battered children, by issuing of a series of circulars giving guidance on the management of cases (DHSS 1970). Suggestions included the need for co-ordination of services through case conferences (*The Battered Baby Syndrome* 1972), the laying down of a structure for reviewing local practices, procedures, management of cases, the reviewing of the work of case conferences, and the drawing up of procedures to be followed by all personnel concerned with aspects of cases through the establishment of Area Review Committees (DHSS 1974). By 1976 all areas of the country had established Area Review Committees with Case Conference procedures and register systems of varying kinds. By 1980 the Department was emphasizing the need to include within the multi-disciplinary approach not only physical injury to children, but also severe and persistent neglect and emotional abuse (DHSS 1980).

The Colwell Inquiry identified as a major area of concern the inexperience and lack of specialist knowledge of those concerned with the child's welfare. This was blamed for errors of judgement in the case. One ot the responsibilities of the Area Review Committees, once established, was to provide education and training programmes to heighten awareness of the problem of child abuse. Local authorities in particular as a number came under scrutiny in the context of statutory inquiries into tragedies involving children, recognized the need for qualified social work staff. In 1972 the number of persons receiving the Certificate of Qualification in Social Work was 2,183; by 1979 there was an increase of more than 50 per cent to 3,592 before restrictions on local government secondment led to a slight fall from that figure (Central Council for Education and Training in Social Work, Annual Statistics). Increasing knowledge from research and experience, greater co-ordination and correlation of information between agencies, and assessment by qualified and experienced staff, led during the 1970s to a greater ability on the part of the professionals involved in child welfare to identify problems at an early stage. These included cases in which abuse to a child had occurred as well as those in which there was a high risk of abuse. And also, most important, those cases in which successful rehabilitation of a child with his birth parents was unlikely and in which permanent arrangements for substitute care were required in the child's interests. Having identified cases in which intervention was required, social workers naturally wished to intervene in order to prevent damage which they were now able to predict would in all probability occur; they then found that the child care legislation in the form of the Children and Young Persons Act 1969 and the Children Act 1948 (now the Child Care Act 1980) was more appropriate for dealing with cases of proven damage rather than helping to prevent damage from occurring.

Social workers and their professional colleagues therefore looked towards their legal advisers for the means to apply their developing expertise to individual cases. Local authorities in particular were increasingly encouraged to approach the Family Division of the High Court of Justice requesting the assistance of that court in the exercise of its wardship jurisdiction over children.

The Family Division of the High Court is the delegate and trustee of the exercise of the Royal prerogative powers by which the Crown claims the right to protect its subjects and in particular to exercise a special parental responsibility towards the minors of the realm. All British subjects who are minors are therefore in a technical sense wards of court. However, the term has acquired a specialized meaning indicating those minors over which the court is exercising jurisdiction in response to an application. The court may, subject to certain self-limiting principles, make any order in relation to a child, subject only to the principle that the court must have regard to the welfare of the minor as the first and paramount consideration. An application to the court for the exercise of the court's jurisdiction in the making of an order may be made by any person having a proper interest in the welfare of the minor. A minor becomes subject to the exercise of the court's jurisdiction on the commencement of proceedings by the issuing of an originating summons and thereafter no steps which materially affect the welfare of the minor may be taken without the leave of the court (Supreme Court Act 1981 S.41). If the court is satisfied that there are exceptional circumstances making it impracticable or undesirable for a ward of court to be or continue to be under the care of either of his parents or of any other individual, the court may if it thinks fit make an order committing the care of the ward to a local authority. If such an order is made the court may direct the manner of the exercise by the local authority of certain of its statutory powers relating to the accommodation and welfare of the ward (Section 7 Family Law Reform Act 1969 and Section 43 Matrimonial Causes Act 1973).

Evidence before the Wardship Court is by way of affidavit and is therefore presented in a considered manner. All parties are served with copies of the affidavits prior to the hearing and the issues before the judge are therefore clear. This is to be contrasted with the *ad hoc* and often haphazard manner in which evidence is adduced before the more usual forum for consideration of such cases, the Juvenile Court. A judge will often reserve a case to himself so that all future applications will be considered by the judge who is therefore familiar with the matter and the reasons behind previous orders and decisions.

That local authorities might have recourse to the wardship jurisdiction became clear from the attitude of the judges of the Family Division who on a number of occasions included in their judgments encouragement to local authorities to approach the court in cases of difficulty. Thus in the case of *Re B (A Minor)* (1974) Mr Justice Lane considered that there might be various circumstances in which a local authority would be grateful for the assistance of the court exercising the wardship jurisdiction. He added:

> 'Local authorities are sometimes faced with difficult and onerous decisions concerning children in their charge; responsible officers of their Welfare Departments may be subject to various pressures from within or from outside the authority itself. I consider that there would be no abandonment of, or derogation from, their statutory powers and duties were they to seek the guidance and assistance of the High Court in matters of difficulty, as distinct from the day-to-day arrangements with which, as the authorities show, the Court will not interfere.'

This indication was cited with approval in a speech by Lord Roskill in the House of Lords in *A* v *Liverpool City Council* (1981). It also became clear that the court was ready to exercise jurisdiction having regard to the welfare of the child as the first and paramount consideration notwithstanding the existence of other legislative provisions apparently providing for the welfare of the child. In *Re D (A Minor)* (1977) Mr Justice Dunn summarized the position in the following way:

> 'Far from local authorities being discouraged from applying to a Court in Wardship, in my judgment they should be encouraged to do so, because in very many of these cases it is the only way in which the Orders can be made in the interests of the child, untrammelled by the statutory provisions of the Children and Young Persons Act 1969.'

It was again emphasized that the value of the jurisdiction lies in the principle applied by the Court which Mr Justice Dunn described as:

> 'the golden thread which runs through the whole of this Court's jurisdiction, the welfare of the child, which is considered in this Court first, last, and all the time. I accept the submission of the County Council that there may be many cases in which the Local Authority is unable to prove one of the conditions in Section 1 of the 1969 Act, and yet it is in the interests of the child that a Care Order should be made.'

The increasing involvement of the local authorities with the wardship jurisdiction is illustrated by the figures for the number of children committed to the care of local authorities under section 7 of the Family Law Reform Act 1969 extracted from the Department of Health and Social Security's Personal Social Services Local Authority statistics for children in care of local authorities. The accuracy of specific figures may be questioned with the usual scepticism of the accuracy of returns, but the trend is apparent. In 1974-75 22 children were committed to care; in 1977-78 this number had risen to 87; by 1980-81 135 children are said to have been committed to care in this jurisdiction.

Those local authorities who have involved themselves in wardship applications have swiftly learned that judges are not prepared to exercise their very personal responsibility towards their wards in these matters lightly. They expect the very fullest information concerning the present circumstances of the child and, if an application is made for the committal of the child to the care of the local authority, they also demand a clear indication of the proposals which the local authority has for the future care of the child. The court continues to exercise a jurisdiction over such matters as access; although it would be wrong for the court to override the views of the local authority unless it were satisfied that the authority's views could not be supported, nevertheless local authority children's officers must accept the fact that where a care order is made they are subject to the court: it is for the court with the assistance of welfare officers, children's officers, and local authority experts to hear both their side and the parents side of the case, before making such order as it thinks right in the interests of the child (*Re Y (A Minor)* (1975)). If the court considers it appropriate a direction requiring the local authority to take steps to rehabilitate a child with a birth parent may be given.

The enquiring nature of the proceedings before the Wardship Judge and the continuing responsibility of the court over matters relating to the welfare of the child notwithstanding the making of a care order have been seen by some as a disadvantage and a restriction on the ability of professional social workers to operate. On the contrary, with regard to children who are potentially suitable for adoption it is these requirements of the court that specifically promote satisfactory early decisions in relation to the secure placement of a child while also encouraging clarity in this complex area.

When it is proposed that those caring for a ward of court should make application to adopt the ward, that step, clearly materially affecting the welfare of the child, may not be taken without the leave of the court. The function of a judge in dealing with an application for leave to bring adoption proceedings is not to decide the point which would later determine the result of the adoption proceedings but to consider whether the application is one which reasonably might succeed (*F* v. *S*) (1973). Where it is proposed at the initiation of the proceedings that on the committal of the child to the care of the local authority he should be placed in a home with a view to adoption, that course of action must also only be taken with the leave of the court. These principles received affirmation in the Court of Appeal in the case of *In Re F (A Minor)* 1983 when Lord Justice Cumming-Bruce set out the propositions of law to be applied so that doubts hitherto entertained might be resolved:

'(1) Once a child was a Ward of Court no important step in the child's life could be taken without the Court's approval.
(2) Before adoption proceedings could be instituted an application had to be made to the Wardship Judge seeking permission to institute adoption proceedings.
(3) Before placing a Ward with long-term foster parents with a view to adoption the Local Authority had to obtain leave of the Wardship Judge so to place the child.'

It was further emphasized that the question of access to the birth parents was a matter of such importance that the Wardship Judge should not remain silent but should give directions one way or another.

It is essential therefore that the evidence before the court in the form of affidavits clearly contains the professional arguments in favour of whatever course of action is proposed. There is no doubt that this requirement focuses the professional mind on the issues subject as they are to the scrutiny not only of the judge but also of advocates acting for other parties.

If the court supports the view advanced that the child should be placed for adoption, that placement may then take place on the authority of the High Court Judge's order. Once placed with the prospective adopters the child may not be removed from those adopters without the leave of the court. The approval may also be accompanied if appropriate by an order that there should be no access by the birth parent to the child. The child is not in the sense of the provisions of the Children Act 1975 freed for adoption, but prospective adopters may be approached with the reassurance that the adoption placement has been approved by a High Court Judge and that once placed the child may not be removed from their care without the leave of that judge. The birth parents will have had full knowledge of the local authority's proposals in the matter and full opportunity to oppose the philosophy of the placement. If the placement is consented to by the birth parents, the consent will in most cases be contained within an affidavit filed in the court and will have been given after advice from a solicitor and Counsel instructed in the proceedings. Subsequently, when it is considered appropriate for the prospective adopters to file an application to adopt the child, a further approach must be made to the Wardship Court for leave to file that application. The matter therefore receives further judicial consideration at that stage.

The decision of the Wardship Judge to approve the placing of the child in a long-term home with a view to adoption and subsequently to approve the filing of an adoption application does not prevent the birth parent from refusing to agree to the making of an adoption order if he or she so wishes; it then becomes necessary for the future court considering an adoption application to dispense with that agreement. The parent's ability to oppose the application for the granting of an adoption order is not affected either. However, realistically, where a judicial decision with the authority of the High Court has been to approve such a placement, particularly in the circumstances in which a birth parent has had a full opportunity to argue the case either for the rehabilitation of the child with her or for her to continue to have access to the child, the ability to demonstrate that the parent is unreasonably withholding her agreement to the making of an adoption order and that therefore that agreement should be dispensed with is significantly enhanced.

A major criticism made on behalf of parents who find that their child in the care of the local authority has been placed for adoption without their knowledge or agreement is that such decisions are made administratively. The ability of the parent to challenge those decisions judicially at the time of the consideration of the adoption application is at too late a stage in the proceedings as the child has already become settled. The attempts of the parent to continue or re-establish a relationship with the child may also be frustrated by administrative decisions regarding access. Since those placements and the decisions relating to access may not take place in the case of a ward of court without the leave of the court and therefore without notice being given to the parent who will be a party to those proceedings this criticism is removed. Furthermore, if the arguments raised in favour of severing parental responsibilities are not accepted by the court, possible rehabilitation may be attempted only with the general oversight and approval of the court concerning the arrangements, with the ability to approach the court for further orders in the event of those arrangements proving unsatisfactory in terms of the child's welfare. Thus, both parents and local authority very clearly know where they stand in relation to rehabilitation and access. The very real danger of a rehabilitation attempt which drifts from bad to worse - unfortunately familiar to those involved in the field - often involving foster home breakdowns and recurring moves for the child before the attempts are abandoned at too late a stage, is reduced.

Insofar as the Wardship Court retains the ability to direct matters such as access, the extent of the jurisdiction goes further than that provided for in the legislative provisions relating to the freeing of a child for adoption. In the application of those provisions the parent may successfully oppose an application for an order freeing a child for adoption but must become involved in seeking further remedies in other jurisdictions on the questions of access or rehabilitation. The provisions relating to freeing a child for adoption within the legislation do not adequately provide for the interests of the extended birth family of the child either. Within the wardship jurisdiction the court may not make an order committing the child to the care of the local authority and therefore approve the placement by that local authority of the child in an adoptive home unless there are exceptional circumstances making it impracticable or undesirable for the ward to be or continue to be under the care of either of his parents or of any other individual (Section 7(2) Family Law Reform Act 1969). The court must specifically consider - and therefore the professional evidence given must specifically provide for - the possibility of the care of the child being undertaken by members of the extended birth family or indeed any other individual. Those individuals may make an application to be joined as party to the proceedings.

At this early stage the consideration of alternative caretakers within the family or elsewhere must therefore be considered. Such matters are often raised at the consideration of an application for an adoption order in the form of grandparents offering a home for the child or complaining that they have been prevented from making such a home available by the administrative decision of a local authority to cease arrangements for access by the birth family. Recent advice from the DHSS issued under the statutory authority S.12G of the Child Care Act 1980 seeks to improve practice in relation to access to children in care, but fails to provide a judicial remedy for those other than parents (DHSS 1983). Parental ability to challenge decisions is limited to an application to the juvenile court which does not have jurisdiction to consider applications to free children for adoption.

Where it has been necessary to make application for the agreement of a parent to be dispensed with the most common grounds on which such an application has relied are that the parent is withholding his agreement unreasonably or that he has persistently failed without reasonable cause to discharge parental duties in relation to the child (Section 12(2) Children Act 1975). The evidence to substantiate the existence of those grounds most commonly consists of an indication that the child for a relatively long period of time has been settled in a prospective adoptive home and that there is no prospect of rehabilitation with the birth parent, or that the failure to make proper arrangements for the care of the child has persisted over a similarly long period of time. That evidence is unlikely to be available in order to support an application to free a child for adoption at the early stages of the child's reception into the care of an agency. The difficulty of placing the child with security therefore persists, despite Houghton's emphasis on the importance of making adoption placements early when there may be an inability to prove one of the conditions contained in Section 12 of the Children Act 1975 necessary to dispense with the agreement of the parent (HMSO 1972:155). Nevertheless in such circumstances an approach may be made to the Wardship Court and the security of a placement which that jurisdiction provides may be achieved before approaching prospective adopters.

The Secretary of State has been slow in bringing into effect legislative arrangements concerning the freeing of children for adoption. The courts have responded to the need for such a procedure in such a way that the gaps even in the recent legislation are filled. Professional social workers are often suspicious of the operation of the law in relation to their client's interests. It is to be hoped that the manner in which the wardship jurisdiction has been employed to support professional decision-making and deal with all relevant issues in one jurisdiction may encourage them to view the results of the law not as a restriction on the operation of their professional expertise and judgment but as a help in achieving their professional objectives as well as a spur to the quality of professional decision-making.

References

Adoption (High Court) Rules (1976) S.I. 1976 No. 1645.

Adoption (County Court) Rules (1976) S.I. 1976 No. 1644.

Adoption (Magistrates' Courts) Rules (1976) S.I. 1976 No. 1768.

Berkshire County Council (1979) *Lester Chapman: Report of an Independent Inquiry Commissioned by the County Councils and Area Health Authorities of Berkshire and Hampshire.* Berkshire County Council.

Children Act 1975 and the Adoption Act 1976 (Commencement) Order 1983 S.I. 1983 No. 1946 (C.53).

DHSS (1970) *The Battered Baby.* LHAL 24/70.

______ (1972) *The Battered Baby Syndrome*: An Analysis of Reports Submitted by Medical Officers of Health and Children's Officers. LASSL 26/72.

______ (1974) *Memorandum on Non-Accidental Injury to Children.* LASSL 13/74.

______ (1980) *Child Abuse: Central Register Systems.* LASSL 4/80.

______ (1983) *Code of Practice: Access to Children in Care.* London: HMSO.

Essex County Council (1981) *Malcolm Page: Report of Panel appointed by the Essex County Council and Essex Area Health Authority.* Essex County Council.

HMSO (1972) *Departmental Committee on the Adoption of Children* (The Houghton Committee) Cmnd 5107. London: HMSO.

______ (1974) *Report of Committee of Inquiry into the Care and Supervision provided in relation to Maria Colwell.* London: HMSO.

______ (1975, 1981) *Health and Personal Services Statistics for England.* London: HMSO.

______ (1980) *Report of Committee of Inquiry into the case of Paul Steven Brown.* Cmnd 8107. London: HMSO.

Jones, D.N. (1982) *Understanding Child Abuse.* London: Hodder & Stoughton.

Kempe, H. (1962) The Battered Child Syndrome. *Journal of the American Medical Association* 181, 1:17–22.

Raynor, L. (1971) *Giving Up a Baby for Adoption.* London: ABAA.

Rowe, J. and Lambert, L. (1973) *Children Who Wait.* London: ABAA.

11 Aided conception: the alternative to adoption

PETER M. BROMLEY

Adoption is not a cure for childlessness: it may provide the childless couple with a substitute for their own child. But the diminishing number of children available for adoption whom couples may regard as suitable for this purpose has led many to consider the possibility of resorting to an alternative, for example artificial insemination or *in vitro* fertilization. Having a child conceived in this way may indeed have positive advantages over adoption: the child will be the child of at least one of the couple (or even both of them), the wife has the emotional satisfaction of bearing a child, and the husband shares the experience of her pregnancy and confinement. Moreover, the conception may give emotional help to a sterile husband and, if the way in which it was brought about is kept secret, the world will know nothing of what he may regard as the stigma of his shortcoming.

Considerable public concern has been expressed recently about the social and ethical implications of some of these practices. As a consequence a Departmental Committee has been set up under the chairmanship of Dame Mary Warnock with the following terms of reference: 'To consider recent and potential developments in medicine and science related to human fertilization and embryology; to consider what policies and safeguards should be applied, including consideration of the social, ethical, and legal implications of these developments and to make recommendations'.

The purpose of this chapter is to consider the legal problems.

Artificial Insemination with the Husband's Semen (AIH)

AIH may be resorted to if both parties are fertile and the woman is capable of bearing a child but conception is unlikely or impossible following sexual intercourse. This may be due, for example, to impotence, physical abnormality, or some unusual condition of the husband's semen.

Any child conceived by AIH will be in the same legal position as a child conceived naturally, so that, if the parents are married, he will be their legitimate child. One problem may arise, however. Semen may be frozen and stored, and some men, about to undergo a vasectomy, genital surgery, or therapy likely to produce sterility, request that some of their semen be stored so that they may produce more children later should this be desired. It is thus possible for a child to be conceived after the father's death. Such a child cannot be legitimate because legitimacy requires conception or birth during the child's parents' marriage. (Technically this is not even AIH because the donor is no longer the mother's husband). How does this affect his rights?

Even though a posthumously conceived child is illegitimate, he has the same claim on his father's estate as a legitimate child. He can also claim property settled by anyone else on his father's children (for example, a trust established by his paternal grandfather's will in favour of the testator's grandchildren). The practical difficulty that may arise is that property may already have been distributed on the assumption that all the beneficiaries were known: all the child can then do is to try and recover his share from those into whose hands it has come. Whether he could claim maintenance from his father's estate is more problematical. The Inheritance (Provision for Family and Dependants) Act 1975 provides that if a person is *survived by* a child, the latter may apply for an order if the deceased's will or the law relating to intestacy fails to make reasonable financial provision for him. The term 'child' includes one who has been conceived but not born at the parent's death, and this, coupled with the words italicized, suggests that the child may not claim if he was not conceived when his father died. Even if the court were to interpret the statute in favour of such a child - as it is hoped it would - the latter would still have to obtain leave to make an application, as the six months' period during which he could have applied as of right will inevitably have expired. The court may be reluctant to give leave if the estate has already been distributed; in this case the only action the child could take would be to apply for a variation of an existing order in his favour. It will be appreciated, however, that this would be possible only if an order had already been made for the benefit of another dependant and any variation would have to be at the expense of the latter.

It is suggested that the law should be changed to ensure that children conceived after their father's death remain legitimate. It is believed that this would reflect public opinion. Some limitations would have to be placed on the operation of such a provision: conception would have to take place before the mother's remarriage and within a given period after the father's death - say, two years. Insemination after this time could not reasonably be regarded as AIH and it would be absurd to treat it as such.

The storage of semen raises the further question of the man's subsequent right to determine how it is to be used and when it is to be destroyed. It is possible, for example, that a doctor might wish to use it for the insemination of another woman or that the sperm might still be viable after the man's death. Earlier authorities suggest that it is impossible to own human tissue; this would mean that the man could no longer control the use of his semen as owner of it. These cases might not be followed today, but the legal position is in considerable doubt (Palmer 1979:7-10). To overcome difficulties that may arise, the man and the practitioner involved should enter into a contract indicating the purposes to which the semen could be put and the circumstances in which it is to be destroyed. Even if neither party is in law the owner of it, the man or (after his death) his personal representatives will have a contractual right to have the terms of the agreement carried out.

Artificial Insemination with a Donor's Semen (AID)

If the woman is fertile and capable of bearing a child but the husband is sterile or severely subfertile, they may wish to have a child by AID. An increasingly common reason for seeking this is that the husband has had an irreversible vasectomy during a previous marriage. AID may also be appropriate if the husband is fertile but is likely to transmit an inheritable disorder such as Huntington's chorea or if the spouses are unable to have more children because of Rhesus factor incompatibility.

MEDICAL AND SOCIAL CONSIDERATIONS

When discussing AID we must constantly remember that the woman, the donor, and the doctor are deliberately setting out to create a child. While, therefore, the purpose of AID is to give the persons who consult the doctor the satisfaction of the woman's bearing a child of her own, it is absolutely essential for the doctor to keep in mind the welfare of any child that may be conceived. The responsibility must be his for it is through his agency alone that conception will take place.

His first concern must be to ensure as far as possible that the couple seeking AID are suitable. The criteria currently adopted are set out by Kerr and Rogers (1975) and by Snowden and Mitchell (1981:55): they include the need to make certain that the couple are strongly motivated and have no moral or religious scruples, that they have a mature and stable relationship, and that they are healthy, able to care for a child, and give it a suitable chance in life. Most practitioners will inseminate an unmarried woman living in a stable heterosexual relationship, but the need to try to give the child a 'normal' family life leads almost all to reject as unsuitable an unmarried woman living alone or in a lesbian relationship.

It will be seen that these criteria reflect those applicable when a couple seek to adopt a child. It has been suggested that in case of doubt a doctor might seek the help of a social worker (Sandler 1979:82). The danger here, however, is that, as we shall see, confidentiality lies at the basis of AID and the intervention of a social worker immediately widens the circle of those with knowledge.

The other field in which the practitioner's judgment and experience are critical is in the selection of the donor. The principal criteria are set out by Snowden and Mitchell (1981:64): in particular they include good health, above average intelligence, a stable personality, and a physical resemblance to the husband (for example, in build and colour of eyes and hair). The welfare of the child (as well as the welfare of the mother and her husband) requires the practitioner to take all reasonable steps to eliminate men who might pass on hereditary physical or mental abnormalities; he must therefore take a full medical history of a potential donor's background and subject him to a thorough medical examination.

As we shall see later, successful insemination imposes potential legal liabilities upon the donor. There is also a danger that a donor may later attempt to satisfy a natural curiosity about the development of his offspring. Consequently, in order to protect the donor himself and the spouses and child (into whose family he might otherwise make a sudden and unwanted appearance) it is absolutely essential that neither the donor nor the spouses should ever discover the identity of the other. (There is also a very real danger that it would be impossible to obtain donors if their anonymity could not be guaranteed.) To guard against a possible change in the law which would enable an AID child to discover the identity of his father (as has happened in adoption), some practitioners are apparently destroying records.

The fear is sometimes expressed that AID could lead to unwitting incest. This seems exaggerated: it has been calculated that if 2,000 children are born each year as a result of AID and each donor has five children, an incestuous marriage is likely to take place once in every 50 to 100 years (HMSO 1960: para. 39). Nevertheless the possibility of incest leads most practitioners to limit strictly the number of times they use semen from the same donor.

Probably the most controversial question surrounding AID today is whether the child should be told of his origins. It is believed that most children are not told: the reasons usually given are the difficulty of explaining the position to a young child with resulting increased emotional trauma if he were to be told later, the impossibility of being able to satisfy his curiosity about the identity of his father, and the danger of his becoming the subject of scorn amongst his peers. A more powerful reason in many cases is undoubtedly the desire to keep secret what the husband regards as the stigma of his sterility. Two main arguments are marshalled on the other side. First, it is said that the child has a 'right to know'. This begs the question: why does he have this right and how far does it extend? Would he - and, more particularly, should he - be told if he was the result of a contraceptive failure or of the wife's adultery of which the husband himself was ignorant? The second and more compelling argument is that the deception may undermine the mutual trust on which the structure of the family is based: the child may sense the existence of a secret and there is a real danger that he may discover the truth at a later date either accidentally or as the result of a malicious disclosure on the breakdown of the marriage. 'Truth is violated; credibility is undermined' (Ciba Foundation 1973:48). The problem is compounded by the difficulty of keeping medical records confidential. It is agreed on all sides that in order to put his own mind at rest the child should be told if AID was used because of the danger of the husband's passing on an inheritable disorder. In other cases the spouses are generally left to make their own decision. The position is scarcely satisfactory but secrecy is likely to surround AID until the public becomes better informed about the causes of male infertility and AID becomes a socially accepted practice.

THE NEED FOR COUNSELLING

The difficulties likely to follow if a child is conceived by AID are probably little known to the couple who seek it. This makes skilful counselling imperative. Not only should the practitioner satisfy himself as well as he can that they will be able to cope with the problems when they arise, but the couple should also be made aware of the legal consequences. This is a matter on which a doctor cannot expect to be expert; if he feels that the need for confidentiality makes it undesirable to send them to a lawyer, he should at least be able to give them a document setting out the legal consequences in simple language.

It is also arguable that a potential donor may need counselling before he decides to donate semen. If such a practice is common, it is not referred to in the literature. The donor too should be warned of his potential legal liability. In any event it should be made clear to him and he should be required to sign a consent form indicating that he fully understands the position.

Public ignorance is presumably the reason why AID has not attracted the demand for legal safeguards that surround adoption. This is a point we shall come back to later.

LEGAL LIABILITY OF MEDICAL PRACTITIONER

The doctor carrying out the insemination obviously owes the same duty to his patient to use all reasonable care as a medical practitioner owes to any patient. Thus he would be liable if the woman was injured by a negligent insertion of the syringe or if the resulting pregnancy caused injury to her health due to a pre-existing condition which a reasonably careful doctor would have discovered when examining the patient before performing AID.

The practitioner must also use reasonable care in selecting the donor. It has already been said that he should carry out a full medical examination and take a full medical history of his family. Failure to do so may result in failure to discover that the donor is a potential carrier of some hereditary disorder; if the child develops this disorder as a result and the exercise of reasonable care would have disclosed the danger, the doctor must be liable for his negligence. It should also be appreciated that if the practitioner is unable to take a history (for example, because the donor was adopted), this will not exonerate him. In these circumstances common prudence dictates that that donor should not have been used at all.

A similar duty of care exists to ensure that the semen used is in fact provided by the donor selected. To preserve anonymity and avoid embarrassment, some practitioners permit donors to leave the receptacle containing their semen unobserved at some point where it may later be picked up for use (Snowden and Mitchell 1981:69). The risk of confusion or even of deliberate substitution is greatly increased; if this occurs and, say, the semen of a white donor is used instead of that of a negro donor or vice versa, the practitioner will clearly be liable for failing to exercise reasonable care.

The duty of care is clearly owed to the woman inseminated. If a half-caste or defective child is born as a result of the doctor's negligence, he will be liable for damages for the mother's distress, particularly if it is obvious to all the world that her husband cannot be the father. There seems little doubt that he would also be liable for any additional expense due to the need to care for a disabled child. Whether he could be sued for the physical inconvenience and economic loss due to the pregnancy and birth is more problematical. The mother would have suffered this damage had the doctor not been negligent. It is arguable that she cannot claim compensation for it. It is even less likely that the doctor can be made liable for any further expense, in particular the maintenance of an unwanted child. It has been held that compensation under this last head cannot be recovered by a woman who bore a child after a negligent and unsuccessful operation for sterilization on the ground that it is contrary to public policy to declare a child unwanted by awarding damages for its birth (*Udale* v. *Bloomsbury Area Health Authority* [1983] 2 All ER 522) and the argument applies with equal force if a child is negligently conceived by AID.

It is readily foreseeable that the mother's husband will also suffer distress if, say, the child could not be his. Consequently a court would doubtless hold that the doctor owes a duty of care to him and that he can also recover for the resulting injury (see *McLoughlin* v. *O'Brian* [1983] 1 AC. 410). But as the authorities now stand, the doctor cannot be sued by the child himself. Liability to a child for prenatal injury is now governed by the Congenital Disabilities (Civil Liability) Act 1976 which provides that he can sue only if the defendant's act affected the mother's ability to have a normal healthy child or affected her during her pregnancy. Clearly her ability to have *a* normal child has not been affected since she may later have other normal children; likewise the act in question preceded her pregnancy. Furthermore, the child's complaint will be that he should not have been born at all, for if other semen had been used, a different child would have resulted: this is quite unlike the thalidomide cases where it was alleged that the development of a perfectly normal foetus was adversely affected by the drug. In *McKay* v. *Essex Health Authority* ([1982] QB 1166) the Court of Appeal held that the 1976 Act gave a child no cause of action for 'wrongful life'; had it done so, it would have been impossible to evaluate non-existence for the purpose of assessing damages. In this case an unsuccessful action was brought by a little girl who was born disabled as the result of undiagnosed rubella from which the mother suffered during the third month of her pregnancy; had it been disgnosed, she would have had an abortion. The argument must apply *a fortiori* if the child would never have been conceived at all.

Two practical difficulties stand in the way of a woman or her husband seeking damages for the doctor's negligence in selecting the donor or using the wrong semen. In the first place, they would have to prove that the abnormality was the result of negligence. This means that it must be due to the insemination, and while this could be substantiated if the child was coloured or affected by syphilis (when it would be easy to show that neither the mother nor her husband suffered from the disease), in a case of hereditary disorder it would be essential to rule out the possibility that the mother was the carrier. In many, perhaps most, cases this would probably be impossible. Even if it were possible, the plaintiff would still have to show that the doctor did not exercise reasonable care in failing to discover the danger of transmitting the disorder. The burden of proving negligence is upon the plaintiff and whilst, in an action against the doctor, the mother could force him to disclose the identity of the donor and produce the notes of any history he took, this may not indicate negligence. The donor himself could be called as a witness; while in some cases his evidence might show that the doctor had been negligent, in others a case might be made out only if the donor were to undergo a medical examination which he might very well refuse to do.

The second difficulty is that the symptoms of many hereditary disorders may not appear for many years after the child's birth. Whilst an action could still lie for a further period of three years (under sections 11(4)(b) and 14 of the Limitation Act 1980), the possibility of proving negligence after such a long delay may be remote.

Obviously the practitioner must explain all the risks inherent in the procedure to the mother and her husband and get them to sign a form indicating that they have given 'informed consent'. It should be noted, however, that any attempt to exempt the doctor from *liability for negligence* as a condition of performing AID is made absolutely void by section 2(1) of the Unfair Contract Terms Act 1977.

LEGAL LIABILITY OF THE DONOR

The donor may be equally liable to the mother and her husband if he was negligent in permitting his semen to be used. The question of his liability might arise if the doctor were sued because the latter could then be forced to disclose the donor's identity: indeed the doctor himself might wish to bring the donor in as a third party to the proceedings. If the doctor is not sued, however, the possibility of an action being brought against the donor by one of the spouses is remote because there would then be no way of discovering his identity. If an action were brought, the plaintiff would have to show not only that the donor knew facts which made the use of his semen dangerous but also that he should have appreciated that it should not be used. While a medical student should realize that he should not be a donor if, say, there is a history of epilepsy in his family, it does not follow that a layman would be expected to have this knowledge.

The donor's potential liability to maintain the child will be considered below.

STATUS OF THE CHILD

It has never been doubted that an AID child is the illegitimate child of the mother and the donor and cannot be the legitimate child of the mother's husband. We look only to genetic paternity and the AID child is therefore indistinguishable from the adulterine child for this purpose.

There is a presumption, however, that a child born to a married woman is the legitimate child of her husband. This could obviously be rebutted if it could be shown that the husband is completely sterile. But if he is merely subfertile, there must be doubt relating to paternity if he was having sexual intercourse with his wife at the time of the insemination. In that case the presumption of legitimacy could usually be rebutted only by a blood test ruling out the possibility of the husband's being the father.

If the mother is unmarried, the child must of course be illegitimate in any event. There is not even a presumption that it is the child of the man with whom she is cohabiting.

REGISTRATION OF AN AID CHILD'S BIRTH

By sections 1(2) and 2 of the Births and Deaths Registration Act 1953 the parents are under a duty to register a child's birth. If a child is illegitimate, the duty is cast on the mother alone and the father's name may not be entered on the register unless he consents or the mother has obtained an affiliation order against him (section 10 of the 1953 Act, as amended by section 27(1) of the Family Law Reform Act 1969 and section 93(1) of the Children Act 1975). Consequently if the child *cannot* be the husband's, the mother alone should register the birth and the father's name should not be entered. If the child could be the husband's (however remote the possibility), the presumption of legitimacy should operate in his favour and the husband is then properly named as the father.

In practice, the child is registered as the legitimate child of both spouses even though the husband could not be the father. If the mother and the man with whom she is cohabiting are not married, the child will normally be registered as the illegitimate child of both, in which case both must sign the register or the man must make a statutory declaration acknowledging paternity. If the person giving the information *knows* that the child cannot be the child of the man named as father, he or she will commit the criminal offence of wilfully giving false information to the registrar under section 4 of the Perjury Act 1911 (or of knowingly and wilfully making a false statement in a statutory declaration under section 5 of the Perjury Act).

Some practitioners advise the couple to register the child as the husband's (Sandler 1979:86). If the doctor knows that the husband is sterile, he himself is guilty of the offence of counselling the crime under section 8 of the Accessories and Abettors Act 1861. If he carries out AID knowing that any child conceived will be registered as the husband's but does not actually advise the couple to make a false statement, it is at least arguable that he is guilty of procuring the commission of the offence (Smith and Hogan 1983:126–9). In order to protect himself against possible criminal liability, he clearly ought to advise them *against* this course of action.

In practice, the chances of anyone being prosecuted are in most cases extremely remote. The prosecution must show beyond reasonable doubt first that the statement is false (in other words, that the husband or cohabitant is not the father) and second that it was made wilfully (that is, that the person making it knew that it was false). It is highly unlikely that evidence would be available to the prosecution to rebut the presumption of legitimacy or to prove that the cohabitant was not the father in the case of an unmarried mother. Even if it were, it might still not be possible to prove that this was known to the accused. The danger is that one of the parties might himself or herself give evidence indicating these facts in other proceedings (for example in relation to inheritance or custody of the child) which could be put in evidence as an admission in a subsequent criminal prosecution. It is unlikely that a judge would order the papers to be sent to the Director of Public Prosecutions but, if he did so, it is not improbable that a conviction would result.

CUSTODY OF AN AID CHILD

If the mother's marriage later breaks down, she will prima facie be entitled to the custody of the child as the mother of an illegitimate child (section 85(7) of the Children Act 1975). Her husband will be able to claim custody or access, however, either in proceedings for divorce or judicial separation under section 42 of the Matrimonial Causes Act 1973 or in a magistrates' court under section 8 of the

Domestic Proceedings and Magistrates' Courts Act 1978, provided that in each case he has treated the child as a child of the family. This of course will normally be the case although it should be noted that, if the spouses separate before the child's birth, he cannot claim custody under these provisions because it has been held that *treatment* involves behaviour towards a child in existence (see *A.* v. *A.*, [1974] Fam. 6) and a child cannot become a child of the family after the family has broken up (*Re M.* (1980), 10 Fam. Law 184).

Neither of these Acts applies if the mother is cohabiting with a man outside marriage. In such a case the cohabitant could claim care and control of the child or access to him only by making him a ward of court.

In theory the donor could claim custody or access as the father of an illegitimate child under section 9(1) of the Guardianship of Minors Act 1971. In practice, however, this is extremely unlikely because the donor will be ignorant of the existence of the child and, even if he were not, the chances of his obtaining an order in respect of a child with whom he has had no contact at all are negligible.

MAINTENANCE OF AN AID CHILD

The mother's husband will normally be bound to maintain the child. But if he can rebut the presumption of legitimacy and has never treated him as a child of the family, he cannot be obliged to maintain him at all, any more than can the wife's extra-martial cohabitant.

The wife can also claim maintenance (at least in theory) from the donor in affiliation proceedings. But as she would first have to establish his identity, her chances of success are very remote indeed.

In certain circumstances a claim for financial provision may also be made against the estate of a deceased person. Amongst those to whom the Inheritance (Provision for Family and Dependants) Act 1975 gives this right are a child (legitimate or illegitimate) of the deceased, a person whom the deceased treated as a child of the family, and any other person being maintained by the deceased immediately before his death. This means that the AID child could claim against the estate of his mother, the mother's husband, and (normally, at least) the man with whom the mother was living in a stable extra-marital relationship. He could also in theory claim against the donor's estate.

INHERITANCE AND OTHER CLAIMS TO PROPERTY

So long as the child can rely on the presumption of legitimacy, he can claim property like any other legitimate child. If he is indisputably illegitimate, he can still claim on his mother's intestacy and can also claim any other property as her child. He cannot, however, claim as her *legitimate* child (if that were relevant) nor can he claim on her husband's intestacy or in any capacity as his child. In theory he could also claim on the donor's intestacy or as his child although, as we have seen, such claims are of little practical importance. If the child were to die intestate, his estate would pass to his mother and (in theory) the donor; his mother's husband could claim nothing at all.

It will immediately be apparent that, if the spouses pass an AID child off as their own, claims may be made by him or on his behalf as though he were their legitimate child. This in turn could give rise to criminal liability for obtaining property by deception under section 15 of the Theft Act 1968. This offence is committed if by any deception a person dishonestly obtains property belonging to another with the intention of permanently depriving the other of it, and 'obtains' includes obtaining for another or enabling another to obtain or retain. Thus the mother's husband may be guilty if, for example, he deliberately claims property left in his father's will 'to my grandchildren' on behalf of an AID child, for by stating that the child is his own he is making a wilfully untrue statement with the intention that the child should obtain property as a result. On the other hand, if he believes that the child is legally regarded as his own and is therefore entitled to the property, the husband will commit no offence because he does not act dishonestly. For the same reason if the child claims the property in ignorance of the fact that he is an AID child, he cannot be convicted, although he will be bound to restore the property if the facts come to light.

What is uncertain is whether an offence is committed by spouses who stand by and permit another to transfer property to the child in reliance on a statement made many years earlier that he is their child (which is the more likely state of affairs). In certain circumstances a person is considered to make a statement continuously so that he can be convicted of dishonestly obtaining (see *Ray* v. *Sempers* [1974] AC 370), but if the spouses held the child out as theirs many years earlier with no intention of enabling him to acquire property, a court might well hold that they have not dishonestly enabled him to obtain the property by deception. The point, however, must be regarded as open.

ARE CHANGES IN THE LAW NECESSARY?

Two possible changes should be considered.

The first is that an AID child should be treated as the legitimate child of the mother and her husband. (The question does not arise, of course, if the mother is not married to the accepting father.) A number of reasons can be advanced for this reform. The main one is that this would reflect the spouses' intention and what happens in practice. There would be no element of deception on registering the birth or claiming property and the potential criminal liability discussed above would disappear. Provided that the donor remained anonymous, there would be no risk of the child having two 'fathers'. The alternative way of regularizing the position would be for the mother and her husband to adopt the child, but this would run counter to the whole purpose of AID and would no doubt be ineffective in practice because the spouses would not use it. The removal of the status of illegitimacy is the solution recommended by the Law Commission in Part XII of their Report on Illegitimacy. It is of course central to this that the husband should consent to the insemination: there can be no question of foisting onto him another's child without his agreement. While it is desirable in any event for his consent to be formally obtained before the course of insemination begins, it would be unfair on the child to make his status depend on this, and consequently the Law Commission further recommends that consent should be assumed to have been given unless the contrary is proved (para. 12.17).

A number of objections can be raised to this proposal. The first is that, if legitimacy is based on the husband's freely and publicly treating the child as his own, the same status should be given to the wife's adulterine child if the husband is prepared to condone her adultery and hold the child out as his own. There is obviously a distinction between the two cases: most people probably regard adultery and AID as ethically different, and it is rare for the husband to consent to adultery in advance. It must be admitted, however, that this distinction is a fine one. The second objection is that, unless some note were to be placed in the register of births, the genetic basis of the register would disappear. The Law Commission rejected the suggestion of annotation because they felt that any such requirement would again be ignored and the child would continue to be registered as the biological child of the husband as at present. An acceptable compromise might be to alter the register so that the man is described as 'father or accepting father'. Finally, it could be argued that by changing the law in this way Parliament would be conniving at deception of those whose claims to property are reduced or defeated by the child's being treated as legitimate. The question really is how far intestate succession and other claims to property depending on relationship should be based today on social parentage rather than blood parentage. Whichever way the answer goes, it is difficult to justify special treatment for AID children: either the same rule should be applied to all children treated as the husband's or it should not be applied at all.

On balance, however, the Law Commission's proposals are probably the better. It would legitimize the current practice and thus remove one cause for feelings of guilt which the spouses may harbour. It also reflects the views of the majority who commented on the Law Commission's earlier Working Paper on the subject (Law Commission, para. 12.8).

The second possible change in the law would be to limit the practice of AID to certain registered practitioners. The reason for this is to try to ensure that only suitable spouses and donors are selected, that treatment is given in proper circumstances, and that all parties receive necessary counselling. Two difficulties stand in the way. The first is that, in 1960 at least, the medical profession itself was opposed to restricting AID to approved doctors (HMSO 1960: para. 246); it is of course possible that the profession generally is now alive to the problems and would welcome such a restriction. The second difficulty is that it is so easy to carry out AID - the woman can in fact perform the operation herself - that any restriction might open the door to 'back-street inseminations' akin to the 'back-street abortions' before the passing of the Abortion Act. Even if evasion were easy, however, it is still the function of the law to establish the norm whenever this is socially desirable, and there is a very strong case for having a register of AID practitioners. In a number of states in the USA (for example New York and California) legislation has been passed providing that a child born to a married woman by artificial insemination *performed by a person duly authorized to practise medicine* with the consent of her husband shall be deemed to be the spouses' legitimate child. Such a condition would give an incentive to have the treatment so performed and might be an effective and acceptable compromise if adopted in this country.

In Vitro Fertilization and Embryo Replacement (IVF and ER)

IVF may be carried out if a woman produces fertile ova and is capable of carrying a child but her ova fail to reach her uterus, usually because of occlusion of the Fallopian tubes. Ova are removed and fertilized with the father's semen; twenty-four hours or so later the resulting embryo is then replaced in the mother's uterus. In order to increase the chances of success, the practitioner usually brings about hyperstimulation of the ovaries artificially so that a number of ova are produced; two or three are replaced after fertilization. Although the success rate is still substantially less than 20 per cent, there is a calculable risk that IVF will produce twins or even triplets.

It will be seen that, if the ovum is fertilized with the mother's husband's semen, the child will be the spouses' natural and legitimate child: legally the position is indistinguishable from that of a child produced by AIH. The relationship of the parents to the practitioner is more complex, however, and in some respects resembles rather that which exists in AID. The doctor takes an active part in bringing about the conception of a child and much of what is said above about the social and medical implications of AID applies to IVF. In particular the practitioner must try to ensure that the couple are suitable; skilful counselling is equally necessary; and only married women or those living in a stable heterosexual relationship will normally be fertilized. At present there is no evidence that the proportion of abnormal children born after IVF and ER is any greater than that following normal conception, but spouses must be warned that there can be no guarantee that the procedure will not affect the child. Hyperstimulation of the ovaries also carries a slight risk to the mother and multiple pregnancies carry a higher risk for both mother and children. A difficult ethical problem is also created by the possibility that more ova will be fertilized than needed. Embryos, like semen, may be frozen and stored; the parties may wish the surplus to be kept for further ER; if not, to what extent and in what circumstances is it permissible to use them for the purposes of medical research?

It will thus be seen that, in addition to exercising the degree of care expected of a competent practitioner, it is essential for the doctor to ensure that the risks involved are fully explained to the parties and that they give 'informed consent' not only to the operation but also to the use and destruction of surplus embryos (Royal College of Obstetricians and Gynaecologists 1983: parts 1–4).

In Vitro Fertilization and Embryo Transfer (IVF and ET)

Embryo replacement can be practised only if the mother produces ova and is capable of carrying a child. Obviously it cannot be used if she does not produce fertile ova at all. In such a case the parties may request that one or more ova taken from another woman (the donor) be fertilized *in vitro* with the husband's semen and then implanted in the wife (the recipient) so that she will carry the child. Because of the ethical problems involved some doctors are said to be awaiting the report of the Warnock Committee before carrying out this operation: the present discussion is based on the assumption that the practice may shortly become common.

It is of course the precise counterpart of AID and good medical practice requires the same criteria to be adopted. Again reference should be made to the section above where they are discussed. The more important points are: IVF and ET should normally be carried out only if the recipient is married or living in a stable heterosexual relationship; care must be taken over the selection of the recipient and her husband and of the donor; the latter's anonymity should be preserved; the problem of disclosing the nature of the child's conception must be faced; and all those involved should be carefully counselled. As in AID, the practitioner must exercise all due care in selecting the donor and performing the operation; he should also obtain the 'informed consent' of both spouses and donor to the risks involved and to the future use of surplus embryos.

STATUS OF CHILDREN CONCEIVED BY IVF AND ET

The problem is the converse of that occurring with AID. In ET the child's father is known: the difficult question is whether the donor or the recipient is to be regarded in law as his mother. One's immediate reaction may be to say the donor by analogy with AID. If this is so, a number of startling results follow.

First, the register of births should indicate that the child is illegitimate with no known mother. As the name of the father of an illegitimate child can be registered only with the mother's consent, his name could not appear either. If either spouse registered the child as the legitimate child of both (or as the child of the recipient and her cohabitant), an offence would be committed under the Perjury Act as it would be if an AID child were so registered.

Second, the right to the child's custody would prima facie vest in the donor as his mother and she would be under a duty to maintain him. The corresponding right and duty of the recipient and her husband would arise from their having treated him as a child of the family. If the recipient were not married, the only way in which she could claim care and control or access would be by applying to have the child made a ward of court.

Third, the child could claim no property as the recipient's child, whether on intestacy or under any will or settlement. If the spouses were to make such a claim on his behalf, they would be criminally liable for dishonestly obtaining property by deception as *mutatis mutandis* the parents of an AID child. Similarly the child would have no claim as his father's legitimate child, although in theory he could claim as the donor's illegitimate child.

Most people would find these conclusions so bizarre, if not repellent, as to force them to the conclusion that the law must regard the recipient as the mother. This accords with common sense and reflects the spouses' own intentions and what will happen in practice; as in AID the alternative solution will lead to deception, the commission of one or more criminal offences, and an added burden of guilt. The analogy with AID also breaks down because, whereas the father's part in the process of procreation ceases on insemination at the latest, there must be a bearing mother for the embryo to develop into a viable child.

In the absence of authority, it is believed that an English court is likely to hold that the recipient is to be deemed to be the child's mother. But it must be emphasized that the position is by no means clear and it can be argued with some force that the child has more in common with the genetic than the bearing mother. If he were registered as the recipient's child, the genetic basis of the registration of births would be further undermined; moreover (in the absence of legislation) he could not marry a daughter of the recipient by a different father (with whom he has no genes in common) but could lawfully marry a daughter of the donor (who would be his genetic half-sister). The chances of unwitting incest are probably as slim as they are with AID, and the balance of advantages is no doubt in favour of making the bearing mother the lawful mother. But legislation is clearly needed to clarify the position.

THE CONTROL OF IVF

Just as we have discussed whether the practice of AID should be confined to certain authorized doctors, we must also consider whether IVF should be legally controlled in any way. At the moment the number of practitioners is so small that the question does not arise but it should be faced before it becomes of practical importance. There is no doubt in the writer's mind that control is necessary. All the reasons for exercising control in AID apply; in addition the operation requires great skill, the threat of damage to the embryo is possibly graver, and the ethical problems resulting from the production of surplus embryos are likely to give rise to public concern. A possible solution is that put forward by the Royal College of Obstetricians and Gynaecologists: they recommend that a statutory body should be established to advise the Secretaries of State who should have power to register directors of institutions where IVF is carried out, to license and inspect premises on which they operate, and to forbid IVF to be carried out except under the direction of registered persons in licensed premises (RCOG 1983: para. 14.3).

Surrogate bearing mothers

In vitro fertilization followed by embryo replacement or embryo transfer can obviously be used only if the recipient is capable of carrying a child. If this is impossible owing, for example, to some structural defect or danger of toxaemia, an attempt may be made to use a 'surrogate bearing mother'. If a woman produces viable ova, these can be removed as in ET; they may then be fertilized with her husband's semen *in vitro,* and the resultant embryo may then be implanted in the host mother. (The procedure could also be adopted if the donor was capable of carrying a child but wished to be spared the discomfort and handicap of pregnancy.) If she can neither produce viable ova nor carry a child, the surrogate mother can be artificially inseminated with the sterile woman's husband's semen. In either case the host mother undertakes to hand the child over to the father and his wife at birth and it is usually further agreed that she will be paid for carrying it. This payment may be deferred and made expressly conditional upon her surrendering the child.

If the child is conceived as a result of IVF and ET, the first question that arises again is which of the two women involved is to be regarded in law as the child's mother. For the reasons given in the last section it is believed that this is the host mother in whom the embryo is implanted. This means that the child will be the illegitimate child of her and the father. The next point to note is that, whether the child was conceived by IVF and ET or by AID, the agreement has no legal validity. By section 1(2) of the Guardianship Act 1973 'an agreement for a man or woman to give up in whole or in part in relation to a child of his or hers the rights and authority [relating to the child's legal custody or upbringing] shall be unenforceable' unless entered into between a husband and wife to operate during their separation. This provision merely restates the common law rule by which all such agreements were void as contrary to public policy (*Humphrys* v. *Polak* [1901] 2 KB 385). It follows from this that the mother could not recover the payment promised even if she handed the child over (*Vansittart* v *Vansittart* (1858) 2 De G & J 249; *Walrond* v. *Walrond* (1858) John 18).

If the host mother decides to go back on the agreement and to retain the child, the father could claim custody, as could the genetic mother if the conclusion stated above is wrong and she is held to be the legal mother. Alternatively the father and his wife (whether or not she was the genetic mother) could apply for care and control by making the child a ward of court. Whatever procedure is followed, however, it is inconceivable that a court would award the custody of a newly born child to them save in the most exceptional circumstances. In the only English case known to the writer, the woman with whom the father was living was unable to have any more children. He therefore agreed to pay the defendant £3,000 to have his child which would be conceived by AID and then be brought up by him and his cohabitant. The mother changed her mind during the pregnancy and refused to hand the child over after it was born. The father then sought care and control, or alternatively access, in wardship proceedings. The Court of Appeal refused to give him either on the ground that no good could come from maintaining this artificial and painful tie ([1979] *CLY, unreported case* 176). The result could have been no different if the cohabitant had been the genetic mother: her claim could be no greater than the father of an AID child.

It is clear that arrangements of this sort should never be entered into at all. They are likely to produce nothing but harm: anxiety suffered by the father and his wife during the mother's pregnancy in case she should change her mind, coupled with emotional stress to the mother if she gives up the child and to the husband and his wife if she does not. The Royal College of Obstetricians and Gynaecologists firmly give it as their view that it is unethical to implant embryos conceived by IVF into surrogate mothers (RCOG 1983: para. 716). If the proposed system of licensing and inspecting premises where IVF is carried out were to be accepted by Parliament, failure to observe this limitation might be a ground for withdrawing a licence.

Conclusions

It will be seen that the law needs changing, or at least clarifying, in a number of respects and it is to be hoped that the Warnock Committee will seize the opportunity to make appropriate recommendations. The areas in which legal change may be desirable can be grouped broadly under two heads.

The first relates to the status of the child conceived as a result of AID or IVF and ET. It has already been noted that the Law Commission has recommended that the AID child should be deemed to be the legitimate child of his mother and her husband and it is urged that this recommendation should be implemented provided that the insemination is carried out by a registered medical practitioner. At the same time it is necessary to consider the status of a child born as the result of a widow's insemination by her late husband's semen. In the case of ET it is necessary to resolve the question whether the woman providing the ovum or the woman carrying the child is to be regarded in law as the mother. For the reasons advanced earlier, it is urged that legislation should put the latter's maternity beyond doubt.

The second matter demanding the intervention of Parliament is the control of IVF and ideally of AID as well. The social problems presented by both and the ethical problems presented particularly by IVF are too great to be left to haphazard and possibly arbitrary solution. The skilled counselling and experienced judgment required in each are, in the writer's opinion, sufficient justification to subject them both to the same careful scrutiny as adoption.

References

Ciba Foundation Symposium (1973) *Law and Ethics of A.I.D. and Embryo Transfer.* Amsterdam: Excerpta Medica.

HMSO (1960) *Report of the Departmental Committee on Human Artificial Insemination* (The Feversham Report) Cmnd 1105. London: HMSO.

Kerr, M.G. and Rogers, C. (1975) Donor Insemination. *Journal of Medical Ethics* 1(1):30–3.

Law Commission (1982) *Family Law: Illegitimacy* (Law Com. No. 118). London: HMSO.

Palmer, N.E. (1979) *Bailment.* Sydney: Law Book Co.

Royal College of Obstetricians and Gynaecologists (1983) *Report of the RCOG Ethics Committee on In Vitro Fertilisation and Embryo Replacement or Transfer.* London: RCOG.

Sandler, B. (1979) Adoption and Artificial Insemination by Donor. In S. Wolkind (ed.) *Medical Aspects of Adoption and Foster Care.* London: William Heinemann Medical Books.

Smith, J.C. and Hogan, T.B. (1983) *Criminal Law* (5th edn). London: Butterworths.

Snowden, R. and Mitchell, G.C. (1981) *The Artificial Family.* London: George Allen & Unwin.

12 The role of the court in the adoption process

HUGH K. BEVAN

The primary role of adoption in English law contrasts markedly with that of its counterparts in civil law countries. Whereas in the latter the emphasis has been proprietary - that is, adoption has been seen as a method of securing succession - in English law it has always been personal and social. Indeed, it was not until the Adoption of Children Act 1949 that particular attention was paid to rights of succession. However, any suggestion that foreign adoption laws are more complex because of their strong proprietary element does not bear examination. On the contrary, the strong social content of the English law largely accounts for its complexity, and the continuing change of emphasis in the social functions of adoption has been a major factor.

The object of the earliest Act, the Adoption of Children Act 1926, was to regularize the numerous *de facto* adoptions of orphans and illegitimate children that took place in the aftermath of World War I, and so to give the child and his adopters the security of a permanent relationship. With that purpose fulfilled, the shift of emphasis was towards the dual function of providing a stable home for the unwanted child, especially the illegitimate child, of the 'depression' years of the late 1920s and 1930s and of meeting the needs of the childless couple. The resultant emergence of adoption societies led to their compulsory registration and regulation through the Adoption of Children (Regulation) Act 1939. At the outbreak of World War II adoption was therefore still very largely seen as the Tomlin Committee had seen it in 1925, namely, as 'a legal method of creating between a child and one who is not the natural parent of the child an artificial family relationship analogous to that of parent and child' (HMSO 1925). Since 1945 one of the most significant features has, of course, been the marked increase in adoptions by the birth parent, so much so that immediately prior to the Children Act 1975 over half the annual adoptions were parental. This change first related to the mother of the illegitimate child who saw adoption by her of her own child as a means of escaping the social stigma of illegitimacy and, less importantly, of improving the legal relationship between them. But it was the high incidence of divorce in the 1950s and 1960s, of remarriage and subsequent adoption by the birth parent and step-parent that largely explains the substantial increase.

The legislative response, through the Children Act, to this increase, though to some extent obscure, has resulted in a sharp decline in the number of adoptions. Apart from the restrictions imposed by the Act on step-parent adoptions, there are other factors which suggest that the number of adoption applications may well continue to fall. Although local authorities may constantly be looking for suitable prospective adopters for children in their care, especially for handicapped and coloured children, there is apparently greater reluctance on the part of foster parents to seek adoption (Samuels 1982) and, where this is so, the local authority is not going to press for adoption, particularly if it faces parental opposition. This trend will accelerate when the provisions of the Children Act 1975 for custodianship come into operation, partly because long-term foster parents will see that custodianship rather than adoption may, in their particular circumstances, have advantages for them - for instance where they can realistically expect the court in granting them a custodianship order to order the birth parent to provide maintenance for the child (S. 34) - and partly because the court when hearing an application for an adoption order will be under a duty to consider the suitability of making instead a custodianship order (S. 37).

It is not, however, to be expected that the fall in the number of adoption applications will necessarily lead to a corresponding reduction in the role of the court. On the contrary, a number of factors militate against that possibility. One has just been indicated. The introduction of custodianship as an alternative to adoption is likely to produce initial problems of construction of some of the relevant complicated provisions. Moreover, the power of the court on making a custodianship order, or while such an order is in force, to make accompanying orders relating to access and maintenance, particularly by the mother or father, will involve investigations and issues which do not arise where an adoption order is made.[1] More importantly, the very nature of the adoption process, with its consequent transfer of the rights and duties of the birth parent to the adoptive parent, is such that the court will always have a key function to perform in it. The sensitivity of modern society to the rights of the individual has enhanced that function. Within the context of parental rights that sensitivity has recently been demonstrated by the reaction against the power vested in a local authority by section 3 of the Child Care Act 1980 to pass a resolution vesting in itself the parental rights and duties. The Child Care Bill, sponsored by David Alton MP, sought to abolish the statutory power to pass resolutions and substitute a judicial process requiring the local authority to bring the parent before the juvenile court for it to determine whether one of the conditions required by section 3 has been satisfied and whether the vesting of the rights in the local authority is in the child's best interests.[2] This direct substitution of a judicial process would be a marked improvement on the present procedure, which places the initial burden on the parent to object to the resolution and then on the local authority to try to obtain the court's confirmation (Child Care Act 1980). Whether because of the parent's diffidence or ignorance of his rights, the fact remains that in very few cases are objections made. Nevertheless, there is some right of challenge. Moreover, the parent has the right at any later date himself to apply to the juvenile court for the resolution to be terminated. All this contrasts strongly with adoption. The irrevocable nature of an adoption order[3] makes the case for a judicial process all the stronger.

If this last comment is significant for the birth parent, it is profound for the child. But, from his point of view, how is the judicial process in adoption to be seen? As the furtherance and protection of his rights or the securing of his welfare? Some of the pressures in the 1970s to grant the child wider rights of self-determination[4] may be seen as a 'propagandist exercise' (Eekelaar 1973) but there are certainly firm indications of a movement to conceptualize children's rights. References to the European Commission on Human Rights and the European Court of Human Rights of such matters as illegitimacy, rights of education, and corporal punishment illustrate the trend. Again, the Children's Legal Centre, established in 1979 as a product of the International Year of the Child, is focusing closer attention on the child as an individual under the law and on the need to provide him with new legal remedies. Nevertheless, the task of conceptualizing is formidable, and there is much to be said for a robust pragmatism which emphasizes the needs of the child and the responsibilities of the adult. That, it is suggested, has increasingly been the approach of English law to adoption. Nowhere is this better exemplified than in the court's power to dispense with the parent's agreement to adoption where it is being unreasonably withheld.

One of the inadequacies of the law prior to the Children Act 1975 was its failure to provide positive guidance on the weight to be given to the child's welfare when reaching decisions which might ultimately lead to his adoption. The Adoption Act 1958 merely stated that the court had to be satisified that the adoption would be for the welfare of the child. This inadequacy in particular compelled the courts to find a solution where the point at issue was the unreasonable withholding of parental agreement. The problem demonstrates the impossibility of maintaining a fair balance between parental rights and children's welfare. The earlier judicial solution (*Hitchcock* v. *W.B. and FEB*) emphasized the former by holding that, since the effect of an adoption order is to terminate the parent's rights, it was prima facie reasonable to withhold agreement. Attention was directed primarily to the conduct and attitude of the parent, and the court had to be satisfied that in some way he had been culpable. In *Re L (an infant)*, decided in 1962, the Court of Appeal moved to an objective test for determining whether the particular parent's attitude was reasonable. What would a reasonable parent do in the circumstances? That principle was affirmed and taken further by the House of Lords in 1970 in *Re W* and *O'Connor* v. *A & B*. Those decisions mark a distinct shift of emphasis towards the child's welfare. In applying the objective test his welfare is not the sole consideration, but it is of great importance, for a reasonable parent will give great weight to it. He will take account not merely of the short-term prospects of the child but also the long term. Moreover, because of the weight to be given to the child's welfare, a parent may be acting unreasonably even if there is no element of culpability or of reprehensible conduct in his decision to withhold agreement.

The Children Act 1975 now provides firmer guidance than the Adoption Act 1958 did in the weight to be given to the child's welfare in adoption cases. Section 3 provides that 'in reaching any decision relating to the adoption of a child, a court or adoption agency shall have regard to all the circumstances, first consideration being given to the need to safeguard and promote the welfare of the child throughout his childhood.' However, in *Re P* it was held that the section does not apply to unreasonably withholding agreement, since that is a decision of the parent, not of the court or adoption agency. The decision is open to criticism (Bevan and Parry 1978), but in any event it creates no practical distinction because the effect of the House of Lords decisions in *Re W* and *O'Connor* v. *A & B* is equally to make the child's welfare first but not paramount. What is of practical significance is the way in which those decisions have been applied over the past decade. The courts have paid increasing attention to the child's welfare and, as has recently been suggested (Sachs 1983), the time may well have come for acceptance of the same principle as governs custody, guardianship, and wardship matters, namely, that the child's welfare is first and paramount. As Ormrod has indicated on more than one occasion,[5] the courts are moving in that direction. The current judicial approach has recently been well summarized (Hayes and Williams 1982).

Nowadays it appears that a court is liable to dispense with a mother's agreement although she has not been culpable and although only a relatively short time has elapsed since her child was placed with the adopters, in a case where she is poor, or very young, where she has had a number of 'boy-friends', where she has little family support, and where her background and mode of life are likely to lead her into further 'trouble'. The baby's position is the court's main concern, and only when it is sure that the child will be well cared for will the court allow the mother to withhold her agreement to the adoption. That, it is submitted, is very close to acceptance of the principle of the paramountcy of the child's welfare

Whatever is or should be the position with regard to unreasonably withholding agreement, it should be remembered that only in about 2 per cent of adoption applications by non-relatives is there a request to dispense with agreement (Grey and Blunden 1971). Section 3 is open to a basic objection. It ignores two facts: (1) that the vast majority of adoption cases do not involve a conflict of interests; (2) that, unlike disputes over custody, guardianship, or wardship, adoption is a protracted process, of which the judicial is only a part. The process calls for the application of different standards at different stages. At the first, before placement, the whole emphasis of the adoption agency's role should be on ensuring that the rights of the birth parent are properly safeguarded. Its subsequent function, once the parent agrees to placement, should be to secure the child's best interests by choosing and monitoring a suitable placement. The court should have the same purpose, both in the investigations through the guardian ad litem and at the subsequent hearing of the adoption application. Under the present law the agency, before placement, must see that the parent is given a memorandum explaining in ordinary language the effect of adoption on his parental rights and calling attention to the process which culminates in the adoption order and to the statutory provisions relating to parental agreement. The parent must sign a certificate to the effect that he has read and understood the memorandum. Although any written agreement to adoption given at the time does not strictly prevent the parent from changing his mind at any time up to the hearing (unless the court dispenses with his agreement) the Court of Appeal has more than once stressed that once the formal, written agreement has been given it becomes progressively more difficult for the parent to show that his change of mind is reasonable.[6] All the more reason, therefore, that the memorandum should explicitly point out the possible effect of the passage of time. Similarly, when the alternative procedure of freeing for adoption comes into operation, the agency ought to have firm responsibilities to the birth parent to see that he fully understands the effect of consenting to the child being freed for adoption. Regrettably the Children Act 1975 fails specifically to impose these obligations on agencies. The omission may be repaired when the appointment of reporting officers, for which the Act provides (sec. 20), is introduced, but that will depend on the duties to be entrusted to these new functionaries. Here, too, the Act is unhelpful, for it fails to define the scope of their role in the adoption process. It refers only to their responsibility of witnessing agreements to adoption; it does not even mention witnessing consents to an application by an adoption agency for an order freeing for adoption. Instead, it leaves it to future Rules to prescribe other detailed functions. It must in particular be hoped that the reporting officer will be given specific advisory functions, requiring him to ensure that the parent fully understands what adoption or freeing for adoption involves. Such functions can, however, only be effectively discharged if his appointment is made obligatory before, or on receipt of, the application for adoption or freeing for adoption.

So far the role of the court in adoption has largely been related to aspects of the substantive law. It is, however, in jurisdictional and procedural matters that the main sources of criticism lie. These stem largely from the fact that the High Court, county courts, and magistrates' courts have, with certain complicated exceptions, concurrent jurisdiction. The wider the variety of courts the more likely the variations in interpretation and administration of the law, a state of affairs which is not helped by having three separate sets of Adoption Rules, which are not uniform. The existence of separate systems of courts can also sometimes cause delays, for example, where the father of an illegitimate child has already instituted custody proceedings in, say, a magistrates' court and then adoption proceedings are brought, say, in a county court. Apart from a few cases heard annually in the High Court, over 80 per cent are brought in county courts and the remainder in magistrates' courts. The choice between a county court and a magistrates' court is sometimes determined, on the advice of the adoption agency, by knowledge of the particular Bench and its attitude to certain kinds of adoptions.

The kinds of problems to which this diversity of systems can give rise have been forcibly illustrated in connection with step-parent adoptions. As part of its policy to reduce such adoptions following divorce, the Children Act 1975 requires the court on an adoption application by the step-parent, whether jointly with his spouse or alone, to dismiss the application if it considers that the matter would be better dealt with under section 42 of the Matrimonial Causes Act 1973, that is, by way of a custody order in the divorce court (Children Act 1975 ss.10(3) and 11(4)). Taking the usual case of a joint application by the stepfather and the birth mother, the question is whether to grant them joint adoption or require them to turn to the divorce court for joint custody. In *Re S (infants) (Adoption by Parent)* the Court of Appeal stated that the effect of the Act was to ask: 'Will adoption safeguard and promote the welfare of the child better than either the existing arrangements or a joint custody order under Section 42?' Since in cases of this kind the child will already have acquired all the material advantages that adoption could provide, 'the advantages of adoption will have to be found, if at all, in the intangible results which might flow from it'. On this test, in the majority of cases the emphasis lies firmly against making adoption orders. However, the early response of many courts to the new law appears to have been variable. One outcome was the sharp drop in applications to magistrates' courts, no doubt the result partly of a DHSS circular discouraging step-parent adoptions and partly of social workers, as guardians ad litem, and justices' clerks referring applicants to county courts (Latham 1982). But within the county courts there does not appear to have been a uniform pattern, even allowing for judicial discretion. After *Re S* some county courts seemed prepared readily to dismiss applications, but there is no evidence of a general attitude of rejection. One of the causes for diversity and uncertainty was the fact that insufficient guidance was given in advance to the courts. This is especially so in regard to the county courts. The difficulties that can arise where one Government Department (in this case the DHSS) is responsible for new legislation and others for court administration - that is, the Lord Chancellor's Department and, for magistrates' courts also, the Home Office - have been highlighted by the new step-parent adoption law. DHSS gave guidance by way of circulars over the new provisions to Social Services Departments, but these circulars were not, it seems, officially sent to county courts and their clerks. Moreover, an amendment was made to the Adoption

Rules of the High Court, county courts, and magistrates' courts, which provides that if it appears that the court may be required to dismiss the adoption application, then the application should not be proceeded with unless the court gives directions as to the further conduct of the application. Unfortunately, the amendment did not specify the procedure to be adopted on the preliminary examination, with the apparent result that different instructions were given by judges. Much has still to emerge about the administration of this area of adoption law. There is an obvious need for continual monitoring of it,[7] especially since the Court of Appeal in *Re D (Minors) (Adoption by Step-parent)* appears to have shifted from its position in *Re S* and no longer requires the court to find that adoption would itself be better than a custody order. But the lessons to be learned may in the long run have wider implications, for the recent experience over step-parent adoptions provides further evidence of the need for a unitary system of family courts.

Pessimism over the possibility of such a system ever being introduced has been slightly lifted by the publication by the Lord Chancellor's Department (in January 1983) of a Consultation Paper on the possible reorganization of the Family Jurisdiction of the High Court and County Courts, including adoption, with a view to closer integration and possibly a new court similar to the Crown Court in criminal cases. The Paper does not cover the domestic jurisdiction of magistrates' courts and there can be little doubt that any attempt to abolish that jurisdiction with a view to the ultimate creation of a family court system would be strongly resisted in some quarters. One is reminded of the criticism generated, especially among magistrates, by the White Paper, *The Child, The Family, and The Young Offender* (HMSO 1965), in its proposal to abolish juvenile courts and replace them with 'family councils' and 'family courts'. But what of the adoption jurisdiction of magistrates' courts? As a spirited defender of their jurisdiction has recently pointed out (Latham 1982), they have in particular the advantages of being less expensive than the county court, and have 'the proved tradition [of being] a tribunal for the unrepresented applicant'. Nevertheless, it must seriously be questioned whether, particularly in the light of the sharp drop in the number of adoption orders made by those courts, the retention of their adoption jurisdiction is any longer needed, and whether it would not be better for the jurisdiction to be absorbed by the county courts. Indeed, if the number of adoption applications has reached a steady state, there is much to be said for concentrating the jurisdiction among a certain number of the judges. That possibility would be strengthened if the proposals outlined in the above Consultation Paper were implemented.

Notes

1 In exceptional circumstances an order granting access to a mother or father may be made when adoption is ordered; see *Re J (Adoption Order: Conditions),* (1973) Fam. 106; (1973) 2 All E.R. 410; *Re S (a minor) (Adoption Order: Access),* (1976) Fam. 1; 1975) 1 All E.R. 109.

2 The Bill would have given the court power to make a care order or a supervision order. For criticism of this 'attempt to equate s.3 resolutions with care orders' see Gallagher, *Parental Rights Resolutions, Natural Justice and the Child Care Bill 1982,* (1983) 13 Fam. Law 54.

3 There is power to revoke in the exceptional case where the order was made in favour of the mother or father alone and the child is subsequently legitimated by the marriage of his parents; Adoption Act 1958, s.26 (as amended).

4 See, for example, the discussion papers of the National Council for Civil Liberties, *Children Have Rights* (No. 5) and *Rights of Children,* and the Draft Charter of Children's Rights prepared by the Advisory Centre for Education, (1971) *Where* p. 56.

5 *Rett* (1977) 2 All E.R. 339: *Re H* (1980) Adoption and Fostering 59; *Re W* (1981) Adoption and Fostering 60.

6 See the cases cited above in n.5.

7 One such research project has already been completed by Judith Masson and Daphne Norbury (1982). It was prepared for DHSS under the auspices of British Agencies for Adoption and Fostering.

References

Advisory Centre for Education (1971) *Where.*

Bevan, H.K. and Parry, M.L. (1978) *The Children Act 1945.* London: Butterworths.

Eekelaar, J. (1973) What are Parental Rights? *Law Quarterly Review* 89:210.

Gallagher, P. (1983) *Parental Rights Resolutions, Natural Justice, and the Child Care Bill.* 13 Fam. Law 54.

Grey, E. and Blunden, R.M. (1971) *A Survey of Adoption in Great Britain,* Home Office Research Study No. 10. London: HMSO.

Hayes, M. and Williams, C. (1982) *Adoption of Babies; Agreeing and Freeing.* 12 Fam. Law 233.

HMSO (1925) *First Report of the Child Adoption Committee* (The Tomlin Committee) Cmd 2401. London: HMSO.

_____ (1965) *The Child, the Family, and the Young Offender.* Cmnd 2742. London: HMSO.

Latham, C.T. (1982) *Adoptions: Jurisdiction and Practice.* 12 Fam. Law 204.

Masson, J. and Norbury, D. (1982) Step-parent Adoption. *Adoption and Fostering* 6(1) 7:10.

National Council for Civil Liberties (1967) *Rights of Children.*

_____ (1977) *Children Have Rights* (No. 5).

Sachs, C. (1983) *Adoption and Dispensing with Parental Agreement - when is agreement unreasonably withheld?* 13 Fam. Law 26.

Samuels, A. (1982) *Adoption: The Social, Professional, and Legal Trends.* 12 Fam. Law 186.

13 Subsidized adoption

MICHAEL D.A. FREEMAN

Subsidized adoption programmes are a relatively new child welfare option for children in need of long-term substitute care. It was not until the late 1950s that a formalized concept of subsidized adoption received serious attention. That was in the United States. In Britain the concept was barely discussed until the early 1970s. The 1958 Adoption Act had continued to ban the payment of any allowance to adopters by imposing a criminal sanction (s.50), and by requiring the court before making an adoption order to be satisfied that the adopter had not received or agreed to receive, and that no person had made or given or agreed to make or give to the adopter, 'any payment or other reward in consideration of the adoption except such as the court may sanction' (s.7(1)(c)).[1] The latter provision contains a loophole which Dr Barnardo's for one were able to exploit: subsidized adoption thus came in through the back door as proposals were put to courts to sanction and this was duly done.

But this practice is strictly peripheral to the main story. Until recently the whole idea of subsidizing adoption was frowned upon. It was felt that to pay adopters went against the grain. If adoptive families were to mirror birth families (and policies and practice until recently were geared towards ensuring this with 'matching' and similar notions), they should be treated as ordinary families were and should accordingly receive no more allowances for the upbringing and support of children they adopted than parents did for their own birth children. It was also argued by opponents of adoption subsidies that allowances increased dependence and this was incompatible with the independence from social work control that adoption was supposed to represent.

The backcloth to this opposition was a very different sort of adoption institution from that we have become used to today. Subsidized adoption became more easily acceptable as the character of adoption itself changed. With the availability of the contraceptive pill, a more liberalized abortion law (introduced in Britain by the Abortion Act 1967), and greater tolerance in a 'permissive' society of the unmarried mother, the supply of healthy white babies dried up. The peak year for adoptions was 1968 (for a good discussion of adoption patterns see Selman 1976). It also saw the highest number of adoptions of illegitimate children where neither adopter was a parent (14,641) but significantly the percentage of such adoptions was already falling (it had been 66 per cent in 1964 and was 59.4 per cent in 1968).[2] Adoptions of legitimate children where one or both adopters was a parent (step-parent adoptions) had already begun to increase by leaps and bounds. They had reached 2,000 for the first time in 1964 (2,291): by 1968 4,038 such orders were registered. In 1974 the total was to rise to 9,114. The tide was stemmed by section 10(3) of the 1975 Children Act but even in 1981 there were over 3,000 step-parent adoptions registered.[3]

It is clear that if adoption were to have continued merely as a service by which infertile couples were supplied with healthy, white babies the institution would be on its last legs. In the absence of profound and totally unexpected social changes there is no reason to believe that adoption would have survived into the next century. That it will do so is the result partly of the large number of divorces and consequent step-parent adoptions (which will continue despite the legislation referred to above; see Rawlings 1982) but preeminently because of a growing belief, supported by empirical data, that older children, children with special needs, black children, and children of mixed race can be adopted. The significance of this should not be underestimated. It means that for the first time content is being given to the idea that adoption is designed to meet the needs of deprived children, rather than those of infertile adults, that it is, in other words, a provision of child care. It also means, of course, that solutions to infertility must be sought elsewhere, in AID (Brandon and Warner 1977; Wadlington 1983), in *in vitro* fertilization (Brahams 1983; Robertson 1983; Harris 1983), and other techniques of genetic engineering, as well as in counselling. Increasing attention will be given to these techniques, but my concern here is with the way in which the change in the character of adoption has smoothed the path to the introduction of subsidized adoption. The idea of paying adopters still meets resistance but the concept is now acceptable to policy-makers. It is now here (the first schemes became operative in Britain in 1982) and can only grow and become a more pervasive part of the social work scene.

In this chapter I examine the case for subsidized adoption. I look at the American experience. I study and evaluate the early British schemes (eighteen were in operation at the date of writing) in the context of social, economic, and legal constraints. Finally, I look to the future and, in particular, to any changes in the law or practice which appear, in the light of my study, to be desirable.

The case for subsidized adoption

In one of the earliest articles written on the subject the case for subsidizing adoption is put in a nutshell: 'Children are our nation's most precious resource. It follows that public funding of adoptions for children who would otherwise be denied real family life is in the public interest' (Goldberg and Linde 1969:98). This statement must be qualified. Adoption is no panacea, nor is it the answer to the problems of all children in long-term care. Many would be better off reunited with their birth families. To ignore this is to engineer policies which may destroy a large number of underprivileged families. But there are many children in long-term care for whom adoption is the answer and whose adoption would be facilitated by financial assistance to prospective adoptive parents. That at root is the case for subsidized adoption.

This point could not, however, be reached until it was accepted that adoption was appropriate for older children. Research from Kadushin (1970), Jaffee and Fanshel (1970), both American studies, and Tizard (1977) shows that older children can be successfully adopted. More recently James has reported on the success of programmes for the adoption of older children. She concludes: 'It is now clear that children previously considered unadoptable can be adopted, that there are people willing to be parents to such children and prepared to work hard to build a family in this different way' (James 1980:195). This contrasts with the adverse findings of a high breakdown rate in the placement of some older foster children (Trasler 1960; Parker 1966; George 1970). Increasingly, older children are being adopted. In 1982, for the first time, adoptions of children under one year of age accounted for less than half (49 per cent) of 'stranger' adoptions (that is adoptions where neither adopter is a parent), 15 per cent were 1–2 years old, 11 per cent 3–4 years old, 17 per cent 5–9 years old, and 9 per cent were 10 years or older. There is no information on the number of adopted children who have mental or physical handicaps, who are black or of mixed race, or who are in sibling groups, This is an unfortunate gap in our knowledge which is likely to be removed if a DHSS proposal for an Adoption Unit Return is accepted.[4]

The impetus towards subdidized adoption comes from a realization that adoptive families can be found for older children and those with special needs. Indeed, the point is commonly made by advocates of subsidized adoption that adoptive families can be found even where foster parents cannot. Thus, David Owen, putting the British Government's case in July 1975, said:

> 'One of the arguments constantly put . . . is that some of these children will stay in care even if fostering is offered. There is a psychological block. If one talks to people now trying to adopt mentally handicapped or severely physically handicapped children, in some cases fostering does not seem to be enough. They want to adopt. If they are willing to make great personal sacrifices in looking after a child . . . they want the certainty that the child will be theirs.'
>
> (House of Commons 1975: col. 471)

In many cases, perhaps most, subsidized adoption will be used to enable foster parents to adopt. Without adoption allowances prospective adopters may not be able to afford considering adoption while at the same time forfeiting boarding-out allowances. In such cases the child may be damaged by belonging to a family psychologically and emotionally without the security of knowing that he also belongs to that family legally. The status of such a child when he reaches the age of majority and ceases to be in care is unsatisfactory. Legally he 'belongs' to the family of his birth, however tenuous the ties: psychologically, he is part of the family in which he has grown up. Some families can apparently afford to adopt if the child leaves school, and obtains employment, so that he becomes in effect self-supporting. It would be regrettable if, for reasons of legal security, pressure were to be brought to bear upon vulnerable sixteen and seventeen-year-olds who might benefit from staying on at school and who, anyway, are likely to find obtaining employment not at all easy.

It is clear that money is a stumbling-block to many adoptions. Agencies commonly report that families discuss adoption with them, only later to withdraw when the financial implications are made clear to them. Children who have been in institutional care are not cheap to support. They may have few belongings. They may be destructive. They may lose things rather more easily than children brought up in normal home settings. Those who oppose the payment of allowances are sometimes expressing a concern that adoption should be undertaken for love and not money. The very idea that adopters can profit from subsidized adoption is, however, far wide of the mark. The sums likely to be paid, roughly commensurate with the boarding-out allowance, fall far short of the actual cost of maintaining a child. It may be that the families who will benefit most from being paid an adoption allowance are large ones, who can often provide the best environment for a child whose previous experiences have been in an institutional setting, but whose financial resources are already fully committed. Phillida Sawbridge of *Parents for Children* is quoted as saying: 'Children who have been in care for a long time often benefit more from going to a larger family, where there is lots of experience and support, from both the parents and other children. Yet it is these families who are probably least able to afford to take another child (in Whitehouse 1982:16).

Opponents of subsidized adoption often seize on two points. Naturally, they refer to its cost. Their arguments here can be readily dismissed. Adoption has been shown to be more cost-effective than other types of long-term programmes (Watson 1972; Young and Allen 1977). It costs £132 a week to keep a child in residential accommodation: this is approximately six and a half times what it costs the community to provide that child with foster parents and if adoption allowances are set at boarding-out allowance rates the figure for adoption will be comparable (DHSS 1981). Of course, there are other consequences detrimental both to the child himself and the community of being in institutional care, but these are not readily quantifiable, though they are well documented (Page and Clark 1977).

A rather different, and more powerful, criticism of the concept of subsidized adoption also rests on economic considerations. Why, it asks, should some adoptive parents be assisted in their nurturing responsibilities by subsidies when the majority of adopters are not helped in this way? The anomaly, if that is what it is, comes out strikingly if the situation is envisaged of two adopted children in the same family, for one of whom an allowance is being paid but not the other. An answer is that an allowance is paid in some cases (for the foreseeable future a small minority) because the child has special needs. There are anyway a whole gamut of allowances paid to people with special needs, for example, attendance allowance and mobility allowance (Lister 1981). There is no evidence that singling out one child in the family for such an allowance either stigmatizes that child or causes any stresses or strains in the family. The criticism is rendered more cogent, however, when the contrast is drawn between adoptive parents who are paid an allowance to adopt a handicapped child in care and that child's birth parents who are not eligible for such favourable treatment but who may have been able to keep the child within the family had they been recipients of the agency's generosity. This discrimination against birth parents was seized on by the British Association of Social Workers in its critique of the 1975 Bill. It argued: 'It would be an intolerable situation if financial resources were made available to subsidize adoption when an allocation of similar resources to the natural parents may have prevented the break up of the family in the first place' (BASW 1975:22).[5] There is considerable force in this criticism and more could certainly be done to prevent children coming into care (Parker 1980). In a sense Section 1 payments[6] are a functional equivalent of adoption allowances.

But none of this alters the fact that the child in question is in care and would benefit from adoption. His parents were not able to cope, for whatever reason, and there are now people who are prepared to try with the help of a subsidy. The important point is that the child, given his present circumstances, is likely to benefit from adoption. Nevertheless, the ambulance waiting at the bottom of the cliff can never be adequate substitute for a fence at the cliff's edge. Adoption allowances must not become a way of cleaning up the mess which, given will, foresight, and adequate anti-poverty programmes, need not have been caused in the first place.

The American experience

The first adoption subsidization scheme began in New York in 1968 (the early history is documented in Katz and Gallagher 1976). The concept has since spread to most other American states.[7] The New York programme was initially limited to foster parents but was amended later to include 'new' parents for children who could not be adopted by their foster parents and who were in residential establishments. The elements within state laws vary but all are intended to increase the number of adoptive homes available for children for whom there are insufficient applicants. Most of the state laws provide for maintenance and medical care.[8] Family income is an eligibility factor in all state laws except Michigan's, where the subsidy attaches solely to the child's condition.

By the end of the 1970s all but seven jurisdictions[9] had some type of subsidized adoption (Howe 1983:189). Most of the programmes follow the Model Subsidized Adoption Act and Regulations (Katz and Gallagher 1976:11). This was commissioned by the Children's Bureau and approved by the Department of Health, Education, and Welfare in July 1975. According to Katz and Gallagher (1976:8) 'permanence and continuation' are basic concepts of the Act. They stress that adoption subsidy programmes are meant to be part of the usual, ongoing child welfare services offered by a state. Since the programmes are designed to reduce foster care caseloads, the Act requires that eligible children be under public or private agency guardianship or care and legally free for adoption. Agencies must first make every effort to place all children under regular adoption programmes and must provide evidence that 'reasonable efforts have been made to place a child without subsidy'. When agency efforts to achieve adoption without a subsidy have been unsuccessful because of one of the following, (i) physical or mental disability, (ii) emotional disturbance, (iii) recognized high risk of physical or mental disease, (iv) age, (v) sibling relationship, (vi) racial or ethnic factors, or (vii) any combination of these conditions, the Act provides that the child is to be certified as eligible for subsidized adoption.

Different state legislation expresses these ideas in different ways. To take one example, in Illinois subsidized adoption is considered when a child can be or is legally free for adoption. Adoption must be both appropriate and in the best interests of the child. Additionally, the child must be 'hard-to-place' and be likely to remain in substitute care until adulthood. A 'hard-to-place' child is defined by the Illinois Child Welfare manual as:

(i) a child who has an irreversible and/or non-correctable physical or mental handicap;
(ii) a child who has a physical, mental, or emotional handicap correctable through surgery, treatment, or other specialized service;
(iii) a child 6 years of age or over;
(iv) a child under the age of 6 years who has been in the same foster home for one year or longer, and remaining with his foster parents is in his best interest; or
(v) a child who, for casework reasons, must be placed with his/her sibling(s)'
(Illinois Department of Children and Family Services 1976).

Despite these criteria a subsidy may be considered for a child who is not 'hard-to-place' within the terms set out above.

Eligibility is determined by the Department of Children and Family Services on the basis of a home study, medical examinations, and personal references. No specific income levels have been set. Illinois legislation provides for three basic types of subsidy (special service, long-term, and time-limited). In practice only the first two are used. Special service subsidy covers such matters as legal fees, medical costs, counselling, and special education. A long-term subsidy is a monthly payment which continues beyond the legal consummation of the adoption. It is subject to annual review (a study in California found that adoptive parents were resentful of this (Waldinger 1982)). The amount of time-limited and long-term subsidies are limited to 'less than the monthly cost of care for the child in a foster home' ('less' meaning at least one dollar less). The specific amount of the subsidy is individually determined. The Department and the adopting parent or parents agree on the type, amount, and duration of the subsidy. The subsidy may continue until the child finishes education or reaches 21, whichever occurs first.

The most recent developments in subsidized adoption in the USA are the passing of the Adoption Assistance and Child Welfare Act of 1980[10] and section 125 of the Economy Recovery Act of 1981. The former was a response to perceived strong federal disincentives to the adoption of children in foster care because, as soon as a foster child was adopted, the state would lose the federal foster care matching funds formerly received for such a child and would have to cover all future subsidy payments solely from state resources. This barrier has been removed by the federal Act of 1980 which allows for federal funding for subsidized adoption through the use of Aid to Dependent Children in Foster Care and Medicaid programmes. Section 125 of the 1981 Act added a new section 222 to the Internal Revenue Code, under which a taxpayer may deduct up to $1,500 of 'qualified adoption expenses' (fees, court costs, attorney fees, and other legitimate expenses) related to the adoption of a 'special needs' child. The new legislation is expected to boost further adoption of 'special needs' children (Waldinger 1982).

The impact of the new legislation cannot yet be estimated. But the programmes as a whole have now considerable experience. Unfortunately, and rather surprisingly, there has been little research in the United States as to the effect of different schemes. The early literature (Goldberg and Linde 1969; Polk 1970; Gentile 1970; Watson 1972) was largely descriptive and from it little about the impact of the programmes emerges. Two more recent studies are, however, an attempt to gauge the impact of different programmes and are rather more valuable as a result.

Shaffer (1981) has reported on subsidized adoption in Illinois. There were almost 1,600 cases in Illinois between 1969 and 1976. Shaffer examined a stratified random 348 (21.5 per cent). Many of his conclusions are at first sight surprising. The subsidy programme is not taking children out of care institutions (60 per cent of the children were being adopted by foster parents with whom they had lived for four or more years); the typical subsidized child did not experience identified physical or psychological handicaps (in 1976, for example, fewer than 20 per cent of the subsidized children had disabilities); handicapped children did not remain in care longer ('the children's handicap status apparently made them highly visible in the worker's caseload' (Shaffer 1981:62)). Given the goal of subsidization the most galling of Shaffer's conclusions was that the existence of the subsidy programmes did not serve as an incentive to shorten the time children were in foster care: on the contrary, 'for children approved for subsidy time in care has increased from almost five years in . . . 1970 to almost eight in . . . 1976, while the mean age of children entering foster care and later adopted through subsidy remains the same, 2.5 years' (Shaffer 1981:65). On the other hand, few teenagers (only 14 per cent in Shaffer's study) were having adoptions facilitated by the subsidy programme. Half of these were adopted by single parents. The acceptance of the single parent as adopter is one of the most interesting developments noted by Shaffer. One in seven of the subsidized adoptions in his study was a single-parent adoption. The typical single parent was female, black, Protestant, widowed, and had children of her own. She was in her late forties and had a very low income (half the mean of two-parent subsidized families). The two-parent families were primarily white, low income, Protestant, in their early forties, and with several children of their own: also, it is clear, far from the stereotypical adoptive parents. The typical subsidized child, if adopted by two parents, was male, six to ten, and not handicapped. He was as likely to be white as non-white. The typical child placed in a single-parent home was female, black, older than other subsidized children, and non-handicapped. Shaffer comments on the 'selective process of discrimination' (1981:61-2) in these placements. Why, he asks, are 'low-income, single-parent homes so often used for older, non-white children. Are these placements made in the best interest of the child or because they are more convenient than other options?' (Shaffer 1981:62). One thing to emerge strongly from Shaffer's study is that adoption is no panacea and that for example other means must be employed to increase the speed with which children move through care and on to permanent placements.

One of these methods features in the other available study by Byrne and Bellucci of the Hamilton County Welfare Department in Cincinnati, Ohio (1982). They stress the importance of computerization in providing information to enable an agency's adoption subsidization programme to grow. 'Computerized demographic data on the child . . . keeps workers abreast of those children who are hard to place and thus . . . targeted for this project in an ongoing way' (Byrne and Bellucci 1982:176). The profile of subsidized adoption which emerges from the Ohio study is somewhat different from the Illinois picture. Thus, a high percentage of the children (72 per cent) are black and many are handicapped (no figure is given but the impression is conveyed by the authors that adoption for such children is a prime object of the programme). Further, the average age of the children is eleven with very few under six years of age. As in the Illinois study, the adoptive families are poor (45 per cent fall below 50 per cent of the state median income); most are foster home adoptions (68.5 per cent); and adoptions by older, retired, and single parents figure prominently (though again the study gives only sketchy information). The authors remark that, with subsidies a recent innovation, their findings are to some extent distorted: in particular they are 'skewed' to adolescence. This is an important lesson to bear in mind. It is almost inevitable that the early reports that the DHSS will get will also reflect this distortion. It would be unwise to base future social policy on unrepresentative data.

Adoption allowances in Britain

Subsidized adoption was already a reality in parts of the United States before it even began to be discussed on this side of the Atlantic. The late 1960s saw serious thought being given to adoption law and practice in Britain (Goodacre 1966; SCSRA 1968; ACCO 1970; Raynor 1970), but the question of paying adoption allowances was not considered. Indeed, the report of the Standing Conference of Societies Registered for Adoption (1968) expresses the hope that any new adoption legislation 'will give both voluntary and statutory agencies much clearer authority to reclaim expenses from adopters', though it concedes 'it is difficult to ask people to pay when they themselves are giving a service' (SCSRA 1968:20).

The introduction of adoption allowances was first mooted in the Houghton Working Paper of 1970 (HMSO 1970: paras. 119-22). It is said that suggestions have been made to the committee that more adoptive homes might be found for children with special needs 'if financial help were available' (para. 120). It is interesting that at this stage Houghton envisaged that courts would be involved in assessing the need for an allowance (para. 121). The Working Paper made no firm recommendation. There might, it noted, 'be a case for introducing subsidized adoption' (para. 122). The final report was published in 1972. This noted that most witnesses to the committee had opposed subsidized adoption. Nevertheless, it advocated 'a period of experiment during which evidence could be gathered' (para. 94); this involved amending the law to permit pilot schemes of payment allowances to adopters under the general oversight of the Secretary of State (para. 95).

Houghton recognized the objection to singling out handicapped children for special payments, though the report does not make it clear why (as indicated earlier, handicapped children are singled out anyway). Houghton, however, thought there was a case for allowances in 'some circumstances, for example, where suitable adopters are available for a family of children who need to be kept together but, for financial reasons, adoption is not possible if an allowance cannot be paid' (para. 94). It is interesting that Houghton stressed the sibling adoption problem, rather than handicap in itself or more generally the 'hard-to-place' child. Like much else in the report (for example, the proposed ban on certain step-parent adoptions and independent placements) the case was not well reasoned. The Committee was clearly aware of the American experiments (they are referred to in the Working Paper, para. 120) but no real attention was given to the programmes that did then exist.

A year after Houghton the influential book *Children Who Wait* was published (Rowe and Lambert 1973). This described Houghton's suggestion as 'helpful'. Like Houghton, Rowe and Lambert stressed the value of subsidies in sibling adoptions and, almost as an afterthought, in enabling foster parents to adopt. They thought it 'a pity' that discussion of subsidized adoption had tended to concentrate on its potential use in finding families for physically handicapped children. They remarked on the absence of a National Health Service in the United States and thought the role of subsidies in Britain to provide expensive medical care 'limited'. (Whether in 1983, with the Thatcher administration bent on pruning the NHS they would draw the distinction as sharply is dubious.)

The concept of adoption allowances was introduced into English law by section 32 of the Children Act 1975 in the face of considerable opposition. It only passed the committee stage in the House of Commons on the chairman's casting vote (although the members of the Committee did not divide on party lines, the provision was in the main supported by Labour members and opposed by Conservative MPs and the single Liberal member of the Committee). The British Association of Social Workers, the National Council for One-Parent Families, the National Board of Catholic Women, and the National Council of Women in Great Britain also opposed the idea. The statutory provision grafts new subsections on to section 50 of the 1958 Act, to which reference was made at the beginning of this chapter. It provides:

> 'If an adoption agency submits to the Secretary of State a scheme for the payment by the agency of allowances to persons who have

> adopted or intend to adopt a child where arrangements for the adoption were made, or are to be made, by that agency, and the Secretary of State approves the scheme, this section shall not apply to any payment made in accordance with the scheme.'
> (Adoption Act 1958: s.50(4))

There is a requirement to monitor the scheme (s.50(6)), and this is being done by the National Children's Bureau (Lambert 1983). Further, the scheme is to expire on the seventh anniversary of its coming into force, unless the subsection providing for expiry is itself repealed (s.50(7)). Should the scheme be terminated at any time, existing adoption allowances are saved (s.50(10)).

The 1975 Act provides no more than a framework. It is silent as to what adoption allowance schemes must contain. It gives no indication as to the criteria to be used by the Secretary of State in approving or rejecting a scheme. The Act says nothing about the type of payment, or its duration. There is nothing about reviewing payments, nor is anything laid down regarding a maximum age beyond which payments cannot be made.

The provision in the 1975 Act was not implemented until February 1982 and the first adoption allowances scheme (Devon County Council) was approved by the Secretary of State in August of that year (Ruber 1982). Since then another seventeen[11] schemes have been approved. Five of these are London boroughs (Brent, Camden, Croydon, Sutton, and the City of Westminster), three are Scottish authorities (Grampian, Lothian, and Strathclyde) and the remainder are county and metropolitan councils spread throughout England (Bolton, Dorset, Kent, Kirklees, Rochdale, Shropshire, Solihull, Somerset, and East Sussex). There are no adoption allowance schemes as yet in Wales. Many more schemes are in the pipeline and it is to be expected that agencies without an allowance scheme will be the exception rather than the rule in due course. The reason why many authorities initially dragged their feet is clear: there was a ruling from the DHSS that adoption allowances were to be deducted from supplementary benefit, though the boarding-out allowance paid to foster parents was not treated in this way (Rose 1982). The law on this was amended in April 1983 (Supplementary Benefit (Resources) Amendment Regulations 1983). A month later it was announced that income tax would not be charged on payments under adoption allowance schemes. These concessions, both of which would have been automatic in any properly thought out and centrally directed project, have enabled serious thought to be given to drawing up allowance schemes.

In constructing allowance programmes authorities have received some assistance from the DHSS (see *Appendix* p. 222), from the British Agencies for Adoption and Fostering (BAAF), which have issued guidelines, and from the National Foster Care Association (NFCA), which has made a number of recommendations. BAAF's guidelines offer advice on how an agency's scheme needs to be set out, how eligibility is to be established, how the scheme is to be funded and allowances paid, as well as proposals for review and monitoring. The NFCA makes the point strongly that families willing to adopt a hard-to-place child should not be expected to reduce their standard of living. In the light of the guidance offered, not surprisingly many of the approved schemes are very similar and some are identical. For example, there is little difference between the schemes in operation in Camden, East Sussex, Brent, Shropshire, and Grampian. Some schemes are set out in legal statute-like language. Others, while equally carefully formulated, are more contextual and orientated towards social work practice. An example of the latter is Somerset. This begins with a statement that adoption can provide the needs for 'love, security, and continuity' which a number of children in its care 'effectively without parents' lack. Included in the scheme is an estimate of the number of children who could benefit from adoption assisted by allowances (30 at present and then fewer than ten a year). The scheme goes on to stress that 'no additional overall costs will arise from the payment of allowances' though it concedes that in the first year or two there will be an additional workload and 'this will limit the pace at which adoptions which have been enabled by the availability of allowances can proceed' (Somerset County Council 1983).

Each of the schemes provides an eligibility test. Brent's is unique in stressing that it cannot 'define any category of adoption where it would, by definition of category, rule out the payment of an adoption allowance' (Brent LBC 1982). The tests in the schemes of Sutton and Kirklees are clearly modelled on the Devon formulation. Those of Camden, Solihull, East Sussex, and Shropshire are virtually identical. The Devon scheme states:

> 'Adopters shall be eligible to be considered for an adoption allowance . . .
>
> (a) Where adoption is in the child's best interests but where the child would not otherwise readily be adopted if an allowance could not be paid.
>
> AND
>
> (b) (i) Where the child has been in the care of the same foster parents for a continuous period of two years or more and significant ties have been established with them.
>
> OR

(ii) Where the child suffers from a significant mental or physical handicap or illness, the nature of which requires an exceptional degree of care.

OR

(iii) Where the child's previous life experience has resulted in significant emotional or behavioural problems.

OR

(iv) Where children form a sibling group who need to be kept together in one family.

OR

(v) Where there are any other exceptional circumstances which, in the opinion of the Adoption Panel, would secure an adoptive home for the child where it could not otherwise be obtained.'

(Devon County Council 1982)

The Strathclyde scheme's categories of children are very similar (mentally or physically handicapped children or emotionally disturbed children; the older child; two or more children; unrelated foster child or those with the prospect of a permanent home with a low-income family) but the style of the scheme is different in that after each category an explanation is provided as to why such children are suitable for a subsidized adoption. The Westminster scheme adds to its eligibility requirements an insistence that the child be in the care of, or the financial responsibility of, Westminster City Council and that the child is resident within the British Isles. The Westminster scheme also lists as one of the 'special circumstances' which may bring the scheme into operation 'factors or a combination of factors of genetic risks (known at the time of adoption and supported by medical opinion) that the child might develop a physical or mental handicap sometime in the future'. It is stressed that the adopters would not actually receive the allowance unless and until the child developed the handicap before it reached nineteen years of age. (City of Westminster 1983) No other scheme recognizes as such the possibility of predictable disability emerging.

Three of the schemes couch the eligibility rule in the vaguest of terms, in each case giving complete discretion to the adoption panel. Rochdale's scheme merely states: 'Eligibility for an allowance . . . will be decided by the adoption panel' (Rochdale Metropolitan Borough 1983). Similarly, that of Kent lays down that 'on application adopters shall be eligible to be considered for an adoption allowance . . . where adoption is in the child's best interests and where the child would not otherwise readily be adopted' (Kent County Council 1983). Dorset's is very similar to Kent's (Dorset

County Council 1982). It is also the only authority to provide in its eligibility rules for the situation where payment is discontinued because of a financial re-assessment with the adopters qualifying for payment again at some time in the future. The respective merits of clearly formulated rules and relatively uncontrolled discretion have been debated elsewhere (Titmuss 1971; Davis 1969; Reich 1964; Jones, Brown, and Bradshaw 1978; Freeman 1980) though not in the context of adoption allowances. The experiences of authorities with different frameworks will be interesting to follow. One final illustration of eligibility rules is in Bolton's scheme. This contains the few examples in any of the approved schemes of a stated exclusion: adoption allowances will not be paid where the child is normally a white healthy baby (Bolton Metropolitan Borough 1983).

The approved adoption allowance schemes follow a pattern on assessment. Thus, with few exceptions, they follow the DHSS guidelines and emphasize that account is taken of the other benefits and resources available to support the child in his adoptive home and the effect on the family as a whole if no allowance were paid. Most pitch the adoption allowance at rates paid for fostering (boarding-out allowances). Not all do. Thus, Croydon provides that the allowance 'shall not exceed two-thirds of the boarding-out allowance which would have been appropriate if the child in care (*sic*) and boarded out by the Corporation'. Their scheme goes on to relate the amount of the allowance to 'the current level of the family's necessary expenditure' (Croydon London Borough 1982). Dorset has a complicated means test: net available income, minus £10 disregard, is divided by the number of persons in the family, including the child to be adopted, and that amount plus child benefit is deducted from the 'Base Rate allowance': the result is the adoption allowance payable. Furthermore, no adoption allowance is payable when the net available income exceeds £60 per week (Dorset County Council 1982). Several schemes (Devon, Kirklees, Sutton) deduct from the boarding-out rate the sum that parents would be liable to pay towards the cost of a child in care.

The most interesting and enlightened of the assessment schemes are those of Rochdale and Somerset. The Rochdale scheme asks prospective adopters to state in writing why they cannot afford to adopt and to estimate the amount and duration of an allowance which would facilitate the adoption in question. The aim is an agreement with the prospective adopters tailored to the individual circumstances (Rochdale Metropolitan Borough 1983). Somerset, like Rochdale, encourages prospective adoptive parents to discuss the allowance with members of the Panel. Its scheme states: 'The level of allowance should not be determined according to any fixed scale, but by a process of open, trusting and practical negotiation with the prospective adoptive parents' (Somerset County Council 1983). The scheme stresses that the allowance should be tailored to the 'subjective' as well as 'objective' circumstances of the family. Somerset's aim is to be involved in the payment of allowances for the 'minimum necessary period'. Its view, which it believes is shared by most adopters, is that the strength of adoption lies in undertaking total responsibility and ridding oneself of professional intervention in family life.

All the schemes have provision for review except Somerset's. This states that annually the authority will write to the adopters 'seeking their confirmation that the child continues to live with them and is their financial dependent. No review of other circumstances will be made, as the only situation in which an allowance will be varied is where adoptive parents feel able to manage with a lower level of subsidy and so notify the County Council' (Somerset County Council 1983). Most schemes provide for an annual review but in several authorities the review is to take place bi-annually. The Camden scheme provides for a review but no period of time is specified. In Shropshire it is provided that reviews should take place every six months. The rapidity of the review in Shropshire does not seem to be motivated by the considerations found in the Somerset scheme: rather it seems to be the product of a small budgetary allocation for payments under the scheme. The schemes say little about the mechanisms of the review. It is clearly going to be an internal one carried on in the absence of the adopters and, where relevant, their representatives. I fear scant regard will be paid to the principles of natural justice and I suspect the courts will not wish to meddle in what Lord Scarman recently called 'the world of social administration.[12]

All the schemes provide for payments to terminate on the occurrence of certain specified events. The most common of these are the child ceasing full-time education and becoming self-supporting through employment or receipt of supplementary benefit. Nine English schemes allow payments to continue beyond the child's eighteenth birthday. For example, in 'exceptional circumstances' Rochdale will allow payments to continue until the age of 21: but only Brent envisages life-long payments where, as in the case of handicapped children, the adopted child is likely to remain dependent permanently. Given that one of the objects of subsidized adoption is to facilitate the adoption of handicapped children, it is rather surprising that only Brent should have thought through one obvious consequence of this.

Space precludes any further analysis of the schemes. Other gaps must, however, be pointed out. The schemes provide for a periodical allowance (sometimes for both a general allowance and an allowance for specific expenses of a recurring nature). What, however, many families taking on several siblings or a handicapped child will need is a large, initial lump sum to buy expensive equipment, to build extensions, to make necessary adaptations to the family home. The schemes are not allowed by the DHSS to provide for this. Another problem which will arise results from an insistence by some authorities to pay allowances only so long as the family remains in the United Kingdom. The first time a military family is posted abroad, an appointment is taken up in the EEC or further afield, or a family of West Indian origin returns to the Caribbean, the penny will drop. The lacuna in the schemes must be filled if such families are not to be penalized.

First impressions of the British schemes in practice

What impact have the British schemes had? The comments that follow can only be first impressions. Many of the schemes have hardly got off the ground, so that worthwhile feedback is as yet limited. But, in the belief that an interim report is better than none, a few comments are offered on what is happening in the London area. London boroughs may not be representative: this caveat must be borne in mind. There are also differences in the experiences of the London boroughs themselves.

The first thing to note is that very few adoption allowances have so far been approved. No accurate figure is attainable but as at October 1983 it would be surprising if there were 100 approvals in the whole country. Close to 20 per cent of these emanate from one London borough (Brent).

Nearly all of the cases so far recommended for an adoption allowance have been in respect of foster children who have been with their foster parents, or at least in care, for some time. In many of these cases the obstacle to adoption was financial. One team leader described to me what was going on as 'mopping up bad practice'. Few of the children being reached through adoption allowances are handicapped but a minority are. In Brent, for example, two of the earliest cases were Downs Syndrome babies whose parents abandoned them in hospital: in both cases the children had been placed in short-term foster homes and adopters were recruited by the use of newspaper advertisements. In both an adoption allowance was discussed before placement and an enhanced rate was paid to meet the extra expenses incurred in taking on a handicapped child.

The vast majority of children whose adoptions are being financially assisted are white. This may be attributable to the fact that in a number of the areas with schemes there are relatively few blacks in the population. It may, however, also partly reflect difficulties in setting up racially compatible adoptions. But in Brent, however, where there is a high concentration of ethnic minorities and where about three-quarters of the children in care are black, an equally high proportion of subsidized adoptions have involved black children of mixed parentage.

The case of adoption of a family of siblings which features so prominently in the propaganda for subsidized adoption seems to occur most infrequently in real life.

If things go on as at present adoption allowances will be used largely to enable long-term foster parents to adopt white children. Early evidence shows that in the main this is what is happening. It would be unfortunate if too much were read into these initial experiences of subsidization in practice. It is inevitable that the first cases will consist of an accumulated backlog, particularly of foster parents who could not afford to adopt previously. The early reports will thus distort what may emerge as the true picture ultimately. This, it is hoped, will be closer to the Houghton conception. Adoption allowances are only an experiment, but once embedded in social work practice they will not be dislodged. The temptation to direct future policy on the results of early monitoring must be resisted if a false trail is not to be followed. In a sense we have done this already by implementing in the 1980s a policy conceived a decade earlier. In the meanwhile practice has moved on: there are fewer children in residential care; the development of specially designed homes for handicapped children has in some places almost upstaged allowances; post-adoption support (Picton 1977; Seager 1977) is well established so that adoption does not necessarily mean the end of contact with social work agencies.

Conclusion

Subsidized adoption is a good idea but it is not a panacea and we must not expect too much of it. It would be surprising if when fully operational through out the country there were ever 500 adoption allowances approved in a year. The introduction of the 'freeing' provisions in the 1975 Act may boost the figures briefly but not meaningfully. Subsidized adoption has enabled some black families to adopt black children, has ensured that some handicapped children grow up in the warmth and security of a family environment, and has given some older children the security of knowing that their psychological parents are their legal parents. It will continue to do so. The current schemes are not beyond improvement: for example, the payment of lump sums should be allowed; payments should not cease if the family takes up residence abroad; what is involved in a review needs to be better thought out (what, for example, is the status of the family in a review and what rights do they have?); reviews are currently scheduled to take place too frequently (every three years or even five years would be sufficient). Most basic of the questions that needs reconsideration is the means test. As indicated the different authorities have different conceptions of what part family income should play in assessment of an allowance. It is my view that it should play no part at all. If subsidized adoption is to be a real child care option, designed for children in need, allowances should attach to the child, not the parents. If a comfortably well off family is prepared to make the personal sacrifices involved in incorporating a hard-to-place child within the family, they should be cushioned against the financial burdens involved. These are matters for consideration when the experiment is reviewed by the DHSS in 1987.

Notes

1 Both these provisions are still good law, now found in Adoption Act 1976 s.57 and s.24(2) respectively.

2 By 1981 when the total number of adoptions had plummeted to 9,284, there were 3,270 adoptions of illegitimate children where the adopter was a parent. The increase in the number of adoptions in 1982 (to 10,240) is largely attributable to an increase in step-parent adoptions.

3 The statistics do not give the exact figure; 3,012 adoptions were registered by joint adopters, at least one of whom was a parent (OPCS 1983).

4 The DHSS is currently piloting a new adoption unit return in a small number of adoption agencies. If successful, the new return will be introduced in England and Wales in 1984 (BAAF 1983).

5 Similar points were made in the debate on the 1975 Bill. See, for example, the impassioned plea by Mrs Millie Miller, Children Bill Standing Committee A, cols. 452–53.

6 Under the Child Care Act 1980 s.1 (formerly s.1 of the Children and Young Persons Act 1963). On this concept in practice see Heywood and Allen (1971), Lister and Emmett (1976), Hill and Laing (1979), Jackson and Valencia (1979).

7 It also exists in Canada (McEwan MacIntyre 1977) and Israel, though not expressly provided for in Israeli adoption law.

8 This is more crucial in an American setting, where a National Health Service does not exist.

9 Arkansas, Guam, Hawaii, Mississippi, Puerto Rico, Virgin Islands, and Wyoming do not have schemes.

10 Public Law 96–272, 17 June, 1980.

11 By April 1984 fifty-eight schemes had been submitted in England and twenty-four approved. Ten agencies were paying allowances.

12 *Lewisham L.B.C.* v. *Lewisham Juvenile Court Justices* [1980] A.C. 273.

Appendix

EXTRACT FROM DHSS CIRCULAR LAC (82) 1

When considering a scheme submitted for his approval, the Secretary of State will have regard to the following matters, and agencies should take them into account in their schemes.

(1) The scheme should indicate the proposed scale of the scheme and any restriction on the category of adopters who will be considered for an allowance.

(2) The scheme should indicate the resources committed to it, in order to demonstrate that it has a satisfactory financial basis and a secure source of funds. If allowances are to be contained within a pre-determined budget, the scheme should specify that the initial award of an allowance is dependent on the availability of resources.

(3) The scheme should include arrangements for the decision on any allowance to be made by the agency's adoption panel.

(4) The scheme should state the terms and conditions on which allowances will normally be paid, any restriction on the maximum amount or duration of an allowance, and the arrangements for the adoption panel to review allowances periodically. The scheme should provide for an allowance to be decreased or stopped only as may be necessary because of a change in the family's circumstances.

(5) The scheme should provide for the adoption panel to satisfy itself, as in all cases where adoption is under consideration, that:

(a) adoption will safeguard and promote the child's welfare throughout his childhood;

(b) these prospective adopters are suitable for this child.

(6) The scheme should provide for the adoption panel to satisfy itself, before deciding on an allowance in any particular case, that the child would not otherwise readily be adopted by these pro-

spective adopters. This will require the agency to assess whether the prospective adopters could afford to adopt the child without an allowance, taking into account:

(a) what other resources or benefits would be available to support the child in his adoptive home;

(b) the effect on the adoptive family as a whole if no allowance were paid.

(7) The scheme should provide for the prospective adopters to be consulted about the amount, frequency and duration of the allowance, and for the final decision on these matters to be taken by the adoption panel.

(8) The scheme should provide for the agency to notify the prospective adopters in writing of the amount, frequency and duration of the allowance, the terms and conditions on which the allowance will be paid, and the arrangements for review and variation of the allowance. The respective commitments and responsibilities of the agency and the prospective adopters should be set out.

(9) The scheme should include arrangements for payments to be continued by the agency if the family moves to another area. The agency remains responsible for the allowance in such circumstances.

(10) Each agency operating an approved scheme will be expected to participate in any research or monitoring instituted by the Secretary of State pursuant to section 50(6) of the 1958 Act, which may be by way of supplying statistical information, providing access to case records, or ensuring that staff of the agency are available for interview. To this end, the scheme should provide for a full record to be kept of each allowance, covering aspects such as the basis on which the allowance was decided, the amounts paid and their duration, and decisions made on review, as well as the usual information about the adoption itself. Whilst adopters should be encouraged to co-operate personally in any research, this should be left to their own discretion.

References

ACCO (1970) *Adoption - The Way Ahead.* London: ACCO.

BAAF (1982) *Guidelines on Approved Adoption Allowances.* London: BAAF.

______ (1983) *News* 12 (September):2.

BASW (1975) *Analysis of Children Bill.* Birmingham: BASW.

Bolton Metropolitan Borough Council (1983) *Scheme for Adoption Allowances.*

Brahams, D. (1983) *In Vitro* Fertilization. *The Lancet,* 24 September.

Brandon, J. and Warner, J. (1977) AID and Adoption - Some Comparisons. *The British Journal of Social Work* 7(3):335-41.

Brent London Borough Council (1982) *Adoption Allowances Scheme.*

Byrne, K.O. and Bellucci, M.T. (1982) Subsidized Adoption: One County's Program. *Child Welfare* LXI(3):173–80.

Camden London Borough Council (1982) *Scheme of Payment of Allowances to Adopters.*

City of Westminster (1983) *Amended Scheme Submitted to the Secretary of State for Social Services for Payment of Approved Adoption Allowances.*

Croydon London Borough Council (1982) *Payment of Allowances to Adopters.*

Davis, K.C. (1969) *Discretionary Justice: A Preliminary Inquiry.* Baton Rouge, Louisiana: Louisiana State University Press.

Devon County Council (1982) *Scheme for Approved Adoption Allowances.* Exeter.

DHSS (1981) *Children in Care in England and Wales, March 1980.* Stanmore, Middx: DHSS.

______ (1982) *Children Act 1975: Further Implementation.* LAC(82) 1. London: DHSS

Dorset County Council (1982) *Adoption Allowance Scheme.* Dorchester.

Freeman, M.D.A. (1980) Rules and Discretion in Local Authority Social Services Departments: The Children and Young Persons Act 1963 in Operation. *Journal of Social Welfare Law* 84–95.

Gentile, A. (1970) Subsidized Adoption in New York. *Child Welfare* XLIX (10):576.

George, V. (1970) *Foster Care: Theory and Practice.* London: Routledge & Kegan Paul.

Goldberg, H.L. and Linde, L.H. (1969) The Case for Subsidized Adoptions. *Child Welfare* XLVIII(2):96–9, 107.

Goodacre, I. (1966) *Adoption Policy and Practice.* London: Allen & Unwin.

Harris, J. (1983) *In Vitro* Fertilization: The Ethical Issues. *The Philosophical Quarterly* 33:217–37.

Heywood, J.S. and Allen, B.K. (1971) *Financial Help in Social Work.* Manchester: Manchester University Press.

Hill, M. and Laing, P. (1979) *Social Work and Money.* London: Allen & Unwin.

HMSO (1970) *Adoption of Children* (Working Paper of the Houghton Committee). London: HMSO.

______ (1972) *Departmental Committee on the Adoption of Children* (The Houghton Report) Cmnd 5107. London: HMSO.

House of Commons (1975) Official Report, Standing Committee A: Children Bill, Ninth Sitting (22 July). London: HMSO.

Howe, R-A.W. (1983) Adoption Practice, Issues, and Laws 1958-1983. *Family Law Quarterly* XVII(2):173–97.

Illinois Department of Children and Family Services (1976) *Subsidized Adoption Program Policies and Procedures.* Springfield, Illinois: IDCFS.

Jackson, M.P. and Valencia, B.M. (1979) *Financial Aid Through Social Work.* London: Routledge & Kegan Paul.

Jaffee, B. and Fanshel, D. (1970) *How They Fared in Adoption.* New York: Columbia University Press.

James, M. (1980) Home-Finding for Children with Special Needs. In J. Triseliotis (ed.) *New Developments in Foster Care and Adoption.* London: Routledge & Kegan Paul.

Jones, K., Brown, J., and Bradshaw, J. (1978) *Issues in Social Policy.* London: Routledge & Kegan Paul (revised edn 1983).

Kadushin, A. (1970) *Adopting Older Children.* New York: Columbia University Press.

Katz, S.N. and Gallagher, U.M. (1976) Subsidized Adoption in America. *Family Law Quarterly* X(1):3-43.
Kent County Council (1983) *Scheme for Approved Adoption Allowances.* Maidstone.
Kirklees Metropolitan Council (1983) *Scheme for Approved Adoption Allowances.* Huddersfield.
Lambert, L. (1983) Monitoring of Approved Adoption Allowances. *Adopting and Fostering* 7(1):5.
Lister, R. (1981) *Welfare Benefits.* London: Sweet and Maxwell.
Lister, R. and Emmett, T. (1976) *Under the Safety Net.* London: Child Poverty Action Group.
McEwan McIntyre, J. (1977) Subsidized Adoption = Love Plus Money? *Perception* (November/December):31-4.
Office of Population, Censuses and Surveys (1983) *Adoptions in England and Wales 1981* (OPCS Monitor FM 3 83/1). London: OPCS.
Page, R. and Clark, G. (1977) *Who Cares?* London: National Children's Bureau.
Parker, R. (1966) *Decision in Child Care* London: Allen & Unwin.
______ (1980) *Caring for Separated Children.* London: Macmillan.
Picton, C (1977) Post-Adoption Support. *Adoption and Fostering* 88:21-5.
Polk, M (1970) Maryland's Program of Subsidized Adoptions. *Child Welfare* XLIX(10):580-83.
Rawlings, R.W. (1982) Law Reform with Tears. *Modern Law Review* 45(6):637-51.
Raynor, L. (1970) *Adoption of Non-White Children.* London: Allen & Unwin.
Reich, C. (1964) The New Property. *Yale Law Journal* 73:733-87.
Robertson, J.A. (1983) Procreative Liberty and the Control of Conception, Pregnancy and Childbirth. *Virginia Law Review* 69(3):405-64.
Rochdale Metropolitan Borough (1983) *Scheme of Payment of Allowances to Prospective Adopters.*
Rose, M. (1982) Adoption Cash Shock for Poor Families. *Community Care* 407:2.
Rowe, J. and Lambert, L. (1973) *Children Who Wait.* London: ABAA.
Ruber, M. (1982) Approved Adoption Allowances: Devon's Scheme. *Adoption and Fostering* 6(4):4.
Seager, M. (1977) Post-Adoption Support in Hounslow. *Adoption and Fostering* 88:26-9.
Selman, P. (1976) Patterns of Adoption in England and Wales Since 1959. *Social Work Today* 7(7):194-97.
Shaffer, G. (1981) Subsidized Adoption in Illinois. *Children and Youth Services Review* 3(1):55-68.
Somerset County Council (1983) *Scheme for Approved Adoption Allowances.* Taunton.
Standing Conference of Societies Registered for Adoption (1968) *Report to the Home Office on Difficulties Arising from the Adoption Act 1958.* Petersham, Surrey: SCSRA.
Strathclyde Rural Council (1982) *Scheme of Payment of Allowances to Adopters.* Glasgow.
Supplementary Benefit (Resources) Amendment Regulations (1983) (S I 1983 No. 503). London: HMSO.
Sutton London Borough (1983) *Scheme for Adoption Allowances.*
Titmuss, R. (1971) Welfare Rights, Law and Discretion. *Political Quarterly*

42(2):130.
Tizard, B. (1977) *Adoption: A Second Chance.* London: Open Books.
Trasler, G. (1960) *In Place of Parents.* London: Routledge & Kegan Paul.
Wadlington, W. (1983) Artificial Conception: The Challenge of Family Law. *Virginia Law Review* 69(3):465-514.
Waldinger, G. (1982) Subsidized Adoption: How Paid Parents View It. *Social Work* 27(6):516-21.
Watson, K.W. (1972) Subsidized Adoption: A Crucial Investment. *Child Welfare* LI (4):220-30.
Whitehouse, A. (1982) Their Future in the Balance. *Community Care* 409: 15-17.
Young, D.W. and Allen, B. (1977) Benefit-Cost Analysis in the Social Services: The Example of Adoption Reimbursement. *Social Service Review* 51: 249-64.

Acknowledgement

The assistance of Tony Hall, Lydia Lambert, Jean Seglow, Jeremy Burns, Margaret Trowell, Barbara Eaton, and Sanford Katz is gratefully acknowledged. My thanks are also due to the many other directors and social services personnel for providing information and answering my queries.

PART III
Transcultural adoption

14 Adoption of black children by white parents in the USA

RITA J. SIMON

Introduction

By 1983 nearly 20,000 black children had been adopted by white families in the United States. Over the past twenty-three years, since organizations such as PAMY (Parents of Adopted Minority Youngsters) and the Open Door Society were founded, beliefs about the wisdom and morality of the practice have undergone considerable reflection, revision, and defection. The practice of placing black children in white homes reached its zenith in 1971, when some 2,500 such placements were made. Since then transracial adoption has declined rapidly, mostly in response to organized opposition and pressure by the National Association of Black Social Workers (NABSW) and black political leaders in the early 1970s. For example from its zenith of 2,574 transracial adoptions in 1971 (and that figure had been preceded by a three and a half fold increase between 1968 and 1971) there was a 40 per cent decline between 1971 and 1972, and a 30 per cent decline between 1972 and 1973. In 1975, the last year the United States government maintained figures on transracial adoption, the Department of Health, Education, and Welfare reported that 104,888 children had been adopted. Black children constituted 11 per cent of those adopted, and transracial adoption .08 per cent (about 830) (Simon and Altstein 1981:55).

At the time my first book on transracial adoption appeared (Simon and Altstein 1977), it seemed as if transracial adoption would disappear. State and local, public and private adoption agencies, as a matter of official policy no longer placed non-white children (that label included American Indian children as well) in white homes. But a few years ago the pendulum began to swing back and at the time this chapter was prepared, public agencies no longer had a policy of forbidding transracial adoptions; they were just more difficult and more time-consuming than inracial adoptions. Nevertheless, several hundred transracial adoptions are completed each year, usually of children who are of school age, and/or with physical or mental handicaps.

Statutes and judicial decisions

As of 1978, there were three states that still 'mentioned race as a criterion for determining the suitability of particular parents as adopters of a particular child' (Day 1979:90). Of the three, Georgia and Michigan do not refer to particular racial groups; South Carolina does. The South Carolina statute permits whites to adopt black children but explicitly prevents blacks from adopting white children.

A federal statute enacted in 1978, 'The Child Abuse Prevention and Treatment and/or Adoption Reform Act', states:

> 'It is, therefore, the purpose of this title to facilitate the elimination of barriers to adoption and to provide permanent and loving home environments for children who would benefit by adoption, particularly children with special needs.'

The statute specifies that the Department of Health and Human Services shall

> 'provide for a national adoption and foster care information data gathering and analysis system and a national adoption information exchange system to bring together children who would benefit by adoption and qualified prospective parents who are seeking such children.'
>
> (Simon and Altstein 1981:86-7)

Since 1975 several state and federal courts have ruled on issues relating to transracial adoption; but they have not spoken with one voice. In 1978 a New Mexico court ruled against the state Department of Human Resources, which had denied a request from a Mormon couple to adopt their nine-month old racially mixed, black and white foster son. The boy had been placed with the family when he was four days old. In opposing the adoption, the Department of Human Resources noted that the Church of Jesus Christ of Latter Day Saints (Mormons) barred non-whites from their priesthood. The trial court judge overruled the department, citing the positive characteristics of the adoptive family. One month prior to this decision, the Mormon church had revoked its long-standing practice of barring non-whites from the priesthood (Simon and Altstein 1981:81).

In 1977 a Georgia county Department of Family and Children's Services denied the petition of Mr and Mrs Drummond, a white couple, to adopt their three-year-old foster son. The child, who was racially mixed, had been placed for temporary care in the Drummonds' home when he was one month old. Within a year the Drummonds requested permission to adopt him. A federal court of appeals upheld the agency denial because of the racial differences between the foster parents and the child. The Court (*Drummond* v. *Fulton County*) contended that in locating the most appropriate adoptive family, legitimate consideration should be given to their respective races. The US Supreme Court later declined to review the decision of the Georgia court. (Justices Brennan and White dissented.) In rendering its decision, the Supreme Court said,

> 'It is obvious that race did enter into the decision of the Department. It appears to the Court that the consideration of race was properly directed to the best interest of the child and was not an automatic type of thing or of placement, that is, that all blacks go to black families, all whites go to white families, and all mixed children go to black families which would be prohibited.'

The Court referred to professional literature on the subject of transracial child placements and claimed that 'a couple has no right to adopt a child it is not equipped to rear' (Simon and Altstein 1981:81–2).

In 1979 a superior court in the state of Connecticut upheld a decision made by the Department of Children and Youth against the petition of white foster parents to adopt the four-month-old black infant placed with them since birth. The court ruled (*Lusa* v. *State of Connecticut*) that it was appropriate for the state to consider the racial background of the child and of the prospective parents in deciding whether to grant the adoption:

> 'The court has no doubt that the plaintiffs are excellent foster parents. Unfortunately, no family in our present society can be an island. Granted that society and the community should not harbor attitudes against interracial mixture, the subject of the foster-home placement and the adoption is the child, whose life will be affected by the community values and prejudices as they exist, not as they ought to be.'
>
> (Simon and Altstein 1981:82)

Opponents and supporters of transracial adoption

Transracial adoption has never been the procedure of first choice by any of the professionals who work in adoption placement. It came about because even though black families have always adopted at a higher rate than white families, there were thousands of black children in institutions or in foster homes who were legally free for adoption. In 1977 of the 500,000 to 750,000 children who were living in out-of-home placements, about 102,000 were available for adoption; approximately 28 per cent of them were black (Simon and Altstein 1981:67).

The heart of the anti-transracial adoption movement as expressed by the opposition to it of the National Association of Black Social Workers (NABSW) is the belief that it is a conspiracy of whites to rob blacks of their children; that it is a legal incursion on the black family. In a letter to *Opportunity,* the President of the NABSW wrote:

> 'NABSW feels that it must reaffirm its stand against transracial adoption. Although we strongly agree that a permanent home for a child is preferable to life in foster care . . . , it does not seem that transracial adoptions are a necessary or viable alternative . . . , as there are many black families willing and able to adopt.
>
> (Simon and Altstein 1981:63)

Opponents of transracial adoption predict family and personal problems as the children become adolescents and young adults. The children will not internalize a social identity or a sense of belonging to those families, and they will reject them when they are old enough to leave and go off on their own. But the adoption experience will have left them unable to cope in a black world and unacceptable to a white society. By being placed in a strange and foreign environment, black children have been condemned to live as pariahs: marginal to both the black and white communities. In response to the argument that transracial adoption is only used as a placement of last resort, that it is preferable to having the child remain in an institution or in foster care, the NABSW and other opponents insist that there are numerous alternatives. The quote below is from the NABSW's letter to *Opportunity.*

> 'Black adoptive homes can be found for black children – thereby negating the need for transracial adoption. . . . [There is] . . . overwhelming evidence from black adoptive projects across the nation that black homes can be found for the so-called "hard to place," as well as easy to place black child. . . . It should be emphasized that the options for children trapped in the Child

Welfare System are not solely between a white adoptive home or a life of institutionalization. There are black families willing and able to adopt.'

(Simon and Altstein 1981:64)

Black social workers and other leaders in the black community assert that many potential non-white adoptive parents are disqualified because of the criteria employed by adoption agencies; criteria that are most applicable to white, educated, middle-class families. They also point out that historically blacks have opted to adopt informally and have preferred not to rely on agencies and courts for sanction. The figures therefore cited by white-run adoption agencies do not reflect the actual number of black adoptions.

These same social workers assert that black families can be found when adoption agencies alter their requirements and methods of procedure. Some of the specific alterations that they have recommended and that have been adopted by various states have been to lower the financial requirements that make families eligible for adoption, to drop or modify the requirements that the mother must remain at home as a full-time mother and housewife, to lower the standards of comfort demanded for the child, such as his/her own room, and - two practices that are much more far reaching in their implications - to place children with single parents and to subsidize adoptions. It is these latter two alternatives that have been the major responses to transracial adoption as viable means for placing black children in black homes.

A few words of explanation about how subsidized adoption actually works. It is a procedure whereby a family legally adopts a child, while the state, via an adoption agency, assumes some part of the financial obligation incurred for maintaining the child. Although the agency continues to maintain a monetary relationship with the family, the legal responsibility for the child shifts from the agency to the family. Almost every state in the United States has passed 'subsidy' legislation. In none of the statutes are the subsidies designed to provide for the child's total financial support. A majority of them link the amount of the payment to the state's foster care scale. A typical statute reads as follows:

'The Department may provide financial assistance, and shall establish rules and regulations concerning such assistance, to persons who adopt physically or mentally handicapped, older and other hard-to-place children who immediately prior to their adoption were legal wards of the Department. The amount of assistance may vary, depending upon the needs of the child and the adoptive parents, but must be less than the monthly cost of

> care of the child in a foster home. Special purpose grants are allowed where the child requires a special service but such costs may not exceed the amounts which similar services would cost the Department if it were to provide or secure them as guardian of the child.
>
> (Simon and Altstein 1977:167)

How will the widespread use of subsidies to prospective non-white adopters affect transracial adoptions? The answer in all probability is that it will tend to reduce their number. White couples who want to adopt a non-white child are likely to be ineligible for subsidies because, as a group, they are usually in the higher occupational and financial brackets and are rarely, if ever, foster parents. The latter usually receive the 'most favored' treatment in subsidy allocation. Although subsidized adoption is not a panacea for the plight of parentless non-white children, the fact that subsidies allow more inracial non-white adoptions, especially by foster parents, tends to work against the transracial adoption of black children by white couples.

Single-parent adoption is the other major innovative replacement for transracial adoption. Where in the hierarchy single-parent adoption falls in relation to transracial adoption is an interesting question. In theory, if a white couple seeks to adopt a non-white child, they will receive priority over a single individual wanting to adopt, even if the latter is racially similar to the child. Whether this in fact occurs is dependent on a host of contigencies. In any event, many observers would seriously question the prevailing assumption that a two-parent family of a race different from the child's is better for a child's development in the long run than a single parent of the same race. As with subsidized adoption and other variants of the historic two-parent inracial matched adoption, the development of single-parent adoption increases the available pool from which potential adoptive parents can be drawn. If eligible black single individuals (of both sexes) are included in this expansion, it further reduces the need for transracial adoption as a method of obtaining homes for black children.

Who are the leading proponents and what are the major arguments in the case for transracial adoption? The majority of organizations that support transracial adoption are child welfare oriented. Their activities are aimed at securing a permanent home for every parentless child. Their goal is to achieve permanence for children who need families. If this can best be accomplished through transracial placement, then that will be the plan of choice. These diverse organizations all had similar beginnings. Groups of concerned families banded together with the common purpose of achieving permanent homes for children in need. Families provided each other with emotional support through meetings and the social networks these meetings created. The groups offered family-centered activities, where adopted children were given opportunities to meet each other. These social activities were particularly valuable for transracially adopted children.

Among the organizations that favor transracial adoption as a viable option is the American Council on Adoptable Children (NACAC). NACAC includes 400 local chapters throughout the United States and Canada and represents a broad coalition of individuals and adoptive parent groups. Their goal is to have every adoptable child adopted.

At a hearing in conjunction with the 1980 White House conference on families, NACAC's president testified:

> 'We believe every child has the right to a loving, "forever" family of his or her own. For a great many children now in foster or institutional care, permanency and love can only be found through adoption. . . .
>
> We are not talking here about the adoption of racially-matched infants by white, middle-class couples. That is not adoption today . . . "Adoptable children" today include many who are older, who are of school age, who are emotionally troubled, physically handicapped, of mixed or minority race, or members of sibling groups. These are "special needs" adoptable children. They need special families. . . . We know such families exist. . . .
>
> However, built into the very system that exists to serve children, there are specific barriers which make permanence difficult or impossible for great mumbers of children. . . .
>
> Criteria and methods for recruiting and approving applicants . . . eliminate, the very people most able to meet the needs of waiting children.'
>
> (Simon and Altstein 1981:71)

What the data tell us about transracial adoption

We turn our attention next to an evaluation of the data that are available on black children who have been adopted by white families. Within the extensive adoption evaluation literature (ably summarized up to 1972 by Professor Alfred Kadushin), there is a relatively small collection of work on transracial adoption (Kadushin 1972). Most of that work has been done in the past decade by Grow and Shapiro (1972), Simon and Altstein (1977 and 1981), and Ladner (1977).

In the early 1970s, Zastrow matched (by the age of the child and the socio-economic status of the parents) 44 white couples who had adopted a black child against 44 white couples who had adopted a child of their own race. Prior to interviewing the parents, he read the agencies' records on the families involved. Zastrow used two measures of parental satisfaction: the parents' own assessment on a five-point scale ranging from extremely satisfying to extremely dissatisfying, and the interviewer's assessment of the parents' overall satisfaction on the same scale. Zastrow found no statistical difference between the two groups of parents and a high rate of successful outcome for both (Zastrow 1977:85–6).

Also in the early 1970s Scarr and Weinberg of the University of Minnesota did IQ tests on 130 black children four years of age and older who had been adopted by whites and were living in Minnesota. They found that the adopted black children had an average IQ of 106, one standard deviation or 15 points above the average IQ of 90, usually achieved by black children living in the North Central region and reared in the homes of their birth. The 99 youngsters they tested who had been adopted at an early age scored even higher, about 110 on the average. Twenty-eight black children adopted by whites and living in the Seattle area wered tested by another researcher, William Womack, who reported that the black youngsters in his study had an average IQ of 115. The scores of the black youngsters in both studies compared favorably with the average score of 113 reported by Leahy for white children adopted by professional families (Day 1979:111).

In 1974, Lucille Grow and Deborah Shapiro of the Child Welfare League of America published the results of their study of 125 families who had transracially adopted black children (Grow and Shapiro 1972). The average age of the children was nine and they had been in their adoptive homes at least three years. The major objective of their study was to assess how successful these adoptions had been. Operationally, success was measured by comparing the scores of transracially adopted children with those of adopted white children on the California Test of Personality. A score above the 50th percentile was defined as indicating good adjustment. The scores of the transracially adopted children and those of the white adopted children matched very closely. Grow and Shapiro concluded that the children in their study made about as successful an adjustment in their adoptive homes as other non-white children had in prior studies. They claimed that 77 per cent of their children had adjusted successfully, and that this percentage was similar to that reported in other studies (Day 1979:110–11).

In 1977 two studies were published on transracial adoption: Joyce Ladner's, *Mixed Families,* and Simon and Altstein's, *Transracial Adoption.* Both studies used the membership lists of the Open Door

Society and the Council on Adoptable Children as their sample frame. Ladner conducted in-depth interviews with 136 parents in Georgia, Missouri, Washington DC, Maryland, Virginia, Connecticut, and Minnesota. Before reporting her findings, she introduced a personal note.

> 'This research brought with it many self-discoveries. My initial feelings were mixed. I felt some trepidation about studying white people, a new undertaking for me. Intellectual curiosity notwithstanding, I had the gnawing sensation that I shouldn't delve too deeply because the findings might be too controversial. I wondered too if the couples I intended to interview would tell me the truth. Would some lie in order to cover up their mistakes and disappointments with the adoption? How much would they leave unsaid? Would some refuse to be interviewed because of their preconceived notions about my motives? Would they stereotype me as a hostile black sociologist who wanted to "prove" that these adoptions would produce mentally unhealthy children?
>
> Prior to starting the interviews I admit to have been skeptical about whether the adoptions could work out well. Because I was reared in the Deep South, with all of its rigid racial segregation, transracial adoption represented, for me, an inexplicable departure from custom and tradition. I would have thought it just as unorthodox for a black couple to adopt a white child. Racial polarization in America sensitizes everyone to the potential hazards in this kind of "mixing" of the races. On the other hand, I was also unwilling to accept the facile cliches the critics used to describe the motives of the adoptive parents. I wanted to find out for myself what kinds of people were adopting and why they did it. What were their day-to-day experiences? How did the adoption affect their biological children? How were the children coping? It was also important to find out the reactions of their families, friends, and neighbors; their philosophies on race relations and black identity; their experiences with the adoption agencies; and their hopes and expectations for their children's future.'
>
> (Ladner 1977:xii–xiii)

By the end of her study, Ladner was convinced that 'there are many whites who are capable of rearing emotionally healthy black children'. Such parents, Ladner continued, 'must be idealistic about the future but also realistic about the society in which they now live'.

> 'To deny that racial, ethnic, and social class polarization exists, and to deny that their child is going to be considered a "black child", regardless of how light his or her complexion, how sharp their features, or how straight their hair, means that these parents are unable to deal with reality, as negative as they might

perceive that reality to be. On the other hand, it is equally important for parents to recognize that no matter how immersed they become in the black experience, they can never become black. Keeping this in mind, they should avoid the pitfalls of trying to practice an all-black lifestyle, for it too is unrealistic in the long run, since their family includes blacks and whites and should, therefore, be part of the larger black and white society.'
(Ladner 1977:255-56)

In their first volume *Transracial Adoption* (1977), Simon and Altstein described the results of a survey of 204 families, each of whom had adopted at least one non-white child. The focus of the survey was on the racial identity, awareness, and attitudes of the adoptive non-white children and their white siblings. In addition to the parents in each of the families, they also interviewed some 388 children between the ages of three and eight years.

The children's responses to various projective tests using dolls, pictures, and puzzles constituted the most important finding to emerge from the study. As a group, the children were more racially color blind and more indifferent to race as a basis for evaluation than any other group reported in any previous study, including studies not only on children in the United States but in Hawaii, New Zealand, and other parts of the world. They found black children who did not think that white children were smarter, cleaner, or more attractive than themselves. They found white children who did not think that black children were dumber, meaner, less attractive, and so on. In other words, their results demonstrated that black and white children responded in similar fashion to traditional questions about which doll or which child they would like to play with, or have as a friend, or looked bad.

They also talked to each of the parents in those 204 families. They found that most of the fathers and mothers believed that race did not figure greatly in how people perceived and evaluated each other or the way they would be likely to relate to each other. They found that on the whole, the parents were extremely optimistic about what relations between different racial groups in the United States would be like in the next one or two decades. They did not seem to be hiding their heads in the sand, disavowing that they, as white parents, would have problems rearing their black children. On the whole, they believed that their problems would not be insurmountable and that their children would grow up to be emotionally healthy, well-adjusted individuals, able to relate to the culture and society of their adopted parents and to the society of their ethnic origins.

Five years later when Simon and Altstein completed the second phase of their study they found that the extraordinarily glowing happy portrait they had painted earlier now had some blemishes on it (Simon and Altstein 1981). It showed some signs of stress and tension. For every five families in which there were the usual pleasures and joys along with sibling rivalries, school-related problems, and difficulties in communication between parent and child, there was one family whose difficulties were more profound and *were believed by the* parents to be directly related to the transracial adoption.

The serious problem that the parents cited most frequently was the adopted children's (usually it was the boys') tendency to steal from other members of their families. They described how bicycles, clothing, and money had been stolen from siblings' rooms and how brothers and sisters had resorted to putting locks on their bedroom doors. Another serious problem was the parents' rather painful discovery that their adopted children had physical, mental, or emotional disabilities that were either genetic, or the result of indifferent or abusive treatment that the children had received in foster homes.

Still a third theme of discontent focused on parental guilt. A few parents felt that by adopting a child of another race they had caused pain, or had inflicted harm on the child or children who had been born to them. The pain was the result either of neglect, because integrating a child of a different race into the family had absorbed so much of their time and energy as not to leave enough for the other children, or because the family had so rearranged its life style (changing churches, friendships, vacations) that the child born into the family felt estranged and left out.

Although Simon and Altstein pointed out the warts and the blemishes in transracial adoption, they did not find that negative feelings and disappointments were overwhelming, or even came close to characterizing the large majority of the families' experiences. Indeed, most of the parents reported that their adoption experiences had brought happiness, commitment, and fulfilment to their lives. Among the twenty-three single-parent families that were found in the second phase (there were no single-parent families in the first phase) almost all the mothers and fathers emphasized that the transracial adoption had enriched their lives and that the tensions and pain leading to the separation or divorce were not related to the adoption.

About the children's performance in school and with peers, 74 per cent of the parents said that their adopted children were doing well in school and that there were no academic problems or difficulties with teachers. The others mentioned lack of motivation and some learning disability problems. Almost all of the parents (85 per cent of them) described their children as not having any difficulty in making friends and being part of a group.

The first time Simon and Altstein contacted these families in 1972, 31 per cent of the parents reported that the grandparents, aunts, and uncles had rejected the adopted children and they (the parents) were not reconciled with the parents. Seven years later, 12 per cent of those families reported that the rift which began with the transracial adoption continued and the family ties had been broken. Fourteen per cent of the parents said that the adoption served to bring them closer to their parents. For the large majority, the adoption of a black child had not resulted in an important change in their family ties. Many of them said: 'Our parents are as loving to their adopted grandchild as they are to their other grandchildren.' The majority of the parents said they still felt as they did seven years earlier that their decision to adopt transracially was among the wisest and most satisfying they had ever made. The children not only provided enormous intrinsic value but they also gave the parents another window through which to view the world. Some reported that the adoption made them realize how prejudiced they had been, and to some extent still were. Now that they were parents of a black child, however, they had to face up to their prejudice and do something about it.

Simply put, their children helped to make their lives more varied, more interesting, and more challenging. Having a black son or an Indian daughter set them apart; and most of the parents enjoyed their special status. Most of them also believed that it was healthy for the other children in their families. It gave them a broader base from which to view and participate in the human experience.

Completing their book at the beginning of 1981, Simon and Altstein noted that transracial adoption had not been completely stymied as they feared it would be in 1975. But they noted that the number of such adoptions continued to be small, and the trend showed no sign of turning upward. Even with the combined efforts of black social workers and child-care agencies, thousands of children, the majority of whom are black, remained in institutions awaiting adoption. The authors ended their second volume as they did the earlier one by emphasizing that the story about these families was not finished and the problem of homeless children living out their childhoods in institutions had not been resolved. They hoped that there would be a relationship between how well the children in their study turn out, how adjusted, how happy, and how emotionally secure they are, and the policies adopted to reduce the number of homeless children.

Conclusion

We conclude this chapter by reiterating that all of the data are not yet in on the issue of greatest concern to the opponents of transracial adoption. How do the black adolescents and adults who have been reared in white families identify themselves; how comfortable are they with their own self-image; is there a conflict between their own perceptions of themselves and the community's? If there is, how do the adoptees respond to this conflict? The fears voiced by Amuzie Chimuzie, for example, that 'black children reared in white families and communities will develop antiblack psychological and social characteristics' have yet to be examined empirically (Simon and Altstein 1981:62). We do not know whether these children will be the 'Oreos' (black on the outside and white on the inside) that the militant black community feared. The parents of these children believe otherwise. They hope and they claim that their black children have integrated, wholesome personalities and the emotional security that will permit them to live in both worlds - the black and the white - and help develop and enlarge that small, but existent community in which the inhabitants are 'color blind'. Color blind in the sense that they do not use race as their basis for evaluation and judgment of the quality and worth of their fellow human beings. Many of these children, their parents believe, will make their way into such communities, and indeed, will provide their leadership. In doing so, the adoptees will be able to live emotionally and socially integrated lives. They will acknowledge and recognize their blackness, join in appropriate 'minority causes', but also retain family ties and social relations with their white parents, siblings, and friends. Rather than the pariah status that the black social workers fear they will hold, these products of transracial adoption will be integrated members of a special and growing world. Ten years from now we shall be able to examine the accuracy of both sides' prophecy.

References

Day, D. (1979) *The Adoption of Black Children.* Lexington: Lexington Books.

Grow, L.J. and Shapiro, D. (1972) *Black Children, White Parents: A Study of Transracial Adoption,* Child Welfare League of America, New York.

Kadushin, A. (1972) *Child Welfare Services.* New York: Macmillan.

Ladner, J. (1977) *Mixed Families.* New York: Anchor Press, Doubleday.

Simon, R.J. and Altstein, H. (1977) *Transracial Adoption.* New York: John Wiley & Sons.

Simon, R.J. and Altstein, H. (1981) *Transracial Adoption: A Follow-Up.*

Lexington: Lexington Books.
Zastrow, C.H. (1977) *Outcome of Black Children - White Parents Transracial Adoptions.* R. & E. Research Associates, Inc., San Francisco.

Acknowledgement

The author and publishers would like to thank Doubleday & Co., Inc for permission to reprint excerpts from *Mixed Families* by Joyce Ladner. Copyright © 1977 by Joyce Ladner.

15 Reflections on bicultural adoption

MARILYN AND LOYAL RUE

It was an evening in October of 1974 when we first considered the possibility of adopting a child from Thailand. We were visiting some neighbors who had just completed such an adoption, and it was from them that we learned that approximately 55,000 orphans under the age of five die each year in Thailand, most of them boys. A depressing statistic. And there, nested in a cradle between these neighbors, was a survivor.

That visit determined the topic of conversation in our home for the next few weeks. At first the issues were clear and simple. We were told that adoptions of infant boys from Thailand were relatively swift and free of bureaucratic irritants. How could we, then, in good conscience, ignore the opportunity perhaps to save a life with so little personal sacrifice? We were childless at the moment but we had always planned to have children. What better time? And what better way? There appeared no reasonable counter-arguments. We began to feel as if we had been delivered a summons.

But then, gradually, the complexities of human responsibility began to emerge and what first appeared to be a straightforward decision became fraught with ambiguities. One worrisome issue gave rise to another. The first involved a re-examination of our motives. Was it possible that we were drawn to this adoption by self-serving motives? Were we really concerned about the benefits to the child or were we seeking some sort of trophy of our own morality? The ambiguity of this issue was never resolved with satisfaction but was something we had to learn to live with. Since having children by birth we have realized that the intermixture of altruistic and self-satisfying motives is a universal characteristic of parenting and *not* unique to adoptive parents. In any event, we regard it as fortunate that we addressed the issue of motives *before* the adoption. If the question had presented itself after the fact there is a good chance that a measure of guilt would have come with it.

At first our deliberations assumed that the only persons who might be affected by our decision were those in the immediate family. But it soon became clear that the extended family (*our* parents and siblings) would play a critical role. We had to consider the possibility that our families would not be enthusiastic about the adoption. If they were to respond differently to this child from the way they would to a biological relative then negative effects upon the child and upon our family relationship would be unavoidable. Whatever slight reservations we might have had over this question were quickly laid to rest by a forthright conversation with our families. Having done this, once the child arrived we found ourselves with quite the opposite problem: his uniqueness made him an easy target for exaggerated affection from grandparents and cousins. Within months, however, the offenders had achieved some perspective on the matter and our son slipped into a niche within the extended family.

As a childless couple we had not been drawn into any more than a cursory acquaintance with research relative to parenting and child development. What we had read, however, seemed to indicate that recent studies were beginning to favor the hereditary side of the old 'nature-nurture' debate. The prevalence of inherited predispositions toward behavior patterns tends to support the conclusion that a biologically related family might be less stressful and, thus, more coherent and stable than an adoptive family. The attitude of social scientists toward this conclusion did not entirely matter to us. The initial plausibility of the conclusion was enough to make it a factor in our discussions. In addition to this, we were beginning to hear a fair amount about the process of 'infant bonding' and its contributions both to good mothering and to the future emotional adjustment of the child.

Research, it seemed to us, did not offer much encouragement to couples who were considering an adoption. And since there was little we could provide by way of theoretical or experimental rejoinder, we did the next best thing: we resolved not to become disaffected by the advice of experts and then changed our reading habits.

After about a month of careful discussion it dawned on us that we had really *made* our decision to pursue the adoption and were seeking ways to rationalize the act. But it was also becoming clear to us that the challenges of adoption (and *bicultural* adoption in particular) required that we be deliberate in our family planning. If adoptions appeared to be discouraged by the bulk of research, then so much the worse for bicultural adoptions where the problems are compounded by the obvious physical differences of the adopted child.

For a while we questioned the wisdom of having additional children by birth. Our reasoning was that our adopted child would be constantly at a disadvantage with his siblings. They would always have the ultimate weapon (his status as a biological alien) at their disposal to bring into the lists when things were not going well. We knew enough about children to know that this feature would be inevitable. But we finally decided that adoption should not be permitted to preclude the arrival of children by birth. In this decision we were mindful of the possibility that we might subconsciously resent the adopted child for denying us the joys of natural parenthood.

But once this decision was made we saw the necessity of *constructing* our family in such a way that we could avoid - or at least effectively compensate for - any possible feelings of alienation that might arise. We reasoned that this objective could only be achieved if we provided our adopted Thai child with the same advantages that would be enjoyed by any eventual birth children. To be more precise, we would be successful if we could equip the rest of the family members with the same *handicaps.* To that end we committed ourselves to the maintenance of a *bicultural family;* that is, a family that affirms a dual heritage. Rather than receive a Thai child into an American home, we wanted to relocate the family itself in some neutral territory. We wanted to construct a Thai-American household in which everyone's heritage was compromised.

This concept is not original. In fact, it is quite a common phenomenon in America. North America is filled with bicultural families: Irish-Americans, African-Americans, Scandinavian-Americans, Anglo-Americans, and the like. We both grew up in Norwegian-American families. Even as children we were aware that Norwegian culture was being affirmed in concert with American culture. And we learned to regard this biculturalism as an advantage, even though it was unclear how it was so.

Of course it was obvious that to construct a Thai-American family would be, in our case, artificial. But we viewed it as the least we could do to provide our adopted child with some of the conditions of personal integrity. It would be one of the ways in which he could find virtue in his uniqueness within a culturally homogeneous community. We also realized that our efforts at maintaining a Thai-American household would be incomplete. Neither of us knew anything about Thai culture and there was no way that we could provide the subtle and habitual influences by which culture is normally transmitted to the young. Nevertheless, we were committed to giving it our best try.

It meant that we would have to find resources for learning about Thai culture and history. It meant that we would have to acquire some Thai art and learn to prepare Thai food. It also meant that we would have to discipline ourselves to keep abreast of current political affairs in Thailand, and to discuss them informally in the family. We knew that it would eventually involve a family trip to Thailand. And we knew that our manner of presenting these influences would have to appear spontaneous, lest they be regarded as token observances. And above all, we realized that we would never have the assurance that our attempts were authentic or sufficient. Yet, in spite of our reservations, we viewed even the shallowest form of biculturalism to be a major responsibility.

As it turned out, what we had been told about the ease and speed of an adoption from Thailand was true. Within six months of our initial inquiry we were on our way to Chicago to meet a flight bound from Thailand. Our son, Boonsong, now eight months old, was being delivered to us there by a Peace Corps volunteer returning to the States from service in the Far East. The moment of arrival remains, for each of us, absolutely unique and special in our experience. Neither of us has since had the experience of being so completely out of control. At that moment we were so emotionally overwhelmed that we were probably not responsible for our actions in a legal sense. And yet we were about to accept the responsibility of a lifetime.

Boonsong was christened Carl Anders Boonsong Rue about a month after his arrival. A friend of ours performed the service during which he read the following baptismal letter to our son:

'Carl Anders Boonsong Rue:

I think the secret is in your name.

Child of the morning,
surrounded by names from evening lands,
brought to this patch-work nation,
itself a child beside the civilizations that gave you life:
world child; earth person!

Today I baptized you,
and I have wondered about that.
I baptized you;
a kind of tribal rite by which we receive you
into this community and this culture.
I have wondered because

I would not want to make your life smaller
than the whole earth to which you and your name belong.

You are not the first to come this way.
The waters between east and west have parted before
for your father's fathers to find this continent
and make this place their home.
Civilizations later, our fathers, too,
rode the sea to this green land.
We have spanned the earth to press in on each other.
Even as you were born, our peoples did in madness collide.
It cannot always be so.
We cannot always be astonished
to meet on the horizons of our cultures,
angry at our own image.
Today we met again.
Like waves from east and west
we have met in you and your name.
With the splashing of primordial waters
we have met in oceanic ceremony and given you name,
and home, and membership among this people.
You are our future;
the promise of larger life and vision;
a plaiting of these cultures into conscious kinship.

Carl Anders Boonsong Rue: world child; earth person!

The secret is in your name.'

In the years since his arrival Carl Boonsong has continued to enlarge our life and vision as the letter promised. And yet it would be misleading if we were to claim that our family life has been without its share of strife. There have been moments of great joy, but there have also been moments of anguish. It is in the nature of a bicultural family that problems are created for all. For Carl there has been insecurity and isolation; for his parents there has been indecision and self-recrimination; and for Carl's two sisters (four and six years younger than he) there has been much confusion resulting from these problems.

We have refined our philosophy of parenting to a single principle: our task is to convince our children, by every means available to us, that the world is a non-hostile place in which to live; and that while dangers exist the world invites and rewards curiosity and ambition. In spite of everything we have done to apply this principle we have frequently felt that we have failed in Carl's case. He has always been, and remains, a reticent and insecure child, vulnerable to any threat of isolation.

When Carl was in his fourth year we announced to him that he was soon to have a new little brother or sister by birth. On one level of feeling he was delighted by the news but as time passed we detected a deeper level at which he was threatened by the prospect of a sibling. This is a typical response even for birth children, but in Carl's situation the news exaggerated his difference and, it seemed to him, jeopardized his position in the family.

The announcement set off a volley of questions which didn't subside for months. Prior to this time Carl had asked only a few general questions about his origins. His physical appearance was obviously different from his parents' and he was fully aware of that from an early age. He also knew that he was originally from Thailand. But now his curiosity was becoming more specific. The idea of a baby growing in mommy's tummy struck Carl as one of the most amusing things he had ever heard. When guests came to our home he would inform them immediately of the process and then become overwhelmed with giggling. One day, however, he became very serious and asked if *he* had once lived in mommy's tummy. When he was told not he asked, 'You mean I was born all alone?'

This was the point at which we had to present a complete, consistent, and constructive story for Carl. We had known from the beginning that this moment would come and we had prepared ourselves by discussing several versions of our 'adoption story'. In spite of our anticipation and preparation we still had the feeling that we had been caught off guard. We told him this: that he had grown in the tummy of a very lovely woman in Thailand; that she loved him very much; that she was extremely poor and unable to care for him; that she wanted to find some people who loved him as much as she did and would also take care of him; that we were the ones. In actual fact, we excluded some of what we knew about Carl's situation in Thailand. Knowledge of his birth parents is forever lost in obscurity. What we know is that he was born in a rural province and passed from family to family until he found himself in the custody of a laborer who was bound for Bangkok to find work. This laborer was subsequently employed on a hospital construction project and made it his practice to bring the child to work with him in a basket. The child eventually became sick and was taken into the hospital. A member of the staff told us that when Carl was admitted to the hospital he was 'covered with mud and Buddhist charms'. He then spent several weeks convalescing in the home of the owner of the hospital, after which he was turned over to a desperately overcrowded orphanage operated by Irish nuns. It was there that he came to our attention.

Occasionally Carl would ask whether or not he had any brothers or sisters living in Thailand. We always reassured him in the negative on this question, but the question remained for a long time. There was even a brief period during which he insisted that he had a twin brother who remained in Thailand. This conviction came to him after seeing a 'NOVA' program about twins. We worried that the idea would continue to haunt Carl but eventually he gave it up. We now regard his 'twin brother notion' as a manifestation of the deep desire in each of us finally to meet up with ourselves.

Before his arrival we underestimated the emotional problems that Carl would come burdened with. After all, he was a mere eight-month-old infant, a *tabula rasa;* what problems could he possibly have? We were naive in thinking that we would be starting afresh. It was not until our first birth child reached the age of eight months that we finally realized how much significant development takes place in such a short period. For eight months Carl had been treated as a parcel and tossed about like a hot potato. It would be out of the question to assume that he could have achieved any semblance of emotional adjustment under these conditions. It is even doubtful that a child with his experience might *ever* become convinced that he is welcome in the world. Carl has always been less affectionate and more dependent than many children who started out in a stable caring environment. These characteristics manifest themselves from day to day in behavior patterns that are sometimes difficult to deal with. As a result, Carl has been in many ways a demanding child. The pathetic irony in a situation like this is that it becomes difficult to welcome a child that does not already feel welcomed. Carl's experiences during his first eight months may have conditioned his attitudes so decisively that our attempts to convince him of the non-hostility of the world are in vain.

But even if our attempts might have been successful there are factors outside the home environment that tend to work against them. Racism has been an especially difficult problem for our family. We live in a homogeneous small town in the middle western United States. There are very few minorities in this community, and those who do live here find themselves targets for a mild form of racism. But racism, even in its non-violent forms, is still pernicious. The difficult thing about racism in our particular situation is that when it is directed at Carl he must deal with it all alone. He does not have the comfort of knowing that the rest of the family shares in his problem. If we were an entire family of minorities, his situation would be much different in this respect. And since neither of us has ever been the victim of racial prejudice we are ill-prepared to help him develop the skills that are useful in combating it.

Racism is discriminatory behavior based on race, and we have found that discriminatory behavior can be expressed as effectively by well-meaning persons as by doctrinaire racists. When Carl was still quite young it happened frequently that strangers would approach us in public and ask where he was from. 'Where did you get him?' is the typical form of inquiry, as if he had been sent out through a mail order catalogue. It strikes us as difficult to see how Carl could interpret this as anything other than an act of aggression. Sometimes children in their innocence would blurt out, 'Hey, look at the brown baby with a white mom and dad.' And even when people did not say anything they often cast glances in Carl's direction which communicated essentially the same message: 'You're different; you don't belong.' As Carl grew older we taught him to volley back the question whenever he was queried about his origins. 'I'm from Thailand, where are *you* from?' We told him that everyone in the United States came from somewhere else, and in fact Carl has received some very interesting responses to his returned question.

It is unfortunate that racism also comes in less innocent forms. The chief offenders in our case are children on the school playground. One morning as Carl was preparing to go to school he said to his mother, 'Mom, I'm a nigger aren't I?'. This was the first indication we had that he was experiencing racist name-calling at school. As we checked into the matter further we discovered that there was a small group of bullies who had been calling Carl and his little Vietnamese refugee friend 'nigger' during the school play periods. Carl is not assertive, so his response to racist forays is not to become belligerent. Instead, he withdraws from the situtation in shame. Shortly after the name-calling began we noticed that Carl was losing his appetite. It finally came to the point where he refused to eat.

At this writing the situation is still unresolved. The school officials have made some modest attempts to intervene and, after losing several pounds, Carl is slowly recovering his appetite. But there are signs that the discrimination persists. And even if it stops on the playground there will be other incidents in other times and places. Our only hope is that Carl will learn to understand racism and to forgive it before he lets it destroy him.

We are convinced that parenthood would become a rare phenomenon if people could learn to appreciate the problems of parenting in advance. And if this were suddenly possible adoptions would soon be unheard of. Of all the parenting problems we have faced, the element of uncertainty has been by far the most difficult to contend with. This is a problem for all parents but the uncertainty is magnified in adoptive families, and even more so in bicultural families.

Adoptive parents seldom have the luxury of knowing when they have been wrong. This may appear an odd assertion but to adoptive parents it will make perfect sense. When Carl's behavior has us at loose ends it would be nice to know if the source of the problem is to be found in our interaction with him or whether the problem is the inevitable result of his first eight months. At first sight this looks like a trivial distinction but in fact it has major implications for our confidence. There is a certain amount of self-doubt expressed in the question 'Where did we go wrong?', but there is infinitely more self-doubt in the question '*Did* we go wrong?'.

The amount of uncertainty in a bicultural situation is much greater than in monocultural families. Earlier we mentioned our belief that a share of Carl's personal integrity depends upon an affirmation of his Thai heritage in addition to his American heritage. However enlightened this may sound in theory it is not a simple principle to put into practice. The situation is saturated with ambiguity. To ignore Carl's Thai heritage would be, in our view, a grave error because it represents an essential element in the process of self-esteem. On the other hand, it would be a mistake to stress his Thai origins to the point where he begins to feel un-American; after all, he *is* an American. The difficult question is when and to what extent we should stress the Thai part of the equation.

To illustrate the risks inherent in this dilemma we relate here the experience of a couple who adopted a young Native American boy. It was the belief of this couple that their adopted son should learn to affirm his American Indian heritage with unmitigated pride. They were correct in this belief, but the actual implementation of the ideal was unfortunate. At one point in the boy's life he started to show signs of self-depreciation. The parents took this as their cue that they should increase the flow of positive information about his origins. They bought dozens of books on Native American culture and went out of their way to see films about American Indians. They even repeatedly visited an Indian reservation of the boy's native tribe. The boy showed some interest at first which reinforced the belief that this was the proper solution. Before long, however, he showed signs of regression and was shortly dysfunctional both in school and within the family. The family eventually sought therapy, when it was discovered that the boy had developed a deep fear that his parents were going to abandon him on the reservation and were preparing him for this by teaching him about American Indian culture.

It is against possibilities such as this that we must decide how to help Carl with his racist problem. Consider the dilemma: children at school single him out for ridicule because of his difference. He begins to think that his oriental features are a curse. The only recourse we have in this situation is to assure him that his Thai origins are intrinsically good; a source of personal pride. But if we go too far with our reassurance we may give him the feeling that he really doesn't belong with us. Anyone considering a bicultural adoption must come to terms with the fact that this dilemma is unavoidable and relentless, and that it is attended by uncertainty and occasional failure. When Carl inquires about Thailand we never know for sure whether his meaning is 'I want to learn more about myself', or 'I want you to reassure me that I belong here and not in some foreign country'.

We have reflected at length upon Carl's position in the family relative to his two younger sisters. They are both, as mentioned, birth children. We have been mindful from the start of the possibility that we might inadvertently show favoritism toward the girls. We are quite confident that charges of unfairness abound in any home where two or more children are present. But in adoptive families where there are also birth children the charge lies closer to the surface. Carl has accused us of showing favoritism very infrequently; no more often, probably, than would be the case if he were a birth child. Yet, we know that his unique status in the family is something of which he is too frequently reminded. This happens, usually, with such subtlety that we can scarcely prevent it. On many occasions, for example, friends or relatives have commented on how much one of the girls resembles her mom or dad. Carl's awareness, when he hears such comments, must focus on how much he *doesn't* resemble either of us. Once, when Carl was experiencing a persistent cough, we took him to our family doctor for a check-up. In the course of the examination the doctor asked us if we had a history of asthma in our family. Carl turned away with an embarrassed smile.

Situations like this come about frequently in spite of our attempts to prevent them. We even create some of them ourselves. When each of the girls was born, for example, we failed to select Thai names for them. Carl had a bicultural name but the girls did not. The oversight was unforgivable . . . twice! We eventually had to legalize the addition of Thai names for the girls at a later date, and we managed to do this in a way that obscured the oversight; the girls' Thai names became official on the same date as Carl's US citizenship became official.

One of our major concerns has been that the cumulative effect of these experiences would be to teach Carl to resent his sisters. The resentment is undeniably there but in no greater measure than is typical of biological siblings. The relationships between these children could easily have been much worse than they are. While Carl's sisters are probably the most constant, yet unwitting, source of his self-consciousness, they are also his greatest source of self-worth. Their regard for him is often nothing short of worship.

We have frequently discussed the similarities and the differences between birthing and adopting, both in terms of process and significance. Adoption proceedings can be compared, in some aspects, with the endurance of a pregnancy. There is after all a certain amount of preparation and anxiety involved in each process. What became clear to us during pregnancy was the fact that the activity of adoption was something that we had shared equally. We had been affected, both physically and psychologically, in precisely the same way because we played precisely the same role. The adoptive process was thoroughly and unmistakably a common experience. But pregnancy was much different. Here there were physical and psychological inequities. During the process of adoption we verbalized every speck of anticipation. Pregnancy, on the other hand, leaves the mother alone in silent conversation with her own body while the father is reduced to the role of spectator, waiting dumbly on the sidelines for reports of the action.

Despite the obvious differences between the process of birthing and the process of adoption, it is our view that the significance of the two is essentially the same. Carl could never be less a part of us than either of his sisters. Our love for him could not be deepened by a mere biological relation. We assert there is no important difference between giving birth and receiving life. Both acts result in the most satisfying of all human experiences: the coincidence of self-fulfilment and self-transcendence.

Our conclusion, for anyone considering an adoption, is that parenting in an adoptive family is more difficult than in a conventional family. This is especially so in the case of a bicultural adoption. In this claim we are not saying that bicultural adoptive families are qualitatively unique - *all* children are vulnerable to insecurity and isolation; *all* parents are plagued by uncertainty and guilt - we are just suggesting that the normal problems of family life become magnified in a bicultural adoptive setting. The problems have the same shape, they are just larger. But there remains a very distinct possibility that the joys of parenting are also larger in an adoptive family. To create life where there was none offers its own rewards, but these are exceeded by the joys of creating hope where there was despair.

16 Parentless refugee children: the question of adoption

RON BAKER

A refugee is any person who

> 'owing to a well founded fear of being persecuted for reasons of race, religion, nationality, membership of a particular social group or political opinion, is outside the country of his nationality and is unable or owing to such fear is unwilling to avail himself of the protection of that country; or who not having a nationality and being outside the country of his former habitual residence as a result of such events is unable or, owing to such fear, is unwilling to return to it.'
>
> (United Nations High Commission for Refugees 1951:12)

Refugee statistics are notoriously unreliable but it has been estimated that there are between 10 and 26 million refugees in the world to-day (US Committee for Refugees 1980; Hartling 1982; Sanders 1982). Approximately half of whichever figure is accepted is made up of children aged 18 years of age and under (D'Souza 1981). It is not known how many of these children are orphans, though many have been parentless for several years. What is known is that in the last thirty years or so several thousand children were brought to the US, Canada, Australia, Holland, Denmark, Sweden, and Britain and were subsequently adopted (Bagley and Young 1982).

Very little detailed information on the outcomes of these adoptions is available, for no systematic monitoring or evaluative procedures were instituted by agencies involved. The United Nations High Commissioner for Refugees (UNHCR) has a protective and overseeing responsibility for 'unaccompanied minors'. Both UNHCR and a number of voluntary agencies involved in the care of parentless refugee children became increasingly concerned about the anomalies and unethical practices that emerged in the process of some of these inter-country adoptions. Cases came to light where parents reappeared to claim their children after they had been legally adopted. A 'market' developed in refugee children in which large sums of money exchanged hands (Gallagher 1975).

> 'The American charter planes which evacuated the supposed orphans were in fact chartered by so called charitable American organizations which sold children at exorbitant prices to cover the budget for their other domestic activities. In addition to these rescue missions, there was a wave of intensive propaganda in favour of adoption which created a fashion to such an extent that it is no exaggeration to say that in those numerous North American and Venezuelan families who were able to pay it was the "in thing" to have one's "Vietnamese".'
>
> (Melone 1976:22)

To prevent situations of this kind and to formulate international principles to cover inter-country adoption a number of seminars were held over a period of twenty years (Moser 1979). These culminated in ten draft principles sponsored and promoted by UNHCR to cover the care and protection of unaccompanied minors (UNHCR 1979). The principles state unequivocally that no refugee child should be considered for adoption until all avenues have been exhausted and every effort has been made to reunite the child with parents or other members of his family, and that if a child is removed to a third country he should be returned to parents or family, wherever they are located, at their request. No time limits are placed on this.

Laudable though this policy appeared to be in protecting the rights of birth parents, there has been little substantive public discussion of it, particularly as it relates to the personality development and mental health of the child and to what extent recent research on inter-country adoption supports or contradicts it. The issue is of importance for two further practical reasons. First, there is a shortage of adoptable children in the developed world and as a result refugee agencies receive constant enquiries asking whether any refugee child is available for adoption. Inevitably these are turned down. Second, at the time of writing there are approximately 4,000 unaccompanied minors living in camps in South East Asia (UNHCR Statistics 1982). The majority of these are boys in the 14-16 age range. Some were sent out by parents to act as 'anchors' for the rest of their family to join them later; subsequently contact was lost deliberately or accidentally in some cases, so that no information is now available as to whether parents are alive or dead. Meanwhile the boys languish in camps, unable to return home and with no prospect of being settled elsewhere. It is not known how many of them are orphans. Though this particular group of youngsters may be better cared for in holding camps rather than being considered for long-term fostering or adoption in a country of secondary asylum because of their age, they highlight a serious policy issue. For it is likely that there are hundreds, if not thousands, of much younger parentless refugee children, under ten years old, in similar or worse circumstances in parts of the world where political instability and war have led to large movements of frightened people and created millions of refugees - for instance Sudan, Eritrea, Lebanon, Vietnam, Sri Lanka, and so on (Khan 1981).

The focus of this chapter is on such young children who became separated from parents in refugee situations, particularly those who have experienced personal threat to their lives. Their plight is especially harrowing. They can find themselves in another country, unable to return home with no prospect of any family reunion. Their parents cannot be traced and are most likely dead. To all intents and purposes the child is alone.

The problem faced by refugee agencies is to decide what kind of help is in the best interests of the child. Currently, the preferred approach is that the child remains in the country of first asylum in a refugee camp and is cared for by selected foster parents or in small groups along with children of similar ethnic background (Campbell 1983). The aim is to protect his ethnic and cultural identity, but the implications of this approach warrant further examination in terms of the child's personality development, mental health, and future life chances. The questions are many, the issues complex and there are no simple answers. I have selected three inter-connected themes central to the issue of long-term fostering and adoption of parentless refugee children in countries of secondary asylum in the following discussion. They are the nature of refugee children's experiences, the relationship of these to identity formation and mental health, and the pros and cons of long-term fostering and adoption of such a child in a country of secondary asylum.

Understanding the experience of some refugee children

The unaccompanied refugee child arouses compassion and concern and rightly so. In many ways they are the most disadvantaged of all children in the world today (Grant 1982).

Consider the nightmare situation in which Indo-Chinese children found themselves in the latter part of the Vietnamese war:

> 'many lost children are treated like stray dogs; travelling in packs and rummaging through garbage they are frequently stoned and if one should happen to be found dead in the street his body is discarded along with the trash. Stealing, prostitution, and begging become means of survival. Charitable homes can offer shelter to only a few. The Director of a wartime Saigon orphanage considered it providential that each night's deaths vacated sufficient space for each morning's new arrivals.'
>
> (Joe 1978:7)

And imagine too the painful reality of a little boy adrift for sixteen days in the China Sea along with other children and a few adults. Five of the children died and the boy tells of how food ran out, how water had to be carefully shared in drops, and how they were forced to drink sea water. The engine broke down several times and this would result in sharks circling their boat. On several occasions larger boats passed but despite their desperate distress signals none stopped. At last they were rescued by an American boat (Zerdoumi 1980).

These are just two examples, there are many others. What goes on in the thoughts and feelings of children who have such experience? What survival strategies do they employ and in what ways are their personalities affected? Loss dominates their world, loss of everything that is significant: parents, family, home, friends, things (Marris 1974). Some have witnessed torture, rape, and dehumanized death. Their hurt can be added to by being neglected or by insensitive handling in holding camps. Trust in adults is massively attenuated or disappears.

As a general rule the younger the child the more difficult it is for him to understand what is happening and why. These generalizations about unaccompanied minors need to be treated with caution. It would be wrong to assume that all refugee children have been seriously traumatized by the refugee experience. The problem is that there has hardly been any research into how the refugee experience affects the unaccompanied child (Gershon 1966; Baker 1982). We know virtually nothing about the significant factors that lead to greater or lesser traumatization if a child remains in a holding camp or is fostered or adopted elsewhere. Often assumptions and generalizations are made as a result which may or may not be true.

It is obvious that significant differences exist between parentless children from different countries and the circumstances in which they lost their parents. The 9,354 children who came to Britain between 1938–40 from east and west Europe were sent out by parents (or concerned others if parents had already been taken away) to save them from extermination in concentration camps (Gershon 1966). A few miraculously survived the horrors of such camps and came to America and Britain after the war (Davidson 1979; 1983; Leitner 1980; Hart 1983). More recently unaccompanied minors have come out of South East Asia, particularly from Korea and Vietnam. They were parentless for a variety of reasons. Some had been sent out with the hope that parents might be able to join them later. Others were abandoned, or wanted to avoid military service, or were hostile to the communist regime (particularly boys aged 13–18). Others still, became 'split off' from parents 'in flight', or were abandoned by them, or saw them killed, whilst others simply fell asleep on a boat they were playing on and found themselves at sea when they awoke.

One would like to know very much more on how these children coped in their new environment and, once they were 'received' in another country, how they responded to the care they experienced (Zigler 1978; Tiborn 1981). As has been observed: 'knowledge about refugee children suffers most critically from the absence of hard data which would permit sophisticated quantitative analysis. Children are in this way too the most neglected part of the refugee population' (Huyck and Fields 1981:247). After initial reception or resettlement, detailed information is needed on how the refugee child establishes himself in a new country, what use is made of educational provision, what occupations are chosen, the ability of the person to form intimate relationships, and what criteria (if any) were arrived at to decide whether group home, family fostering, or adoption was the most appropriate form of help.

A substantive literature on inter-country and inter-racial adoption is available but hardly any of this refers specifically to adoption as this relates to the parentless refugee child. To gain insight into the nature of these children's experiences we can draw from a range of data which includes what the children are able to tell us in words or through their play and drawings, the observations of those who have had close relationships with them, the analysis of agency records (Fry undated), and a few research findings.

Despite national, ethnic, or racial differences, the one thing that all such children have undegone is the refugee experience, and this has occurred at a vulnerable time in their personality development. A serious student of 'refugeeism' writes: 'many of the stages through which the refugee passes in his exodus leave a residue of psychic scar tissue and continue into his present day life to affect his perceptions, values, and attitudes' (Keller 1975:87). Keller's research is based on adults, but his observations may be even more pertinent for the child refugee. There seems little doubt that the child experiences a serious assault on his identity as a direct result of becoming a refugee. There also seems agreement among refugee workers that many of these children become psychologically scarred, some perhaps for life. The picture they present soon after the experience is one of personal and social crisis: they are confused, disorientated, psychically numbed, emotionally drained, and some release their stress in explosive 'acting out' behaviour.

A psychologist with experience of Kampuchean refugee children writes:

> one is not long in the company of these children before becoming aware of their continuing emotional struggle to recover from the past. Recurring nightmares plague many children, especially those who have witnessed the death of a parent. Sometimes they wake from these night terrors with somatic complications: headaches, stiff necks, respiratory ailments, or occasionally the temporary loss of eyesight or hearing unconnected to organic impairment. And given paper and crayons, these children spend hours making what psychologists refer to as "catastrophic drawings". This same behaviour was observed in children liberated from Nazi concentration camps.'
>
> (Boothby 1982:1)

And another painfully vivid picture from the same author:

> 'Mom is one of more than 3,500 Khmer children who have entered holding centres inside Thailand since 1979 without their parents. A few of these children were in severe shock seeing a parent bayoneted to death or a brother or sister blown apart in a landmine explosion. Many suffered from prolonged malnutrition. All had emerged from years of continual violence and upheaval.'
>
> (Boothby 1982:1)

I wish now to consider the effects of such experiences on the identity formation and mental health of the unaccompanied refugee child.

Identity, mental health, and the traumatized refugee child

Identity refers to a sense of 'I' or 'oneness' that the individual develops particularly in the early formative years of his life. How it occurs is complex and little understood but comprises physical, psychological, and socio-cultural elements which are inextricably connected. Gaining insight into the feeling and fantasy state of the refugee child is extraordinarily difficult. Few are open enough or articulate enough to allow this to happen. Even fewer helpers can have real empathy for what the child has gone through and continues to go through.

We can gain glimpses into the child's world by carefully noting his behaviour and play. Commonly such a child is hypersensitive to other people and situations. An obvious survival strategy has forced him to function like an emotional radar screen identifying nuances of feeling which 'normal' children would not recognize, and which he interprets often rightly. Relationships with others are characterized by mistrust and suspicion and reflect the cluster of feelings which the child struggles to come to terms with - loss, anger, fear, panic, alienation, confusion, guilt, and emptiness. It may be said with truth that all deprived children struggle with such feelings, but the traumatized refugee child feels them with greater intensity (Lindemann 1944).

To illuminate further the dynamics of the refugee child's situation and how his identity is seriously threatened, I draw on a simple framework which I have referred to elsewhere as a 'relationship web' (Baker 1983).

In this it is suggested that a person's identity is formed and maintained by a range of factors which interact to provide structure and meaning throughout life, as shown in *Figure 1*.

Figure 1 Central components of the 'relationship web'

A

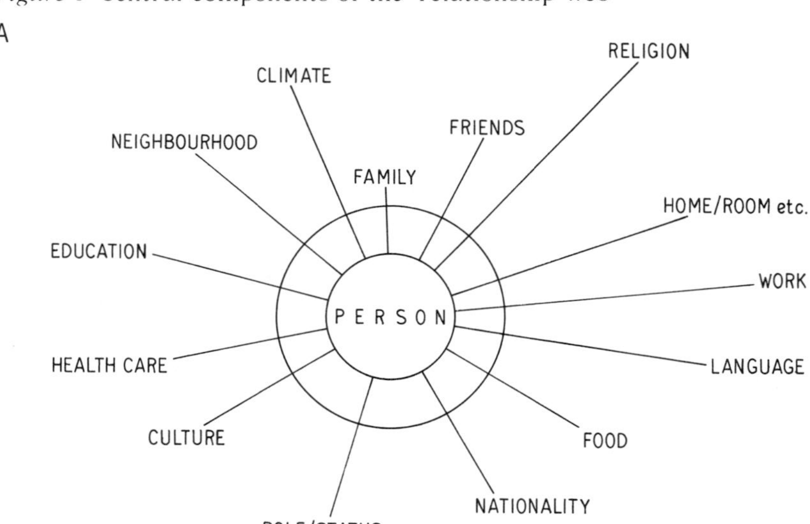

As is depicted the person is normally 'held in position' by affiliations that include other people, institutions, societal structures, norms, and assumptions. To strip these away suddenly is to put the person into a state of crisis and serious psychological risk. The picture then becomes totally different (B).

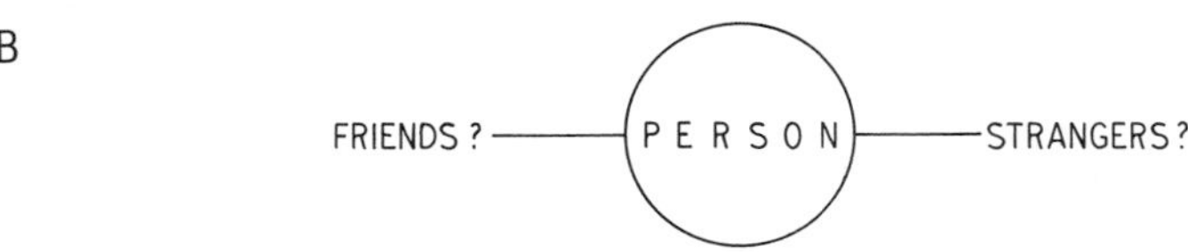

There is no relationship web to speak of. Assistance for such a person requires that the relationship web is now respun by the combined efforts of the individual and those who assist him. This process is likely to take considerable time.

The unaccompanied refugee child who is dramatically transported to a country of secondary asylum is in this position. He finds himself in a strange land, often unable to communicate at all and, worse still, unable to decode other people's messages to him. Everything is different, food, climate, and surroundings, and there is little sense of belonging. Like a piece of driftwood in the sea he feels powerless. Such a child differs significantly from one who is orphaned in his own country. The latter at least retains some affiliations which provide a 'part web' and make for a degree of continuity.

On this basis it may be argued that it is preferable for the child to remain in a holding centre in a neighbouring country close to his country of origin, because at least a 'part web' can be retained and built on, rather than being considered for fostering or adoption elsewhere. But the central issue must be, what *on balance* is in the child's long-term interests? Is he more or less likely to develop normally in a holding centre, or by being fostered or adopted? There are indeed many questions to which at this stage we have few answers. What can be said is that to make such judgements involves very careful and systematic assessments by skilled workers who need to take crucial factors into account such as the age of the child, his physical and psychological state, the relationships (if any) he retains with significant others, his future life chances if he were to remain in a holding centre or go to a country of secondary asylum, and the motivation and resources of those who would care for him in the latter.

It is known that identity formation and mental health are closely connected. In her substantive review of the mental health literature Jahoda cites numerous research findings which show the connection between self-esteem, self-acceptance, and an integrated personality structure (Jahoda 1958). A person with a sense of self-worth is clear about his identity, has basic trust in himself and others, and a range of realistic purposes and goals.

The concept of identity has always been difficult to define. Numerous attempts have been made by psychologists (Erikson 1968, 1971; Maslow 1968; Rogers 1961), sociologists (Cooley 1922; Mead 1962; Goffman 1959, 1968), and social workers (Perlman 1968; Dixon and Sands 1983). Erikson is possibly the most influential and often quoted writer on this subject. In his 'eight-stage model of man' he suggests that identity is formed and consolidated throughout the life cycle. The individual's identity is confirmed or weakened as he moves through a series of 'psychosocial crises' in which a number of ego characteristics (trust, autonomy, initiative, identity, intimacy, generativity, integrity) and ego qualities (perception, reasoning, memory, judgement, tension tolerance, impulse control, and so on) become part of the personality structure (Hollis 1982:182). Erikson sees the development of identity as a process which is 'located in the core of the individual and yet also in the core of his communal culture' (Erikson 1971:22). Thus psychological and socio-cultural elements combine and contribute to the individual's identity.

Four core factors can be identified in the vast literature on identity formation which are of direct relevance in understanding the situation of the refugee child. It is clear that mental health and a sense of identity are based on the following:

a) a feeling of continuity with the past and present - 'knowing one's roots';
b) an awareness of an essential 'I' which remains the same in different situations;
c) being 'at home' and identified with a particular social group;
d) feeling significant and acknowledged by others.

The refugee child is hardly ever in the position to feel positive on any of these counts. His grip on the past and present is often fluid and tenuous, rarely is a reference group available (unless these are other children in a similar position to himself), 'significant others' have disappeared, and he is dependent on strangers.

Drawing on Erikson's insights, Dixon and Sands offer a useful analysis of the relationship between identity and the experience of crisis:

> 'during crisis situations the vital centre of a person - his or her sense of identity - is threatened. . . . When coping methods fail, the "person" [writer's change from "client"] experiences feelings of identity loss or diffusion. This experience involves feelings of worthlessness, loss of purpose and meaning, and a sense of non-

being that erode cognitive and emotional faculties and result in a crisis state.'

(Dixon and Sands 1983:227)

Three other important aspects of identity need to be mentioned which are of particular relevance for the unaccompanied refugee child. These are the racial, ethnic, and 'adoptive' aspects of his world. They represent the totality of his life and what he has to integrate.

The notion of a racial identity is controversial. Here it simply means the obvious physical characteristics that distinguish one group of people from another, that is to say skin colour, hair, facial and other bodily features. To acknowledge differences in no way implies that either one group or another is superior or inferior. The racially different refugee child has to develop survival strategies (and needs help to do this) to cope with people and a community that may harbour strong hostility towards him (Chestang 1972). It has been suggested that 20 per cent of British people are blatantly racist, wanting no contact with racial minorities, 60 per cent hold assimilationist views, which mean they are prepared to tolerate minorities only if they submerge their cultural characteristics, and 20 per cent are pluralistic (Bagley and Young 1982:84). Other research supports the view that there are strong racist elements in British society (Scarman 1982; Cheetham 1982). Any discussion on the wisdom of transracial adoption of refugee children in Britain and principles of good parenting practice must take those unpleasant facts into account.

Whereas physical differences are obvious, ethnic identity is not nearly so clear, yet its retention is central to the child's identity. For some children who have not been helped to retain an awareness of and pride in their roots the price in terms of their mental health can be high (Ladner 1977). Research on transracial adoption in the US shows that, on the whole, black and oriental children have made a successful adjustment (Kim 1978; Silverman and Feigelman 1981). However, Dong Soo Kim cautions that the long-term implications of this apparent success are uncertain. He comments: 'From a mental health perspective the term adjustment has questionable validity because it may be a matter of relative or subjective judgement without sufficient reference to the internal definition of well-being of the children themselves' (Kim 1978:480).

Our attention is drawn to an important point which is that we need to ask the children themselves how they feel and not merely rely on 'external' indicators which are likely to be biased in favour of success. It seems quite possible for a child to appear fully acculturated yet not really to have integrated his ethnic, racial, and adoptive identities. (In adults it has been suggested that this can result in 'identity guilt' (Keller 1975:91).) The result could be a child whose identity becomes split. It may also link to a comment occasionally made by refugees themselves and refugee workers, 'once a refugee always a refugee'. This is yet another issue that warrants research.

Lastly 'adoptive' identity. This broad concept includes all that the child must absorb by way of language, norms, values, new relationships, and so on in the new country. Naturally, it incorporates his adoptive family if he is adopted. A range of factors will influence the speed with which this can occur – the quality of care he experiences, the relationships he makes, peer group affiliations, school, and so on. Generally speaking, the older the child and the greater the difference between the host country and himself, the more complex and lengthy the process will be (Hochfeld 1960; Cederblad 1981).

To summarize this section: unaccompanied refugee children are uprooted physically, psychologically, and socio-culturally. To a greater or lesser extent this is a traumatic experience which impedes the child's identity development at a particularly crucial point in life. In the process he may be left confused about who he is, where he belongs, and what the future holds. A sense of loss dominates his feelings, his ego boundaries are blurred, and his sense of 'I' is seriously under threat. He needs help to overcome his losses, to rebuild his life, and to integrate the racial, ethnic, and adoptive aspects of identity (Comité Inter-Mouvement Auprès des Evacués 1978; Vasquez 1981). Though it may take years to achieve, the ideal outcome for such a child is a fully acculturated person who has knowledge of and genuine pride in his origins. The position taken here is that because of the nature of his refugee experiences the parentless refugee child is in a 'special' category and has more than the usual developmental tasks to achieve (Sterba 1949). This is so whether he remains in a holding centre or goes to a country of secondary asylum.

The issues relevant to the long-term fostering or adoption of refugee children will now be discussed.

Parentless refugee children: should they be adopted?

It is of course impossible to generalize; some children benefit from adoption whilst others do not, but the research outcomes on inter-country adoptions show that on the whole they are successful.

> 'all studies of adoption outcome, regardless of the nature of the sample - white infants, older, foreign, handicapped, transracial, independent - have high success rates. A major negative finding is that no study has yet succeeded in identifying variables either in the child or adoptive parents that consistently predict success or failure, suggesting that most adults who wish to do so can adopt successfully and that most children are indeed adoptable.'
>
> (Shapiro 1982:101)

Alongside this there is considerable concern among a number of researchers who show that some adoptive parents and agencies avoid acknowledging and supporting ethnic and racial differences (Kim 1977; Ladner 1977; Bagley and Young 1979: Gill and Jackson 1983). This can leave the child with identity problems and lacking effective coping mechanisms when he meets a hostile racist world. Physically and intellectually transracially adopted children do as well if not better than their contemporaries. To what extent this is true for the adopted refugee child is not known, for virtually none of the research refers specifically to him or the problems that his foster or adoptive parents might have to deal with. Hence it needs to be used with caution. What is required are in-depth studies on refugee children themselves, how they experienced the range of different forms of care, what were the policies and principles that were used to decide whether they were kept in community homes, family fostered, or adopted. Further we need to study whether the long-term outcomes of different approaches were significantly different, and what was the experience of adoptive parents or others who looked after these children. A study along these lines, which may produce some useful insights, is now in progress (Ressler, Boothby, and Steinbock 1984).

Within refugee organizations and among refugee workers, different views are apparent. The Ockenden Venture has over thirty years of experience in dealing with unaccompanied minors in Europe, Tibet, Africa, Indo-China, and the UK. Having evaluated this work, Joyce Pearce, Ockenden's Executive Chairperson concludes,

> 'It is our firm conviction on humanitarian grounds that any policy which places a child from an alien culture immediately into a family fostering situation is wrong. We recommend a group home system from which real and natural relationships can be formed at the child's own pace without external pressures and when sufficient adjustment to a new life style has been made for there to be as little trauma as possible.'
>
> (Pearce 1981:3)

This position is much in line with the UNHCR draft principles and would find considerable support among refugee workers. The statement does not explicitly rule out family fostering or adoption but discussion with Joyce Pearce confirms her view, that in the short term neither of these alternatives is in the child's best interests. She believes that the child should form close and 'natural' relationships at his own pace with prospective foster or adoptive parents and that this could take several years to achieve. There is little doubt that the quality of 'community home' care that Ockenden has been able to offer has been of a very high order. However, it does beg the question to what extent are other organizations (statutory and voluntary) able to provide the loving and committed care so ably demonstrated by Joyce Pearce herself, and whether they would be as prepared to allow potential adoptive parents and refugee children to ease into a significant relationship over such a considerable time.

Another perspective is provided by Christian Outreach, a UK agency with substantial experience of facilitating the adoption of South East Asian children found in the 'life and death situations' described earlier. From the mid-1970s this organization has been involved in the adoption of 120 babies and older children and reports that 'in general they have been very very successful' (written communication 1983).

There are obviously no hard-and-fast rules that ought to be applied. Circumstances of life and death demand immediate action and flexibility in approach seems to be what is required in working out what best to do. The key factor is careful, comprehensive, and systematic assessment of each child's needs, so as to match these against the resources and alternatives available, and to do this in circumstances where the child feels secure, cared for, and as far as possible involved in decisions about his future. The arguments for and against the adoption of unaccompanied refugee children can be summarized as follows.

AGAINST ADOPTION

1 Adoption is final. It is frequently impossible to be sure that the child's parents are dead. If they reappear and claim him, a 'tug of war' over the child can occur and legal battles follow which can seriously affect his development (Zwerdling and Polansky 1949).

2 Refugee children (of 'knowing age') are too traumatized to benefit from the kind of parenting that the majority of adoptive parents are able to give.

3 Adoption locks the child legally into a relationship which inevitably is complex and which he may come to resent as he gets

older (McWhinnie 1967; Triseliotis 1973; Raynor 1980). (Several acquaintances of mine who were fostered refugee children recall now how pleased they were that they had not been adopted because they were enabled to retain a sense of independence, particularly at those times when they were not getting on with foster parents. 'It was good to know that they were not my real parents or that I was not legally bound to them at times.')

4 Adoption does not readily enable the child to retain and develop his cultural roots and ethnic identity.

5 In principle such adoptions should not occur because:

(i) the child is better off in his own country and culture, as inadequacy of care is essentially seen through western eyes. One writer views it as another form of imperialism and asserts:

> 'a society where adoption hardly exists in practice should not when attacked from all sides suffer further from the very persons who profess to be coming to its aid, but because of their traditions, own needs and legal policies, impose structures which are the very negation of indigenous traditions.'
>
> (Melone 1976:25)

(ii) inter-country adoption results in a 'market' for refugee children. At the same time it exploits poor countries, indulges the wealthy, and reduces the guilt of the rich countries (Melone 1976; Resnick & de Rodriguez 1982).

FOR ADOPTION

1 For full psychological bonding to occur, the child and the adoptive parents need to know and feel that they have a total commitment to each other. Without the certainty of a legal contract, this is less likely to occur. The adoption gives full entitlements, responsibilities, and controls over the child, clearly establishes in law what the child is entitled to, and also legally protects him.

Adoption is therefore a necessary (but not sufficient) prerequisite for the loving care the child needs to develop (Bowlby 1971, 1975, 1981; Goldstein, Freud, and Solnit 1973, 1980).

2 The refugee child's special developmental and identity needs require constant, consistent, and nurturing parental figures with whom very special relationships can be developed. These may be needed for many years if not for the rest of their lives. Arrangements outside adoption for these children are less likely to provide this.

3 To adopt a refugee child is the ethical thing to do and helps to create a multiracial society.

Summary

The controversial question of the adoption or long-term fostering of refugee children in countries of secondary asylum bristles with psychological, ethical, legal, and practical issues, all of which require further analysis and empirical research.

For the parentless refugee child the question of who he is and what he is to become are crucial. Most of these children desperately need to belong to someone. They need the security and warmth of stable close relationships, not only to grow emotionally, but to work out the significance of their losses with people they have learnt to trust. Sometimes they need the opportunity to grieve months or years after brutalizing events they experienced, because it was too dangerous or confusing to do this when they were 'in flight'. To be able to 'work through' the painful reality of their refugee experience the options for these children are varying forms of care and assistance within refugee holding camps or being brought to a country of resettlement where a community home, family fostering, or adoption are all possibilities. On balance it would seem that adoption should be seen as a viable option only in special circumstances and that long-term community care should be used in the first instance.

What is clearly evident is that in western countries there are people of goodwill, sound motivation, and resources who want to care for and love the parentless refugee child and be loved by him in return, whether this is on a fostering or adoption basis. On the sensitive issue of the adoption that some of these children experience, research and common sense suggest that in special circumstances some of them would benefit enormously from the love and security that very carefully selected adoptive parents could give, as long as they had appropriate support and advice from skilled child carers (Michaels 1952; Montalvo 1959: Kirk 1964: Silverman and Feigelman 1977; Bagley and Young 1979; Costin and Wattenberg 1979).

An issue which is currently arousing a lively debate in the general field of adoption is the suggestion that there comes a time when it may be in the child's best interests to be adopted, even if it is known that the parents are alive though they may have had no contact with their child for several years (Tizard 1977). This recognizes the significant difference between biological and psychological parenting. Whether it warrants thinking about in relation to refugee children who may languish in camps for years is a matter of conjecture. Through the eyes of a parentless refugee child, who has little contact with family or whose parents and family whereabouts have been unknown for years, it may matter very little whether his developmental needs are met by black, brown, yellow, or pink people as long as they are met by someone.

Hawaii recognized the special needs of some refugee children by changing its adoption laws several years ago. It placed on statute that children who came into the country in 'extraordinary circumstances', and where 'the existence, identity, and whereabouts of the child's parents are not reasonably ascertainable', could be adopted after a one-year waiting period (Sanders 1978). To my knowledge the outcomes of these adoptions have not been reported and it would be helpful to know what problems and issues became apparent in following such a policy.

In conclusion it seems apparent that a policy has evolved to keep parentless refugee children in holding camps in first countries of asylum. Other options, such as moving these children to countries of secondary asylum where they could be offered 'community home' care, long-term family fostering, or adoption, are much less favoured. To what extent present policies are in the best interests of some of the most needy children is not known. Careful examination and empirical research into the implications and outcomes of these alternative forms of care are needed.

References

Bagley, C. and Young, L. (1979) The Identity Adjustment and Achievement of Transracially Adopted Children: A Review and Empirical Report. In G.K. Verma and C. Bagley (eds) *Race, Education and Identity.* London: Macmillan.

______ (1982) Policy Dilemmas and the Adoption of Black Children. In J. Cheetham (ed.) *Social Work and Ethnicity.* London: Allen & Unwin.

Baker, R. (1982) *The Refugee Experience: Communication and Stress.* Paper presented at the International Association of Schools of Social Work Research Seminar, University of Sussex, August 1982. In Press. Also available from the author.

______ (1983) *The Psychosocial Problems of Refugees.* British Refugee Council/European Consultation on Refugees and Exiles, Bondway House, 3-9 Bondway, London SW8 1SJ.

Boothby, N. (1982) Khmer Children: Alone At The Border. *IndoChina Issues* No. 32:1-7. Centre For International Policy, Indochina Project.

______ (1983) The Horror, The Hope. *Natural History* 1(83):64-9.

Bowlby, J. (1971) *Attachment and Loss,* vol 1. Harmondsworth: Penguin.

______ (1975) *Attachment and Loss,* vol 2. Harmondsworth: Penguin.

______ (1981) *Attachment and Loss,* vol 3. Harmondsworth: Penguin.

Campbell, P. (1983) Unaccompanied Minors: The Issues. *Refugees.* News from the United Nations High Commissioner for Refugees, No. 17, May.

Cederblad, M. (1981) Getting An Identity: Transracial Intercountry

Adoption. In L. Eitinger and D. Schwartz (eds.) *Strangers in the World.* Amsterdam: Huber.

Cheetham, J. (1982) *Social Work and Ethnicity.* London: Allen and Unwin.

Chestang, L. (1972) The Dilemma of Biracial Adoption. *Social Work* 17: 100-15.

Comité Inter-Mouvement Auprès des Evacués (1978) The Influence of Political Repression and Exile on Children. In *Mental Health and Exile,* World University Service, May 1981, 20 Compton Terrace, London N1 2UN.

Cooley, C.H. (1922) *Human Nature and The Social Order.* New York: Scribner's.

Costin, L.B. and Wattenberg, S.H. (1979) Identity in Transracial Adoption, a Study of Parental Dilemmas and Family Experiences. In G.K. Verma and C. Bagley (eds) *Race Education and Identity.* London: Macmillan.

Davidson, S. (1979) Massive Psychic Traumatization and Social Support. *Journal of Psychosomatic Research* 23:395-402.

______ (1983) The Psychosocial Aspects of Holocaust Trauma in the Life Cycle of Survivor - Refugees and Their Families. In R. Baker (ed.) *The Psychosocial Problems of Refugees.* British Refugee Council.

Dixon, S.L. and Sands, R.G. (1983) Identity and the Experience of Crisis. *Social Casework* 64(4):223-30.

D'Souza, F. (1981 rev. ed.) *The Refugee Dilemma: International Recognition and Acceptance.* Report No. 43, Minority Rights Group, 36 Craven Street, London WC2N 5NG.

Erikson, E. (1968) *Childhood and Society.* New York: Norton. (A complete bibliography of all of Erikson's work is contained in H.M. Mair (3rd edn.) *Three Theories of Child Development* 1978:276-80.)

______ (1971) *Identity Youth and Crisis.* London: Faber.

Fry, P. (undated) *Children Caught Between Countries.* Unpublished but available from the author.

Gallagher, U.H. (1975) What's Happening In Adoption. *Children Today* Nov/Dec.

Gershon, K. (1966) (ed.) *We Came As Children: A Collective Autobiography.* London: Gollancz.

Gill, O. and Jackson, B. (1983) *Adoption and Race.* London: Batsford in association with BAAF.

Goffman, E. (1959) *The Presentation of Self in Everyday Life.* New York: Doubleday Ruckor.

______ (1968) *Stigma: Notes on the Management of Spoiled Identity.* Harmondsworth: Penguin.

Goldstein, J., Freud, A., and Solnit, A. (1973) *Beyond the Best Interests of the Child.* New York: Free Press.

______ (1980) *Before the Best Interests of the Child.* London: Burnett Books/ Deutsch.

Grant, J.P. (1982) *The State of the World's Children 1981-82.* UNICEF, 866 UN Plaza, New York, NY 10017, USA.

Hart, K. (1983) *Return to Auschwitz.* London: Granada Publishing.

Hartling, P. (1982) From Tragedy to Hope. *Refugees.* News from the United Nations High Commissioner for Refugees, No. 1, January. Nobel Peace Prize Lecture delivered in Oslo 10/12/81.

Hochfeld, E. (1960) In the Adoptive Family: The Alien Child. *Social Casework* 41 (March 3rd edn.) 123-27.

Hollis, F. (1982) *Casework: A Psychosocial Therapy* (3rd edn). New York: Random House.

Huyck, E.E. and Fields, R. (1981) Impact of Resettlement on Refugee Children. In *International Migration Review,* Special Issue, Refugees Today, ed. B.N. Stein and S.M. Tomasi. vol 15 (53-4):246-54.

Jahoda, M. (1958) *Current Concepts of Positive Mental Health.* New York: Basic Books.

Joe, B. (1978) In Defense of Inter-Country Adoption. *Social Service Review* 52 (March):1-20.

Keller, S. (1975) *Uprooting and Social Change: The Role of Refugees in Development.* Delhi: Manohar Book Service.

Khan, A.S. (1981) *Study on Human Rights and Massive Exoduses.* UN Economic and Social Council, Commission on Human Rights, 38th Session, United Nations.

Kim, D.S. (1977) How they Fared in American Homes: A Follow Up Study of Adopted Korean Children. *Children Today* 6 (March/April):2-6.

______ (1978) Issues in Transracial and Transcultural Adoption. *Social Casework* 59(8):477-86.

Kirk, H.D. (1964) *Shared Fate.* New York: Free Press.

Ladner, J. (1977) *Mixed Families Adopting Across Racial Boundaries.* New York: Anchor/Doubleday.

Leitner, I. (1980) *Fragments of Isabella: A Memoir of Auschwitz.* London: New English Library.

Lindemann, E. (1944) Symptomatology and Management of Acute Grief. In H.J. Parad (ed.) *Crises Intervention: Selected Readings.* New York: Family Service Association of America.

McWhinnie, A.M. (1967) *Adopted Children: How They Grow Up.* London: Routledge & Kegan Paul.

Marris, P. (1974) *Loss and Change.* London: Routledge & Kegan Paul.

Maslow, A. (1968) *Toward a Psychology of Being.* New York: Reinhold.

Mead, G.M. (1962) *Mind, Self and Society.* Chicago: University of Chicago Press.

Melone, T. (1976) Adoption and Crises in the Third World, Thoughts on the Future. *International Child Welfare Review* 29(June).

Michaels, R. (1952) Special Problems in Casework with Adoptive Parents. *Social Casework* 33 (Jan):18-24.

Montalvo, F.F. (1959) Casework Consultation in Overseas Adoption. *Social Casework* 40 (March):129-36.

Moser, A. (1979) International Perspective: *Adoption and Fostering* 1, 1:44-8.

Pearce, J. (1981) *The Ockenden Venture (UK) Programme for Unaccompanied Children.* Mimeograph. Available on request from the Ockenden Venture, Guildford Road, Woking, Surrey, U.K.

Perlman, H.H. (1968) *Persona.* Chicago: University of Chicago Press.

Raynor, L. (1980) *The Adopted Child Comes of Age.* London: Allen & Unwin.

Resnick, R.P. and de Rodriguez, G.M. (1982) *Intercountry Adoption Between the United States and Colombia.* International Social Service, American Branch, and Latin American Regional Office.

Ressler, E.M., Boothby, N., and Steinbock, S.J. (1984, research in progress) *Unaccompanied Children in Emergencies.* Research co-ordinated by E. Ressler, Institute Henry Dunant, 114 Rue de Lausanne, 1202 Geneva, Switzerland.

Rogers, C. (1961) *On Becoming a Person* Boston: Houghton Mifflin.

Sanders, D. (1978) The Interdisciplinary Approach in Work with Vietnamese Refugees. *International Social Work* 21(4).

______ (1982) *New Developments in International Refugee Work: A Challenge to Social Work Education.* Paper presented at XXIst International Congress of Schools of Social Work, University of Sussex, Brighton, UK, August.

Scarman, L.R. (1982) *The Scarman Report.* Harmondsworth: Penguin.

Shapiro, D. (1982) Minority Interests in Adoption. In *The Social Welfare Forum 1981,* National Conference on Social Welfare (108th), Columbia University Press.

Silverman, A.R. and Feigelman, W. (1977) The Impact of Political Conflict on Transracial Adoption: The Case of Vietnamese Children. *Group* 1(4):253-64.

_____ (1981) The Adjustment of Black Children Adopted by White Families. *Social Casework* 62(9):529-36.

Sterba, E. (1949) Emotional Problems of Displaced Children. *Social Casework* 30(May):175-81.

Tiborn, K. (1981) *A Follow Up of the Conditions of Unaccompanied Minors and Handicapped Persons Among Refugees from Vietnam Resettled in Sweden.* National Board of Health and Welfare, Sweden.

Tizard, B. (1977) *Adoption: A Second Chance.* London: Free Press.

Triseliotis, J. (1973) *In Search of Origins: The Experiences of Adopted People.* London: Routledge & Kegan Paul.

United Nations High Commissioner for Refugees (1951) Text of the 1951 Convention Relating to the Status of Refugees. In *Convention and Protocol Relating to the Status of Refugees.* United Nations, 1981.

_____ *Draft Body of Principles On The International Protection of Unaccompanied Minors,* UNHCR Circular to Governments - mimeograph.

UNHCR Statistics (1982) *Report on Numbers of Unaccompanied Minors in Camps of First Asylum Having a UNHCR Presence.* October. UN Circular.

US Committee for Refugees (1980) *World Refugee Survey.* 1970, New York.

Vasquez, A. (1981) Adolescents From the Southern Cone of Latin America in Exile: Some Psychological Problems. In *Mental Health and Exile.* World University Service, May 1981, London.

Zerdoumi, N. (1980) Refugee Children. *Refugees.* News from the United Nations High Commissioner for Refugees, No. 5, December.

Zigler, E. (1978) America's Baby Lift of Vietnam's Children: What Is To Be Learned For a Psychology of Change. In J. Anthony and C. Chiland (eds.) *The Child in His Family: Children and Their Parents in a Changing World.* London: Wiley.

Zwerdling, E. and Polansky, N. (1949) Foster Home Placements of Refugee Children. *Social Casework* 40:277-82.

17 Latin American children in intercountry adoption

ROSA PERLA RESNICK

Introduction

The adoption of Latin American children by adoptive parents from the developed countries of the world is examined in this chapter as a recent phenomenon of growing significance. Drawing on the findings and recommendations of a 1982 study, *Intercountry Adoptions between the United States and Colombia*, (Resnick and Rodríguez 1982) this paper focuses specifically on the practices and procedures involved in the intercountry adoption process and its related cross-cultural and racial problems. Reference is also made to the recommendations that emerged from the Interamerican Interdisciplinary Expert Group Meeting on Adoption, held in Quito, Ecuador, in March 1983, where there was a strong support for legislation to safeguard children's rights at the international level (Calvento Solari 1982; Opertti Badan 1982).

An overview

While adoption is as old as mankind, the adoption of children by parents living not only in other communities, but in other countries, is a new concept. Without attempting to delve into history, but in order to place Latin American adoptions in perspective, it is appropriate briefly to remark that the modern practice of intercountry adoption emerged after World War II when the disruption of families in war-torn countries left behind a considerable number of orphans and abandoned children. Intercountry adoption of those children took place first between European countries, and later, between those countries and the United States (Joe 1978; UNICEF 1979).

By 1950, the number of European children available for adoption began to decrease as a consequence of various factors such as widespread sex education, implementation of family planning practices, growing sterility among childbearing couples, increasing social acceptance of unmarried mothers, and extensive legalization of abortion. Therefore, couples interested in adopting children turned to the less developed countries of the Third World. In the years 1955-75, Asian countries became the predominant source of children for adoption by prospective parents from developed countries. In Asia, as well as in other parts of the Third World, poverty and overpopulation contributed to child abandonment while, in countries such as Korea and Vietnam, the devastating impact of war generated large numbers of abandoned, orphaned, and rejected children. Originally, certain Asian governments, namely Korea and Vietnam, authorized intercountry adoptions, particularly with the United States (Chakerian 1966; Kramer 1975).

As a result of these developments, a number of social agencies emerged in the United States and Third World countries to deal with this new trend, although the sending countries appeared to have reservations about the practice (Melone 1976). Some of the arguments used to justify these reservations were related to the fact that, being poor and underdeveloped, there was some fear of being exploited by the rich countries and of the impact on population trends of the loss of infants and young children. Another concern was related to the poor national image that could emerge if international adoptions were perceived as the result of the inability of developing countries to meet the needs of their underprivileged children. Ethical considerations also came to the fore when international adoptions were criticized as financial transactions in a children's market. Selling children for large sums cast suspicion on intercountry adoptions and the reliability of those who sponsored them.

With these criticisms in mind, social agencies such as International Social Service, the Centre International de l'Enfance, the Adoption Resource Exchange, and others tried to develop policies and procedures in order to safeguard the security and the legal rights of children adopted between countries. However, such adoptions were hampered by the fact that there were differences in the adoption laws of various countries. As a consequence, the first World Congress on Adoption and Foster Placement held in Italy in 1971 petitioned the United Nations to convene an international conference for the purpose of establishing a World Convention on

Adoption Law and formulating a new code.

However, despite these efforts, to date no final decisions have been reached on international regulations governing these adoptions. Further efforts are currently aiming to establish much needed safeguards so that the rights and social wellbeing of the children are protected. An international meeting of experts convened by the United Nations in Geneva, in December 1978, produced a 'Draft Declaration on Social and Legal Principles Relating to Adoption and Foster Placement of Children Nationally and Internationally'. This has already been reviewed by twenty-eight member states and is on the agenda for discussion at the 1983 session of the General Assembly (Pilotti Davies 1983).

Adoption of Latin American children

By 1975, Latin American countries had become the main source of adoptable children for prospective parents from developed countries. This resulted to a considerable extent from the fact that South Vietnam in 1975 and Korea in 1980, in their concern at losing their children, began to implement new policies that would eventually put a stop to the emigration of children for adoption. Furthermore, abortion legislation in Singapore, Hong Kong, and Korea had significantly reduced the number of unwanted children. In addition, rapid economic development and more liberal social attitudes were bringing about an improvement in the social welfare programs and living conditions in oriental countries, thus limiting the number of children likely to be given up for adoption.

In the United States, a shortage of white children and particularly of young babies was a major reason why prospective adoptive parents turned to Latin America. Furthermore, factors such as the following account for Latin American countries currently becoming a significant source of adoptable children: patterns of industrialization have broken down the traditional extended family; difficult socio-economic conditions have affected many families and have been particularly hard for abandoned or unmarried mothers; and the social services are in short supply for everyone.

In *Table 1* below Colombia emerges as the Latin America country sending the largest number of children to the United States, a number that increased every year. In 1980, Colombia rated second among all countries in the world, sending abroad over 650 children or 13 per cent of the total number. At the regional level, Colombia contributed 44 per cent of the 1498 children leaving Latin America for the United States; Mexico rated second in 1973 and third in 1980.

Table 1 *United States: Orphans adopted abroad*[1] *or admitted for adoption, by country or region of birth, 1973, 1975, 1980*

country or region of birth	*1973*	*year 1975*	*1980*
Total, all countries	4,015	5,633	5,122
Latin America & Caribbean: total	332	977	1,498
Brazil	20	26	49
Chile	n.i.	n.i.	97
Colombia	107	379	659
Costa Rica	14	94	49
Ecuador	21	61	42
El Salvador	n.i.	69	183
Guatemala	n.i.	31	82
Honduras	13	n.i.	19
Jamaica	7	25	29
Mexico	85	162	116
Nicaragua	2	15	8
Panama	13	21	23
Peru	7	15	70
Rest of L. America & Caribbean	43	79	72
Asia: total	2,976	4,221	3,414
Korea	2,183	2,913	2,693
Philippines	205	244	255
India	8	37	317
Thailand	70	139	12
Vietnam	324	655	1
Rest of Asia	186	233	136
Europe	388	265	127
Africa	13	21	21
Oceania	17	16	1
Canada	289	133	61

n.i. = no information
Source: This table originally presented in Spanish in F. Pilotti Davies (1983) is now reproduced in English by permission of the Sección de Estudios Juridicos y Sociales, Instituto Interamericano del Niño. The data for 1973 and 1975 came from International Year of the Child, *Adoption*, New York, 1979, pp. 20-1. The data for 1980 came from the US Department of State, Bureau of Consular Affairs, *Statistics on Immigrant Visa Issuances During Fiscal Year 1980*, October 1981.

In that year it was displaced by El Salvador, presumably as a consequence of the political, social, and economic crises in that country. Data contained in this table show that Latin America is the only region in the world where the number of children being adopted abroad is increasing, from 8.4 per cent in 1973 to almost 30 per cent in 1980. In the light of current world circumstances, it can be predicted that the number of children coming from Latin America for adoption will increase, primarily as a result of the policies of countries in the Far East to limit this activity during the last decade (Pilotti Davies 1983).

PROBLEMS

As the number of intercountry adoptions originating in Latin America increases, there has been a growing concern on the part of Latin American governments and responsible groups in both the sending and the receiving countries about the purpose and the procedures for such adoptions.

At present, prospective parents use different means to contact the children, such as social agencies, independent intermediaries, and voluntary associations. The countries from which the children come have different regulations and services in relation to adoption. In short, there is no uniform procedure through which the adoption of Latin American children is carried out.

With regard to legal aspects, the diversity of laws and regulations is even more complicated, because adoption legislation in the United States, for example, is a matter of state rather than federal law. In Latin American countries there is no single legal approach to adoption. It is also necessary to take into account the fact that intercountry adoptions involve not only legislation on adoption itself, but also regulations on migration in both the sending and the receiving countries. The diversity of procedures and regulations makes it difficult for agencies to operate with clear guidelines and this gives rise to serious concern about possible questionable activities surrounding a number of these adoptions.

As noted in the International Social Service report on Colombian adoptions, the public outcry for meaningful improvements in the intercountry adoption process, particularly between the United States and Latin America, has grown increasingly loud in recent years. Scores of documented cases of scandalous abuses of parents and children have continued to emerge in both continents. Widening recognition of such conditions has led in the past to the establishment of adoptive guidelines and procedures, such as the *Intercountry Adoption Guidelines* prepared by the American Public Welfare Association (and published by the United States Department of Health, Education, and Welfare in March 1980). It was recognized by all, however, that while these guidelines were well received, they were not mandated by law to be implemented. However, a number of corrective strategies and resources, many of which were activated by the adoptive parents themselves through their own organizations and various advocacy interest groups around the United States, have evolved in recent years with some success.

In contrast with the wealth of studies on the adoption of oriental children, there is a conspicuous lack of research on Latin American adoptions. The newness of the phenomenon, coupled with the controversies involved and the importance given to other priorities in the field of child welfare, may account for the inadequate attention to this subject.[2]

Intercountry adoptions between the United States and Colombia

A study, completed under the sponsorship of the American Branch and Latin American Regional Office of the International Social Service, attempted to examine systematically the practices and procedures in effect for the adoption of Colombian children by American parents (Resnick and Rodríguez 1982). Its purpose was also to identify similarities and differences in the respective laws and their enforcement, as well as contradictions and/or weaknesses that could jeopardize the security and wellbeing of the children involved. An examination of the attitudes and opinions of all participants in the process was also part of the study. Its ultimate objectives were to identify the possible problems emerging in the intercountry adoption process between the United States and Colombia and to contribute to a set of recommendations that would be helpful for future practice as well as holding implications for future policy formulation.

The research was carried out simultaneously in the United States and in Colombia through interviews and mailed questionnaries in English and Spanish. In the United States the respondent groups included adoptive parents, agency personnel, and judicial, immigration, and consular authorities. In Colombia, judicial authorities, staff of public and private agencies, health professionals, and consular officials were involved.

The findings and recommendations that emerged from the study are here summarized in the form in which they were published in the report (Resnick and Rodríguez 1982):

PROCEDURES IN THE ADOPTION PROCESS FOR COLOMBIAN CHILDREN

According to Colombian law an abandoned child must be declared legally abandoned in order to be available for adoption. This declaration must be requested by the agency from the judicial authorities.

While only half of the Colombian personnel thought that most children had the declaration of abandonment, most of the adoptive parents believed that the majority of children did have such a declaration. However, there is a time element involved in this procedure, because the declaration of abandonment should be requested three months after the child's arrival at the agency, but it is usually requested after six months. Also, the judicial authorities commonly delay action on this request.

The problem concerning the declaration of abandonment leads to the first recommendation emerging from this study:

Recommendation 1: Any intercountry adoption program with Colombia must inform prospective adoptive parents in full detail about the need to obtain a legal declaration of abandonment for children who have been abandoned, and has to involve attorneys in the US, preferably with experience in intercountry adoptions and corresponding Colombian professionals as required by Colombian law.

If the child is not abandoned, consent for adoption is necessary. There was wide belief across all respondent groups that this consent was usually given by the biological mother, but in some cases it is issued by the agency.

Initial Contacts with Adoptive Parents

Contacts between adoptive parents and children were made through different systems of communication. Adoptive parents contacted both Colombian and American agencies, but most of the children were actually made known to them directly by Colombian agencies. This raises the question of whether the American agencies had any information available to give to the parents. There is reason to believe that adoptive parents and 'individuals interested in adoptions' were the main sources of information to American agencies. The 'individuals' display their work openly, outside the agency system, and although they are considered important contacts by Colombian staff, they are not thought to be ideal sources of information. They are not regarded as illegal operators, but their activities are likely to create risks for parents and children.

It seems from the data that the formal systems of Colombian and American agencies, as well as adoptive parents' groups, actually appear to be the principal resources for contact between parents and children. This apparently contradicts the popularly supported notion, so widespread in the media, that adoptions in Colombia are mainly carried out through the intervention of particular intermediaries, but since 'individuals interested in adoptions' come from an informal outside system that is likely to bring problems to the child, the following recommendation is made:

Recommendation 2: An effort should be made to establish a Center of Information for American and Colombian agencies, as well as for prospective parents, regarding the laws and procedures in force in both countries. This would make the 'outside' informal system of information unnecessary. An international social agency would be an ideal organization to fulfill this function.

Criteria in Selecting Adoptive Parents

Adequate financial resources are regarded as a very important factor by all respondents except the lawyers and the adoptive parents themselves.

Family structure as a criterion for selection was perceived differently by Colombian staff and by American parents and staff. While there appears to be a trend in Colombia to prefer childless couples, this element is considered unimportant by the United States respondents.

The age of the prospective parents did not seem to be an important criterion on the part of the American respondents. However, the Colombians expressed a preference for couples between 30–35 years of age, which would suggest that adoptive parents older than biological mothers were preferred.

The capacity for good social relations was considered to be very important, but the religious affiliation of the adoptive parents was regarded in both countries as unimportant.

Criteria based on similarity of race traits point up important issues. In spite of the fact that the parents were not asked about their race, parents adopting Colombian children are white and are seeking children who have features similar to theirs. This may eventually bring about problems both in Colombia - leaving behind children 'hard-to-place' because they do not have 'white' features - and in the US, where parents may become aware of racial differences only when the children grow older, because these differences are not apparent at an early age.

Recommendation 3: Any intercountry adoption between Colombia and the US must respect the values and cultural patterns of both countries. The procedures for selecting the children should not create new problems.

Criteria and Procedures for Assigning the Child to Adoptive Parents

Criteria concerning the children's good physical health and physical characteristics were generally observed, but the legal situation of the child was the criterion most frequently used to select him/her for adoption.

The Home Study

Although the importance of conducting a home study of the adoptive parents clearly emerged from the data, this research did not investigate the conception or the content of it in the two countries. There was widespread agreement across all respondent groups that a home study of the prospective parents should be done by an American social agency before starting adoption procedures, but the Colombian agencies also indicated a desire for some participation in the preparation of the home study. This reflects the conflicting criteria that have been noted.

Recommendation 4: A system should be established to facilitate discussion and exchange of views between Colombian and American agencies so that better safeguards and controls may be applied at both ends on behalf of parents and children.

Information Received by Adoptive Parents

Adoptive parents generally received adequate information about the physical characteristics of the child but less information about his/her emotional nature. Previous experiences of the child were often disclosed, but the motives of biological parents for releasing children for adoption were not so frequently revealed. Information concerning the child's family background or socio-economic status was provided only sometimes. Lawyers, perhaps being overly concerned about confidentiality, did not allow agencies to share full information with the prospective parents, preventing them from acquiring a better understanding of their future child.

There was full agreement that parents received complete information regarding the documentation required in Colombia and in the United States.

The role of judicial authorities and judges in Colombia appeared to be well understood by many adoptive parents. However, the role of the Colombian Institute of Family Welfare or the US Consulate in Bogota was not so clear to adoptive parents.

Voluntary associations of adoptive parents, Colombian agencies, 'individuals' involved in adoptions, and American agencies were the most important sources of information about Colombian adoptions.

In summary, information received by adoptive parents, which was provided by various sources, was generally incomplete, not only regarding the child, but also regarding the procedures to follow. The respondents recognized the problem of insufficient or distorted information; limited information is available in agencies in both countries.

Recommendation 5: A system should be established to convey clearly to Colombian and to American agencies, as well as to adoptive parents, background information concerning the child's origin and life experience, with due regard for confidentiality, in order to enable parents to reveal to the child a real picture of his/her past history when it becomes appropriate to do so.

Termination of the Adoption Process

There was a tendency to consider the trial period of the child in the adoptive home as essential before the adoption was completed. However, some respondents thought adoption should be completed at the time of placement, and many respondents, particularly Colombian lawyers and agency staff, did not answer the question. In any case, there was general agreement that adoptions should be completed in both countries, that a follow-up period is necessary, and that this should be done mainly by an American agency.

The adoption process generally took one year at most, contradicting the media, which reported that cases were resolved in just one month. The latter were considered to be exceptions.

The total cost of the adoption process ranged between $2,000 and $6,000. Inflation and differences in the time period of the adoption might account for this spread.

From the comparative analysis of the laws of Colombia and the US it was concluded that the adoption should be legally finalized in both countries. This is indeed the only means to prevent legal risks to children and parents. The laws as well as the opinions of most of the respondents identified the possibility of a legal limbo for the child, otherwise.

Recommendation 6: An American agency should assume the responsibility of conducting a trial period in the adoptive home and making sure that the adoption is finalized in the US.

Cross-cultural and racial issues

Issues related to differing cultures and races become apparent in the process of selecting Latin American children as well as in the process of their integration and adjustment into a society that is socially, culturally, racially, and linguistically different. However, the wealth of follow-up studies done so far on Asian children adopted by American and European parents suggest that their early adjustment to their new environments has generally been a happy and positive experience (Andersson 1982; Bagley and Young 1980; Kim 1978).

As already noted, no research has been produced on any aspect of Latin American adoptions other than statistical tables, let alone the follow-up on the integration of the adopted children into their new foreign families. A number of experiences have been reported in a recent book:

> 'Some of the prospective parents who contacted us expected me to describe what a typical Colombian child looked like. There was no way I could. The population of Colombia, and of most other Latin American countries, is even more racially mixed than that of the United States . . . I advised prospective parents who insisted upon adopting white children to go to Argentina, Chile, Costa Rica, or to the old colonial cities of Colombia to personally select the children they wanted. . . . [The same authors report that] discrimination was apparent in the questions of many prospective parents . . . in most cases adoptive parents gave a great deal of thought to the interracial and cross-cultural implications of Latin American adoptions.'
>
> (Erichsen and Erichsen 1981:54)

In the end, through careful in-depth examination of feelings and attitudes, many parents do reach the decision to adopt a racially and culturally different child with the conviction that the child will be welcomed into their families. It is important to point out that in the United States there is a large network of adoptive parent groups, organized as self-help groups, which conduct a series of workshops, seminars, lectures, social gatherings, in order to help both parents and children to become acculturated to each other's customs and behaviors (Resnick 1982).

The International Social Service study revealed that there were different attitudes to racial issues. Most of the Americans in the sample, in contrast to some of the Colombians, considered that the 'parents' race should be similar to the child's' (Resnick and Rodríguez 1982). A striking finding relates to the religious affiliation of the adoptive parents, which does not seem to play an important role in their selection of children, although it is a well-known fact that a majority of Colombians belong to the Roman Catholic faith.

These issues are indeed controversial and difficult to resolve. No generalizations can be made about the motivations of adoptive parents in the selection process, in order to increase the possibility of a successful adoption.

Recent developments

As mentioned earlier there is no international legislation governing the adoption of children between countries. There are only bilateral agreements such as those between Sweden and Korea.[3] In Latin America, Colombia and Ecuador have studied the possibility of a similar arrangement with Sweden.

As a result of this serious gap, an Interamerican Interdisciplinary Expert Group Meeting was convened in Quito, Ecuador, in March 1983, by the Organization of American States, Washington, DC; the Interamerican Institute for the Child, Montevideo, Uruguay; the Swedish Government; and by several Latin American and European international organizations, public as well as private. The purpose of the meeting was to review the legal and social aspects of adoption in order to stimulate the updating of current legislation, particularly in the field of previously enacted international private law.

This meeting came about as a result of the Xth General Assembly of the Organization of American States (OAS) in 1980, which recommended that the adoption of minors be included as the only topic of family law to be considered by the projected Interamerican Conference on International Private Law (Conferencia Interamericana Derecho Internacional Privado) in early 1984.[4] A similar interest was expressed by the XIth General Assembly of the OAS held in Santa Lucia in 1981 supporting an initiative of the Interamerican Institute for the Child (Montevideo, Uruguay) along the same lines.

The agenda included three basic themes: 1) socio-medical-psychological aspects in adoption; 2) national or domestic law; 3) private international law. These themes were discussed during the one-week deliberations by more than sixty experts coming from most of the Latin American countries, from the United States, and several European nations.

Some of the most important recommendations emerging from that meeting follow:

1 Every effort should be made to strengthen family life in the children's own country before any consideration is given to putting the child up for adoption.
2 If adoption is considered, priority should first be given to prospective parents in the child's own country.
3 If this proves to be unsuccessful and intercountry adoption is resorted to, procedures should be developed through private or public licensed agencies with experience in the social welfare international field.
4 The security of the adoptee will depend on national legal norms, as well as on the international private laws that the countries involved in intercountry adoptions decide to follow.
5 Interdisciplinary teams of lawyers, medical doctors, psycholo-

gists, and social workers should be involved in the intercountry adoption process so that each individual case may be accurately evaluated from every professional perspective in order to come up with the best possible solution.

Conclusion

Latin American adoptions are today on the forefront of the international child welfare scene due to the increasing number of children adopted by foreign parents. While there is a dire need to stimulate Latin American countries to modernize their laws and regulations for domestic adoptions, it is also true that social, economic, and political developments around the world call for improvements in intercountry adoption legislation with Latin America.

Although guidelines and practices have been established in the past on behalf of children, a UNICEF document indicates that

> 'to the detriment of many children, safeguards so clearly spelled out in official documents dating back two decades and observed in intercountry placements have been many times totally ignored in intercountry arrangements . . . in the absence of adequate and carefully structured research, false myths are perpetuated and harmful and ineffective practices are repeated.
>
> (UNICEF 1979:5, 13)

In 1982, International Social Service, in its research on intercountry adoptions, took the first step on behalf of Colombian children adopted by American parents. There is hope that the awareness raised by the study will stimulate further research and discussion about the still *terra incognita* field of Latin American adoptions, and that it will also have an impact on the entire social welfare field as systems are developed in other parts of the world.

Notes

1 United States Immigration and Nationality Act, Sec. 101 (b) (1) (F): 'a child, under the age of 16 at the time a petition is filed in his behalf to accord a classification as an immediate relative under sec. 201 (b), who is an orphan because of the death or disappearance of, abandonment or desertion by, or separation or loss from, both parents, or because the sole surviving parent is incapable of providing the proper care and has in writing irrevocably released the child for emigration and adoption.'

2 A series of twenty-seven documents produced in Spanish for the Interamerican Interdisciplinary Expert Group Meeting on

Adoption, Quito, Ecuador, March 1983, will contribute to a better understanding of intercountry adoption in Latin America. Available from the Interamerican Institute for the Child, Av. 8 de Octubre 2904, Montevideo, Uruguay.

3 Treaty of 15 December, 1966 between the National Social Welfare Board of Sweden and the Child Placement Service in Korea. Renewed on 7 April, 1975 between the same Swedish organization and the same Korean agency, whose name was changed to Social Welfare Society (Korea). Still in effect. (Data provided by the Swedish Consulate in New York City.) On 17 December, 1979, the National Board of Health and Welfare in Sweden authorized the Swedish Organization Adoption Centre to grant intercountry adoption assistance to Swedish families residing in Sweden, who want to adopt a minor child of Korean nationality.

4 Draft conclusions from the Quito, Ecuador, meeting held in March 1983. Final Report published in late 1983. *Reunión de Expertos sobre Adopción de Menores, 7 al 11 de Marzo de 1983, Quito, Ecuador,* by the Instituto Interamericano del Niño, OEA, Sección de Estudios Juridicos y Sociales, Montevideo, Uruguay.

References

American Public Welfare Association (1980) *Intercountry Adoption Guidelines.* Washington DC: Department of Health, Education, and Welfare.

Andersson, Gunilla (1982) *Intercountry Adoption in a Swedish Perspective.* Paper presented at the International Congress on Adoption, Eilat, Israel, 9-14 May.

Bagley, C. and Young, L. (1980) The Long Term Adjustment and Identity of a Sample of Intercountry Adopted Children. *International Social Work* 23(3):16-22.

Calvento Solari, U. (1982) Hacia un Nuevo Derecho de la Adopción. *Boletín del Instituto Interamericano del Niño* 56(218):17-24. Montevideo, Uruguay.

Chakerian, C.G. (1966) *Children of Hope.* New York: Immigration Services Church World Service and Chicago: Department of Church and Community, McCormick Theological Seminary.

Conferencia Interamericana Derecho Internacional Privado III (1984) (Interamerican Conference International Private Law), held at La Paz, Bolivia, April.

Erichsen, J.H. and Erichsen, H.R. (1981) *Gamines: How to Adopt from Latin America.* Minneapolis: Dillon Press.

Joe, B (1978) In Defense of Intercountry Adoption. *Social Service Review* 52(1).

Kim, D.S. (1978) Issues in Transracial and Transcultural Adoption. *Social Casework* 59(8):477-86.

Kramer, B. (ed.) (1975) *The Unbroken Circle.* Minnesota: OURS (Organization for a United Response).

Melone, T. (1976) Adoption and Crisis in the Third World: Thoughts on the Future. *International Child Welfare Review* 29, June:20-5.

Opertti Badan, D. (1982) La Adopción Internacional en el Derecho Internacional Privado. *Boletín del Instituto Interamericano del Niño* 56(218):25–35.

Pilotti Davies, F. (1983) *Las Adopciones Internacionales en América Latina: Antecedentes Sociales, Psicológicos e Históricos y Sugerencias para su Reglamentación*. Montevideo, Uruguay: Sección de Estudios Jurídicos y Sociales. Instituto Interamericano del Niño.

Resnick, R.P. (1982) *Adoptive Parent Self-Help Groups in Latin American Adoptions*. Paper presented at the XXIst Congress of Schools of Social Work, Brighton, England, 23-7 August.

Resnick, R.P. and Rodríguez, G.M. (1982) *Intercountry Adoptions between the United States and Colombia*. New York: International Social Service, American Bank.

UNICEF (1979) International Year of the Child *Adoption*.

Acknowledgement

The author and publishers would like to thank the International Social Service, American Branch for permission to reproduce recommendations made in Resnick and Rodríguez (1982:129-35).

18 The influence of western adoption laws on customary adoption in the Third World

MAEV O'COLLINS

Adoption as a social transaction is a subject of interest to anthropologists and jurists, in part because the range of adoption practice is as varied as the societies in which it is a frequent, or at least unremarkable, event. This very range and diversity increase the difficulties inherent in a comparative cross-cultural study of adoption, as rural communities in Europe or North America share many common features with their counterparts in Third World countries. Urbanization and industrial development have brought changes in family structures and attitudes towards parenthood in western and non-western societies. The process of change and adaptation of customary laws has been a continuous one but this discussion will not attempt to consider the situation in societies in the Third World prior to the introduction of western legal systems. It will focus on the colonial and post-colonial period when customary adoption laws and practices came in contact with the different attitudes and historical traditions reflected in western law.[1]

Other papers in this volume are concerned with the current adoption debate in western societies as western adoption laws are also under pressure to change in order to reflect changing societal values and social conditions. The focus here will be on western laws which were introduced in or which influenced Third World societies, although they may represent an outdated version of present practice in their countries of origin.

Introduction

'Adoption was the ancient, as it is the modern, method of creating by law, the relationship of parent and child.'

(Abbott 1930:460-61)

The creation of a new relationship seems a universal and accepted element of adoption transactions. However, the corollary that existing parental ties are always broken does not hold for all adoptions. In some societies adopted children continue to have regular and meaningful contacts with their biological parents and kin, and adoptions are ways of enriching and strengthening ties between two family groups. Western adoptions tend, at least in ideal terms, to make the welfare of the child the paramount concern, although dispensing with the consent of a parent is viewed as a serious matter which must only be done in carefully circumscribed situations. In some non-western societies, however, adoption is the initiation of a gift relationship, one which reflects well on the person who gives as well as the recipient. The birth parents display their generosity or sympathy towards the relative or clan member who adopts their child. To *refuse* an adoption request may be a serious matter leading to family or group tension. Once again this is very different from the pervasive, if unspoken, feeling that a parent who gives up his or her child is somehow less loving or less responsible. The feeling that those who adopt are acting generously is a more universal sentiment as adoption carries with it the gloss of caring and giving freely to the child, whatever the reality may be in particular situations.[2]

Adoption norms and practices reflect different attitudes to parenthood and parenting behaviour. In many small-scale societies adoption is between relatives; is not always permanent although this may be the intention at the time of adoption; does not involve cutting off ties with the birth parents; and may involve continuing or additional inheritance and successional rights. It is clear that this is a very different approach from that of formal non-relative adoption in modern western societies. One can appreciate the despairing comment of Robert Lowie that in Third World traditional societies 'adoption customs rest on a mental attitude difficult to conceive for those nurtured in western traditions' (Lowie 1930:460).

Modern western adoption laws were formalized in the late nineteenth and early twentieth centuries, at a time when many western legal systems were introduced as part of colonial laws or as the majority law in settler-dominated countries. How successful has this process been in changing the flexible, varied and ambiguous nature of customary adoption practices? To what extent have these western attitudes and legal practices altered the way adoption transactions are carried out? Are there other influences, religious as well as secular, which need to be taken into account? Is western adoption practice itself under review and are traditional attitudes and norms less exotic and perhaps more understandable than in 1930?[3] Lowie's comments are particularly apposite to this discussion as, although customary adoption practice will be considered in a broader comparative perspective, a major focus will be on the South Pacific. This is because the writer's experience as an adoption worker, and in teaching and research, has been in this region. In addition, societies scattered across the South Pacific which form the broad groupings of Micronesia, Polynesia, and Melanesia, share a greater acceptance of adoption as a normal feature of social life. It is as true today as in 1930 that: 'Oceania as a whole represents a main center for adoption carried to unusual lengths' (Lowie 1930:460).

Adoption practice: diversity and change

Before discussing the special features of adoption practice in Oceania, customary adoption in Africa and Asia will be considered, the effects of religious and administrative influences, and the relationships between different systems of law.

Adoption practice in Africa

Writing in 1897, the first indigenous barrister from the then Gold Coast (now Ghana) described customary adoption among the Fanti in these terms:

> 'Adoption is practised by persons who have no next of kin to succeed to their property. The person adopted is usually of the same clan as the person adopting, but if of a different clan, he assumes the name given him and becomes a member of his clan. To make adoption valid it must be done publicly and the person who wishes to adopt must not only get the consent of the family and parents whose child is about to be adopted, but he must clearly state before witnesses his desire and intention.'
>
> (Sarbah 1968:34)

Shared clan membership, a public statement of intent, and the need for family as well as parental consent are common features of customary adoption in Africa. Other writers refer to adoption in times of war or famine and to the changes in adoption practice during times of civil disturbance (Cotran and Rubin 1970:60–6). Different legal mechanisms had been instituted by the colonial administration whereby disputes regarding adoption could be heard and adjudicated, but the persistence of customary practice was noted. When discussing the adoption of children among the Kikuyu of Kenya, one writer stated:

> 'This article is not concerned with the substantive law of adoption in Kenya, which is contained in the Adoption Ordinance, 1958. Section 36 of the Ordinance recognises the impossibility or inexpediency of applying the general law to all races in the Colony, and adoption among Africans continues to be regulated almost entirely by the provisions of tribal custom.'
>
> (Simmance 1970:69)

Rights on both sides are usually not completely transferred by adoption and a child adopted by friends will not be cut off from contact with natural parents or kin. Tswana customary adoption might involve a direct request for a child, or parents might themselves initiate an adoption of a child by relatives or friends (Schapera 1970:65). Rights of inheritance may depend upon whether the adoption is recognized by elders in the community. Birth sons born after an adoption have pre-emptive rights to inherit property or land (Cory and Hartnell 1970:65–6).[4]

The development of parallel legal systems, with customary and introduced laws existing in an uneasy relationship, began with European colonial expansion and may also be found in nation states which were not formally colonized by European metropolitan countries. In a comprehensive treatment of legal pluralism, Hooker concludes that received English law and common law principles, interacting with diverse customary laws, resulted in a complex amalgam of laws and procedures which defy orderly interpretation. He points out that:

> 'Tanzania and Ghana exemplify post-independence attempts to establish a body of common law which will include statutory received English law and customary law. . . . Adoption has been influenced but probably less than other areas of law as "through enabling legislation the traditional position in regard to the definition of legally recognized personal relationships was preserved within general limits".'
>
> (Hooker 1975:183–85)

Nevertheless, the move towards codification of laws, establishing of precedents, and uniformity in such matters as succession and inheritance of property, has affected more flexible, if sometimes ambiguous, customary adoption practices. Disputes over adoption are now heard in western-style courts, precedents are established and determine later cases. Customary law, as Sarbah noted in 1897, speaks of what *usually* happens and uses broader concepts of family or parental consent. It is inevitable that as unification and co-ordination proceed and civil law becomes the preferred method for determining social rights and obligations, there will be a shift away from diversity and a narrowing of interpretation in adoption matters (Van Tromp 1970).

INTERACTION OF RELIGIOUS, SECULAR, AND CUSTOMARY LAWS

Customary adoption laws and practices have been influenced, not only by western laws, but also by religious codes which exist alongside secular legal systems. In discussing customary law in the Punjab, Diwan describes the Hindu institution of adoption where, if a man has no sons an adopted son provides great spiritual benefit for his adoptive father (Diwan 1978).

Under the Hindu Adoptions and Maintenance Act 1956, changes took place and a wife can now veto an adoption where formerly her consent was not necessary. Rights of succession and inheritance of property are described as absolute and are contrasted with the less formal Punjabi customary adoption where an heir is appointed but without changing rights of collateral succession (Diwan 1978:98–124). The introduced English system of courts and judicial interpretation of laws adds another dimension to adoption as court orders and registration of adoptions provide evidence of the validity of an adoption. Nevertheless, customary adoption has continued as the practice of choice and Diwan states that: 'the custom of adoption, both formal and informal, has been almost universal, so much so that *it has been held in a series of cases* that burden of proof lies on the person who asserts that there is no custom of adoption' (Diwan 1978:112–13, emphasis added).

The effect of legal interpretations has been to strengthen the position of formal adoptions as being more certain and recognizable, although this has been questioned on the grounds that they are essentially different concepts and that legal interpretation has failed to recognize these fundamental differences (Diwan 1978:124).

The influence of a plural legal system on adoption practices is described by Tambiah in his discussion of Sinhala laws and customs in Ceylon (now Sri Lanka). English court systems and judicial interpretation of the facts of adoption have altered adoption practices. For example:

> 'The necessity for a public declaration by the adopting parent to constitute a valid adoption has been stressed in many decisions, but the Courts after a period of vacillation have now veered round

to the view that a public declaration by the adopting parent is not necessary.'

(Tambiah 1968:109)

It should be noted that for Sinhalese, as for Punjabi and Fanti, adoption by one adoptive parent (usually an adoptive father) seems to be the rule rather than the idea of adopting parents replicating biological parenthood.

In adoption, as in other areas of personal and family law, the move towards codification and unification of the law may weaken the position of customary law and lead to a greater acceptance of European-based civil law. Customary or *Adat Law* in Indonesia and Malaysia is complicated, not only by the influence of Dutch civil law but also by the application of Islamic law (Ter Haar 1962). Hooker reports that it seems 'settled law now that adopted children will not succeed to an intestate in Malaya' (Hooker 1975:175). Adat and Islamic Law differ in respect to inheritance by adopted children, but he cites a case in the period of Dutch colonial rule of Indonesia when the strength of Adat Law was reflected in a decision in which 'The court recognized the claim of an adopted son of a deceased woman to share in her estate according to local *adat*. At Islamic law, an adopted child had no claim' (Hooker 1975:272).

While in some societies Islamic Law has gained a position of dominance over customary law, Indonesian national sentiment and post-colonial revision of Dutch Civil Law have sought to maintain Adat Law, and Islamic law appears to have remained in a subordinate position. However, as Hooker cautions, 'discussion of Adat, inter racial law or Islamic law necessitates a consideration of the other two, even if only to exclude them' (Hooker 1975:284).

In the examples so far customary adoption has involved a public, or at least a verifiable, statement of intent in which community leaders, witnesses, or other regulatory mechanisms exist to ensure that an adoption transaction has taken place. However, in Japan prior to World War II:

> 'Adoption was simply a private transaction. . . . Often between the two family heads concerned, conceivably without regard to the wishes of the adoptee. There was no judicial control whatever, and adoption could thus be used to cover the sale of a human being for purposes of gain and exploitation.'
>
> (Watanabe 1963:369)

The introduction of a new family law in 1947, and other changes in the Civil Code at that time, emphasized individual rights and greater equality in decision making. Watanabe, in describing changes in the status of family members, notes that:

> 'the institution of adoption, once a device to secure the continuation of a House, is now an instrument of child welfare. The adoption of a child below the age of majority can no longer be made by simple agreement of the natural and adoptive parents, but requires the approval of the Family Court, which must determine whether the adoption will promote the best interests of the child.'
>
> (Watanabe 1963:375–76)

This last example is the most explicit evidence of the effect of western-style thinking and legal regulation on traditional or customary adoption. It is noteworthy that these changes occurred in the immediate post-war years when Japan was under American military occupation.

ADOPTION IN THE SOUTH PACIFIC

A pervasive western attitude is that adoption is unusual or in some way exceptional and worthy of particular comment or question. This may explain why the South Pacific is seen as a remarkable area for the study of customary adoption where many family groups in a community may be involved in one or more adoption transactions. Before describing the frequency of adoption in Torres Straits societies, Lowie commented: 'In some regions of the globe, however, adoption is practised on a scale wholly disproportionate to any rational grounds therefore' (Lowie 1930:460).

Two collections of articles on adoption in Oceania have documented the wide range of adoption practices which exist in non-western societies in the South Pacific (Carroll 1970; Brady 1976). The fluid boundary between adoption, with its implications of permanent and changed relationships, and fosterage, or temporary or partial changes in parental rights and responsibilities, makes it impossible to generalize even for small societies sharing similar cultural values and social structures. In one society 'a conspiracy of silence surrounds the adoption and it is considered to be very bad taste to tell a child he is adopted' (Marshall 1976:35). In another: 'The adoptee's continuing relationship with his natural parents may range from infrequent to almost daily contact' (Morton 1976:78). While for another it has been observed that 'Although young children are made aware at an early age who their adoptive parents are, that is, who they "belong" to, they are never forced to reside with them against their will' (Tonkinson 1976:233).

The transfer of major parental responsibilities to the adopting parents exists side by side with a continuing link with the child's biological kin. Adoption in Manihi Atoll, in the Tuamotu Archipelago to the east of Tahiti, exemplifies these dual obligations: 'While the natural parents are expected to show continued affection and interest in their child, the child's first obligation is to the adoptive parents' (Brooks 1976:53).

The concept of adoption as a transaction which involves social exchanges is found in many South Pacific societies.[5] In Truk it is reported that gifts to the family of the child are given by the adopting family. 'As tokens of their future intentions, and also to obligate the real parents before the child arrives, they bring little presents to the family, particularly the pregnant mother' (Goodenough 1970:324).

These gifts are not seen as payments for the child but rather as a necessary cement to make the transaction real and lasting. In many societies it is a common practice to exchange gifts as part of any serious social transaction - marriage, the birth of the first child, as part of funeral ceremonies. These exchanges are meant to build up and make permanent relationships between family groups. In adoption transactions this becomes important as the ties which bind natural and adopting parents and their kin help prevent problems arising later on. There is a belief that:

> 'it is easier to deal with people with whom one already has an established account of reciprocal rights and obligations. Hawaiians feel that conflict is less likely with such people and that any problems which do arise can be more easily mediated. If the natural parents are neither relatives nor friends, there is a lingering fear that the contract will be broken either by them or the child.'
>
> (Howard *et al.* 1970:32)

In discussing adoption in Hawaii the authors state that Hawaiians fulfil social needs through personal transactions and use these rather than the formal western institutions. Similarly, Tahitian adoption has been contrasted with western adoption by Levy, who concludes that:

> 'In form, Polynesian and Micronesian adoption is relatively frequent, public, casual and involves only partial transfer of the adopted child to the new family. Western adoption is relatively infrequent, private, formal, and involves an almost complete transfer.'
>
> (Levy 1970:83)

In Papua New Guinea, adoption encompasses a wide range of practices which have been recorded by observers since European colonial administration in the 1890s. One observer who worked among the Gunantuna of the Gazelle Peninsula from 1899 to 1914 described payments of traditional money and complete secrecy as being the feature of adoption within the same society (Meir 1929:35). More than fifty years later, adoption on the Gazelle Peninsula was described as a way by which the generosity and 'big man' status of a Tolai leader had been publicly demonstrated. 'His household is now replete with adopted children and dependent male relatives. He is the epitome of the traditional Tolai big man' (Salisbury 1970:326).

Adoption carried out within a group may mask the differences which exist between adoptive and biological ties. Fortune noted that in Dobu it was considered that 'adoption is never felt to be as binding a tie as blood kinship' (Fortune 1963:17). On the other hand, retaining biological kin ties but gaining recognition in a new kinship group is reflected in practices where adopted children use kinship terms for both adopted and biological kin (Du Toit 1975:93). Certainly, in the past adoption by complete strangers was a rare event except in times of warfare or social disruption when children who had been orphaned or captured might be adopted into a family.[6] Among the Melpa of the Western Highlands for example, a man might take over children 'in the past usually refugees of war, to be his own children' (Strathern 1972:106).

Influence of western adoption practices

What happens when western-style laws and attitudes converge with traditional, more flexible approaches to adoption? It has been noted by a number of commentators that those involved in an adoption transaction distrust the more rigid and remote procedures associated with western courts. Registration as a 'customary adoption' or in the land courts provides a halfway meeting ground but even here the gradual development of systematic procedures and precedents tends to make customary practice less flexible as it is recorded and used as the basis of later judgments. The introduction of national written constitutions and political government has also served to standardize adoption through legislation. For example, following disputes over succession and appeals from the Tongan Land Court, the Tongan Legislative Assembly passed a constitutional amendment to the effect that: 'A male child of the adopted title holder would not succeed to his father's title. Instead, on the death of an adopted holder, the title would return to a successor in the original blood patriline' (Marcus 1977:236). This illustrates how western-style procedures tend to lessen the ambiguities which have been a central feature of adoption practices in traditional societies.

Adoption in the Ellice Islands (now Tuvalu) consists of both legal and customary procedures. These may be either (a) a legal contract, in which the adoption event is negotiated through the island government and registered with the local Lands Court or (b) a customary contract, in which the adoption event is negotiated orally and independent of the court. The main elements that make up the adoption transaction are 'mutual consent, firm land allocations, and appropriate behavior', but it has been observed that the introduced system is less acceptable as 'Adoption legislation does not take traditionally ambiguous adoptions into account' (Brady 1976:139).

The same view was expressed, albeit in different terms, by Mr Justice Smithers of the Supreme Court of the then Territory of Papua New Guinea, when considering whether a financial payment could be made as part of adoption proceedings. Evidence was given that it was customary practice in the particular society for payments to be made to the female line by the father of a male child. He concluded that there was 'nothing reprehensible in the mother receiving, and the applicant paying an amount of money in connection with this major event in their lives and the lives of their children. It is not something upon which the law should frown' (*Papua New Guinea Law Reports* 1965–66:58).

This example illustrates how customary attitudes and practices have also modified and influenced introduced western-style adoption. The Papua New Guinea Adoption of Children Act 1968 has been used to a very limited extent.[7] The Adoption of Children (Customary Adoptions) Act 1969 provides for a more flexible arrangement where the period of adoption may be stated and property rights and other limitations or conditions recorded. Registration of a customary adoption is made through the lower courts with minimal formality. The 1967–68 Annual Report of the Child Welfare Council noted some disquiet that 'Adoptions by custom are a growing source of difficulty. . . . there should be no intervention in custom although the nature of the custom in force should be declared at the time of adoption' (Papua New Guinea Child Welfare Council 1968:3).

The Council commented on the Customary Adoption Ordinance as legislation which would serve as a:

> 'bridge between traditional procedures and the highly legalised adoption laws which provide a complete and final change of legal status. There is endless variety in customary practices relating to fostering, guardianship, and adoption of children; unlike legal adoption, which makes confidentiality a basic principle, the parties to customary adoption are known to each other, the child usually knows both its natural and adoptive parents, and the concept of a final separation is generally not involved.'
>
> (Papua New Guinea Child Welfare Council 1970:10)

The avoidance of western-style adoption procedures has been noted throughout the South Pacific. In French Polynesia:

> 'Under the civil code it is possible to adopt a child legally through the offices of the French courts. However, this method is not generally used by Polynesians, in part because the criteria for legal acceptability of the parties involved (such as age of adoptive parents) differ from local norms but also because the court system is seen as foreign and capricious.'
>
> (Brooks 1976:55)

A study of eighty-one adoptions in Tonga showed that 'Few applications for legal adoptions are made to the courts because the circumstances of Tongan adoptions are often incongruent with the European model of adoption applied in the courts' (Morton 1976:65).

Western adoption and traditional practice: New Zealand, Australia, and Papua New Guinea

Adoptions involving Maori and Aboriginal communities reflect the existence of a similar interplay between customary practice and introduced legal systems. An additional feature is that these traditional societies are minority groups under direct and indirect pressure from western-style laws and attitudes. Hooker states that:

> 'Prior to the Native Land Act of 1909, Maori adoptions were a matter of custom, and the courts relied upon this in establishing the validity and effect of any adoption . . . . After 1909, all adoption by Maoris had to be effected by orders of adoption made by the Maori Land Court, and since the passing of the Adoption Act of 1955 the same law is applied to Maoris as to Europeans except that for Maoris the Maori Land Court has jurisdiction and not the Magistrate's Court . . . . This legislation is in line with the increasing Europeanization of Maori affairs in New Zealand.'
>
> (Hooker 1975:335)

Adoption practice in Australia and New Zealand follows a similar pattern to European and North American adoption practice. Papers presented at the First Australian Conference on Adoption held in 1976 illustrate the different approach taken in child-centred adoption practice, compared to the family-centred approach of societies in Oceania. The weight to be given to the interests of all parties must be resolved time and again but, as one review of Australian Adoption Law comments, 'declaring that the child's welfare is paramount does not really resolve these dilemmas' (Hambly 1976:97).

An important part of this conference was the discussion of the relationship between Australian adoption law and agency practice and the value and attitudes held by Aboriginal communities. The writer's experience as an adoption worker for more than a decade in a large Australian family welfare agency is reflected in the 'common themes' recorded from a workshop where it was noted that: 'Viable alternatives to legal adoption through the white system must be available so that placement of each individual child is determined by the needs of that child and his family, rather than by the *straitjacket of bureaucratic procedures*' (Sommerlad 1976:163, emphasis added). The nature of community responsibility for children, and the importance of retaining contact with their community if children are adopted, were stressed and reflect similar feelings from Papua New Guinea, Eastern and Western Oceania, and the Maori community in New Zealand. The idea that adoption means that the child is lost forever was considered intolerable, not only for the immediate family but for the wider kinship network, as the adoption of the child diminishes the family group and is a loss for the wider society.

Australian adoption law has greatly influenced legal adoption in Papua New Guinea as laws during the period of Australian administration were based on those current at that time in the State of Queensland. In addition, legal training followed the Australian pattern; most magistrates and judges were Australians; and English case law and its variations in the Australian states were used as precedents.

Since Independence in 1975, Papua New Guinean judges have been appointed but, in interpreting adoption legislation, courts have continued to rely on western-style interpretations. In an appeal by Australian adoptive parents against a decision refusing their application to adopt a Papua New Guinean child, expert witnesses were called by both the applicants and the Director of Child Welfare (who opposed the application). The court found that there was no substantiated evidence that the child would face a conflict of identity in Australia, and the adoptive parents won the case. The decision as to what was in the best interests of the child could not be made from legislation, as there is no legal bar to expatriate couples adopting Papua New Guinean children. It was stated in one of the accompanying judgments that: 'If there is any deliberate policy of preventing expatriates from adopting Papua New Guinean children then this policy should be written into the Act' (Kapi 1981:21). At the present time most formal court adoptions involve applicants who are not closely linked to traditional Papua New Guinean societies or where one or both adoptive parents are expatriates, so it is not surprising to find western attitudes and values as the overall frame of reference.

Traditional and western adoption: change and continuity

In this discussion it is clear that the effect of western adoption laws on customary adoption in the Third World has been the development of a duality of approach characteristic of most former colonies. In situations where colonial interest was less affected many matters were left to customary practice or were subject to the decisions of 'native' courts. The significance of adoption for land rights, determination of inheritance, and rights of succession led to the transfer of adoption practices from being a matter of 'custom' to a matter for adjudication by more formal and rigid legal institutions. Even where the intention has been to acknowledge 'custom' the process of establishing the facts in customary adoption through court proceedings leads to a less flexible situation. Customary adoption continues, however, to remain the preferred transaction in many South Pacific societies.

In his opening discussion on the meaning of adoption, Carroll notes the difficulties in a comparative treatment of adoptions in Oceania if they are to be measured against the values and practices set forth as ideals by such agencies as the Child Welfare League of America or the United Nations Department of Social Affairs (Carroll 1970:3-17).

In many societies jural parenthood may be shared and so it would be unthinkable that adoption could mean severance of contact between birth and adopting parents. Complete secrecy is impossible where adoption involves a public statement of intent, as it did for the Fanti in 1897 and many South Pacific societies today.

Claims of adopting parents must be strengthened by care and nurturance of the child and may have a time limit in which parental duties and responsibilities must be performed. In these situations:

> 'The rights and duties of jural parenthood change throughout the lifetime of the child. The successor to jural parenthood acquires only those duties in relationship to the child that still remain to be discharged and only those rights that are appropriate to the child's age and station in life.'
>
> (Goodenough 1970:403)

Many of these ideas are inconceivable in western-style adoption. Yet it is only in recent times that policies of complete separation, secrecy, total transfer of rights, and absolute permanency of the transaction have become standard practice in western adoption. Adoptions between relatives or those known to each other are closer to elements of adoption in traditional Third World societies. The adoption agency or professional middle man or woman is now a feature of western adoptions where impersonal transactions are preferred, but this trend has been questioned by those who see adoption arrangements as too rigid and artificial.

In discussing the various ways in which western adoption practices have influenced Third World societies it is not possible to compare the apparent rapid change in Japan after World War II with the gradual formalization of adoptions in Ghana or Kenya or Indonesia. It is even less possible to compare adoption in these countries with the relatively unchanged patterns of customary adoption practices in many of the small societies in Oceania or the particular situations of embattled minority cultures in the settler states of Australia and New Zealand.

In countries with minority immigrant cultures, the differences in attitudes to adoption are no less significant. Birth and adoptive parents may come from different cultural backgrounds and, even if separated by time and circumstance from their society of origin, they may retain many of the norms and values of the community from which they or their parents moved. These values will form the conceptual basis from which they view the partial or complete, temporary or permanent, abrogation of parental rights. In these situations those who are involved in managing the adoption transaction, as well as those who are party to it, need to have a clear understanding of the differences which exist. Otherwise the presence of western-style adoption legislation in a society may be accepted at face value and so mask the persistence of traditional adoption practices and the real depth and vitality of custom. Understanding of these differences may also make it possible for other models of adoption to become an important perspective from which to view western adoption attitudes and practices.

Notes

1 An earlier version of this discussion was presented at a seminar held on 14 March, 1983 at the University of Papua New Guinea. The writer wishes to express her appreciation of the contributions and suggestions made by participants. Several speakers noted the importance of stressing that the focus on adoption refers to the period after the introduction of western legal systems to Third World countries.

2 The problem of relating theory and practice was noted by the

writer when she was an adoption officer in a large family welfare agency. Many adoptions conform to the ideals set down in legislation and procedural guidelines but the complexities of balancing the rights of different individuals have been described as 'the adoption dilemma' (Frankel 1972:772–80).

3 For example there is the idea that adopted children may need to establish or maintain contact with their biological parents, as seen from a study of adopted children who sought to obtain more information from birth records (Triseliotis 1973).

4 A communal sense of collective guardianship which is part of tribal custom may also mean that the concept of adoption only becomes important in times of social dislocation. The group may normally look after its own without the necessity of a formal adoption ritual (Kirkpatrick and Broder 1976).

5 The concept of exchange does not only refer to the transfer of material resources. Shore considers that Samoan adoption involves exchange as it reflects the creation of new alliances. Samoa is also different from other Polynesian societies as adoptions are more frequently carried out by non-biological kin (Shore 1976:164).

6 While in many societies those captured in warfare would have usually been killed, oral traditions of group origin and clan genealogies contain references to adoption of adults, as well as children. How often this occurred cannot be determined with any degree of accuracy nor whether the immediate effect of colonial law was to increase the frequency of adoption.

7 The 1972 Annual Report of the Papua New Guinea Child Welfare Council stated that 47 adoption orders were made during that year. Official court records show that the number has declined markedly since Independence in 1975. Approximately 142 adoption orders were made in the period 1972–76, but only 45 orders were made in the next five-year period 1977–81.

References

Abbott, G. (1930) Adoption: Modern. In E.R. Seligman and A. Johnson (eds) *Encyclopaedia of the Social Sciences*. New York: Macmillan.

Brady, I. (1976) Socioeconomic Mobility: Adoption and Land Tenure in the Ellice Islands. In I. Brady (ed.) *Transactions in Kinship*. Honolulu: The University Press of Hawaii.

Brooks, C.C. (1976) Adoption on Manihi Atoll, Tuamotu Archipelago. In I. Brady (ed.) *Transactions in Kinship*. Honolulu: The University Press of Hawaii.

Carroll, V. (1970) Adoption on Nukuoro. In V. Carroll (ed.) *Adoption in Eastern Oceania*. Honolulu: University of Hawaii Press.

Cory, H. and Hartnell, M.M. (1970) Customary Law of the Haya. In E. Cotran and N.N. Rubin (eds) *Readings in African Law* vol. II. London: Frank Cass.

Cotran, E. and Rubin, N.N. (eds) (1970) *Readings in African Law*. London: Frank Cass.
Diwan, P. (1978) *Customary Law*. Chandigarh: Panjab University.
Du Toit, B. (1975) *Akuna: A New Guinea Village Community*. Rotterdam: Balkema.
Fortune, R.F. (1963) *Sorcerers of Dobu*, revised edn. London: Routledge & Kegan Paul.
Frankel, S.F. (1972) The Adoption Dilemma: Divergence of Theory and Practice. *Brooklyn Law Review* 38:772–80.
Goodenough, W.H. (1970) Epilogue: Transactions in Parenthood. In V. Carroll (ed.) *Adoption in Eastern Oceania*. Honolulu: University of Hawaii Press.
Hambly, D. (1976) Balancing the Interests of the Child, Parents, and Adopters: A Review of Australian Adoption Law. In C. Picton (ed.) *Proceedings of First Australian Conference on Adoption*. Sydney: The Committee of the First Australian Conference on Adoption.
Hooker, M.B. (1975) *Legal Pluralism*. Oxford: Clarendon Press.
Howard, A., Heighton, R.H., Jordan, C.E., and Gallimore, R.G. (1970) Traditional and Modern Adoption Patterns in Hawaii. In V. Carroll (ed.) *Adoption in Eastern Oceania*. Honolulu: University of Hawaii Press.
Kapi, M. (1981) Supreme Court Judgment 207. In *Supreme Court Judgments 1981*. Port Moresby: Government Printer.
Kirkpatrick, J.T. and Broder, C.R. (1976) Adoption and Parenthood on Yap. In I. Brady (ed.) *Transactions in Kinship*. Honolulu: The University Press of Hawaii.
Levy, R.I. (1970) Tahitian Adoption as a Psychological Message. In V. Carroll (ed.) *Adoption in Eastern Oceania*. Honolulu: University of Hawaii Press.
Lowie, R.H. (1930) Adoption: Primitive. In E.R. Seligman and A. Johnson (ed.) *Encyclopaedia of the Social Sciences*. New York: Macmillan.
Marcus, G.E. (1977) Succession Disputes in Modern Tonga. *Oceania* 47(3): 220–41.
Marshall, M. (1976) Solidarity or Sterility? Adoption and Fosterage on Namoluk Atoll. In I. Brady (ed.) *Transactions in Kinship*. Honolulu: The University Press of Hawaii.
Meir, J. (1929) Adoption among the Gunantuna. *Catholic Anthropological Conference* (1):1–98.
Morton, K.L. (1976) Tongan Adoption. In I. Brady (ed.) *Transactions in Kinship*. Honolulu: The University Press of Hawaii.
Papua New Guinea Adoption of Children Act 1968 (1976). In *Revised Laws of Papua New Guinea*. Port Moresby: Government Printer.
Papua New Guinea Adoption of Children (Customary Adoptions) Act 1969 (1976) In *Revised Laws of Papua New Guinea*. Port Moresby: Government Printer.
Papua New Guinea Child Welfare Council (1968–72) *Annual Reports*. Port Moresby: Government Printer.
Papua New Guinea Law Reports (1965) 66:58. Port Moresby: Government Printer.
Salisbury, R.F. (1970) *Vunamami*. Melbourne: Melbourne University Press.
Sarbah, J.M. (1968) *Fanti Customary Law*, 3rd edn. London: Frank Cass.
Schapera, I. (1970) A Handbook of Tsawana Law and Custom. In E. Cotran and N.N. Rubin (eds) *Readings in African Law*, vol. II. London: Frank Cass.
Shore, B. (1976) Adoption, Alliance, and Political Mobility in Samoa. In

I. Brady (ed.) *Transactions in Kinship*. Honolulu: The University Press of Hawaii.

Simmance, A.J.F. (1970) Adoption of Children among the Kikuyu of the Kiambu District. In E. Cotran and N.N. Rubin (eds) *Readings in African Law*, vol. II. London: Frank Cass.

Sommerlad, E. (1976) Homes for Blacks – Aboriginal Community and Adoption. In C. Picton (ed.) *Proceedings of First Australian Conference on Adoption*.

Strathern. A. (1972) *One Father, One Blood*. London: Tavistock Publications.

Tambiah, H.W. (1968) *Sinhala Laws and Customs*. Columbo: Lake House.

Ter Haar, B. (1962) *Adat Law in Indonesia*. (Trans.) In E. Adamson Hoebel and A.A. Schiller (eds). Djakarta: Bhratara.

Tonkinson, R. (1976) Adoption and Sister Exchange in a New Hebridean Community. In I. Brady (ed.) *Transactions in Kinship*. Honolulu: University of Hawaii Press.

Triseliotis, J. (1973) *In Search of Origins*. London: Routledge & Kegan Paul.

Van Tromp, J. (1970) Xhosa Law of Persons. In E. Cotran and N.N. Rubin (eds) *Readings in African Law*, vol. II. London: Frank Cass.

Watanabe, Y. (1963) The Family and the Law: Individualistic Premise and Modern Japanese Family Law. In A. Taylor von Mehren (ed.) *Law in Japan*. Cambridge: Harvard University Press.

Name index

Abbott, G. 289
Achenbach, T.M. 84
Adcock, M. 61
Allen, B.K. 207, 222
Alstein, H. 229, 230, 231, 232–35, 238–39, 240–41
Andersson, G. 282
Ansfield, J.G. 122
Anthony, S. 149
Aponte, J.F. 114, 116, 117

Bacon, R. 34, 57–8
Bagley, C. 119, 254, 263, 265, 268, 282
Baker, R. 254–72
Baran, A. 41, 43
Baumrind, D. 89
Bean, P.T. 1–5
Bell, R.O. 88
Bellucci, M.T. 211
Benet, M.K. 9, 19, 20, 21
Berkovitz, B.J. 156
Bevan, H.K. 194–202
Birch, H.G. 88, 92
Bissett-Johnson, A. 147, 156
Blunder, R.M. 198
Bodenheimer, B. 156
Bohman, M. 75, 117, 120
Boothby, N. 259, 265
Borgatta, E.F. 114, 116
Bowlby, J. 87, 94, 267
Bradshaw, J. 217
Brady, I. 294, 297
Brahams, D. 204
Brandon, J. 204
Brenner, R.F. 117
Broder, C.R. 302
Bromley, M. 24–37
Bromley, P.M. 174–93
Brooks, C.C. 295, 298
Brown, J. 217
Byrne, K.O. 211

Caldwell, B.M. 88
Calvento Solari, U. 273
Campbell, P. 256
Carroll, V. 294, 300
Castanos, J.N. 91
Cederblad, M. 264
Chakerian, C.G. 274
Chatterton, S.G. 147, 153
Cheetham, J. 263
Chess, S. 88, 92
Chestang, L. 263
Clark, G. 207
Clarke, A.D. 87
Clarke, A.M. 60, 72, 87, 118
Clive, E. 154
Colman, M. 118
Cooley, C.H. 261
Coopersmith, S. 94
Coote, A. 14
Cory, H. 291
Costin, L.B. 268
Cotran, E. 290
Coussins, J. 14
Crook, J.A. 132

Cross, L.A. 114, 116, 117

Davidson, S. 258
Davis, G. 154
Davis, K.C. 217
Davis, L. 76
Day, C. 47, 49, 50, 51, 74, 121
Day, D. 230, 236
Defries, J. 75
Diwan, P. 292
Dixon, S.L. 262
D'Souza, F. 254
Du Toit, B. 296

Edelbrock, C.S. 84
Eekelaar, J. 154, 196
Elonen, A.S. 117
Emmett, T. 222
Erichsen, H.R. 283
Erichsen, J.H. 283
Erikson, E. 40, 123, 261, 262

Fahlberg, B. 77
Fanshell, D. 114, 116, 117, 120, 205
Feigelman, W. 263, 268
Fields, R. 258
Fish, A.D. 115
Fisher, F. 41
Fortune, R.F. 296
Foster, A. 124
Frankel, S.F. 302
Fratter, J. 77
Freeman, M.D.A. 13, 14, 203-26
Freud, A. 14, 23, 157, 267
Fruin, D. 15, 54, 71
Fry, P. 258

Gallagher, P. 202
Gallagher, U.H. 208, 255
Gasbarro, D.T. 114, 115
Gentile, A. 210
George, V. 136, 205
Gershon, K. 257, 258
Gill, O. 11, 72, 265
Gluck, M.R. 114, 115
Goffman, E. 262
Goldberg, H.L. 205, 210
Goldhaber, D. 118
Goldstein, J. 14, 23, 157, 267
Goodacre, I. 29, 122, 150, 211
Goodenough, W.H. 295, 300
Goodman, L. 25
Goodwin, D.W. 120
Goody, J. 132
Grant, J.P. 256
Grey, E. 198
Grow, L.J. 235, 236

Hall, E. 44
Hall, T. xiv-xvii, 79
Hambly, D. 298
Hapgood, M. 54-82
Harlow, H.F. 94
Harper, L.V. 88
Harris, J. 204
Hart, K. 258
Hartling, P. 254
Hartnell, M.M. 291
Hayes, M. 198
Herbert, M. 83-99
Heywood, J.S. 222
Hill, M. 222
Hochfeld, E. 264
Hoffman, M.L. 90
Hogan, T.B. 183
Hoggett, B. 131-45
Hollis, F. 262
Holman, R. 15, 137
Hooker, M.B. 291, 293, 298
Howard, A. 295
Howe, R.A.W. 208
Humphrey, M. 9, 84, 114, 115, 116
Hussell, C. 81
Huyck, E.E. 258

Iwaniec, D. 89

Jackson, B. 11, 72, 265
Jackson, L. 114, 116
Jackson, M.P. 222
Jaffee, B. 117, 120, 122, 205
Jahoda, M. 261
James, M. 205
Joe, B. 257, 274
Johassohn, K. 115
Jones, D.N. 165
Jones, K. 217
Jordan, B. 60-1

Kadushin, A. 116, 118, 119, 120, 205, 235
Kapi, M. 299
Katz, S.N. 208
Keller, S. 258, 263

Kellmer Pringle, M.L. 10, 15, 117, 118
Kempe, H. 165
Kennell, J.H. 92-3
Kerr, M.G. 117
Kety, S. 120
Khan, A.S. 256
Kim, D.S. 263, 265, 282
Kirk, D. 115
Kirk, H.D. 121, 123, 269
Kirkpatrick, J.T. 302
Klaus, M.H. 92-3
Koller, K.M. 91
Kornitzer, M. 117, 150
Kramer, B. 274

Ladner, J. 235, 237-38, 263, 265
Laing, P. 222
Lambert, L. 12, 13, 30, 57, 58, 61, 67, 75, 119, 124, 137, 149, 162, 213, 214
Latham, C.T. 200, 201
Laurance, J. 14
Lawder, E.A. 117
Lebens, K. 62-3, 64, 67, 79, 137
Lee, S.G. 88
Leeding, A.E. 47, 49, 50, 74, 121
Leete, R. 147, 149
Leitner, I. 258
Levy, R.I. 295
Levin, B. 84, 114, 115, 116
Lewis, D.O. 116
Linde, L.H. 205, 210
Lindemann, E. 260
Lister, R. 207, 222
Lorenz, K.Z. 86
Lowlie, R.H. 289, 290, 294

McClearn, G. 75
McEwan, Mc. J. 220
Macleod, A. 154
MacLeod, V. 16, 19
McWhinnie, A. 26, 40, 117, 120, 266
Maddox, B. 146, 147, 156
Maher, B.A. 125
Mandell, B.R. 15, 17
Marcus, G.E. 296
Marshall, M. 295
Marshall, T.H. 12
Marris, P. 257
Maslow, A. 261
Masson, J.M. 146-60, 202
Mead, G.H. 261
Mech, E. 117
Meir, J. 295
Melone, T. 255, 267, 274
Menlove, F. 114, 116
Michaels, R. 268
Mitchell, G.C. 177, 179
Monaghan, B. 81
Morgan, P. 86
Morton, K.L. 295, 298
Moser, A. 255
Munsinger, H. 119
Murch, M. 154

Newton, D. 77
Norbury, D. 147, 148, 153, 155, 202

O'Collins, M. 288-304
Offord, D.R. 84, 114, 116, 117
Opertti, Badan D. 273

Page, R. 207
Palmer, N.E. 193
Pannor, R. 41, 43
Parker, R. 65, 80, 205, 208
Parry, M.L. 197
Pascall, G. 9-23
Paton, J.M. 40
Patterson, G.R. 89
Pearce, J. 265
Peller, L.E. 122
Perlman, H.H. 262
Picton, C. 41, 121, 220
Pilotti Davies, F. 275, 277
Plomin, R. 75
Polansky, G. 266
Polk, M. 210
Priest, J. 155

Rawlings, R.W. 154, 155, 204
Rawstron, D. 13
Raynor, L. 52, 70, 73, 74, 75, 76, 120, 121, 122, 162, 211, 266
Reece, S.A. 84, 114, 115, 116
Reich, C. 217
Resnick, R.P. 267, 273-87
Ressler, E.M. 265
Richards, K. 32
Ripple, L. 117
Robertson, J.A. 204
Rodriguez, G.M. 267, 273, 278, 283
Rogers, C. 117, 261

Rose, M. 214
Rosenthal, D. 120
Ross, A.O. 96
Rowe, J. 12, 13, 24, 26, 27, 30, 32, 34, 57-8, 61, 63, 67, 136, 137, 162, 213
Rowlands, O. 61
Ruber, M. 214
Rubin, N.N. 290
Rue, L. 243-53
Rue, M. 243-53
Russell, J. 51
Rutter, M. 87, 91

Sachs, C. 198
Salisbury, R.F. 296
Samuels, A. 195
Sanders, D. 254, 269
Sandler, B. 177, 183
Sands, R.G. 262
Sants, H.J. 40, 114
Sarbah, J.M. 290, 292
Sawbridge, P. 66, 81
Scarman, L.R. 263
Scarr, S. 74
Schaffer, R. 87
Schapera, I. 291
Schechter, M.D. 114, 115, 122
Schorr, A. 16, 17
Schwartz, E.N. 117
Seager, M. 220
Seglow, J. 10, 15, 94, 117, 118
Selman, P. 204
Senturia, A. 114, 115, 116
Shaffer, G. 210, 211
Shaffer, H.R. 43
Shapiro, D. 235, 236, 264-65
Shapiro, M. 114
Shaw, M. 62-3, 64, 67, 79, 113-27, 137
Shawyer, J. 12
Shinegold, D. 77
Shore, B. 302
Sigvardsson, S. 75, 117, 120
Silverman, A.R. 263, 268
Simmance, A.J. 291
Simon, N. 114, 115, 116
Simon, R. 229-42
Skeels, H.M. 117, 118
Skodak, M. 117, 118
Sluckin, A. 92, 93, 94
Sluckin, W. 86, 92, 93, 94
Smith, J.C. 183
Snowden, R. 177, 179
Solnit, A.J. 14, 23, 157, 267
Sommerlad, E. 299
Sorosky, A.D. 41, 43
Spicer, D. 161-73
Steinbock, S.J. 265
Sterba, E. 264
Stone, F.H. 40
Strathern, A. 296
Streather, J. 75, 119, 124, 149
Sweeney, D.M. 114, 115

Tambiah, H.W. 293
Ter Haar, B. 293
Theis, S. van S. 117
Thomas, A. 88, 92
Thomson, H. 147, 150
Tiborn, K. 258
Titmuss, R. 217
Tizard, B. 11, 12, 71, 72, 74, 93, 94, 119, 136, 137, 205, 268
Tonkinson, R. 295
Toussieng, P.H. 114, 115
Trasler, G. 205
Triseliotis, J. 38-53, 63, 74, 121, 122, 124, 138, 266, 302
Tunnard, J. 14
Turner, M. 73, 79

Valencia, B.M. 222
Van Tromp, J. 292
Vasquez, A. 264

Wadlington, W. 156, 157, 204
Wainwright, D. 31
Walby, C.M. 47, 50, 51
Waldinger, G. 210
Warner, J. 204
Watanabe, Y. 293, 294
Watson, K.W. 207, 210
Wattenburg, S.H. 268
Wedge, P. 10, 15, 117, 118
Weidell, R.C. 45
Weinberg, R. 74
White, R. 61
Whitehouse, A. 207
Wilding, P. 9, 17
Williams, C. 147, 157, 198
Wilson, E. 20, 21
Witmer, H.L. 117
Wright, D.S. 90

Young, D.W. 207
Young, L. 254, 263, 265, 268, 282

Zastrow, C.H. 236
Zerdoumi, N. 257
Zigler, E. 258
Zwerdling, E. 266

Subject index

access by birth parents 140-41
access to birth records, numbers of 47-8; *see also* birth certificates
Adoption Act (1926) 1, 113, 132, 194
Adoption Act (1958) 25, 133, 134-36, 139, 143, 149, 202, 203
adoption, as a child care option 27, 136-37, 139-43, 204-05, 221; as a solution to childlessness 10-11; outcome 10, 113-27; *see also* numbers of children adopted in England and Wales
Adoption Assistance and Child Welfare Act (1981) (in USA) 210
adoption of children in Northern Ireland 39
adoption, cost 207
adoption, definition of 115, 194
adoption law, object of 131-35; in Oceania 290-92; in Africa 290-92
adoption, legal effect of 132-35
Adoption Resource Exchange (ARE) 25, 27, 32, 274
Adoption Rules 200; County Court 163; High Court 163; Magistrates Court 163
Adoption Unit Return 205
aided conception 174-93; counselling for 178-79; custody of child 183-87; legal liability related to 179-82; registration of child 182-83; social considerations 176-78; status of child from 182; *see also* artificial insemination
allowances, on adoption 139; in subsidized adoption 217-20
American Public Welfare Association 277
Area Review Committees 165
artificial insemination 174-87; by donor (AID) 176-87; by husband (AIH) 174-76
assessment: of adoptive parents 73-5, 280; of children for adoption 69-76, 280-81
Australia, adoption in 298-99

battered child syndrome 165
Be My Parent 30
Berkshire County Council, adoption policies of 165
birth certificates, obtaining them by adopted children 38-53, 121; in Third World countries 290-96
Brent London Borough Council, adoption policies of 215
British Adoption Project 27
British Agencies for Adoption and Fostering (BAAF) 26, 32, 35, 58, 60, 214-15, 221
British Association of Social Workers (BASW) 208, 213
boarding out, of children 64
Bolton Metropolitan Borough,

adoption policies of 217
bonding 86-7, 91-5

Canada, adoption in 156-57
casework, with adoptions 62-6
Child Adoption 24, 27, 29, 30, 31
Child Care Act (1980) 196
Child Treatment Research Unit 89, 95-8; reports from 97
Child Welfare League of America 42
Children Act (1926) effect on step-parent adoptions 148
Children Act (1975) 25, 32, 38, 43-51, 63, 121, 133, 134-36, 138, 140, 142-43, 153, 154, 172, 183, 197, 199, 200, 213, 214
children in care, cost of 207
Ciba Foundation, law and ethics on AID 178
clinical studies of adopted children 113-17
Colwell, Marie, Report of Committee of Enquiry into 164-65
Colombia *see* Latin America
Comité Inter-Mouvement Après des Evacués 264
comparative studies, of adopted children 116-17
Congenital Disabilities (Civil Liability) Act (1976) 180
conduct disorders 83-5, 89-94
consent, parental to adoption 139-45; *see also* freeing for adoption; wardship
Court of Appeal, decisions in adoption cases 154-55
courts in adoption 194-202; numbers of adoptions in types of court 199
crime, and adoption 116-17
Croydon London Borough, adoption policies of 217
Curtis Report 136
custodianship 138, 144, 154, 195; in Scotland 153

Department of Health and Social Security (DHSS), Children's Division 24
Devon County Council, adoption policies of 214-16
Doncaster Adoption and Family Welfare Society Ltd 34
donors *see* artificial insemination
Dorset County Council, adoption policies of 216

El Salvador *see* Latin America
Essex County Council, adoption policies of 81, 165
embryo replacement 187-92; status of child in 189-92
ethics, in adoption 59-62
experience of adoption 120-21

family courts, effects on adoption proceedings 201
Family Division, of the High Court 166
Family Law Reform Act (1969) 167, 171, 182
Family Rights Group 61
Feversham Report 177-78, 187
five-year rule 139
freeing the child for adoption 142-43, 164, 172; *see also* consent
fostering, compared with adoption 137

general practitioners 101-02
genetic anxiety 117
guardian *ad litem* 135, 155
guardianship 152-53

hard to place child, defined 209
Houghton Committee 24, 28, 44, 133, 134, 136, 139, 151, 152, 161-64, 212-13
Hurst Committee 40, 44

identity, in adopted children 38-53, 94-5, 124
Illinois Child Welfare Manual 209
imprinting in children 86-7, 93
in vitro fertilization 187-92; control of 190-91; status of child in 189-92
infantile attachment *see* bonding
information, received by adoptive parents 281-82
informed consent 181; *see also* consent
Inheritance (Provisions for Family and Dependants) Act (1975) 175

intelligence, of adopted birth parents 118; of adopted children 118-19; of adoptive parents 117-20

Japan, adoption in 293-94

Kent County Council, adoption policies of 216
Kirklees Metropolitan Council, subsidized adoption scheme 217
knowledge base, of adoption 68-79

Latin America, children for adoption from 275-76, 278-85
Law Commission, Report on Illegitimacy 186-87
local authorities, in wardship cases 168

management of adoption placements 77-8
matching, of children and families 75-6
maternal deprivation, and future development 85-6, 91-2
medical liability *see* artificial insemination
Mexico *see* Latin America

National Association of Black Social Workers, in USA 229, 232
National Child Development Study 85, 118-20, 137
National Children's Bureau 65, 214
National Council for Civil Liberties 202
New Zealand, adoption in 298-99
numbers, of children adopted in England and Wales 7, 204

Oceania, adoption in 294-96
Office of Population, Censuses and Surveys (OPCS) 1, 221
older children, adoption of 3-4, 10-11, 54-82, 120-21, 204-05; number of adopted 30, 55-9, 205
Ontario, Law Report Commission 156; Ministry of Community and Social Services 39; *see also* Canada
origins, search for 38-53, 121
outcome of adoption 113-27
Owen, Dr David, and Children's Bill 45, 206

Papua New Guinea, Child Welfare Council 297; Law Reports 297
Parent to Parent Information on Adoption Services (PPIAS) 25, 29, 35
parental agreement 139-43, 162-64
parental rights, versus children's welfare 197
Parents for Children 24, 25, 28
parents, of adopted children 96-8
permanence, in older child adoptions 60-1
private adoptions 131-33
professionalization, in adoption matters 134-35
psychiatric conditions, and adoptions 114-15, 119-20

rearing adopted children 88-9
refugees, adoption of 254-72; arguments for adoption of 267; numbers available for adoption 255-56; policy relating to 255-56
relinquishment, of children for adoption 163-64, 264-67
rights, of both parents 15; of children 12-15
risk factors, in adoption 117-20
Rochdale Metropolitan Borough 216
Royal College of Obstetricians and Gynaecologists, Report on *in vitro* and embryo transfer 192

Scotland, law on adoption 58, 153
Seebohm Report 28
selection, of children for adoption 69-71; of families for adoptive children 65-7, 73-5
social administration, and adoptions 9-23
social class and adoptions 15-16
social work and services, in adoption 2-3, 31, 56-8, 66-7, 105-12, 166; staff 65
Somerset County Council, adoption policy of 217
Soul Kids Campaign 34

South Pacific *see* Oceania
special needs adoptions 1, 30, 55; *see also* older children
Standing Conference of Societies Registered for Adoption 151, 212
statistics, on adoption 1-2, 29
status of child, in AIH and AID 182; *in vitro* fertilization 189-90; in embryo transfer 189-90
statutory agencies, compared with voluntary agencies 34-5
step-parent adoptions, defined 146-49; effects of Children Act (1975) 154-55, 200; numbers of 149, 204
subsidized adoption 146-60; in Britain 212-20; case for 205-08; DHSS proposals 224-26; Strathclyde Rural Council 216; Sutton London Borough 217; in USA 233
success, in adoption 117-20
surrogate bearing mothers 191-92

telling children of adoptive status 121-23; of origins 178
termination of adoptive process 282
third-party adoption 25-6
time spent on selection for adoption 80-1
Tomlinson Committee 132, 194
transracial adoption 27, 229-42, 243-53; legal statutes 230-35; opponents and supporters of 232-35; results of 235-40; in USA 229-42

United Nations Draft Declaration on Social and Legal Principles Relating to Adoption 275
United Nations High Commission for Refugees (UNHCR) 254-55
United Nations International Year of the Child 276

vetting *see* assessment
voluntary societies 24-37

wards of court: and adoption proceedings 169-70; number of 168; and parents 170-71
wardship 137-38, 161-73
Warnock Committee 174, 188-89
Westminster London Borough Council 216